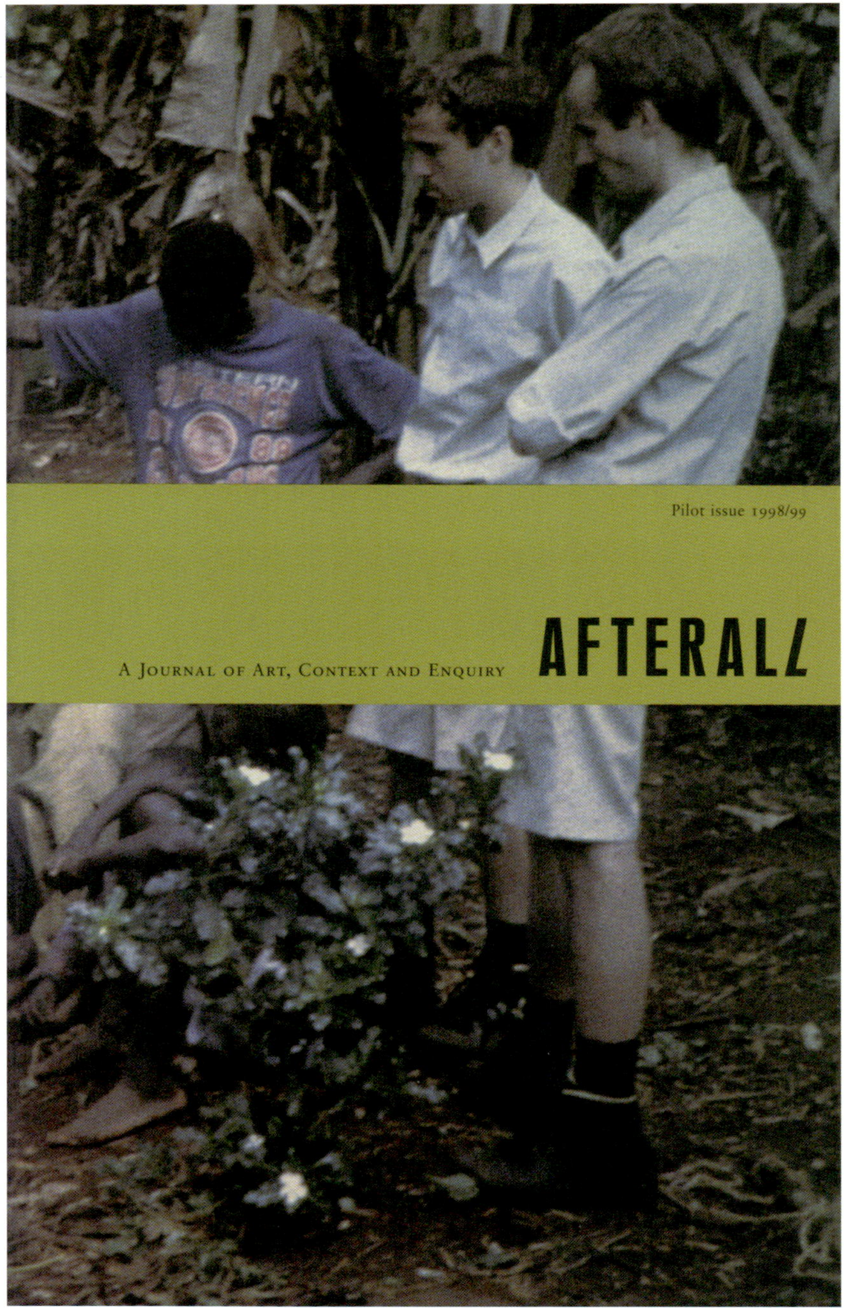

Cover image of the first issue.
Afterall, Issue 0, Spring/Summer 1998–99

THE IMPERCEPTIBLE TREMBLING OF THINGS
Mark Lewis, for the editors

Amy Hempel's very short eponymous story (it's barely eight lines long) from her recent collection *Sing to It: New Stories* (2019), opens with the following: 'At the end, he said, No metaphors! Nothing is like anything else.'[1] *Nothing is like anything else.* Some years ago, a friend shared an odd experience she had on a plane, flying from Toronto to Saskatoon, Saskatchewan. She was sitting next to a young man from Pakistan, aged around 22 or 23, en route from Karachi to take up a graduate scholarship at the University of Saskatchewan. He had the window seat; my friend had the aisle. As they were getting close to their destination, the young man tapped my friend on the shoulder and asked: 'What is all that whiteness down there?' My friend leaned over and looked out the window and of course everywhere down below was carpeted with snow. When I have retold this story, people have usually thought it can't be true as they assume almost everyone, especially those travelling to Canada for postgraduate studies, would know what snow was, how it looked, that it was white. And sometimes I have thought that maybe I have got the story wrong, that I've forgotten a detail or indeed made something up.

But recently I was flying to Saskatoon, probably on the same scheduled flight as my friend and the young man from Pakistan. I was going to Saskatchewan to make a film, and as I needed lots of snow, I was travelling there in the middle of winter. As the plane approached Saskatoon, I too looked out the window and for the first time I think I understood why that young man had been puzzled by what he saw. There was indeed snow, lots of it, everywhere. But there was a strangeness to what I saw and this was not simply due to the fact of snow. Saskatchewan is almost completely flat (there are no mountains, barely any hills) with a tiny population (it's exactly five times the size of England with less than one million people) and there are few cities and towns. Looking out the plane window, the whiteness seemed to me to go on and on forever with little articulation. It didn't really look like 'snow' at all. Rather it appeared as a strange and unworldly whiteness, with its own peculiar perspectival and spatial laws. It was strange too because it was not completely unfamiliar: there were still a few roads, buildings, occasional trees, etc., but nothing looked exactly right. A modern populated region almost completely covered with snow is not the same as an empty Arctic expanse. And if I wasn't so accustomed to the sight, I might well have asked the person next to me what it was I was looking at.

In March, the initial experience of the Covid-19 pandemic – international lockdowns, a disaster mise-en-scène – felt to me a little like going to bed one night, with everything outside clearly articulated, sharp contours as normal, and waking up and realising that while I slept the world had been carpeted with a deep layer of snow. Many of the usual markings, divisions between spaces, recognisable signs of life were gone. In this way there had been a kind of magical defamiliarisation of the earth and all its formal, social and political consequence. But in some ways, many things still looked the same – unfamiliar while remaining somewhat familiar. The Russian formalist Viktor Shklovsky describes this device – *ostranenie* – as the quintessential art effect, the *work* in the work of art – the work, that is, of making the world, or some aspect of it, strange. When looking at a work of art, you know what you are looking at, but somehow you also don't. Recognition, misrecognition is a trope, given substantive value by Sigmund Freud in his description of *disavowal* as the work of the unconscious in the face of a different kind of strangeness – sexual difference. With both defamiliarisation and strangeness, certain things – difference, history, repression, etc. – are revealed, often as if for the first time. Or at least they can be if one pays close attention. It's an effect that can be both political as well as psychoanalytical. It's what Freud, in another text, called the *Unheimlich*, the uncanny.

In a way this strangeness means that the world looks back at the viewer, challenges them to see difference, to see something new, as if the world's very form (in all of its complexities) has been overdetermined by something homologous to this aesthetic effect. This might explain why for some it seems so difficult to imagine what an artistic or aesthetic response to the pandemic might be. For a long time, many artists couldn't go to their studios. Some couldn't go outside. Many lost their income. Dozens of art institutions that have heretofore supported and presented their works have since shrunk and even disappeared. Perhaps some will not even be artists anymore. It's an unfamiliar landscape.

But the idea of a 'response' is far too transactional, too myopic, and would instinctively miss the radical possibilities of this new, changing landscape. Perhaps it's the instinct that needs to be resisted here. Do we, for instance, really need works of art that play coy creative with the mask motif? Probably not, or not yet anyway. What, then, is to be done? It's a familiar question, that even at the 'best of times' is troubling, enigmatic and hard to grasp, but now is differently torqued. How to imagine an art that can be contemporary with this new world form – able to respond to the pandemic phenomenon's own seemingly totalising aesthetic. It might be a question, for instance, of how we make that defamiliarising effect have an impact and consequence adequate to the differences it exposes. Art can make things strange; but if everything is now strange, then what? How can artists depict, transliterate, ponder, muse, reckon with this devastating snow storm that has transformed our landscape beyond recognition and, temporarily at least, revealed through amplification societies' racist divisions and diminishing social and economic prospects for the many as the *sine qua non* of comprehensive nefarious political repressions?

Certainly a defamiliarising effect can enable an opportunistic disenchantment. If, for instance, we have wondered, as most have, whether things will ever 'return to normal', we have at least been forced to consider how such nostalgia is simply a longing for something that never really existed, at least uniformly, consistently or satisfactorily for many. Normal for a few; hell for others. In the context of the pandemic's divisions, 'normal' reveals its contradictory, complex meaning and erasures. Some have been excited by this effect, not necessarily happy or pleased, but excited nevertheless – awake, temporarily at least, to the dreary, contingent and reactionary 'normal' of their lives. And for some, even those who don't exactly glimpse possibility, pessimism has certainly become an engine, *un cri perçant*. Pessimism, as Eugene Thacker has characterised it, is an enchantment with disenchantment, 'an ecstasy of the worst'.[2] So while some remain anxious (still longing perhaps for that impossible normal), others have become exhilarated, angry and defiant. The pandemic has erased our normal, made the latter, at least for now, palpable and tendentious

Sometimes you need real darkness to see something different, to experience invention. Creativity, as Peter Wollen once wrote, 'always makes use of what it can scavenge by night'.[3] Henry James writes that 'the rarest works pop out of the dusk of the inscrutable, the untracked'.[4] Light wages war with itself, I read somewhere, and if you are looking for new planets in distant galaxies, you understand that all the wonderful magical light from a billion stars, both dead and alive, is simply pollution that stops you seeing. If you want to see something, really see it, you need to see past the light, and catch the dark precarity. Darkness, like silence, is a location: full of meaning, full of possibility. Darkness is doubt, an unsettling uncertainty, a lack of self-confidence – what Maurice Merleau-Ponty found in Paul Cézanne, for instance: a doubt without end. When we look into the dark, when we look attentively, 'normal' explodes; it disintegrates; we lose our balance.[5]

I believe that the chill I feel in this darkness is the thrill of contemporaneity. The feeling that this space, this out of time moment, will breathe into the future as a vital memory of now, of something that happened, that evolved somewhere, where *you* are. This chill then connects you to this moment, makes you feel more than a witness, but part of its essential form. I think you can feel this thrill, or rather its evanescence, in that momentary and profound disappointment you experience when you finally find something you had thought for a moment you had lost, and that if you *had* lost would have imposed difficulty at best, devastation at worst. You found what you were looking for, what you *needed* to find, but somehow you wish you hadn't. For that material loss would seem hardly worse than the disappearance of the momentary thrill you experienced that something wholly unpredictable was about to change the course of (your) history, before the light returned and a kind of adjectival normal was imposed. Holding that moment in suspended animation, now that's an effort of invention. In Raymond Carver's short story 'Cathedral',[6] Robert, a blind friend, persuades the narrator to draw a cathedral with his eyes closed, so that he can experience the creative act in darkness, like a blind person might. When the drawing is finished, Robert tells the narrator to open his eyes and see what he has made. But the narrator doesn't; he keeps his eyes closed, to extend the moment, to experience his own drawing in total darkness for a little longer. The story ends with the blind Robert asking the narrator if he's now in fact looking at the drawing. The narrator, his eyes still shut, only darkness at his fingertips, replies, 'it's really something.'

Things now are 'extraordinary' – palpable, deep, layered and most of all strange. There might even emerge the feeling that if, day by day, things weren't made strange afresh, then this would itself be truly strange. This strangeness, then, is itself *really something*. It really 'is'. Its darkness, the resistance, no matter how short-lived, to any return to normal, means we all have to engage in a reckoning. With dizzying, minatory inequality, in disease as in life. Black Lives Matter. Monuments to slavery impose. There remain, of course, agents – states, those with ill-considered stakes – who insist on the return of some status quo ante, or preach 'tolerance' as panacea. Tolerance can certainly be a virtue, but as Michael Wood reminds us, 'all kinds of things which are not virtues can hide in its skirts, and […] tolerance itself may be indistinguishable from condescension.'[7]

In an opinion piece in the *New York Times*, 'You Want a Confederate Monument? My Body Is a Confederate Monument', the poet Caroline Randall Williams writes: 'The black people I come from were owned and raped by the white people I come from […]. I have rape-coloured skin. My light-brown-blackness is a living testament to the rules, the practices, the causes of the Old South. Who dares to tell me to celebrate them?'[8] To argue now for historical context, tolerance, the specificity of prior aesthetic judgement and so on, feels blind, completely out of context, violent even. Williams might well have quoted Fyodor Dostoyevsky in *Crime and Punishment* (1866): 'In place of dialectics, life has arrived.' Art's complicity. Art's failure. And finally, art's opportunity.

For this, our 50th issue of *Afterall*, the seven editors have each written texts and commissioned essays, responding independently to the particularities and the strangeness of these critical, strange and darkened times. Each has brought their own history, geography and practice to this editorial septuple; and each has also chosen seven works of art that seem significant, powerful and appropriate now. When we were planning this issue we had initially thought that when all the essays were written and works of art chosen, that we would then round up the selection of artworks by choosing a 50th. Fifty works for issue 50. But we unexpectedly stumbled. We realised that in the spirit of this issue's editorial idea, that the 50th, final work would really need to be chosen by all of us together. Yet this would have undermined, contradicted even, the predicate of the editorial imperative. On reflection the lacuna here seems appropriate, consequential. Perhaps it can stand in for all the important and significant works made in both the glare and shadow of this past year's strangeness, works that have been produced but have not yet been recognised as such.

Finally we want to acknowledge the instrumental and creative energy of Ute Meta Bauer. Ute joined *Afterall* four years ago and jointly edited and guided the development of all issues since then, including both this and the next, issue 51; but sadly, Ute and NTU Centre for Contemporary Art Singapore are leaving *Afterall* at the end of this year. Ute and her team will be greatly missed. We also want to acknowledge the important intellectual work of Ana Bilbao, Charles Esche, Anders Kreuger and David Morris in developing the journal over the years. With this new issue we warmly welcome our new editors: Amanda Carneiro, Nav Haq, Amber Husain and Adeena Mey. Elizabeth Karp-Evans and Adam Turnbull of Pacific have produced this issue's innovative design.

1   Amy Hempel, *Sing to It*, New York: Simon and Schuster, 2019, p.2.

2   Eugene Thacker, *Infinite Resignation*, London: Repeater Books, 2018, p.271.

3   Peter Wollen, *Raiding the Icebox: Reflections on Twentieth Century Culture*, London: Verso, 1993, p.210.

4   Henry James, 'Letter to Graham Balfour', November 1901.

5   But there is room for caution here too. Roland Barthes warns against the night, when 'the adjectives return, *en masse*' (*Roland Barthes by Roland Barthes*, trans. Richard Howard, London: Papermac, 1995, p.115). For Barthes, the adjective is enlisted to rob things of their truth – it reassures us, it pits language 'against', and hides the meaningless of meaning as everything becomes pithy, trite.

6   Raymond Carver, 'Cathedral', *Cathedral*, New York: Knopf, 1983.

7   Michael Wood, 'The Meaninglessness of Meaning', *London Review of Books*, vol.8, no.17, 1986.

8   Caroline Randall Williams, 'You Want a Confederate Monument? My Body Is a Confederate Monument', *The New York Times*, 26 June 2020, available at https://www.nytimes.com/2020/06/26/opinion/confederate-monuments-racism.html (last accessed on 7 October 2020).

Alain Resnais and Marguerite Duras, Isaac Julien, Chantal Akerman, Raoul Peck, Zarina Bhimji, Amar Kanwar, Pier Paolo Pasolini

Hannah Arendt; Seyla Benhabib; Stuart Hall; Michael Hardt and Antonio Negri; Frantz Fanon; Paul Gilroy; Chantal Mouffe; Edward Said; Peter Weiss; Cornel West

Why Is It So Difficult to Love the World?

Ute Meta Bauer & Ana Salazar

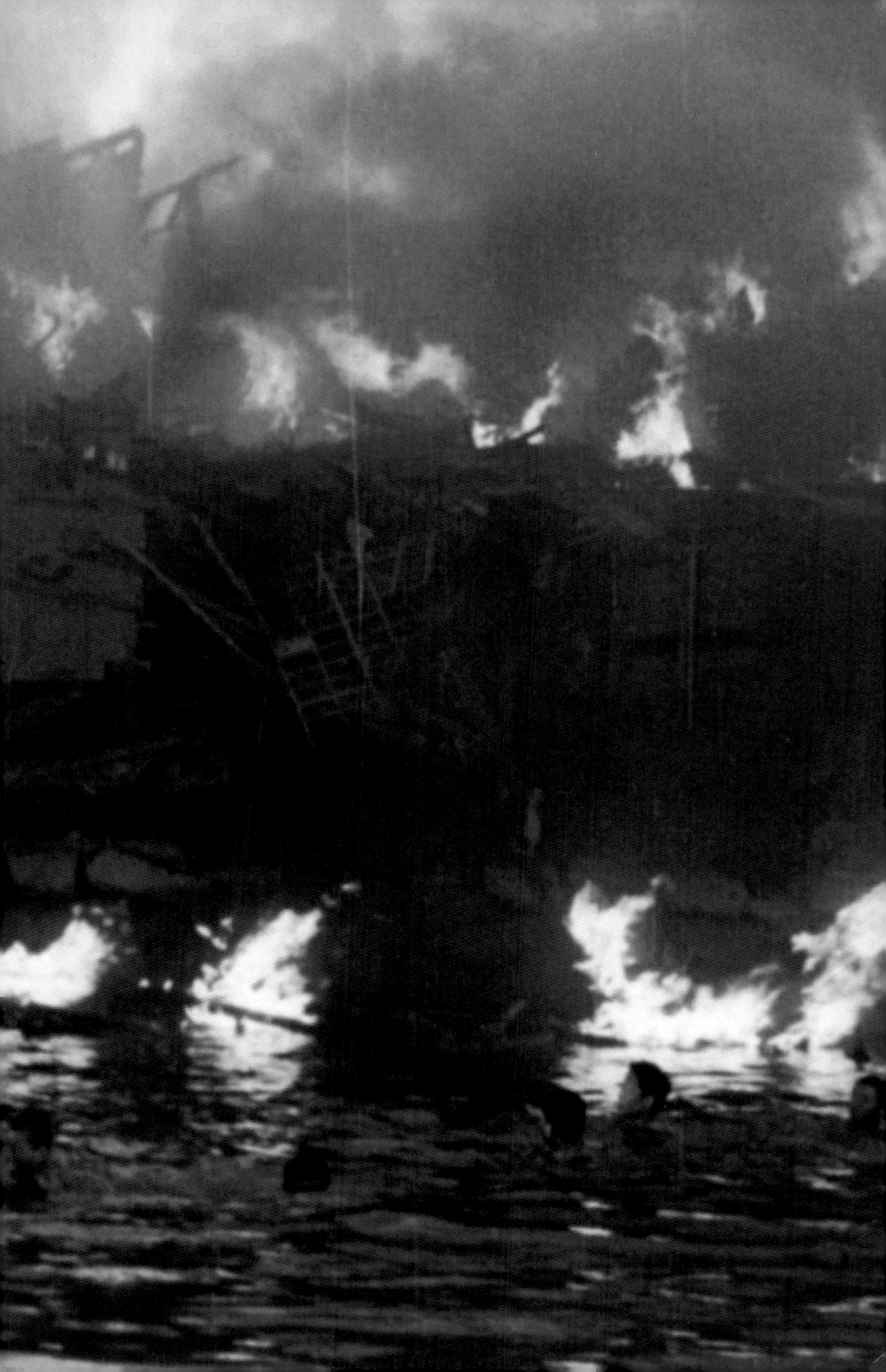

In her life's work on political thought, German philosopher Hannah Arendt questioned the origins of violence and authoritarianism. *Amor mundi* (love of the world) – an early possible title for *The Human Condition* (1958) – is at the core of this thinking. In her journal she once asked: 'Why is it so difficult to love the world?'[1] To look at it differently, we could ask the question in reverse: 'Why is it so easy to hate the world?' It often seems that any path that prioritises love, justice, respect and the defence of dignity for all life can only be forged through constant struggle, while a path that reproduces hate and violence is already there in front of us. We have lived through many vicious cycles of violence in human societies, which have generated an established, systemic violence. What is it possible to do within human power?

This 50th edition of *Afterall* responds to the situation created by Covid-19 – a consequence of humanity's treatment of its environment and other species. The pandemic has also boldly highlighted entrenched socio-economic inequalities. Artists, however, have long been engaged in making such 'invisible' issues visible – a major reason art plays such a fundamental role in societies. For this piece, we juxtapose seven moving-image artworks that dwell on systemic violence and oppression, with excerpts from texts by philosophers and theorists who offer new perspectives on these issues and generate much needed discourses for a movement towards global equality.

Afterall was born some twenty years ago, at a time when cultural studies was at a global peak. The field had strong roots in the UK since the 1980s through the Centre for Contemporary Cultural Studies at the University of Birmingham, founded in 1964. BBC Four was then promoting multiculturalism as the 'new paradigm' for Britain, which accordingly understood and constructed itself as a multicultural society. This didn't happen without struggle and negotiation, of which one of the leading voices was that of the late cultural theorist Stuart Hall. He describes the overall context in which he found himself at the time as that of a *Familiar Stranger*.[2] A public intellectual and spokesperson of the Windrush generation – those arriving from the ex-colonies of the Caribbean to the UK between 1948 and 1970 – Hall influenced many young artists and practitioners, including Isaac Julien, then a young painting and film student.

Julien was deeply involved in the political struggle that took place in 1980s Britain, at the height of punk, the New Romantics and dub music, and closely followed happenings around Notting Hill Carnival, an annual event in West London. *Territories* (1984), his first film and his final degree work at Central Saint Martin's School of Art, juxtaposes archival footage of demonstrations and clashes between the police and Black people at Carnival, portraying the experience of racism in the UK. Using the testimonies of protestors as soundtrack and exposing how the police tried to banish participants from the streets, the film's title refers to territories of race, class and sexuality – a triangulation that Hall considered intrinsically connected. In Julien's later film, *Frantz Fanon: Black Skin, White Mask* (1996), he examines similar ideas around discrimination in the context of the French colony of Martinique, in which Fanon – a psychiatrist by profession, and political leader by choice – was born. His film *Looking for Langston* (1989), however, has a more abstract, surreal setting, and while highlighting the specific predicament of queer people of colour, articulates how racism cuts across class, gender and sexuality, sparing not even the privileged, affluent members of the Black community.

Arriving in Texas with the intention of filming America's South and tracing the movements of writers James Baldwin and William Faulkner, Belgian film-maker Chantal Akerman found herself confronted with the news of a Black man having been brutally murdered by three white men. *South* (1999) portrays the story of James Byrd Jr., who was beaten, chained to a pickup truck and then dragged to his death. The camera mercilessly follows the truck's five-kilometre route in long landscape shots, interrupted by interviews and images of Byrd's funeral, evoking the climate in which such a hate crime could and did happen. For the African-American philosopher, political activist and author Cornel West, racism is part and parcel of the constitution of the United States. The global movement to end racism and oppression has been silenced over and over in an endless cycle, seemingly impossible to break. Yet, the fight has never ceased. Hence British historian and academic Paul Gilroy calls for a new name for the movement beyond anti-racism, which he considers inadequate to describe the ongoing violence, repression and inequalities suffered by Black people around the world.

In *Lumumba, la mort d'un prophète* (*Lumumba, the death of the prophet*) (1990), Haitian-born film-maker Raoul Peck, who grew up in the Belgian Congo, examines how Patrice Lumumba, one of the most charismatic figures of the African Independence Movements, was ruthlessly undermined when he became the first elected Prime Minister of the Independent Republic of the Congo in 1960. In this documentary with diverse archival footage, Peck unveils how Western and specifically Belgian political and economic interests never intended to give up control over the Congo, ultimately leading to Lumumba's covered-up murder in January 1961. Frantz Fanon, who became a leader of the Algerian revolution, accurately elucidates how the independence of African countries took place, echoing what is stated in *Lumumba*: independence was given with one hand and taken with the other. Leaving Africa exploited and destroyed, the European colonisers saw no need for reparations. In this regard for Fanon, as he points out in his book *The Wretched of the Earth* (1961), the redistribution of (global) wealth is of the utmost importance.

Fanon suggests the physical and psychological wounds of the victims of impunity can only heal through collective violence against the oppressor. Hand in hand with racism and classism, violence against women is committed around the world with a similar sense of impunity. *The Lightning Testimonies* (2007), by Indian film-maker and artist Amar Kanwar, sheds light on the history of systemic sexual violence inflicted on Indian women across regions and generations. Projected over eight screens, their bodies become sites of memory and resistance, both individual and collective.

Oppressions, of course, have their own complex histories and contexts. In 1972, President Idi Amin of Uganda ordered the expulsion of all its ethnically Asian citizens within three months. As a child, the Ugandan Asian artist Zarina Bhimji and her family stayed on in Uganda until 1974, hiding in a small village before finally fleeing to the UK. Bhimji returned to Uganda for the first time in 1998, driven by an interest in places that bear traces of war. She started photographing, and on her second journey, slowly began filming her family home, the school and the mosque of her childhood. In a deserted Uganda, she filmed the eerie interiors of abandoned buildings, military barracks and bloodstained prison cells. The mesmerising pans in *Out of Blue* (2002), devoid of people, accompanied by the sounds of human humming and breath as well as the music of Pakistani singer Abida Parveen, become a solemn portrayal of the extermination and cultural erasure.

Alain Resnais, director and
Marguerite Duras, screenplay,
Hiroshima mon amour,
1959, film, colour, 85min

The traumatising experience of losing one's citizenship is exacerbated by a complete loss of human rights. Hannah Arendt came to this realisation while observing how the Jewish population in Germany became stateless during World War II. The practice is enforced in certain countries towards First Nations, Roma, Sinti and Palestinian people to this day.

In other parts of Europe different histories were being played out. *Salò, or the 120 Days of Sodom* (1975) was Pier Paolo Pasolini's last film before he was murdered. The film's story, a loose adaptation of the 1785 book by the Marquis de Sade, follows four wealthy Italian libertines during the fascist Republic of Salò (1943–45), who kidnap eighteen teenagers and proceed to mentally and physically torture them over a period of four months. The extreme violence and sadism that unfold throughout the film mirror the political corruption and authoritarianism that continues in post-Mussolini Italy, while also pointing to moral corruption and nihilism. A critique of capitalism and consumerism, Pasolini's *Salò* depicts the epitome of lust for power that extends itself into a violent power manifested in domination and sexual abuse.

The impact of any conflict is long-lasting. With screenplay by Marguerite Duras and direction by Alain Resnais, *Hiroshima mon amour* (1959) is a meditation on memory – on how (not) to forget the atomic bomb thrown by the U.S. Air Force onto Hiroshima on 6 August 1945, killing hundreds of thousands of civilians and devastating the city and its inhabitants with interminable consequences. The traumatic history of Hiroshima's nuclear bombing is narrated through personal conversations between a French actress and a Japanese architect, who become briefly involved during the actress's stay in Japan. In these compressed, sharp historical constellations, any division between the personal and the political collapses. In the film, this is made apparent by how the damaged body becomes a wounded, war-torn landscape.

2020 commemorates 75 years since the nuclear bombing of Hiroshima and Nagasaki. Sadly, we are closer than ever to a nuclear war with major arms control treaties being withdrawn and hard-won victories towards the elimination of atomic weapons being squandered. The all-destructive bomb is the ultimate instance of imperial biopower – control over life, as argued by Michael Hardt and Antonio Negri in *Empire* (2000).

The attempt to reinstall imperialisms – currently to be witnessed in various parts of the globe – has nurtured a fertile ground for neo-fascism, the normalisation of state violence and the abuse of state power, including in countries with democratic constitutions. The ongoing widening of the socio-economic gap has accelerated during the current pandemic, and the impact on those who can't afford to isolate or work from home is devastating. The human right to protection and care is clearly not extended to all.

Invited by *Afterall* to select works of art that are relevant at this moment, in the attempt to understand the gravity and scale of the crisis we have revisited and cited texts that inquire specifically into systemic economic inequalities and state violence, which are once again resurfacing. As Arendt pointed out in *The Human Condition*, what is required in order to break the spirals of violence and divide is the re-emergence of unconditional love for this world and, we would add, all its life forms.

Once we acknowledge the dimension of 'the political' we begin to realise that one of the main challenges facing democratic politics is how to domesticate hostility and to defuse the potential antagonism in all human relations. The fundamental question for democratic politics is not how to arrive at a rational consensus, that is, a consensus not based on exclusion: this would require the construction of an 'Us' that did not have a corresponding 'Them'; an impossible feat because – as we have seen – the condition of the constitution of an 'Us' is the demarcation of a 'Them'. The crucial issue for democratic politics, instead, is how to establish this 'Us'-'Them' distinction in a way that is compatible with pluralism. The specificity of modern democracy is precisely its recognition and legitimation of conflict; in democratic societies, therefore, conflict cannot and should not be eradicated. Democratic politics requires that the others be seen not as enemies to be destroyed but as adversaries whose ideas should be fought, even fiercely, but whose right to defend those ideas will never be questioned. Put differently, what is important is that conflict does not take the form of 'antagonism' (struggle between enemies) but of 'agonism' (struggle between adversaries). The aim of democratic politics is to transform potential antagonism into agonism.[3]

*

Antonio Gramsci has made the useful analytic distinction between civil and political society in which the former is made up of voluntary (or at least rational and noncoercive) affiliations like schools, families and unions, the latter of state institutions (the army, the police, the central bureaucracy) whose role in the polity is direct domination. Culture, of course, is to be found operating within civil society, where the influence of ideas, of institutions and of other persons works not through domination but by what Gramsci calls consent. In any society not totalitarian, then, certain cultural forms predominate over others, just as certain ideas are more influential than others; the form of this cultural leadership is what Gramsci has identified as *hegemony*, an indispensable concept for any understanding of cultural life in the industrial West.[4]

*

As the postcolonial and post-Cold War model of global authority takes shape and reconfigures relationships between the overdeveloped, the developing and the developmentally arrested worlds, it is important to ask what critical perspectives might nurture the ability and the desire to live with difference on an increasingly divided but also convergent planet. We need to know what sorts of insights and reflection might actually help increasingly differentiated societies and anxious individuals to cope successfully with the challenges involved in dwelling comfortably in proximity to the unfamiliar without becoming fearful and hostile. We need to consider whether the scale upon which sameness and difference are calculated might be altered productively so that the strangeness of strangers goes out of focus and other dimensions of a basic sameness can be acknowledged and made significant. We also need to consider how a deliberate engagement with the twentieth century's histories of suffering might furnish resources for the peaceful accommodation of otherness in relation to fundamental commonality. In particular, we need to ask how an increased familiarity with the bloodstained workings of racism – and the distinctive achievements of the colonial governments it inspired and legitimated – might be made to yield lessons that could be applied more generally, in the demanding contemporary settings of multicultural social relations. This possibility should not imply the exaltation of victimage or the world-historic ranking of injustices that always seem to remain the unique property of their victims. Instead of those easy choices, I will suggest that multicultural ethics and politics could be premised upon an agonistic, planetary humanism capable of comprehending the universality of our elemental vulnerability to the wrongs we visit upon each other.[5]

The history of migration can't be comprehended without the imperial connection. Jamaicans came as colonials, drawn by an invisible gravitational pull to the 'absent centre' which had defined life in the colony for centuries. They came, as Ashis Nandy felicitously put it, as 'intimate enemies'. The unequal relations of power, wealth and authority separated the colonised from the British. But colonisers and colonised were locked in struggle with each other in a re-enactment of Hegel's master-slave dialectic. This was a relationship, in other words, which could not be transcended. It could only be fought to the death.

Those who had made the journey from the Caribbean could be understood as symbolically enacting the third, long-postponed and final leg of the historic process of unequal exchange known as 'the triangular trade'. This had originally taken British traders and trinkets to Africa, followed by the transportation of the enslaved to the Caribbean, and then lastly the shipment of rum, sugar and profits produced by forced labour back to England's seaports. The new generation of Caribbean migrants, on the Windrush and on the many vessels which followed, were 'completing' that shattering Middle Passage, bringing it all back 'home' where it belonged. History was turning back against itself.[6]

*

'Look, a Negro!' It was an external stimulus that flicked over me as I passed by. I made a tight smile.

'Look, a Negro!' It was true. It amused me.

'Look, a Negro!' The circle was drawing a bit tighter. I made no secret of my amusement.

'Mama, see the Negro! I'm frightened!' Frightened! Frightened! Now they were beginning to be afraid of me. I made up my mind to laugh myself to tears, but laughter had become impossible.

I could no longer laugh, because I already knew that there were legends, stories, history, and above all *historicity*, which I had learned about from Jaspers. Then, assailed at various points, the corporeal schema crumbled, its place taken by a racial epidermal schema. In the train it was no longer a question of being aware of my body in the third person but in a triple person. In the train I was given not one but two, three places. I had already stopped being amused. It was not that I was finding febrile coordinates in the world. I existed triply: I occupied space. I moved toward the other [...] and the evanescent other, hostile but not opaque, transparent, not there, disappeared. Nausea…

I was responsible at the same time for my body, for my race, for my ancestors. I subjected myself to an objective examination, I discovered my blackness, my ethnic characteristics; and I was battered down by tom-toms, cannibalism, intellectual deficiency, fetichism, racial defects, slave-ships, and above all else, above all: 'Sho' good eatin'.[7]

Isaac Julien, *Territories*, 1984,
16mm film, colour, sound, 24min 6sec.
Courtesy the artist and Victoria Miro,
London/Venice

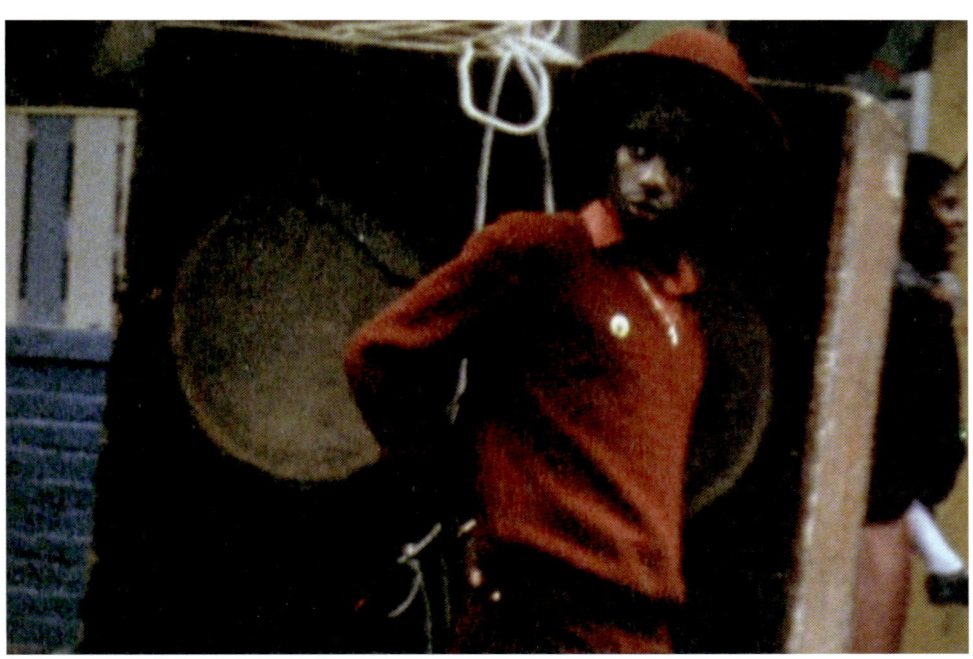
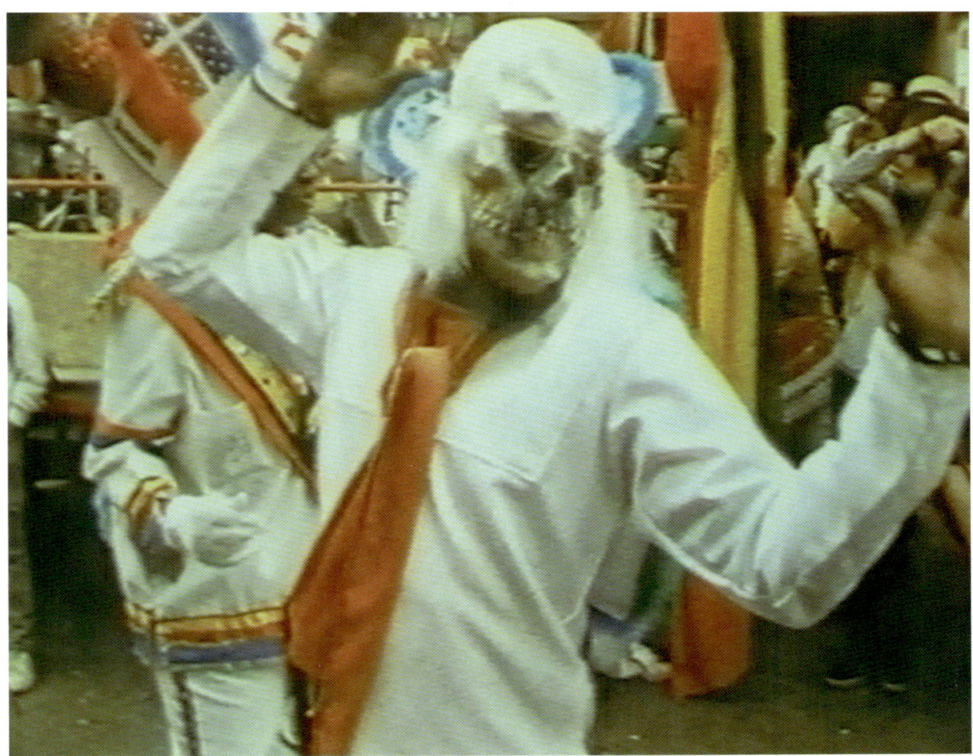
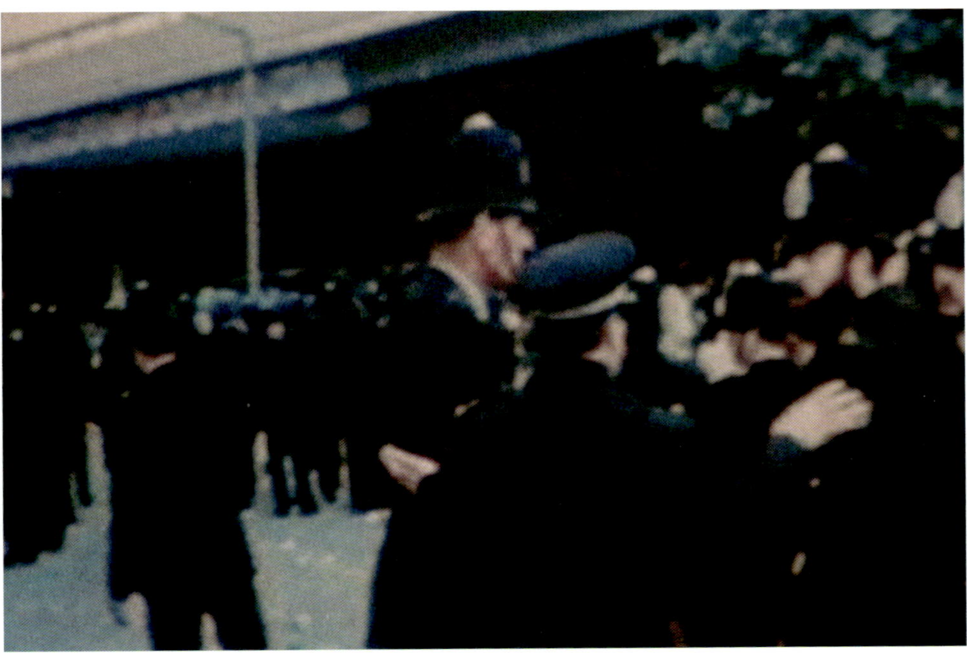

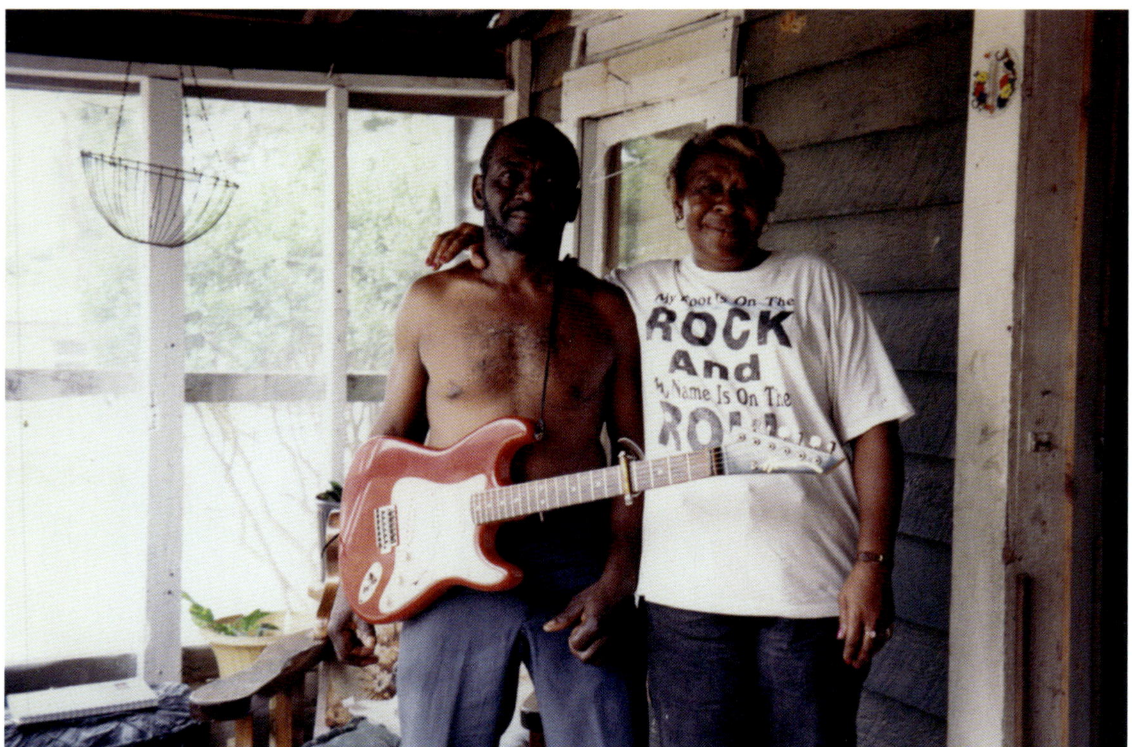
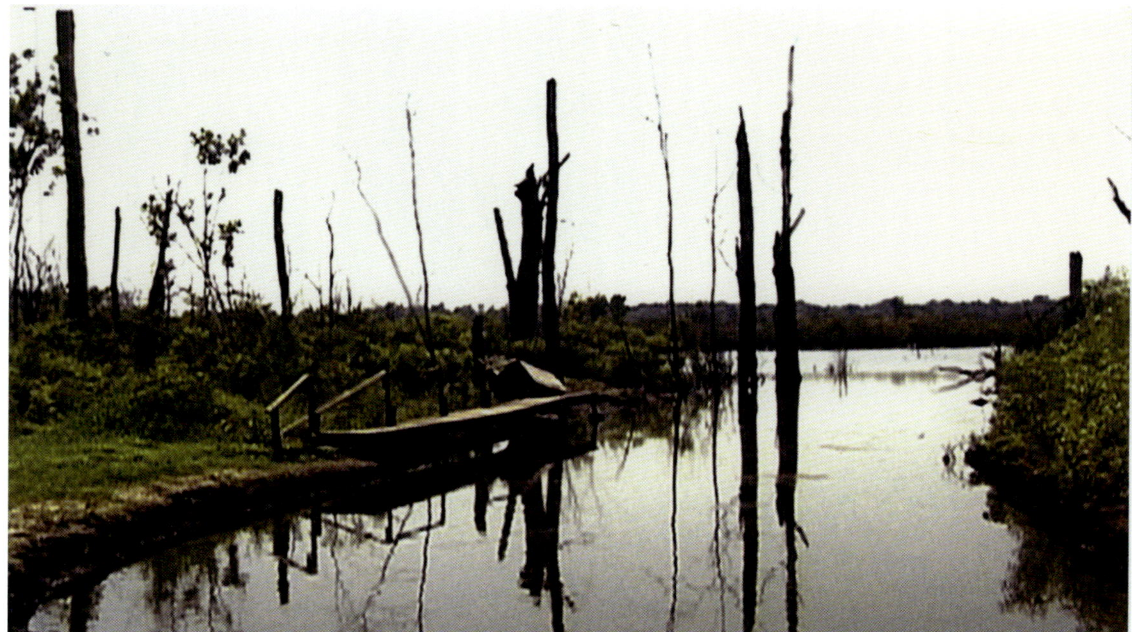
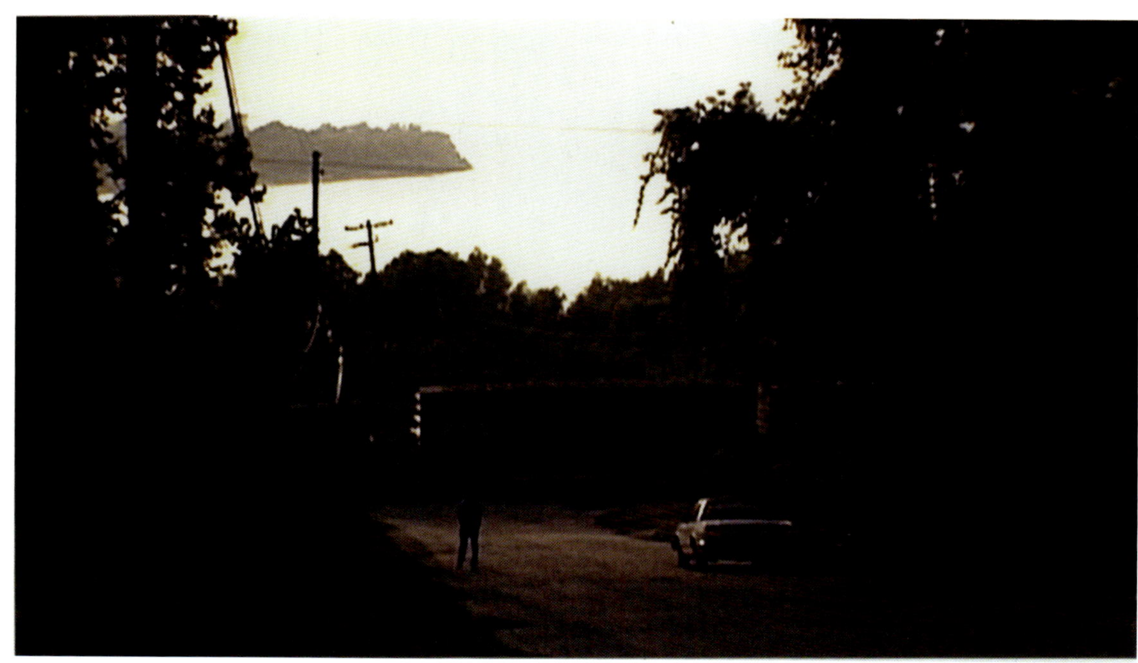

To talk about race and empire in America is to talk about how one musters the courage to think, care and fight for democracy matters in the face of a monumental eclipse of hope, an unprecedented collapse of meaning and a flagrant disregard for the viewpoints and aspirations of others. Niggerization in America has always been the test case for examining the nihilistic threats in America. Yet we rarely view niggerization as constitutive of America – just as we rarely think nihilism is integral to America. For so long niggerization has been viewed as marginal and optimism central to America. But in our time, when we push race to the margins we imperil all of us, not just peoples of colour. If we are to grapple with the contemporary forces of evangelical, paternalistic and sentimental nihilism prevailing in the country today, we must draw on the deep well of insight into the scars of our racism and imperialism to be found in the democratic tradition that has run alongside those nihilistic forces. The voices and views of nihilistic imperialism may currently dominate our discourse, but they are not the authentic voice of American democracy.[8]

*

If we are going to interrupt the romance of racial and ethnic absolutism at last, we will need to find an explanation for how that telling blockage has damaged the planetary movement we should probably no longer refer to minimally and apologetically as antiracism. In recognition of the need for more assertive and wholeheartedly political moods and tactics, we should become prepared to acknowledge the extreme difficulty as well as the great value of moral and political enterprises that require the systematic denaturing of 'race' as part of confrontations with the alienated sociality that absorbs the cries of those who suffer by making the sound less than human.[9]

Chantal Akerman, *Sud*, 1999, film, colour 71min. Collection Cinematek. Courtesy Chantal Akerman Foundation-Amip

In the opening sections of 'Imperialism', Arendt examines the European 'scramble for Africa'. Her thesis is that the encounter with Africa allowed the colonising white nations such as the Belgians, the Dutch, the British, the Germans and the French to transgress abroad those moral limits that would normally control the exercise of power at home. In the encounter with Africa, civilised white men regressed to levels of inhumanity by plundering, looting, burning and raping the 'savages' whom they encountered. Arendt uses Joseph Conrad's famous story, *The Heart of Darkness*, as a parable of this encounter. The 'heart of darkness' is not in Africa alone; twentieth-century totalitarianism brings this centre of darkness to the European continent itself. The lessons learned in Africa seem to be practised in the heart of Europe.[10]

*

Today, national independence and the growth of national feeling in under-developed regions take on totally new aspects. In these regions, with the exception of certain spectacular advances, the different countries show the same absence of infrastructure. The mass of the people struggle against the same poverty, flounder about making the same gestures and with their shrunken bellies outline what has been called the geography of hunger. It is an under-developed world, a world inhuman in its poverty; but also it is a world without doctors, without engineers and without administrators. Confronting this world the European nations sprawl, ostentatiously opulent. This European opulence is literally scandalous, for it has been founded on slavery, it has been nourished with the blood of slaves and it comes directly from the soil and from the subsoil of that under-developed world. The well-being and the progress of Europe have been built up with the sweat and the dead bodies of Negroes, Arabs, Indians and the yellow races. We have decided not to overlook this any longer. When a colonialist country, embarrassed by the claims for independence made by a colony, proclaims to the nationalist leaders: 'If you wish for independence, take it, and go back to the middle ages', the newly independent people tend to acquiesce and to accept the challenge; in fact you may see colonialism withdrawing its capital and its technicians and setting up around the young state the apparatus of economic pressure. The apotheosis of independence is transformed into the curse of independence, and the colonial power through its immense resources of coercion condemns the young nation to regression. In plain words, the colonial power says: 'Since you want independence, take it and starve.' The nationalist leaders have no other choice but to turn to their people and ask from them a gigantic effort. A regime of austerity is imposed on these starving men; a disproportionate amount of work is required from their atrophied muscles. An autarkic regime is set up and each state, with the miserable resources it has in hand, tries to find an answer to the nation's great hunger and poverty. We see the mobilisation of a people which toils to exhaustion in front of a suspicious and bloated Europe.

Other countries of the Third World refuse to undergo this ordeal and agree to get over it by accepting the conditions of the former guardian power. These countries use their strategic position – a position which accords them privileged treatment in the struggle between the two blocs – to conclude treaties and give undertakings. The former dominated country becomes an economically dependent country. The ex-colonial power, which has kept intact and sometimes even reinforced its colonialist trade channels agrees to provision the budget of the independent nation by small injections. Thus we see that the accession to independence of the colonial countries places an important question before the world, for the national liberation of colonised countries unveils their true economic state and makes it seem even more unendurable. The fundamental duel which seemed to be that between colonialism and anti-colonialism, and indeed between capitalism and socialism, is already losing some of its importance. What counts today, the question which is looming on the horizon, is the need for a redistribution of wealth. Humanity must reply to this question, or be shaken to pieces by it.[11]

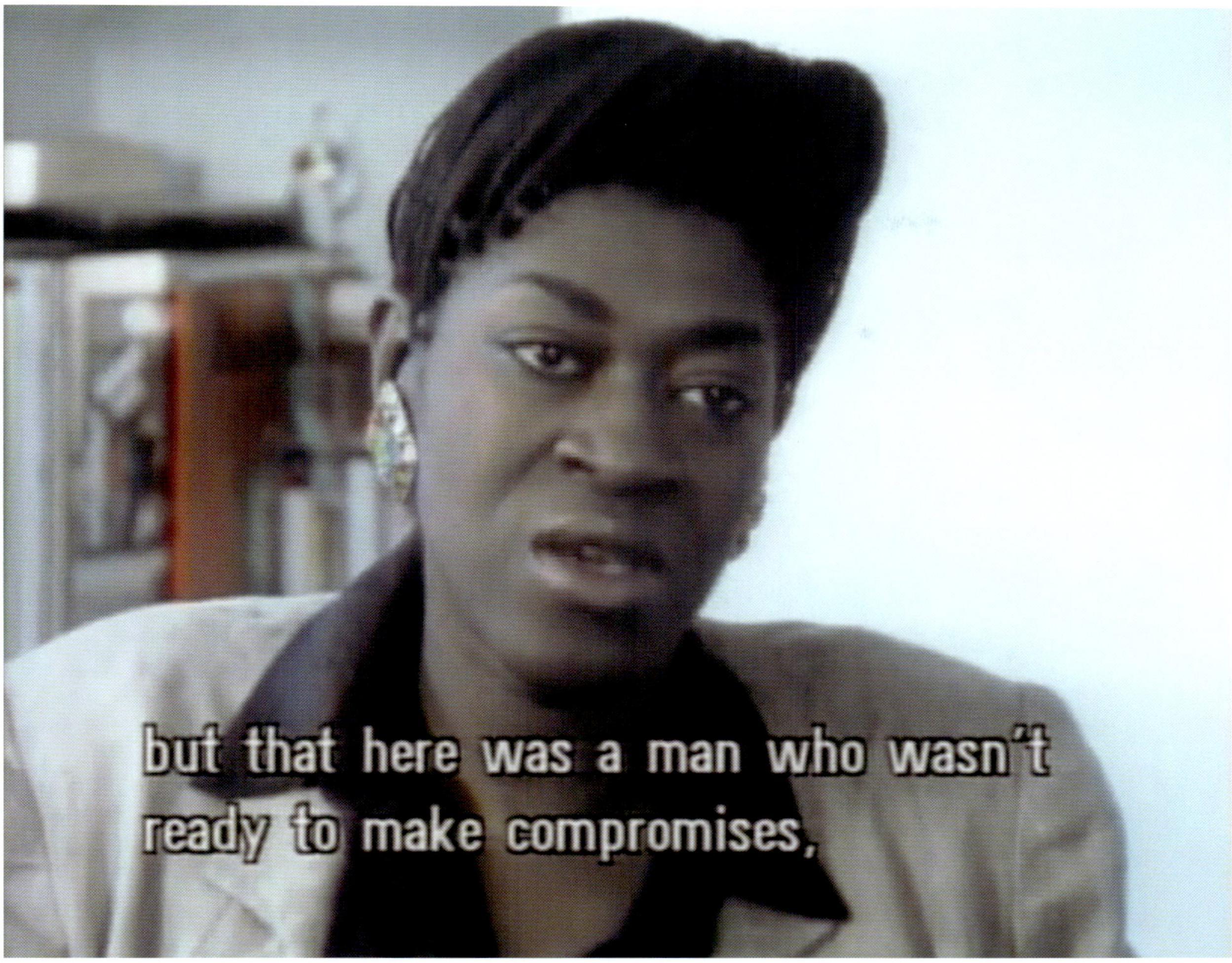

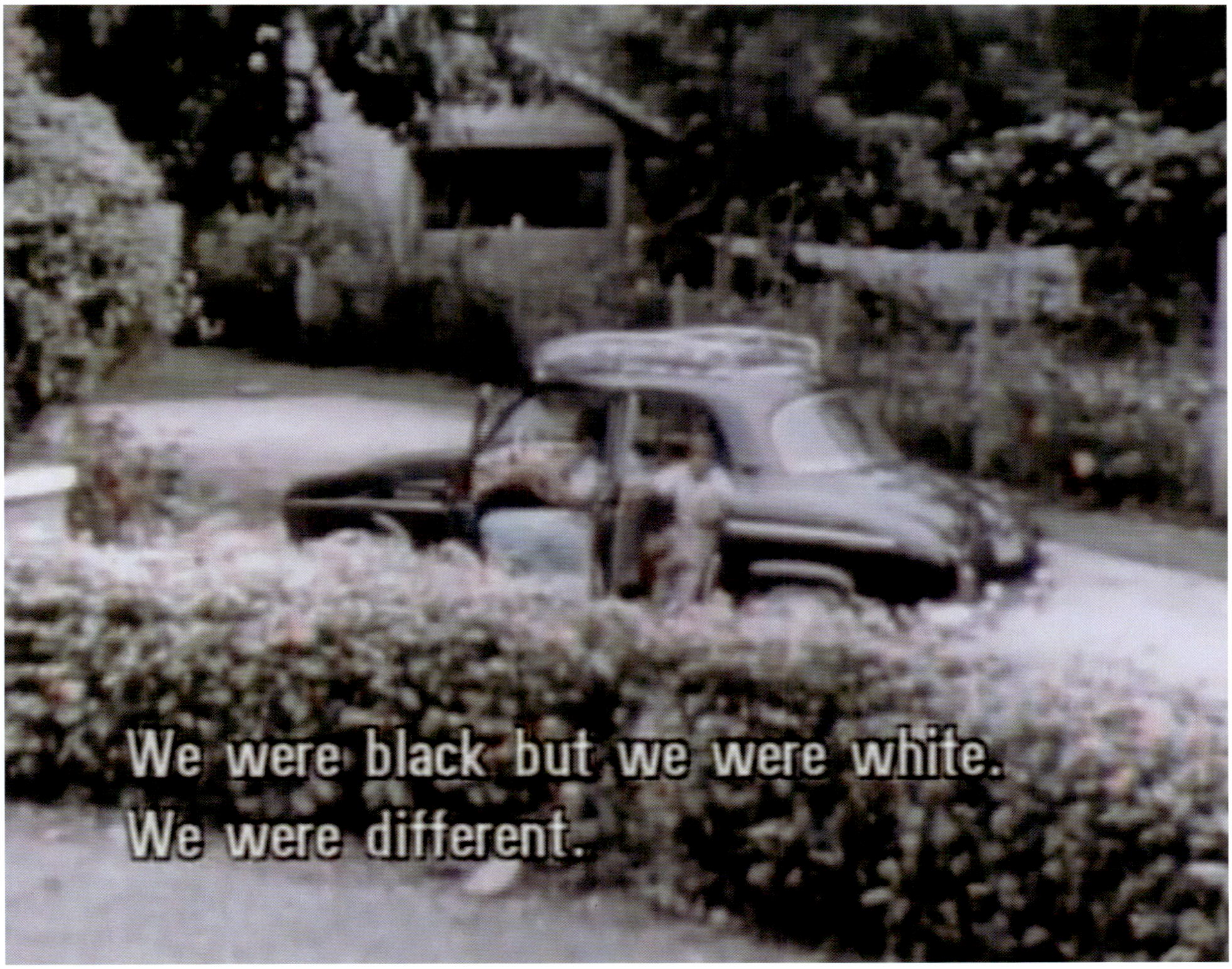

Raoul Goulard, *9000.000: Congo An I*, 1961,
included in Raoul Peck, *Death of a Prophet*, 1990,
film, black and white, 69min. Courtesy SONUMA-RTBF

Raoul Peck, *Death of a Prophet*, 1990,
film, black and white, 69min.
Courtesy Velvet Film, Paris

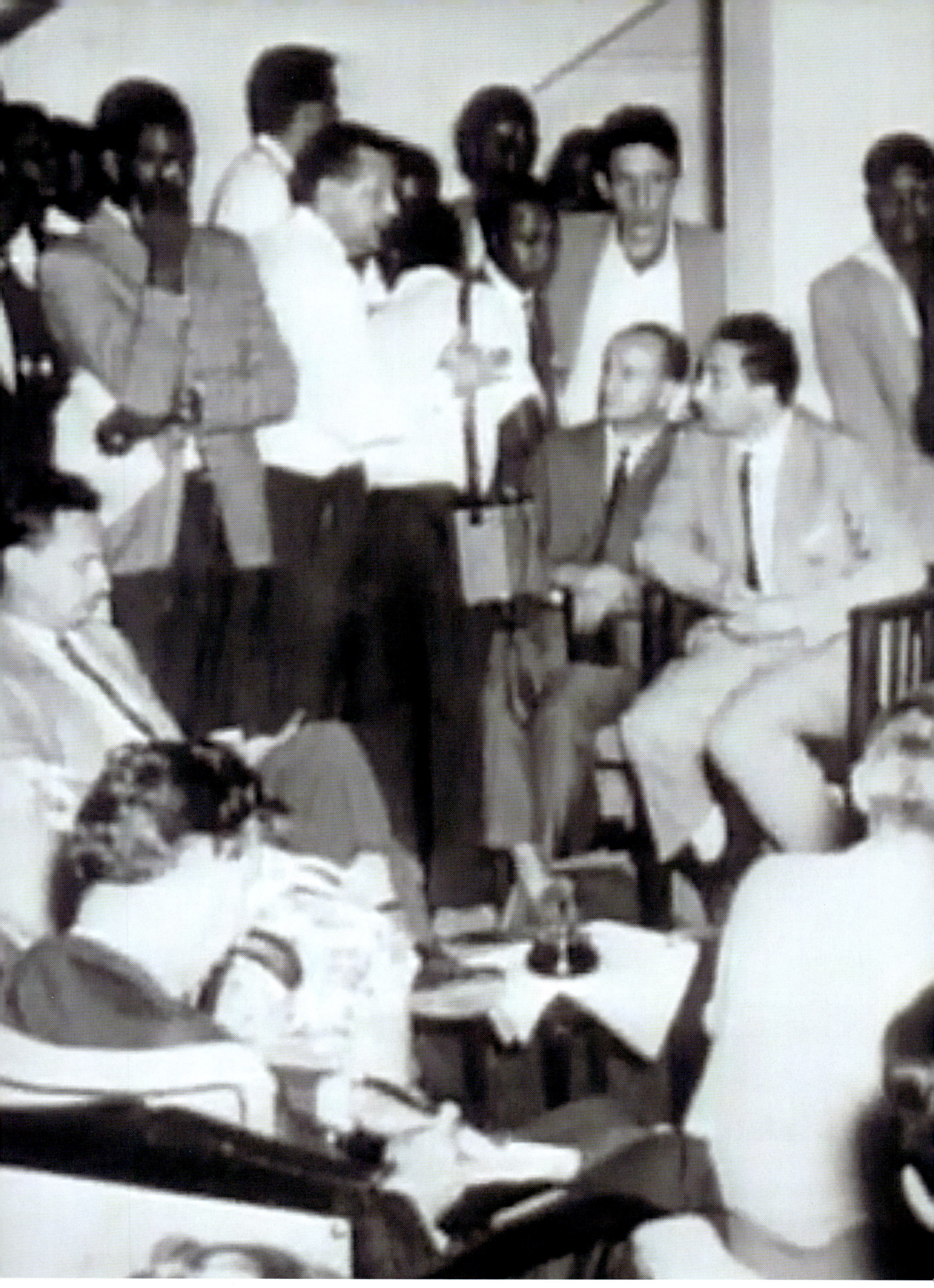

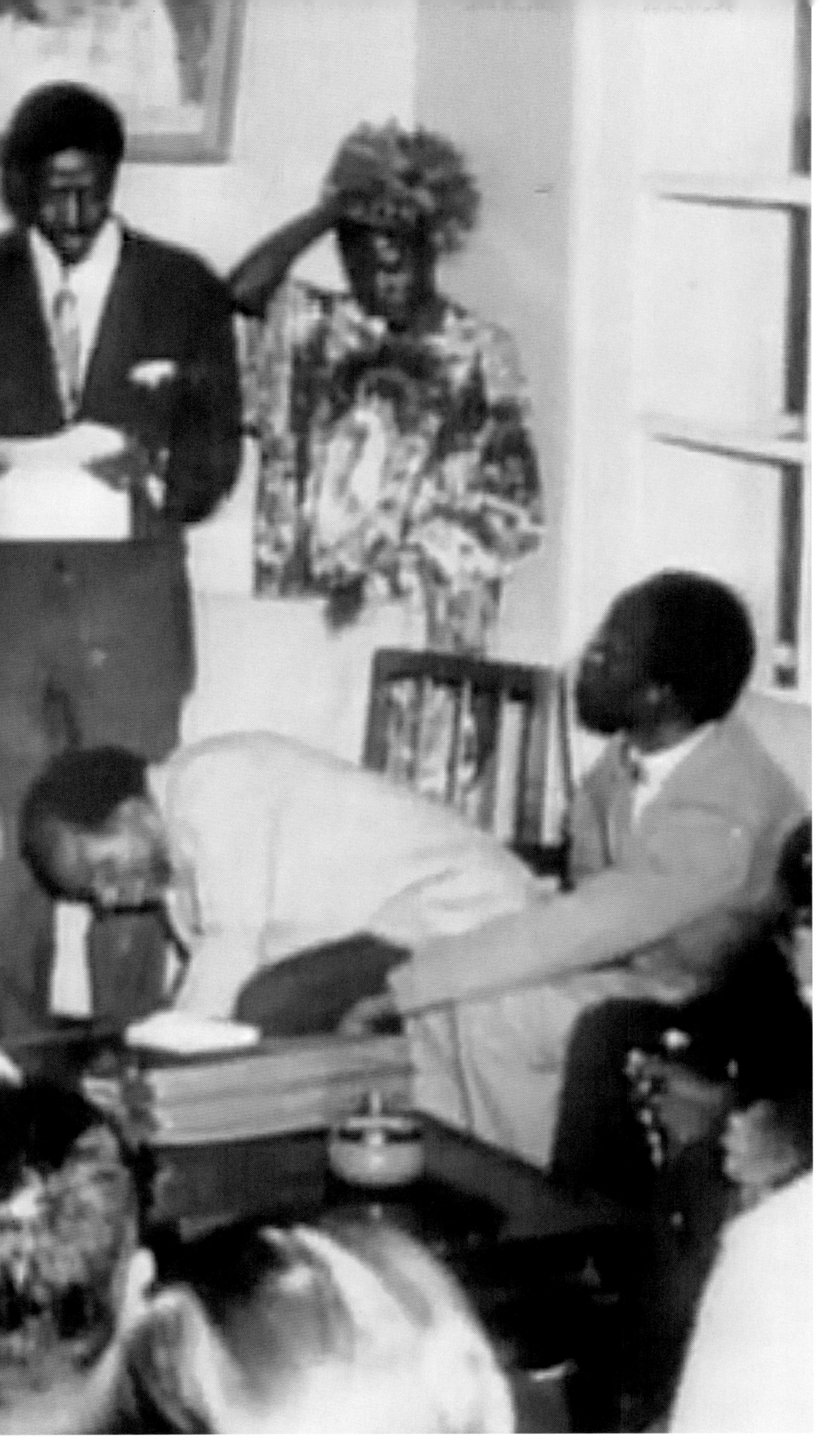

Raoul Goulard, *9000.000: Congo An I*, 1961,
included in Raoul Peck, *Death of a Prophet*, 1990,
film, black and white, 69min. Courtesy SONUMA-RTBF

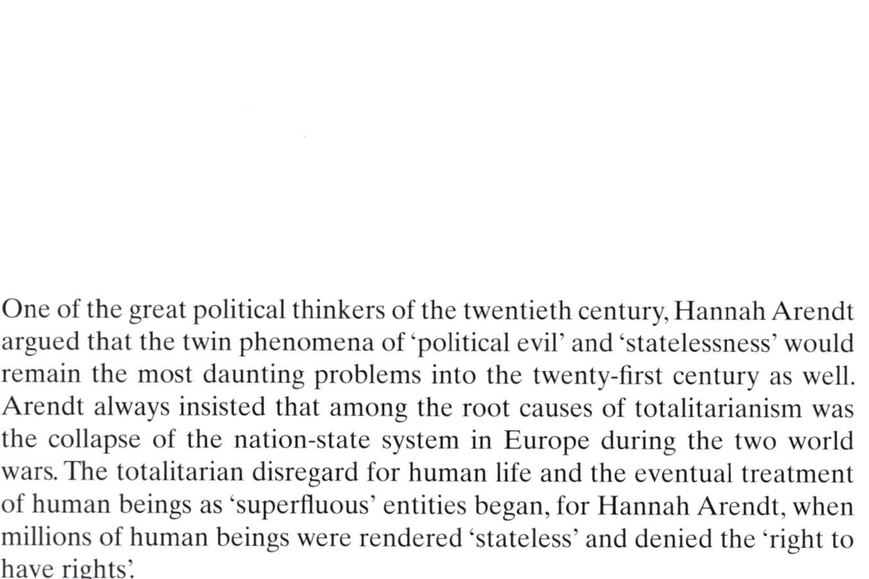

One of the great political thinkers of the twentieth century, Hannah Arendt argued that the twin phenomena of 'political evil' and 'statelessness' would remain the most daunting problems into the twenty-first century as well. Arendt always insisted that among the root causes of totalitarianism was the collapse of the nation-state system in Europe during the two world wars. The totalitarian disregard for human life and the eventual treatment of human beings as 'superfluous' entities began, for Hannah Arendt, when millions of human beings were rendered 'stateless' and denied the 'right to have rights'.

Statelessness, or the loss of nationality status, she argued, was tantamount to the loss of all rights. The stateless were deprived not only of their citizenship rights; they were deprived of any human rights. The rights of man and the rights of the citizen, which the modern bourgeois revolutions had so clearly delineated, were deeply imbricated. The loss of citizenship rights, therefore, contrary to all human rights declarations, was politically tantamount to the loss of human rights altogether.[12]

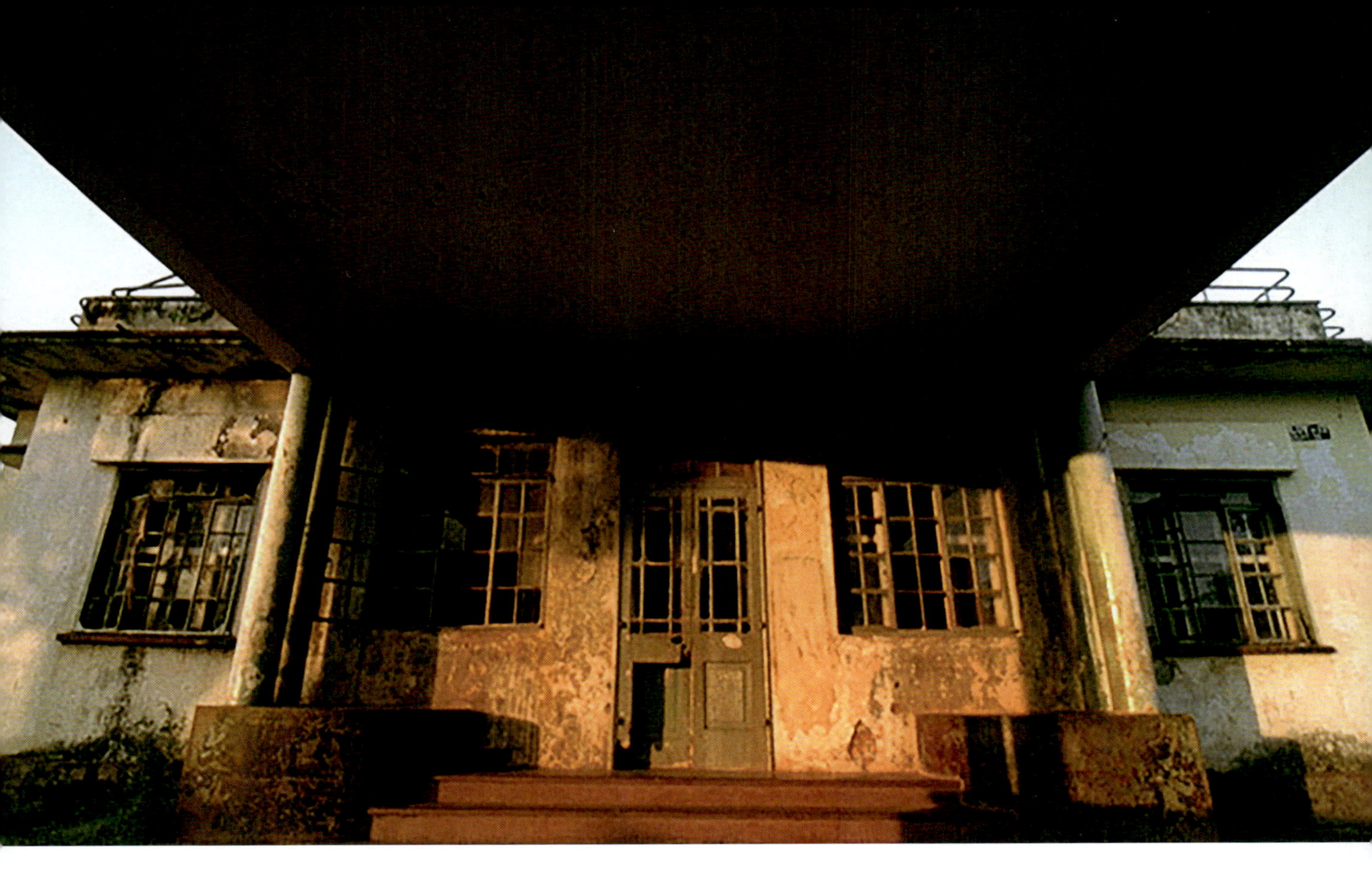

Zarina Bhimji, *Out of Blue*, 2002,
super 16mm film, shown as video,
projection, colour and sound (stereo),
24min 25sec. © Zarina Bhimji.
Courtesy, DACS/Artimage 2020

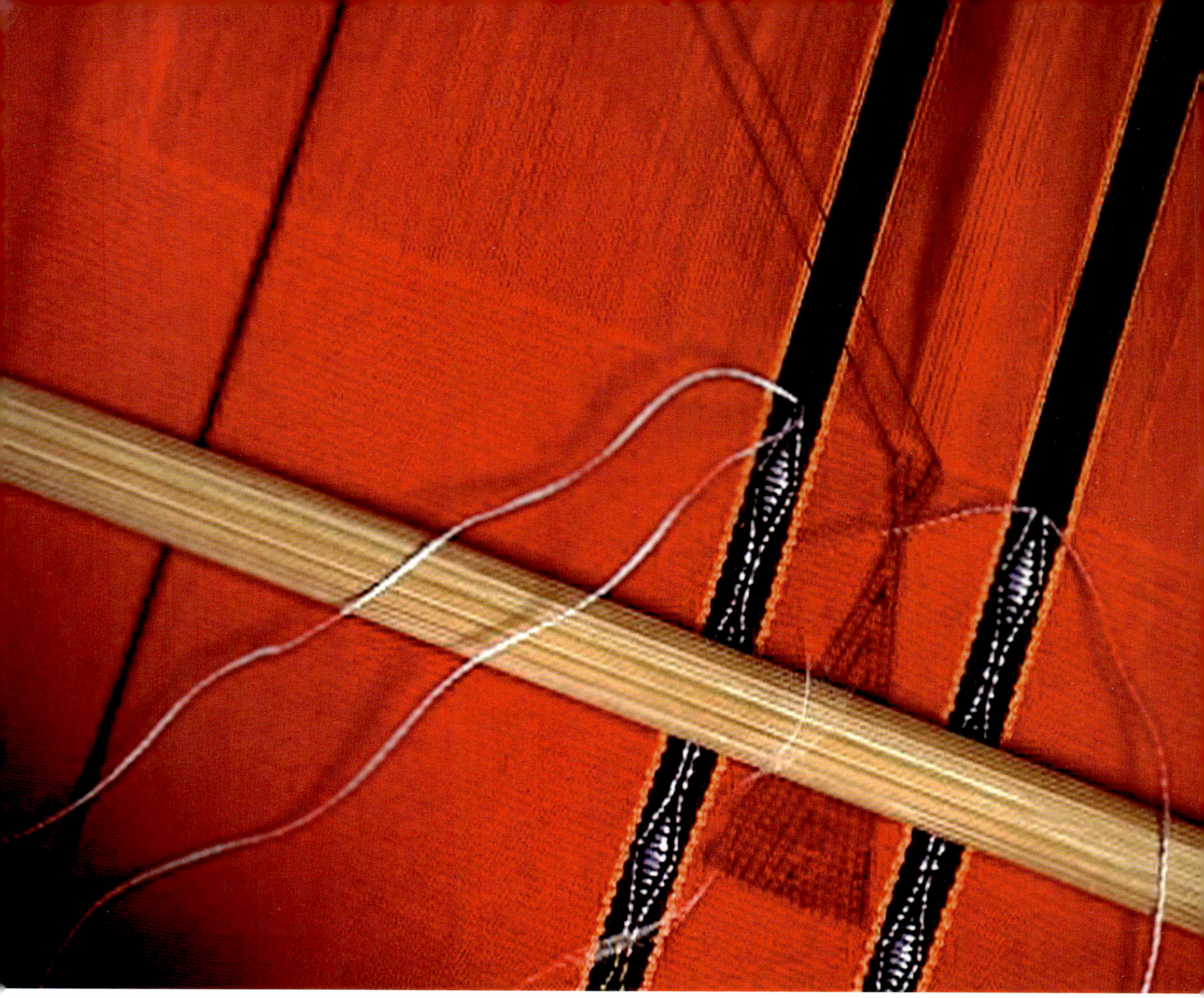

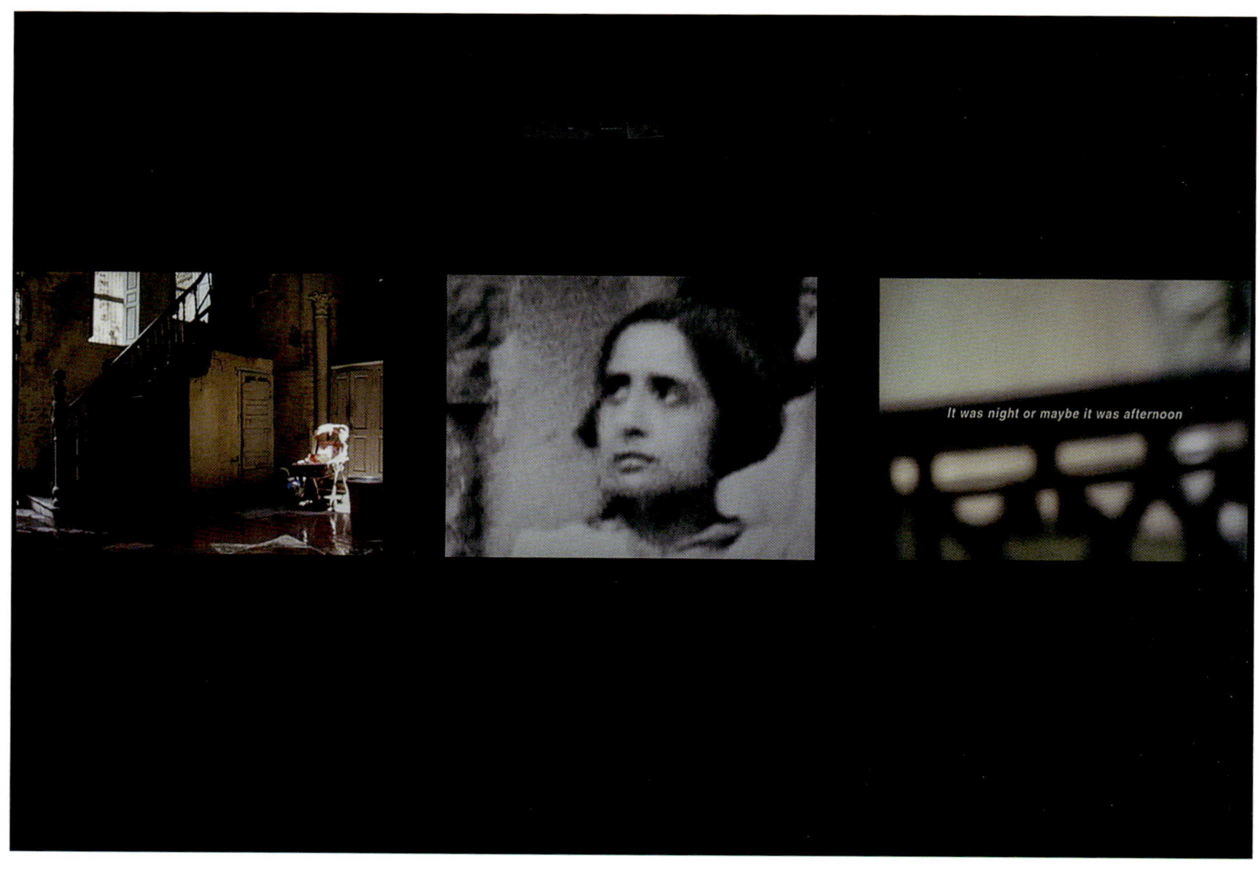

It was night or maybe it was afternoon

When the native is tortured, when his wife is killed or raped, he complains to no one. The oppressor's government can set up commissions of inquiry and of information daily if it wants to; in the eyes of the native, these commissions do not exist. The fact is that soon we shall have had seven years of crimes in Algeria and there has not yet been a single Frenchman indicted before a French court of justice for the murder of an Algerian. In Indo-China, in Madagascar or in the colonies the native has always known that he need expect nothing from the other side. The settler's work is to make even dreams of liberty impossible for the native. The native's work is to imagine all possible methods for destroying the settler. On the logical plane, the Manichaeism of the settler produces a Manichaeism of the native. To the theory of the 'absolute evil of the native' the theory of the 'absolute evil of the settler' replies.

[…]

But it so happens that for the colonised people this violence, because it constitutes their only work, invests their characters with positive and creative qualities. The practice of violence binds them together as a whole, since each individual forms a violent link in the great chain, a part of the great organism of violence which has surged upwards in reaction to the settler's violence in the beginning.[13]

Amar Kanwar, *The Lightning Testimonies*, 2007, video, 8 projections, black and white and colour, sound, 32min 31 sec. Courtesy the artist

THE PEOPLE'S REACTION

The Four Singers: *[With musical accompaniment]*
Why do they have the gold
Why do they have all the power
Why do they have friends at the top
Why do they have jobs at the top
We've got nothing always had nothing
Nothing but holes and millions of them

Kokol: Living in holes
Polpoch: Dying in holes
Cucurucu: Holes in our bellies
Rossignol: and holes in our clothes
The Four Singers & Chorus: Marat we're poor and the poor stay poor
Marat don't make us wait any more
We want our rights and we don't care how
We want our Revolution NOW

Marat: These lies they tell about the ideal state
The rich will never give away their property
of their own free will
And if by force of circumstances
they have to give up just a little
here and there
they do it only because they know
they'll soon win it back again

[…]

Because if you believe them
[turns towards the audience]
they will be completely in charge
in their marble homes and granite banks
from which they rob the people of the world
under the pretence of bringing them culture
  [Coulmier *leaves the platform and hurries*
  towards Sade. He speaks to him. Sade does
  not react]
Watch out
for as soon as it pleases them
they'll send you out
to protect their gold
in wars
  [Sade *rises and moves to the arena*]
whose weapons rapidly developed
by servile scientists
will become more and more deadly
until they can with a flick of a finger
tear a million of you to pieces[14]

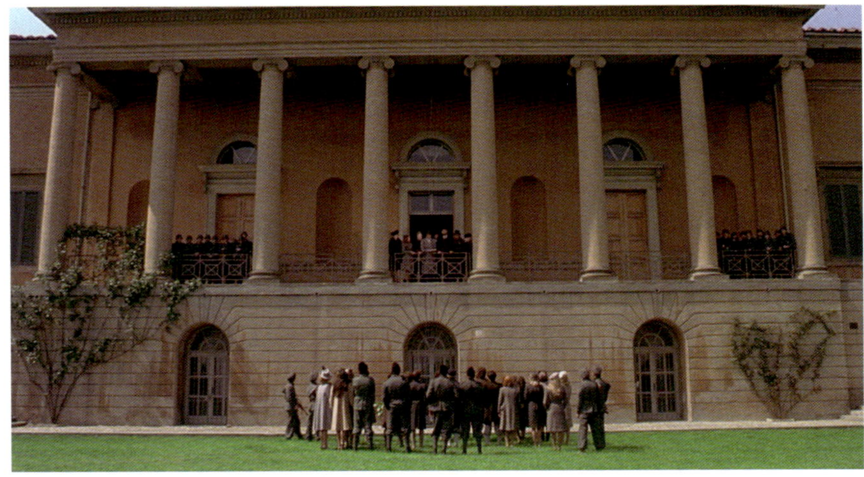

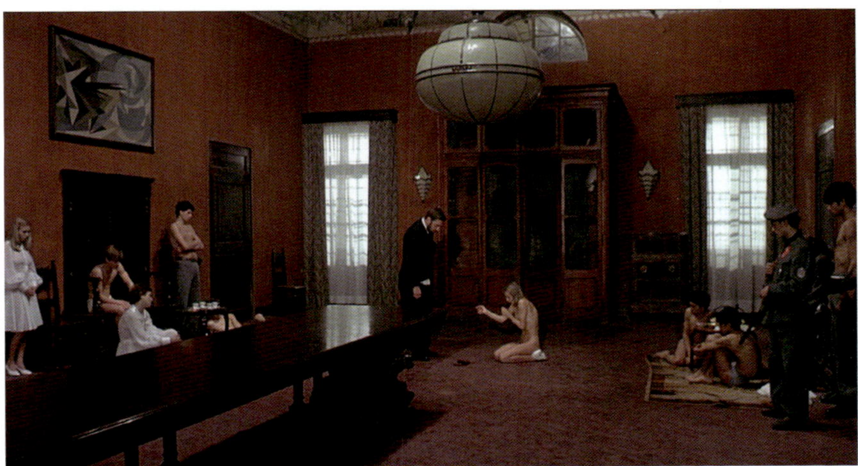

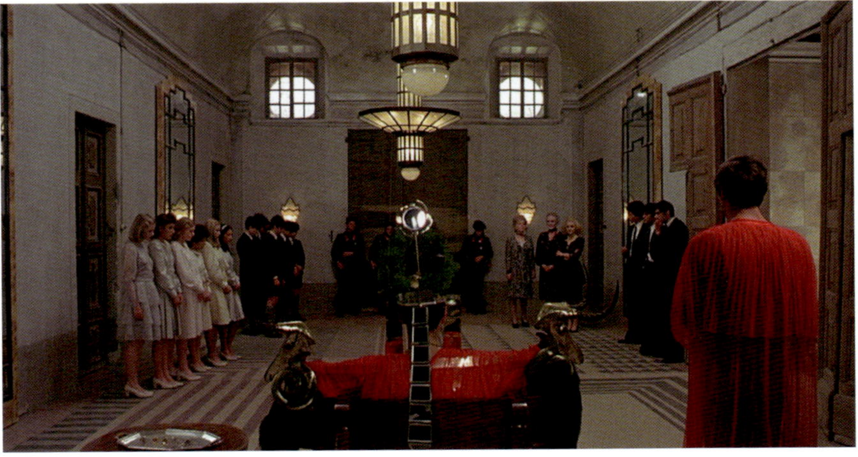

Hegemony is leadership which is in control, and that is what hegemony means: mastery. It means continually exercising the mastery of a situation. It entails forms of domination, if you will, that are not explicitly repressive. The notion that once hegemony is established it goes on forever is also quite foreign to Gramsci's conception. Hegemony is difficult work. It always has to be won. A dominant bloc has to constantly work for the establishment and continuation of its hegemony. It has to occupy the spaces which are required to reproduce its authority in the society. And what it gains is leadership and the containment of alternative forces. It need not incorporate or destroy them. It has enormous space within it for those who cannot live within the system. It is perfectly capable of tolerating marginals and deviants. It boxes them in, partly by the iron fist and partly by the velvet glove. But the fact that those open spaces exist is a testimony to its capacity to rule.[15]

*

Imperial control operates through three global and absolute means: the bomb, money and ether. The panoply of thermonuclear weapons, effectively, gathered at the pinnacle of Empire, represents the continuous possibility

Pier Paolo Pasolini, *Salò, or the 120 Days of Sodom*, 1975, film, colour, 185min.

of the destruction of life itself. This is an operation of absolute violence, a new metaphysical horizon, which completely changes the conception whereby the sovereign state had a monopoly of legitimate physical force. At one time, in modernity, this monopoly was legitimated either as the expropriation of weapons from the violent and anarchic mob, the disordered mass of individuals who tend to slaughter one another, or as the instrument of defence against the enemy, that is, against other peoples organised in states. Both these means of legitimation were oriented finally towards the survival of the population. Today they are no longer effective. The expropriation of the means of violence from a supposedly self-destructive population tends to become merely administrative and police operations aimed at maintaining the segmentations of productive territories. The second justification becomes less effective too as nuclear war between state powers becomes increasingly unthinkable. The development of nuclear technologies and their imperial concentration have limited the sovereignty of most of the countries of the world insofar as it has taken away from them the power to make decisions over war and peace, which is a primary element of the traditional definition of sovereignty. Furthermore, the ultimate threat of the imperial bomb has reduced every war to a limited conflict, a civil war, a dirty war, and so forth. It has made every war the exclusive domain of administrative and police power. From no other standpoint is the passage from modernity to postmodernity and from modern sovereignty to Empire more evident than it is from the standpoint of the bomb. Empire is defined here in the final instance as the 'non-place' of life, or, in other words, as the absolute capacity for destruction. Empire is the ultimate form of biopower insofar as it is the absolute inversion of the power of life.[16]

*

Lest you think, to paraphrase Gramsci, my optimism of the will has now completely outstripped my pessimism of the intellect, let me add a fourth element that comments on the moment. For, if the global postmodern represents an ambiguous opening to difference and to the margins and makes a certain kind of decentring of the western narrative a likely possibility, it is matched, from the very heartland of cultural politics, by the backlash: the aggressive resistance to difference; the attempt to restore the canon of Western civilisation; the assault, direct and indirect, on multi-culturalism; the return to grand narratives of history, language and literature (the three great supporting pillars of national identity and national culture); the defence of ethnic absolutism, of a cultural racism that has marked the Thatcher and the Reagan eras; and the new xenophobias that are about to overwhelm fortress Europe. The last thing to do is read me as saying the cultural dialectic is finished.[17]

1   Hannah Arendt, *Denktagebuch. Bd. 1: 1950 –1973* (ed. Ursula Ludz and Ingrid Nordmann), Zürich: Piper, 2002, p.522.

2   Stuart Hall's memoir of that name was published posthumously by Allen Lane in 2017.

3   Chantal Mouffe, *Hegemony, Radical Democracy, and the Political* (ed. James Martin), London: Routledge, 2013, p.185. Reproduced with permission of the licensor through PLSclear.

4   Moustafa Bayoumi and Andrew Rubin (ed.), *The Edward Said Reader*, New York: Vintage Books, 2000, p.73.

5   Paul Gilroy, *Postcolonial Melancholia*, New York: Columbia University Press, 2004, p.3.

6   'Caribbean Migration: The Windrush Generation', in Stuart Hall and Bill Schwarz (ed.), *Familiar Stranger*, pp.173–202. © 2017 Stuart Hall Estate. All rights reserved. Republished by permission of the copyright holder and the publisher Duke University Press.

7   Frantz Fanon, *Black Skin, White Mask*, New York: Grove Press, 1967, p.111. English translation © 2008 Richard Philcox. Used by permission of Grove/Atlantic, Inc. Any third-party use of this material, outside of this publication, is prohibited.

8   Cornel West, *Democracy Matters*, New York: Penguin Press, 2004, p.60. © 2004 Cornel West. Used by permission of Penguin Press, an imprint of Penguin Publishing Group, a division of Penguin Random House LLC. All rights reserved.

9   P. Gilroy, *Postcolonial Melancholia*, op. cit., p.57.

10 Seyla Benhabib, *The Rights of Others: Aliens, Residents and Citizens*, Cambridge: Cambridge University Press, 2004, p.51.

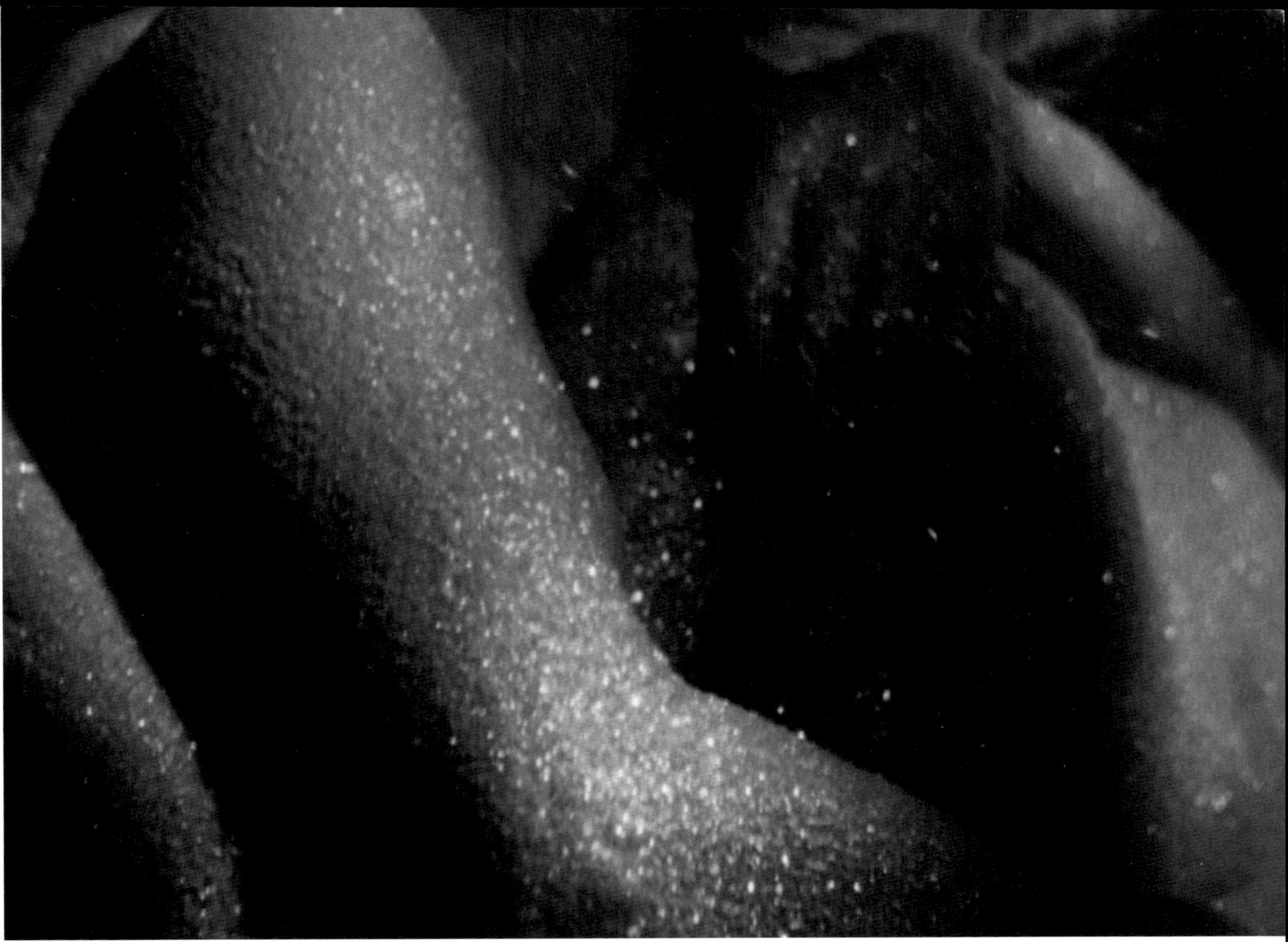

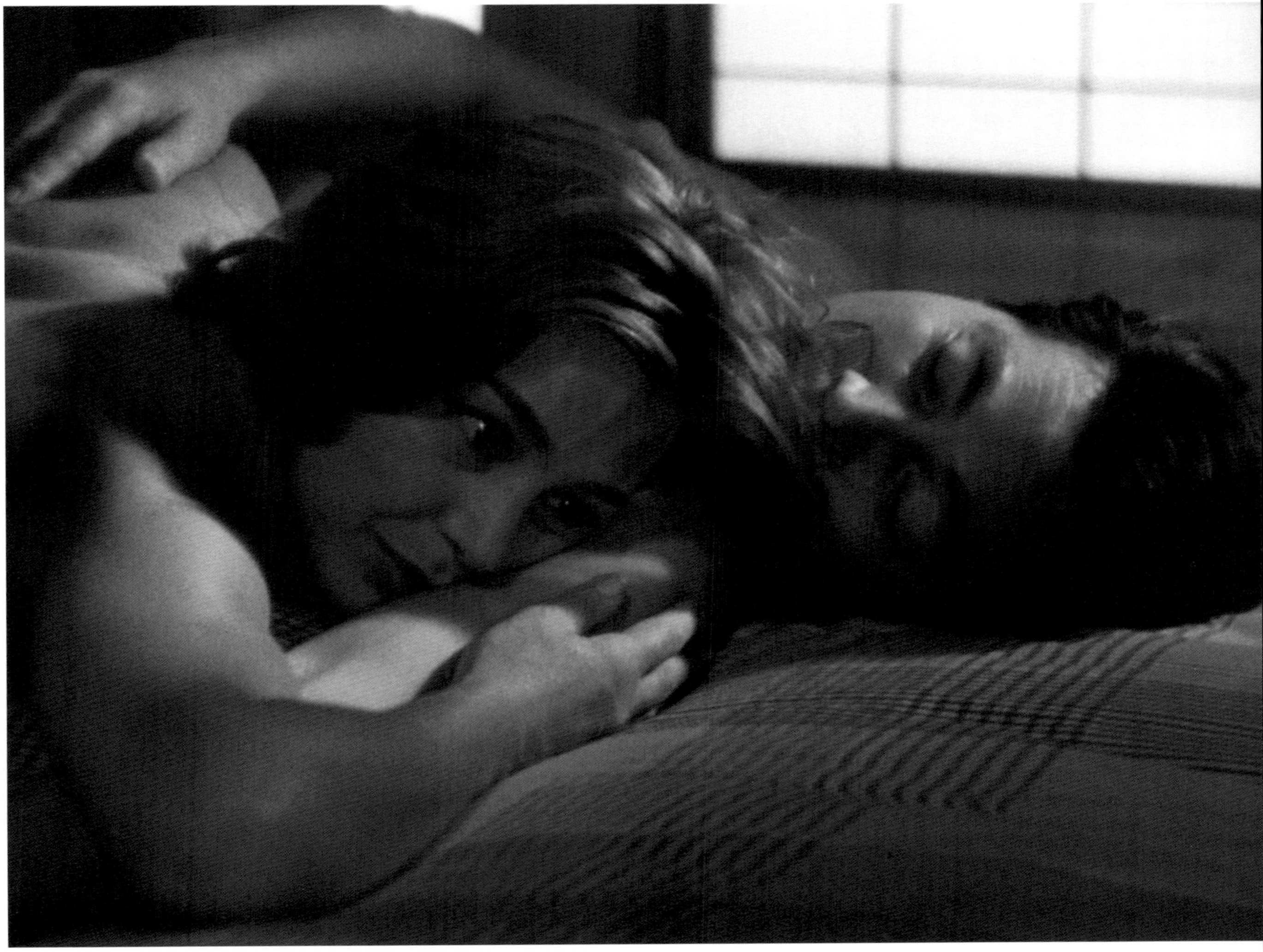

Alain Resnais, director, and Marguerite Duras,
screenplay, *Hiroshima mon amour*, 1959,
film, colour, 85min

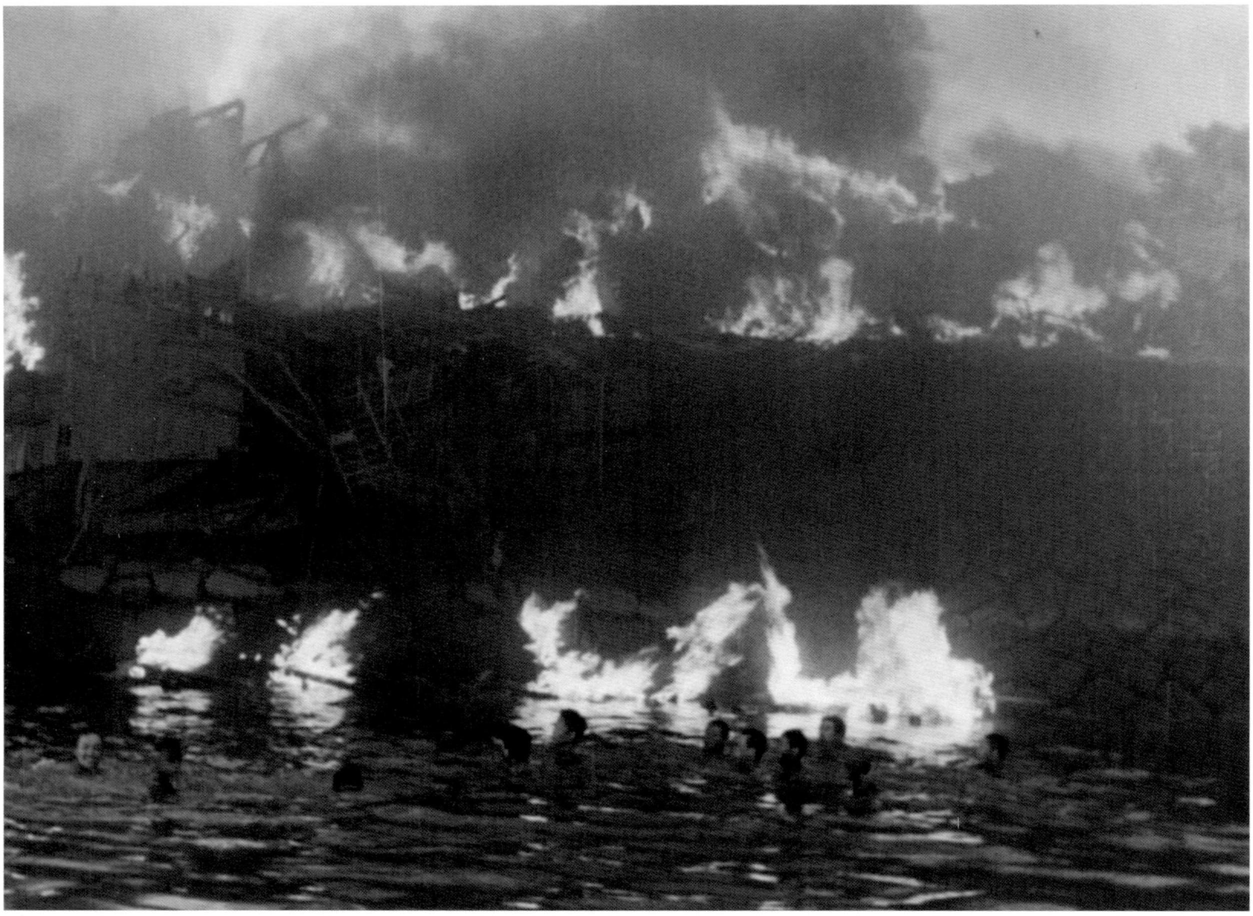

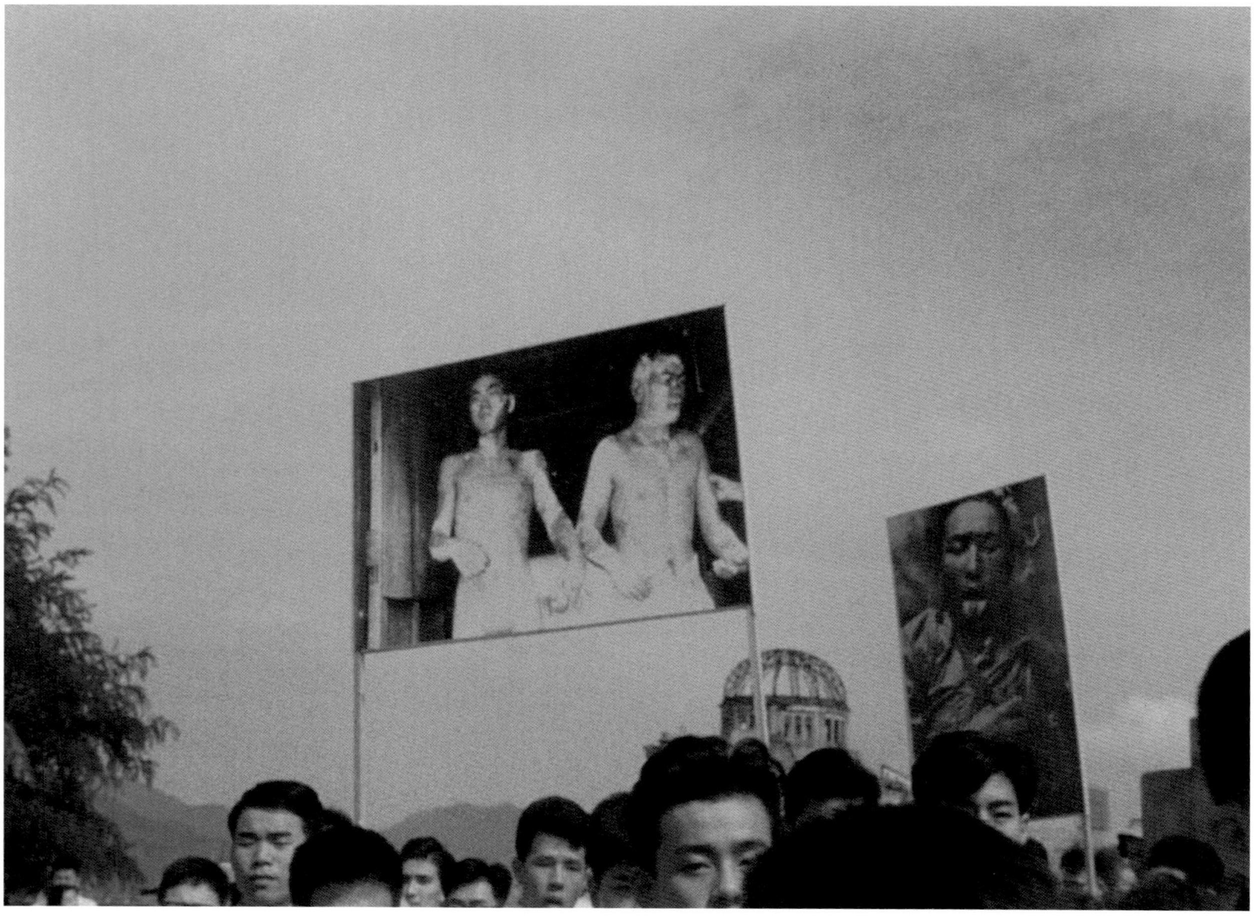

Ute Meta Bauer & Ana Salazar

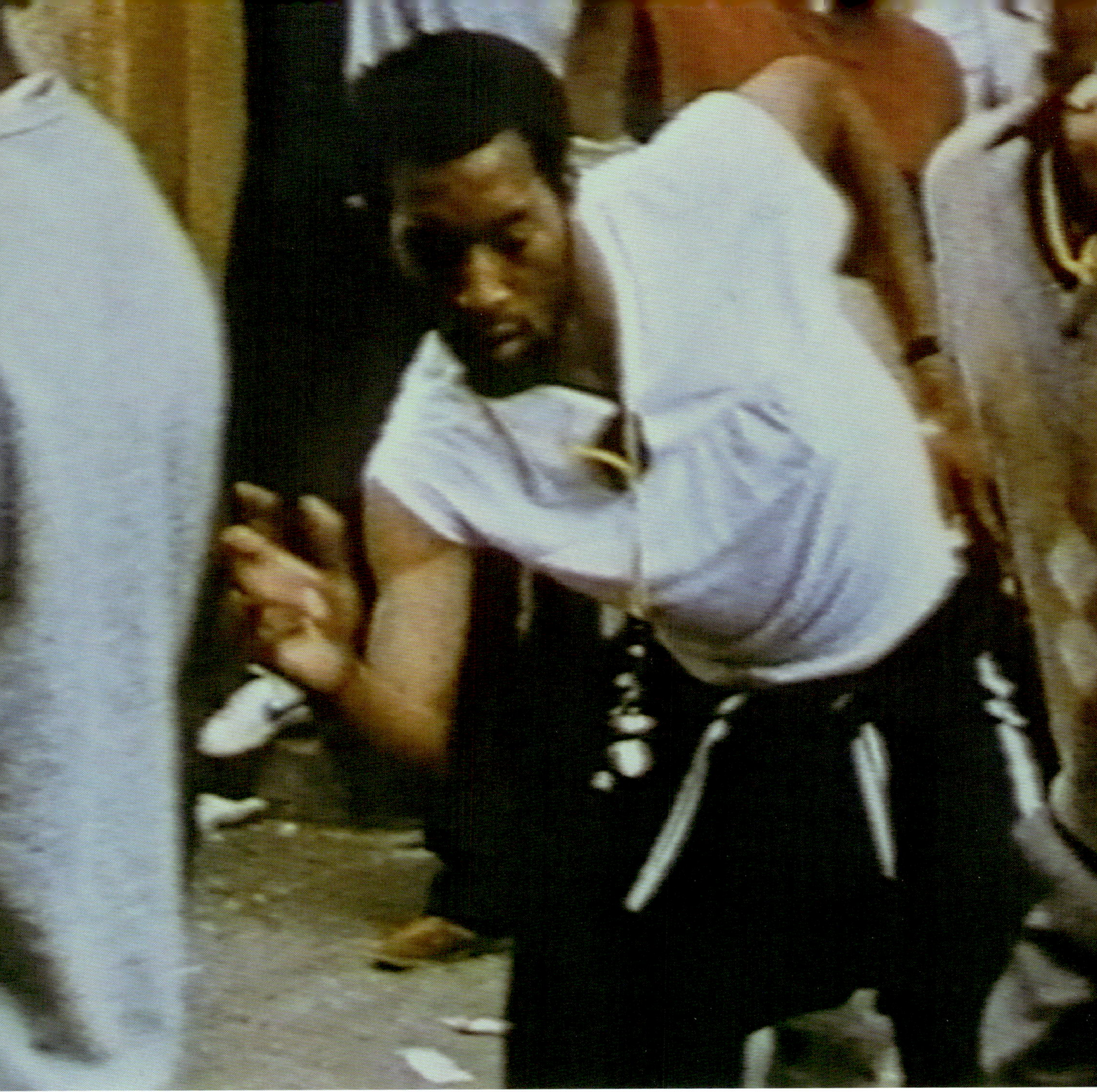

**Isaac Julien, *Territories*, 1984,
16mm film, colour, sound, 24min 6sec.
Courtesy the artist and Victoria Miro,
London/Venice**

11   Frantz Fanon, *The Wretched of the Earth*, London: Penguin Books, 2014, p.76. ©
     1963 Présence Africaine. Used by permission of Grove/Atlantic, Inc. Any third-party
     use of this material, outside of this publication, is prohibited.
12   S. Benhabib, *The Rights of Others*, op. cit., p.49.
13   F. Fanon, *The Wretched of the Earth*, op. cit., p.73.
14   Peter Weiss, Marat/Sade, *The Persecution and Assassination if Marat as
     performed by the inmates of the Asylum of Charenton under the direction of the
     Marquis de Sade*, London: Marion Boyars, 1982, p.43 and p.62.
15   S. Hall, 'Domination and Hegemony', *Cultural Studies 1983: A Theoretical History*
     (ed. Jennifer Daryl Slack and Lawrence Grossberg), Durham, NC: Duke University
     Press, pp.155–79. © 2016 Stuart Hall Estate. All rights reserved. Republished by
     permission of the copyright holder and publisher Duke University Press.
16   Michael Hardt and Antonio Negri, *Empire*, Cambridge, MA: Harvard University
     Press, 2000, p.345. © 2000 the President and Fellows of Harvard College.
17   S. Hall, 'What is this "black" in black popular culture?', *Stuart Hall: Critical Dialogues
     in Cultural Studies* (ed. David Morley and Kuan-hsing Chen), London and New
     York: Routledge, 1996, pp.465–75. Reproduced with permission of the licensor
     through PLSclear.

Adrian Piper, Belkis Ayón, Dalton Paula, Arthur Bispo do Rosário,
Rosana Paulino, Black Quantum Futurism, Lorna Simpson
With a poem by Fred Moten

Time Will Tell

Amanda Carneiro

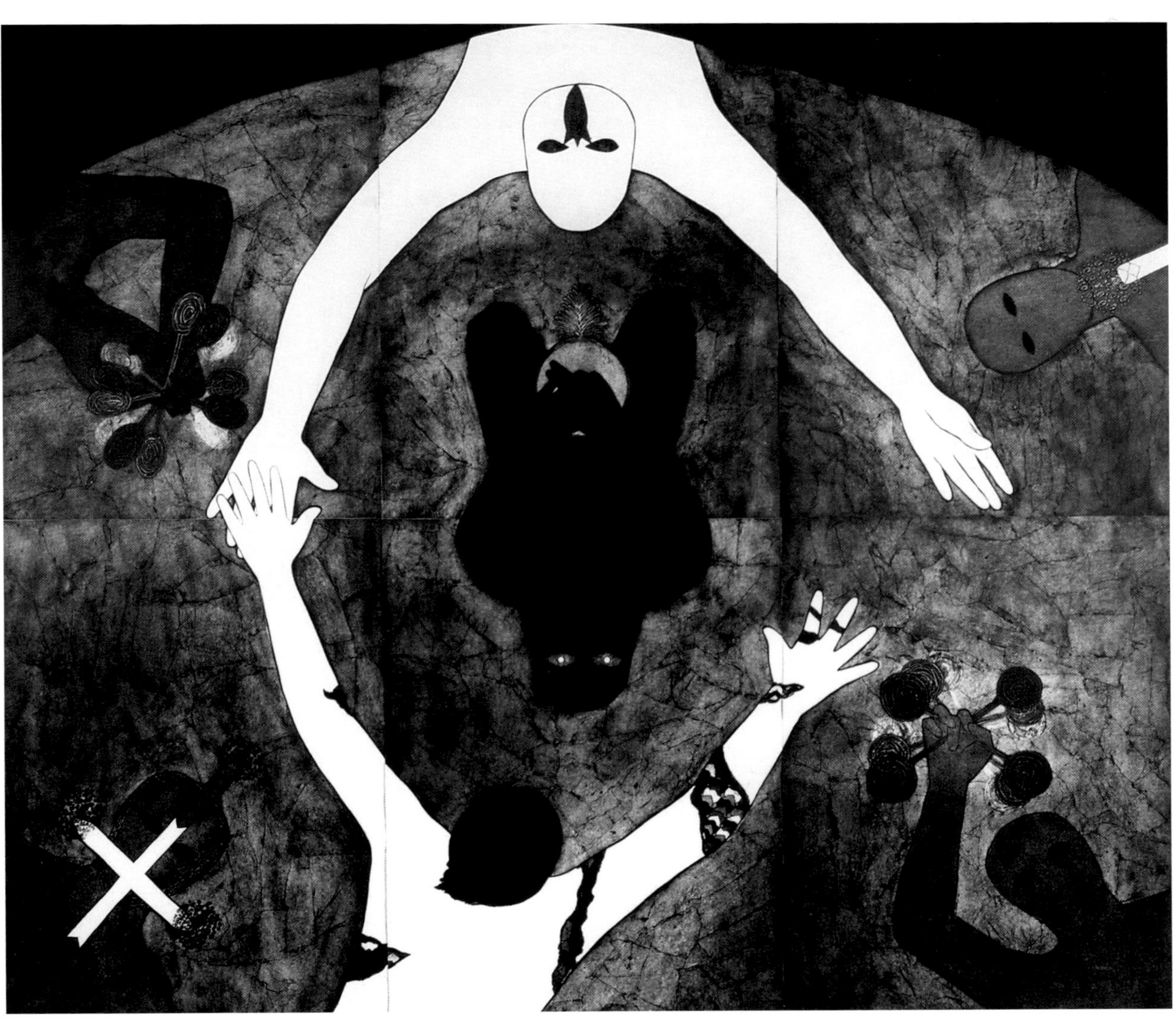

Belkis Ayón, *Ya estamos aquí*
(We are here already), 1991, collography.
Photograph: José A. Figueroa.
Courtesy and © the Belkis Ayón
Estate, Havana, Cuba

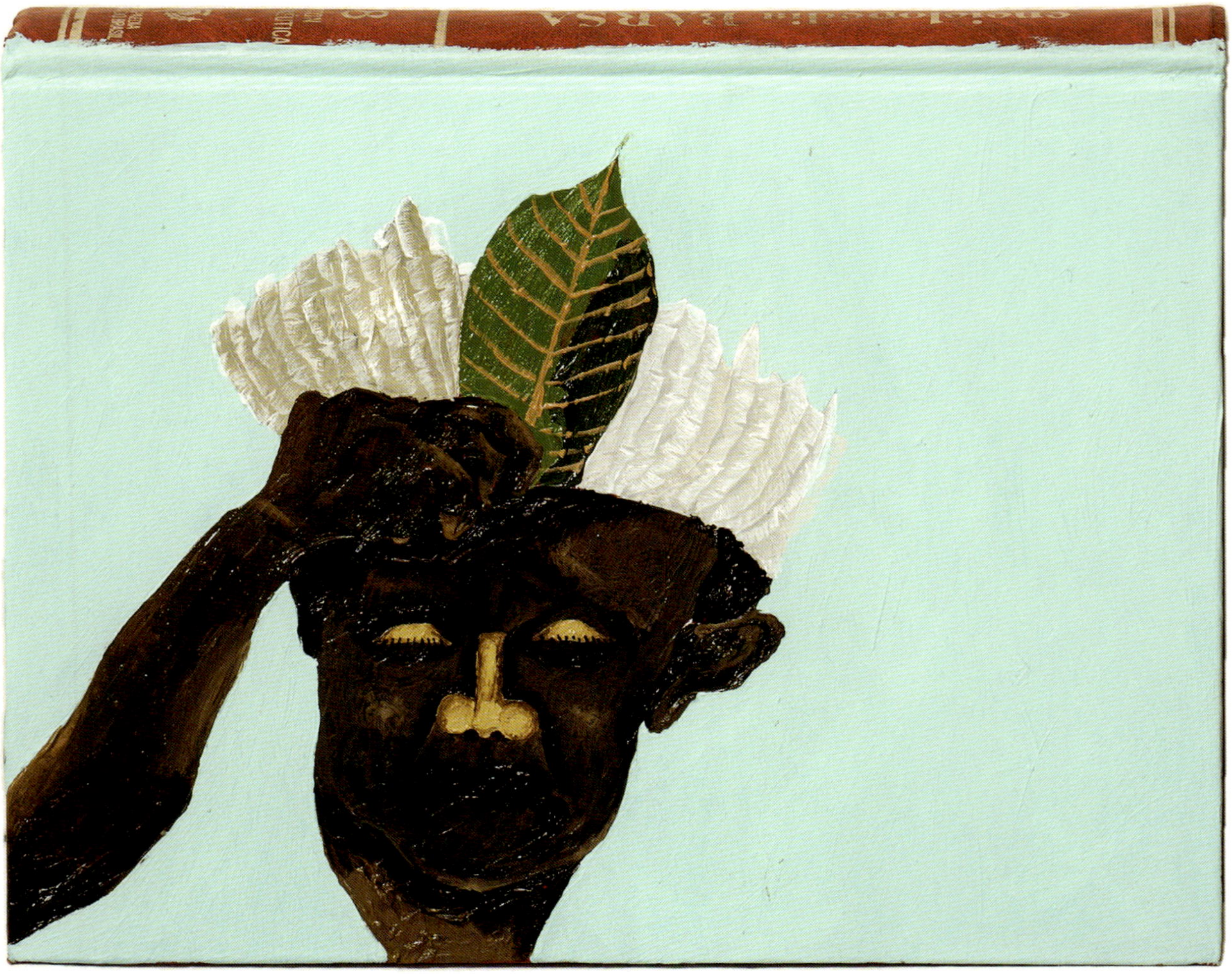

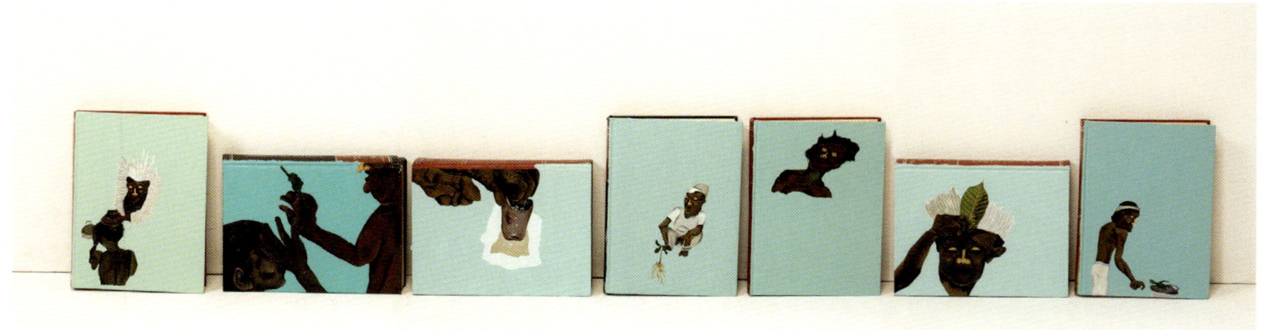

Dalton Paula, *Cura B*, 2016,
oil on seven books.
Photograph: Paulo Rezende.
Courtesy the artist

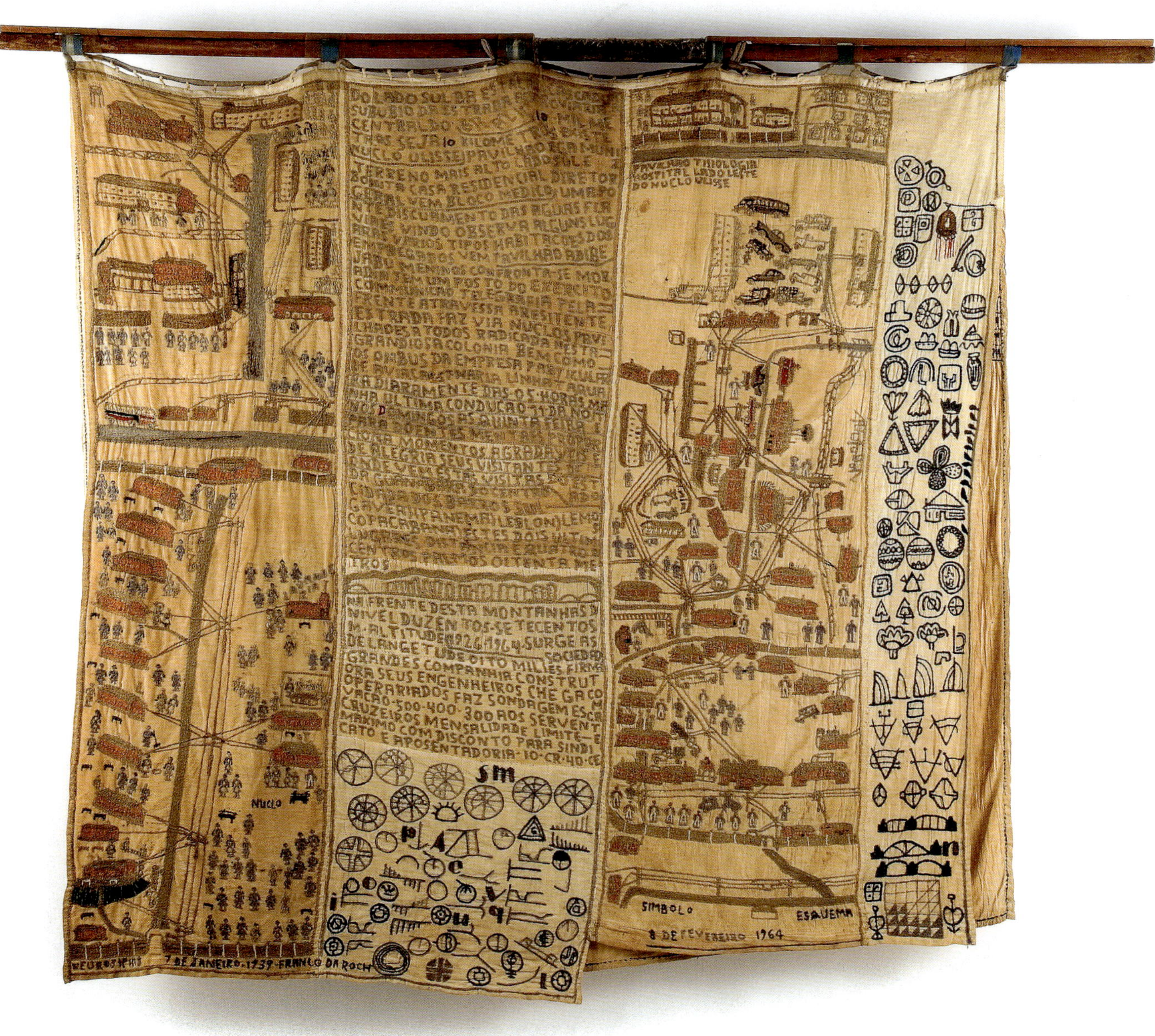

Artur Bispo do Rosário,
Eu preciso destas palavras. Escrita.
(*I need these words written down.*), undated.
Courtesy Museu Bispo do Rosário Collection.

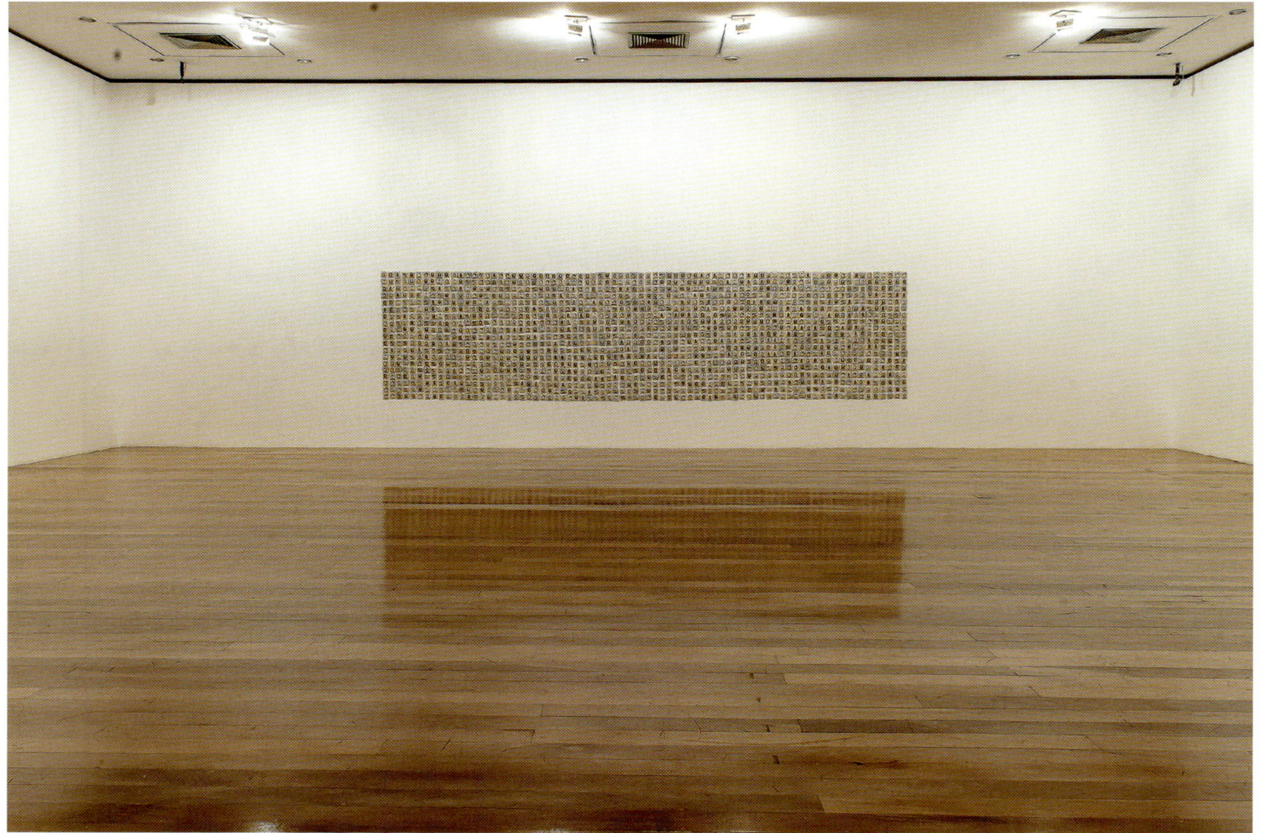

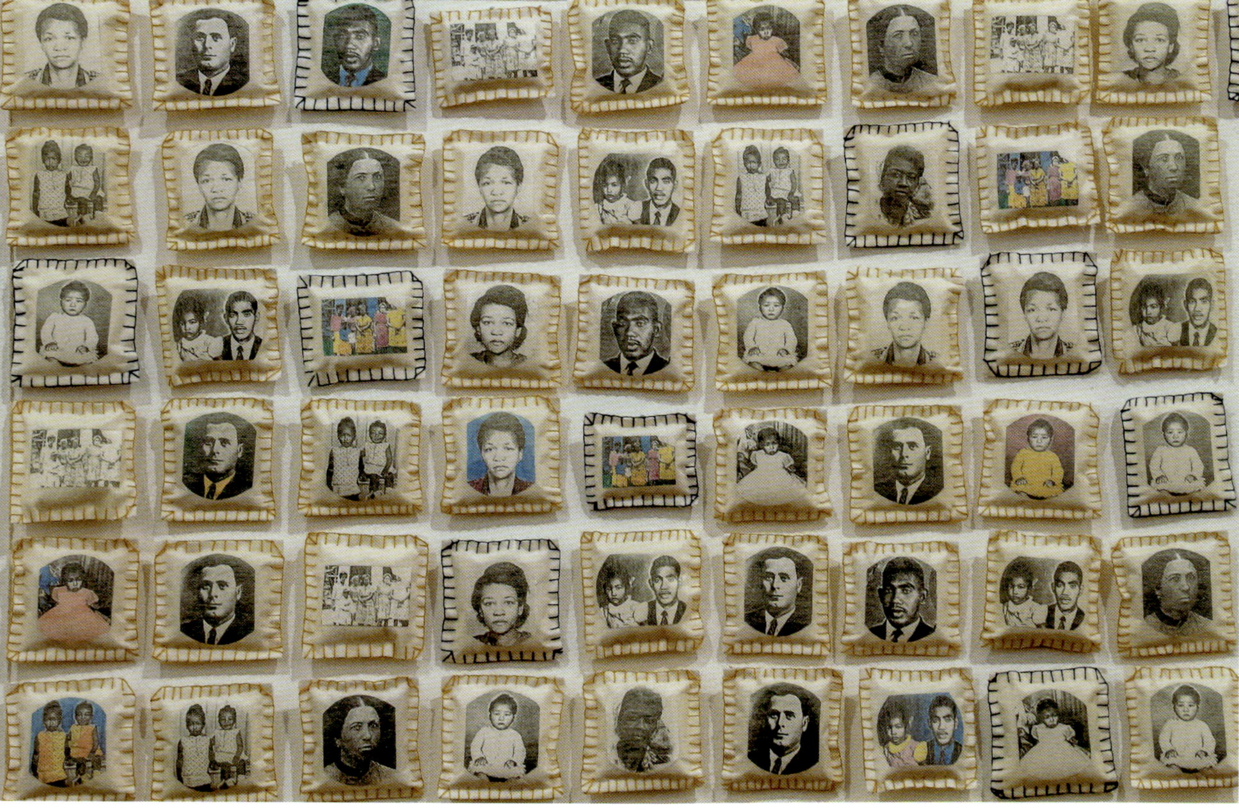

Rosana Paulino, *Parede da memória*
(*Memorial Wall*), 1994–2015.
Courtesy the artist

wait for it

you remain the future in our present like an accent pause that gramsci had to measure. living better now that double tap stop till then till that is your time we're in love with waiting. we can't so we can surprise so we can

attend and take urgent care. the erotic cure, which shows up as, which gives us, so that it ought to give us,

pause is our propulsion. who do what's been done can't wait for it and can't walk off. who recognize the

future don't wait on us, but because they don't know about service, about what it is to be an instrument,

decide they just ain't gon' wait. they miss something, they missing something, our liveness in reverb, this re:

that we refer to something, that we regard something, that we in regard to something else. they tell us what they think they know and we wait till they understand. I'm tired of waiting till they understand. see you later.

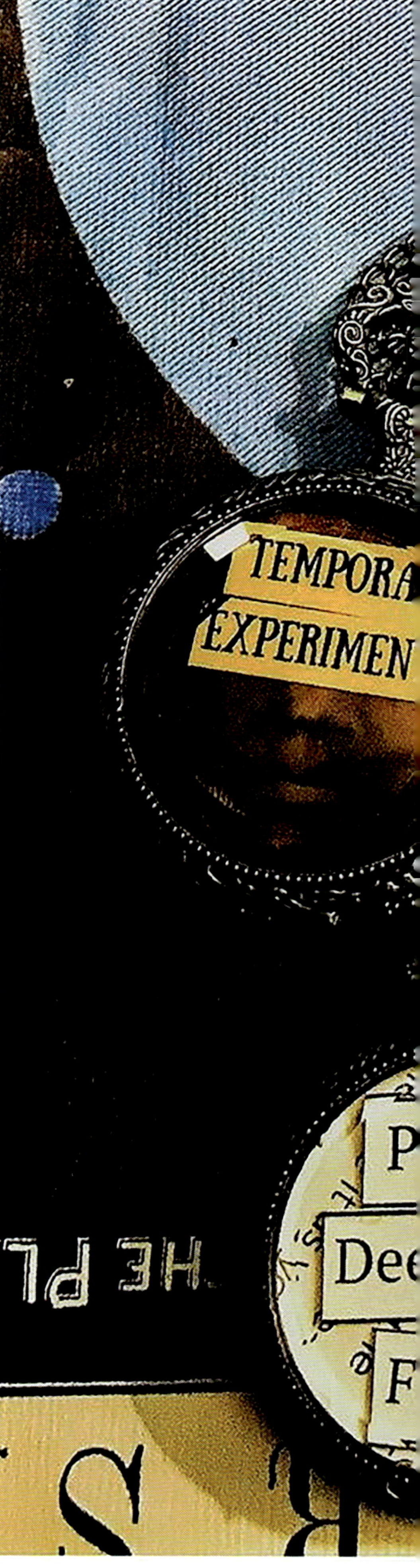

Black Quantum Futurism,
The Temporal Disruptors, 2018,
archival collage paper on found objects.
Courtesy the artists

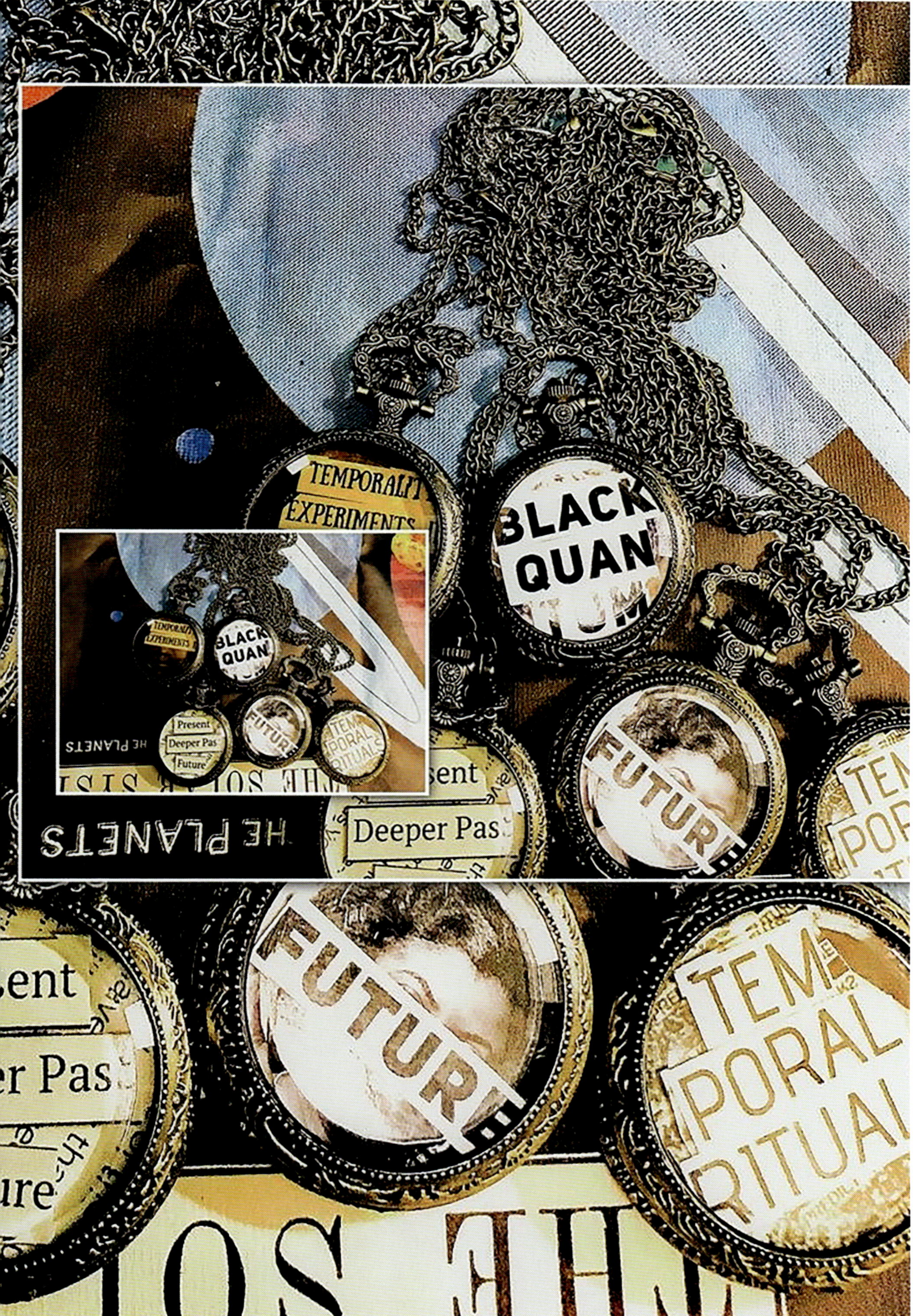
TEMPORALIT
EXPERIMENTS
BLACK
QUAN
FUTUR
TEM
POR
RITUAL
TEMPORAL
RITUALS
Present
Deeper Pas
Future
HE PLANETS
THE SOLAR SIS
Deeper Pas
sent
THE SO

Shilpa Gupta, Derek Jarman, Jeremy Deller, Nam June Paik, Robert Cailliau,
Sergey Kuryokhin and Sergey Sholokhov, Laura Grace Ford

Dark Matter, or the Infinite Reservoir of Black Swans

Nav Haq

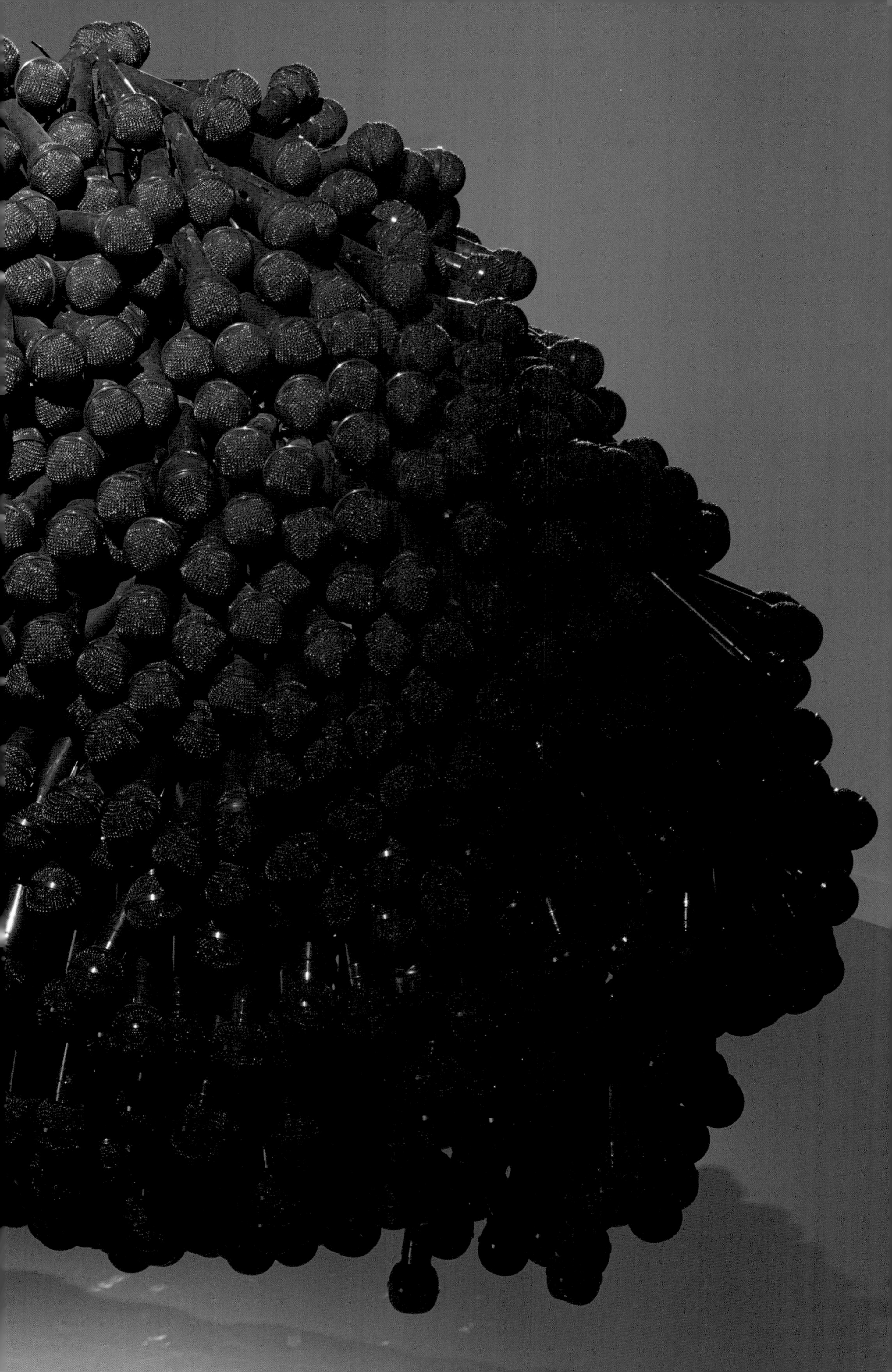

World War I. The discovery of penicillin. The AIDS epidemic. The development of the World Wide Web. The dissolution of the USSR. The attacks on the World Trade Center in New York on 11 September 2001. The financial crashes of 1987 and 2008. The Indian Ocean earthquake and tsunami of 2004. Donald Trump's win in the 2016 US election. The Covid-19 pandemic of 2020. All events within living memory to which the label of 'black swan' has been applied.

'The black swan theory' posits that the events that have the deepest impact on society and history are those that are unpredictable or highly improbable. Developed by writer and former risk analyst Nassim Nicholas Taleb in his influential 2007 book *The Black Swan: The Impact of the Highly Improbable*, the theory proposes that almost all of the most 'consequential' events in history are unexpected, and that humans only later convince themselves that these events are explainable. Taleb regards most major scientific discoveries, historical events and even artistic accomplishments as 'black swans' – both consequential and unpredicted. The notion of 'our blindness with respect to randomness, particularly large deviations' summarises the central idea of his thesis.[1]

The term 'black swan' derives from the Latin expression *rara avis in terris nigroque simillima cygno* (a rare bird in the lands and very much like a black swan) to describe something so rare or improbable as to have precluded contemplation of its existence prior to its appearance; when the Latin phrase was coined, black swans were presumed not to exist at all. Indeed, all *known* swans (and therefore in the public imaginary *all* swans) were white until a black variety was discovered in Australia by Dutch explorer Willem de Vlamingh in 1697. As Taleb puts it, before this discovery the idea that all swans were white was:

> an unassailable belief as it seemed completely confirmed by empirical evidence. The sighting of the first black swan [...] illustrates a severe limitation to our learning from observations or experience and the fragility of our knowledge. One single observation can invalidate a general statement derived from millennia of confirmatory sightings of millions of white swans. All you need is one single (and, I am told, quite ugly) black bird.[2]

Thus, the infallibility of a 'known fact' was undone once its fundamental postulate was disproved. The black swan is an oft-cited reference in philosophical discussions of the improbable.[3] Since the observation of the first black swan represented the undoing of an entire epistemology – the belief in empirical evidence as a guarantee of human knowledge – the metaphor, when applied to other instances of the unexpected, points to the black swan's exposure of the limitations of human knowledge.

Taleb's theory ultimately aims to make a claim about *the human condition* – specifically the rationality of the modern human mind in processing our known universe. 'Histories and society do not crawl', he writes, '[t]hey make jumps. They go from fracture to fracture, with few vibrations in between. Yet we (and historians) like to believe in the predictable, small incremental progressions.'[4] It is in undermining this kind of thinking, which Taleb takes to be a structuring principle of most societies, that the black swan exposes the fragile nature of thought systems in general. Though societies, he observes, adopt a general pretence towards progress, the unsoundness of dominant thought paradigms can lead not only to life-changing innovations, but also to great inequalities and violence. The human tendency, Taleb argues, is to paper over the unknown, and to create narrative fallacies with the things we recognise. 'We do not spontaneously learn that *we don't learn that we don't learn.*'[5]

Of course, as those drastic divisions and inequalities exacerbated by the Covid-19 pandemic suggest, universalising invocations of human nature are limited in their use, and the tendency towards labelling crises 'black swan events' is itself exposed as a folly. Indeed, from the outset of this pandemic, Taleb himself has been quick to qualify his theory as a call to strengthen societies' defences, not as 'a cliché for any bad thing that surprises us'.[6] With that, and a degree of criticality in assessing what counts as 'unpredictable' in mind, there is nevertheless perhaps value at this moment in revisiting Taleb's theories. For they ask us to look towards, rather than away from, the unknown. They ask, in a sense, that we consider the ambiguous, the consequences of which can amount to infinitely more than that which seems 'known', or empirically explainable. Such ambiguity is the equivalent of dark matter, which while representing 85% of the matter in the universe, having a major influence on the universe's evolution, cannot be explained by known theories. Taleb's is a demand for a paradigm shift. How can societies exercise the capacity and imagination for considering, even embracing, ambiguity and the unknown?

The artistic field, including that of contemporary art, is in itself an ambiguous presence. Not only aesthetically, but also ontologically speaking, modern and contemporary art has a particular status as its own category of experience, distinct from other practices, beliefs and rituals.[7] This can often result in high levels of societal intolerance of art, as many find great difficulty in rationalising or justifying its existence. Art, nevertheless, maintains a certain capacity to influence society by providing exposure to ambiguity, and thus increasing openness to the not-quite-understood. Art, and more specifically artistic imagination, often investigates what is invisible, causal and complex in the world. Examples might include Kazimir Malevich's Suprematist painting *Black Square* (1915), with its ground-breaking use of pure abstraction, seeking to transcend the objective perceptual world; the corporeal self-exploration of Carol Rama in the era of Italian fascism; the visceral, cultural Cartesianism of Damien Hirst's *Natural History* series of dead animal installations; the anti-modern propositions of Joseph Beuys' art and activism; or Susan Hiller's Paraconceptual (paranormal and conceptual) investigations of perception and the mind. Many of these artists might themselves be thought of as 'black swans', producing, through the unexpected, new directions for art and its discourses. Art, though still perhaps only notionally comprising an avant-garde, and furthermore one that is often circumscribed and undermined by market and state forces, retains a claim on the ambiguous. It thus remains both challenging and horizon-broadening. Its presence in society is a marker of a certain liberalisation of perception. What we can extrapolate from this is a new use or value for art – *to help us become more susceptible to, and curious about, ambiguity.*

Artists have themselves frequently reflected on supposed 'black swan' events, and offered unique deconstructions of the relations between the invisible and the visible in that these diverge from the discourses of media and scientific analysis. 'Can we understand health without considering wild diseases and epidemics? Indeed the normal is often irrelevant', writes Taleb.[8] We might think here of Derek Jarman's film *Blue* (1993), a meditation on how the artist's life was affected by HIV/AIDS. A single shot of a blue surface, *Blue*'s focus is a backdrop with an invisible subject. Its narrative references world events, from conflict in the former Yugoslavia to the advent of rave counterculture. Here, we experience the expression of someone coming towards the end of their life, avoiding the fallacies supplied by such institutions as that of religion, and seeking instead a deeper kind of understanding.

Previous: Shilpa Gupta, *Singing Cloud*, 2008–09 (detail), object built with thousands of microphones with 48 multi-channel audio. Photograph: M HKA. Courtesy the artist.

In particular, the role of human agency in 'black swan' events is a subject for artistic exploration. The artist Nam June Paik is credited with the very term 'electronic superhighway', adopted to describe the internet. Proposing a global system of communication and exchange, his works envisioned a near future of rapid transformation. *Electronic Superhighway: Continental U.S., Alaska, Hawaii* (1995–96), produced a few years before the invention of the World Wide Web by Tim Berners Lee (supported by Robert Cailliau), can be seen to portray, even predict, the human role in the generation of unexpected yet profound societal change. We might also think here of Sergey Kuryokhin and Sergey Sholokhov and his infamous film *Lenin Was a Mushroom* (1991), broadcast on Leningrad television during a period of reform in the late USSR, which aimed to mirror the (humanly constructed) narrative fallacies behind those seemingly impersonal ideologies that hold up our known world. Kuryokhin, impersonating a historian, narrates his discovery that Vladimir Lenin consumed enough psychedelic mushrooms to become one himself. Arriving at his conclusion through an unlikely but possible chain of facts and events, he manages to create a plausible account. The work came at a key moment, towards the dissolution of the USSR, for cutting through illusions of ideological power. In that same moment, it conjured a whole other sphere of thought and causality.

'Any reduction in the world around us can have explosive consequences', wrote Taleb, 'since it rules out some sources of uncertainty; it drives us to a misunderstanding of the fabric of the world. For instance, you may think that radical Islam (and its values) are your allies against the threat of Communism, and so you may help them develop, until they send two planes into downtown Manhattan.'[9] *It Is What It Is* (2009) is a 'mobile museum' created by the artist Jeremy Deller. There is often a simplicity in Deller's projects, which create encounters with things so loaded that we are prompted by little more than the encounter itself to think about the relationships that underlie them. The centrepiece of *It Is What It Is* is an exploded car in the aftermath of a suicide bomber's detonation in Iraq. Transported through art-institutional settings as a 'readymade', the object was discussed in conversations arranged by the artist, bringing participants to think about the car's wider context (decades of foreign policy and intervention in the Middle East) and the profound destabilisation, resulting from this context, that continues into the present. *It Is What It Is* offers us the opportunity to think in complex ways, beyond facile framings of a so-called 'War on Terror', directing attention towards the eventual outcomes of long-running hegemonic worldviews.

Contemporary artworks such as these point us towards the question of temporality in our understanding of events around us. Artistic imagination is often prompted by concerns about such constructs as that of time, which shape the human environment. Shilpa Gupta's *Singing Cloud* (2008–09) was built upon an analysis of various facets and processes of the human mind, among them that of temporality. A large amorphous shape, constructed using four-thousand microphones, the work considers the psychological impact of today's highly mediated information landscape, which cultivates suspicion and fear. Developed through a collaboration with Mahzarin Banaji, a professor of psychology at Harvard University, *Singing Cloud* considers the multilayered alterations that take place in human perception following exposure to media images, when a drop in individual consciousness of the self filters out to the level of collective conscience. The work reflects not only on the psychology of fear, but also on the desire to understand and prepare oneself for the future's abstract possibilities. Gupta interprets her research in this area into a soundtrack made from hypnotic fragments of speech. The microphones are reverse-wired – rather than being used to record sound, they instead emit a soundtrack, designed to 'sing' and ripple over the surface of the work. As Taleb puts it:

> Alas, we are not manufactured, in our current edition of the human race, to understand abstract matters – we need context. Randomness and uncertainty are abstractions. We respect what has happened, ignoring what *could have* happened. In other words, we are naturally shallow and superficial – and we do not know it. This is not a psychological problem; it comes from the main property of information. The dark side of the moon is harder to see; beaming light on it costs energy. In the same way, beaming light on the unseen is costly in both computational and mental effort.[10]

In *Singing Cloud*, a black amorphous mass, evoking simultaneously cloud, brain and organism, seeks to shine a light on what is typically located in the darkness of human perception.

In Taleb's understanding, black swans are appearing with increasing frequency, perhaps in conjunction with our accelerating, hyper-connected world, and it has become evident that our political institutions are ill-equipped to deal with them. This puts the onus on societies to be able to withstand upheaval, which in turn points to the significance of cultural practice. Do societies possess the intelligence and critical tools to think about the kind of ambiguity that is central to existence, and to process more productively that which they fail to predict? The artistic sphere is here indispensable in looking to address and embrace ambiguity, interrogating systems of knowledge. Independent of other more empirical fields, art provides unique aesthetic and thereby philosophical lenses on complex events and occurrences, shining a light on the vast dark matter of perception. Art, in this way, has a singular value in society. It can help us to *learn that we can learn.*

1   Nassim Nicholas Taleb, *The Black Swan: The Impact of the Highly Improbable*, New York: Random House, 2007, p.xix.

2   *Ibid.*, p.xvii.

3   See, for example, Karl Popper, *Conjectures and Refutations: The Growth of Scientific Knowledge*, London: Routledge & Kegan Paul, 1963.

4   N. N. Taleb, *The Black Swan*, op. cit., p.11.

5   *Ibid.*, p. xxi.

6   Quoted in Bernard Avishai, 'The Pandemic Isn't a Black Swan but a Portent of a More Fragile Global System', *The New Yorker*, 21 April 2020, available at https://www.newyorker.com/news/daily-comment/the-pandemic-isnt-a-black-swan-but-a-portent-of-a-more-fragile-global-system (last accessed on 12 October 2020.

7   I take particular inspiration from the writings of Thierry de Duve on the question of the status of art.

8   N. N. Taleb, *The Black Swan*, op. cit., p.xxiv.

9   *Ibid.*, p.16.

10   *Ibid.*, p.132.

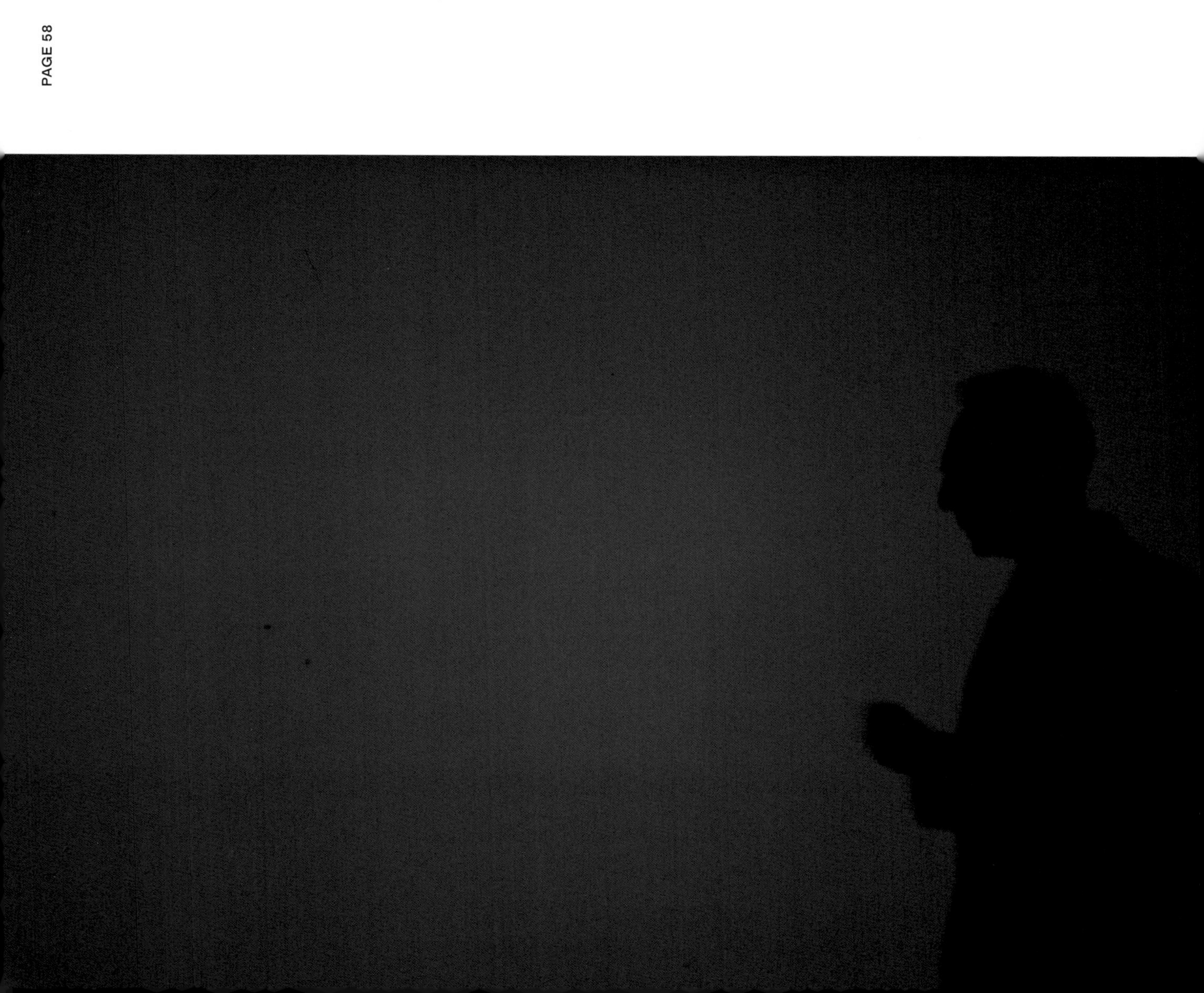

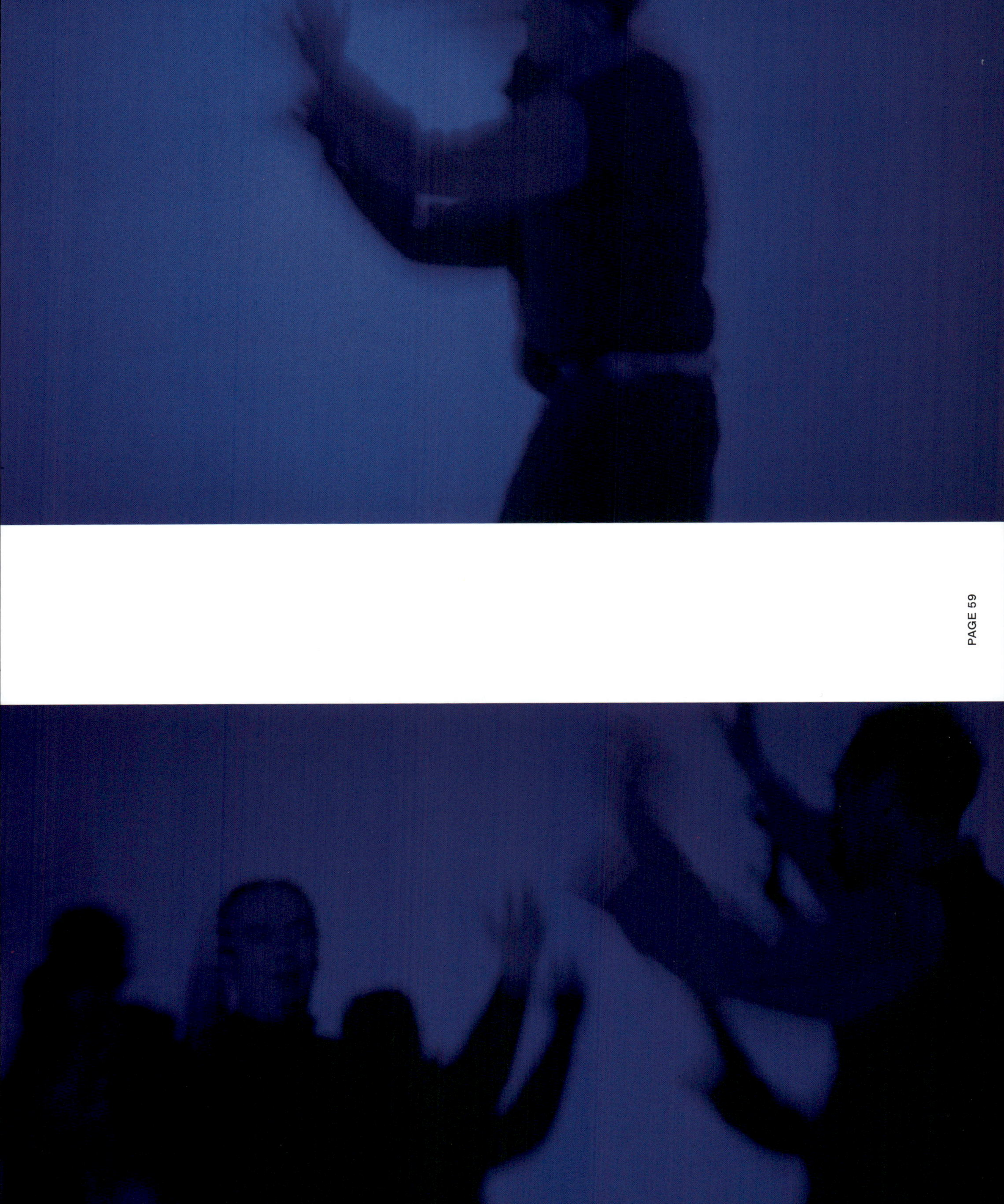

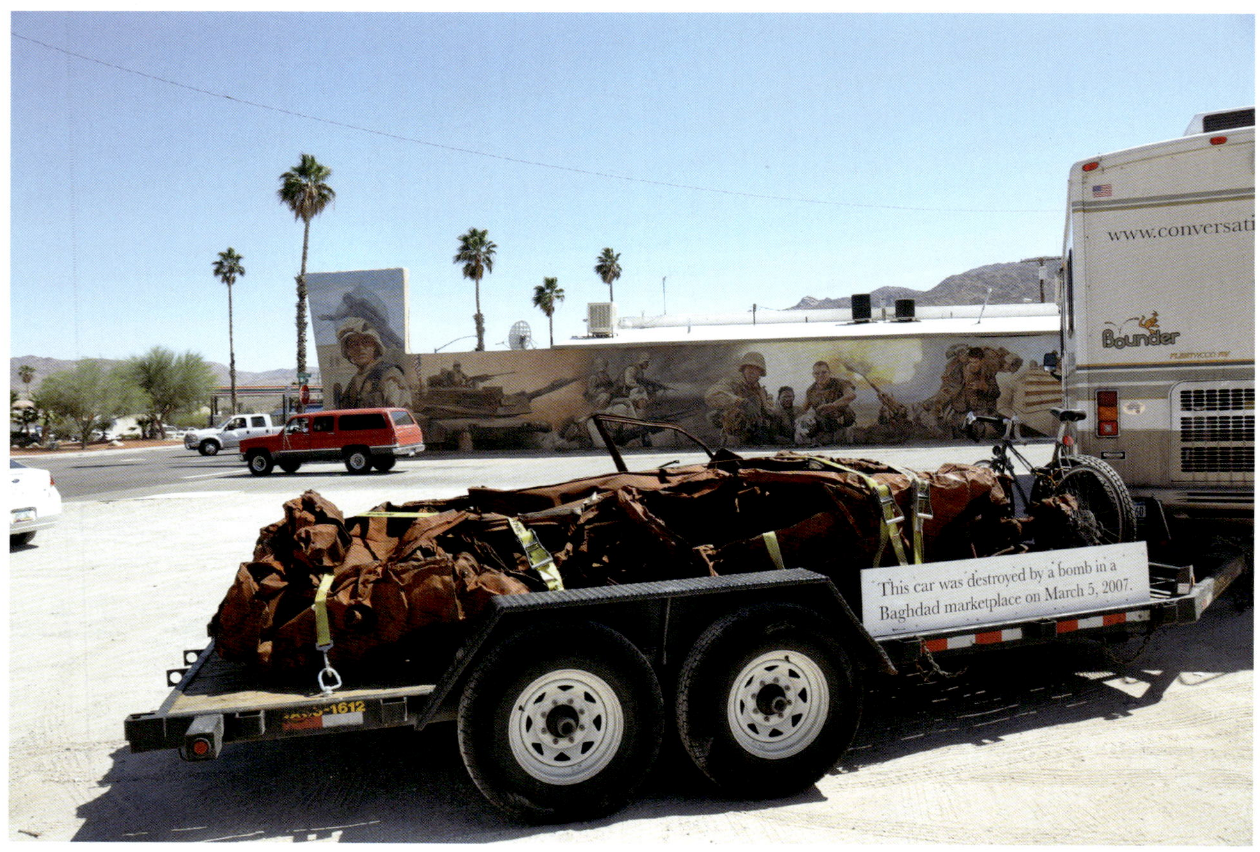
www.conversati
Bounder
This car was destroyed by a bomb in a
Baghdad marketplace on March 5, 2007.

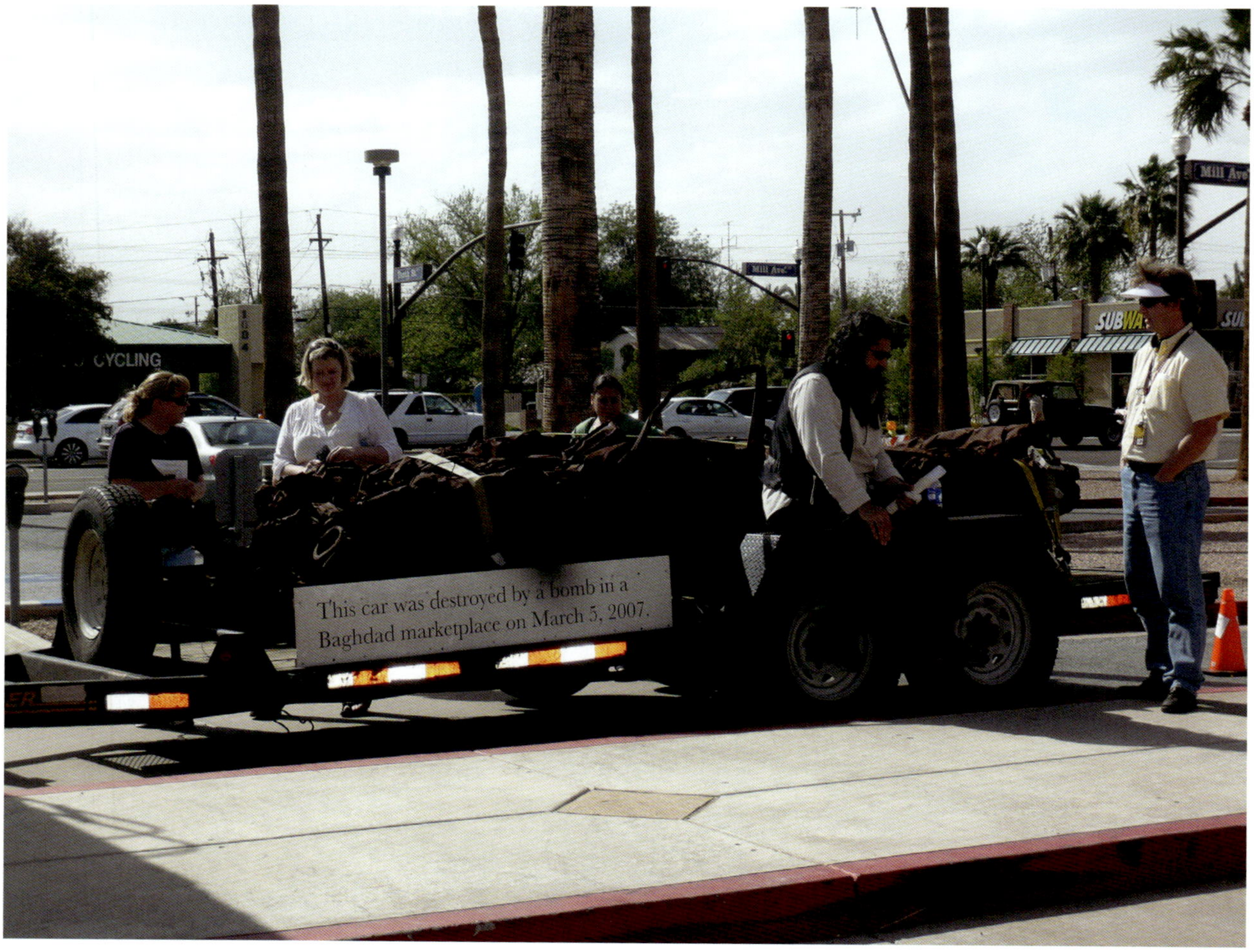

Mill Ave
CYCLING
SUBWA
This car was destroyed by a bomb in a
Baghdad marketplace on March 5, 2007.

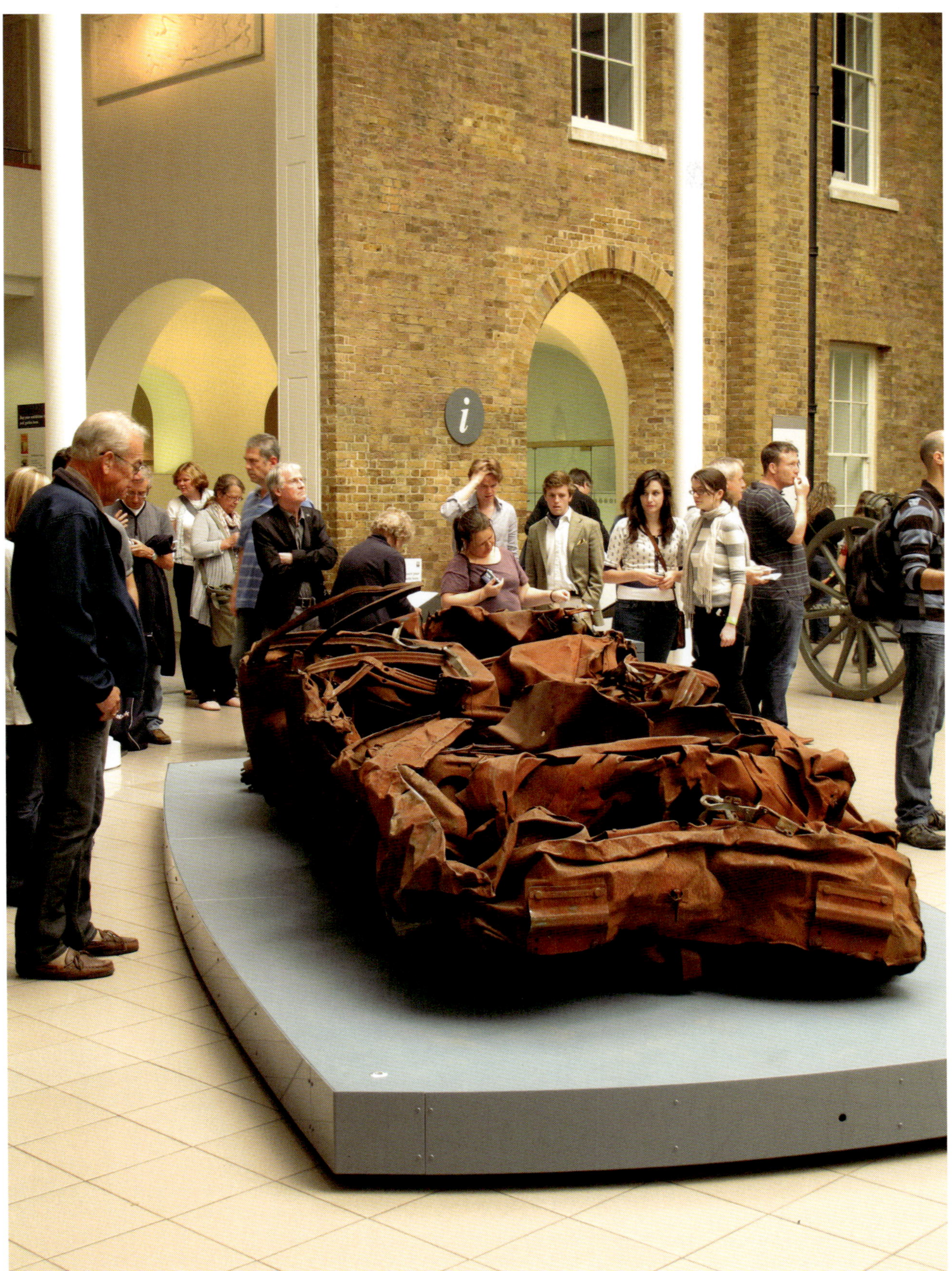

(above left) Jeremy Deller, *It Is What It Is*, 2009,
Palms Marine Base, CA. Photograph: Jeremy
Deller. Courtesy the artist and Creative Time

(below left) Jeremy Deller, *It Is What It Is*, 2009,
Phoenix, AZ. Photography: Jeremy Deller.
Courtesy the artist and Creative Time

(right) Jeremy Deller, *It Is What It Is*, 2009,
installation view, Imperial War Museum, London.
Photograph: Jeremy Deller. Courtesy the artist
and Creative Time

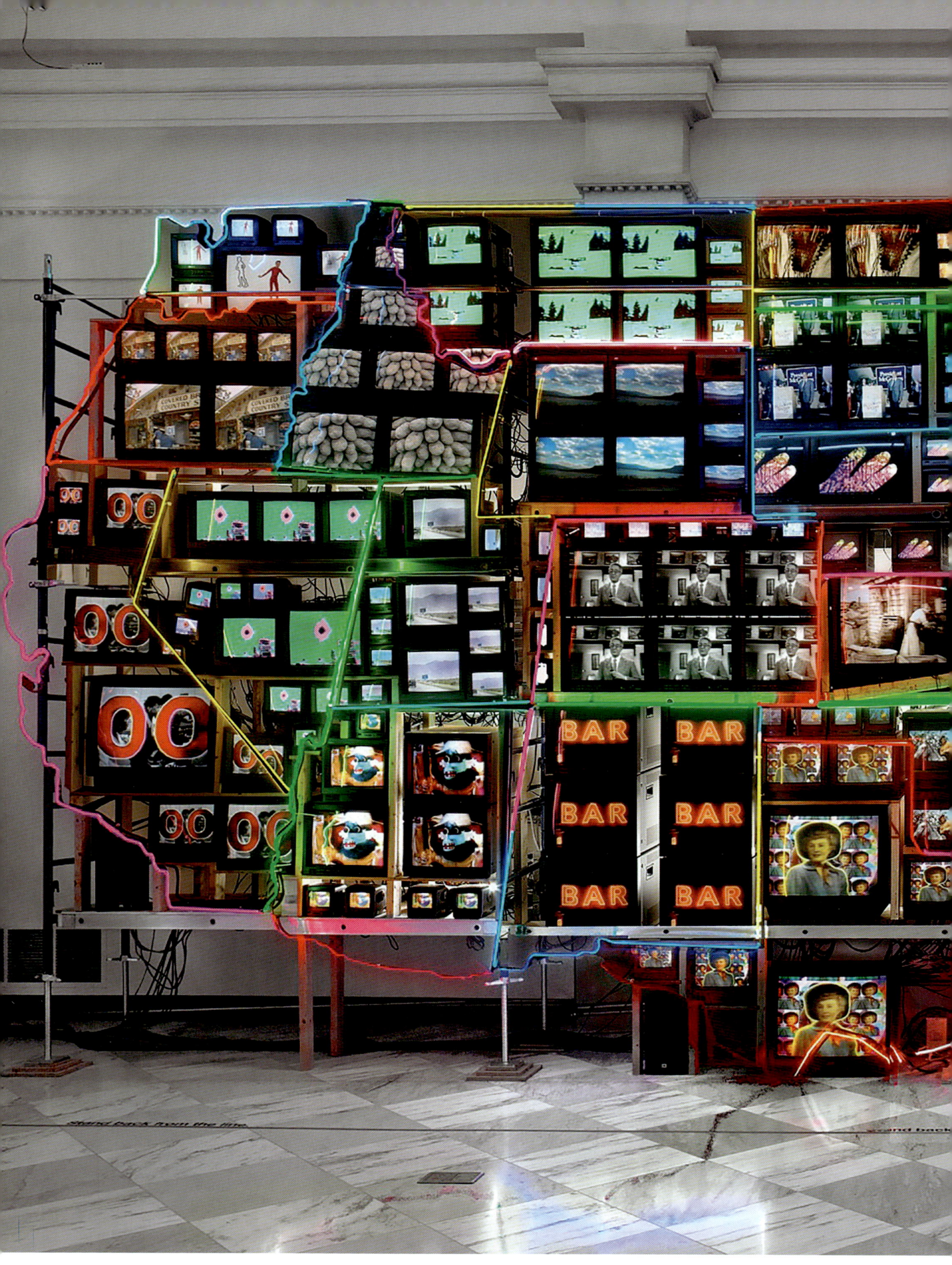
COVERED BRIDGE COUNTRY S
BAR
BAR
BAR
BAR
BAR
BAR

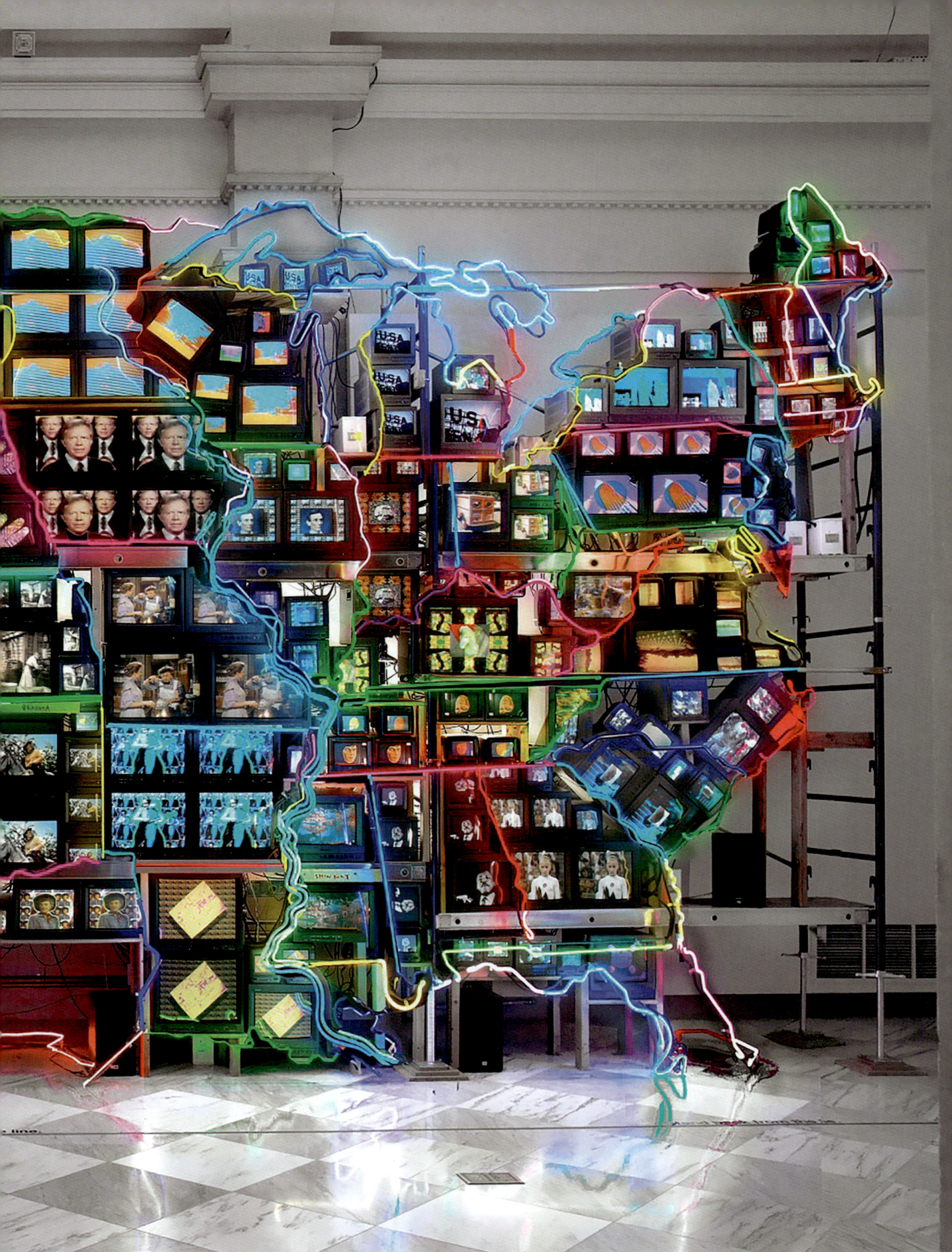

Nam June Paik, *Electronic Superhighway:
Continental U.S., Alaska, Hawaii*, 1995,
51 channel video installation
(including one closed-circuit television feed),
custom electronics, neon lighting, steel and
wood; colour, sound, Smithsonian
American Art Museum.
Courtesy the artist. © Nam June Paik Estate

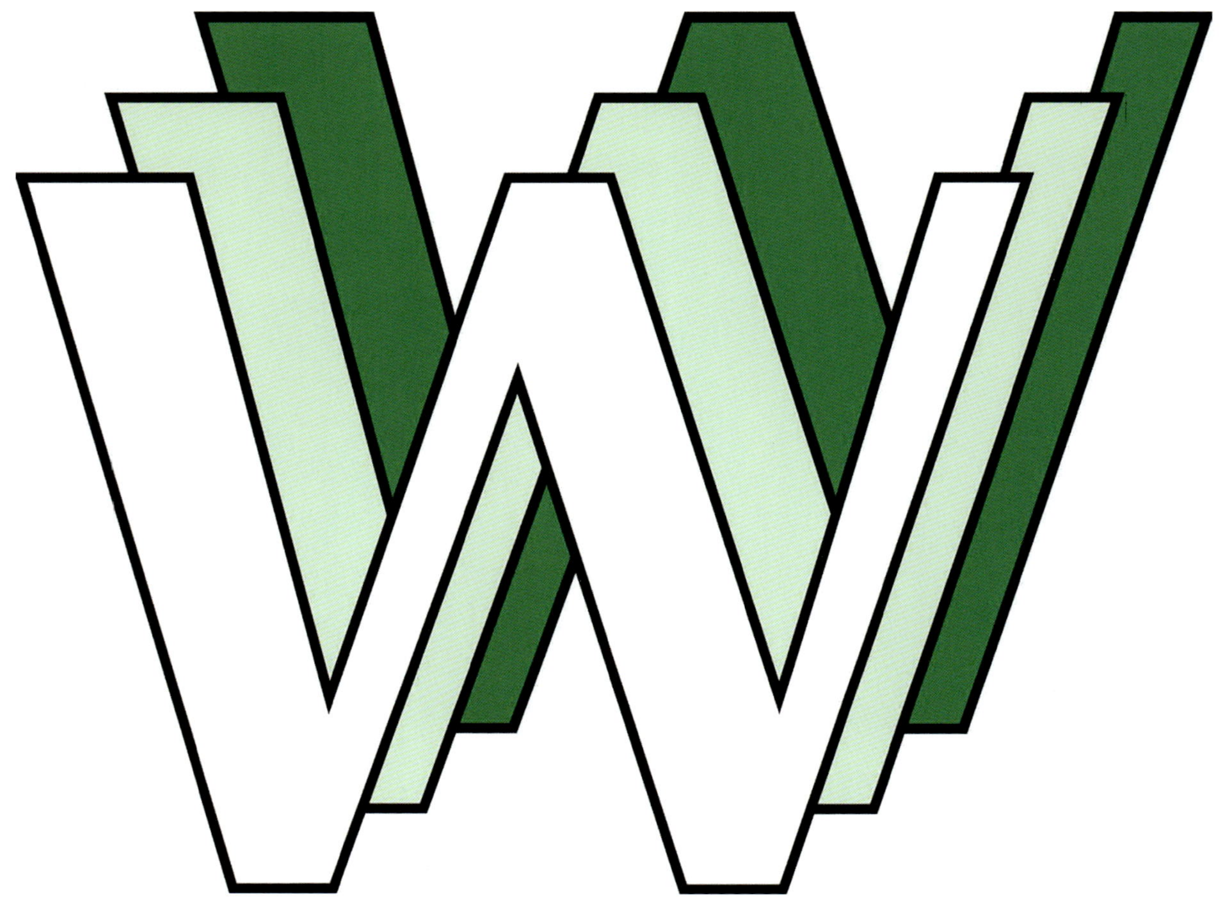

Robert Cailliau, World Wide Web
'historical' logo, 1990, composed of
three 'W's using the Optima Bold
font, according to Cailliau himself

Sergey Kuryokhin and Sergey
Sholokhov, *Lenin — Mushroom*, 1991,
stills from television broadcast.
Archive of Anastasia Kuryokhina

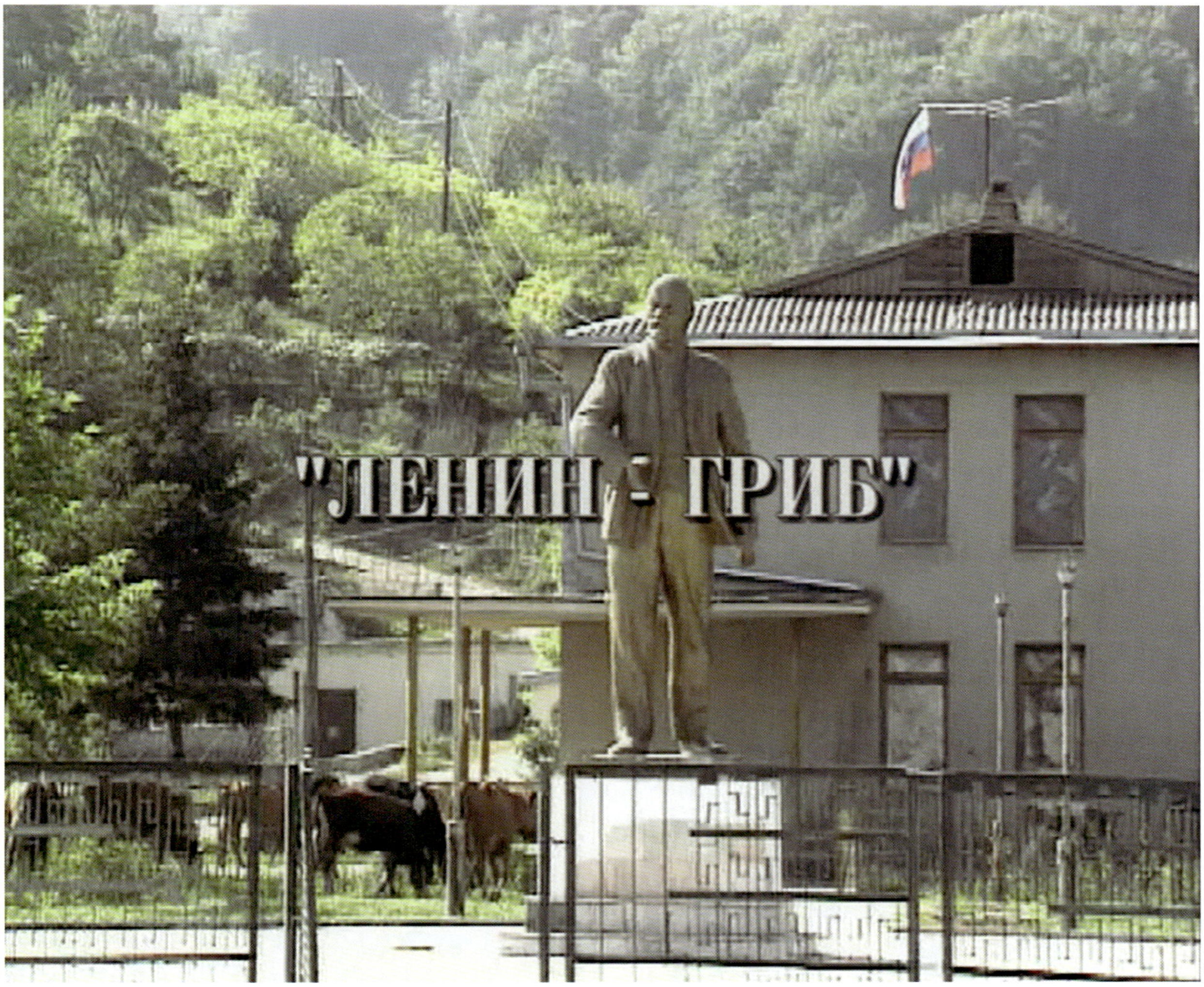

"ЛЕНИН - ГРИБ"

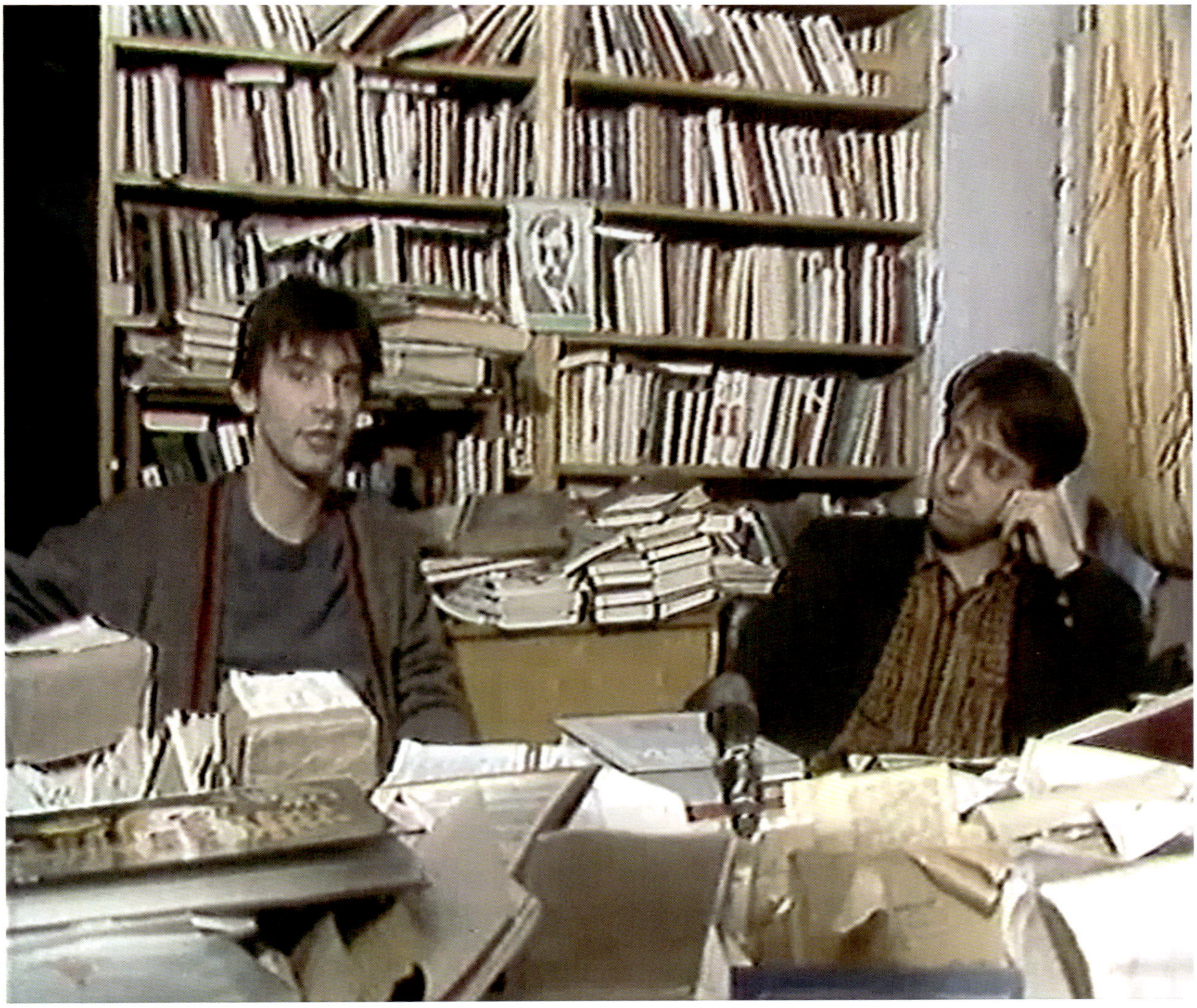

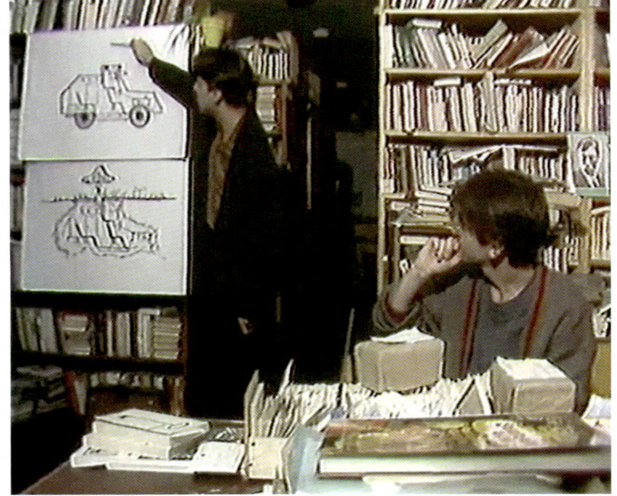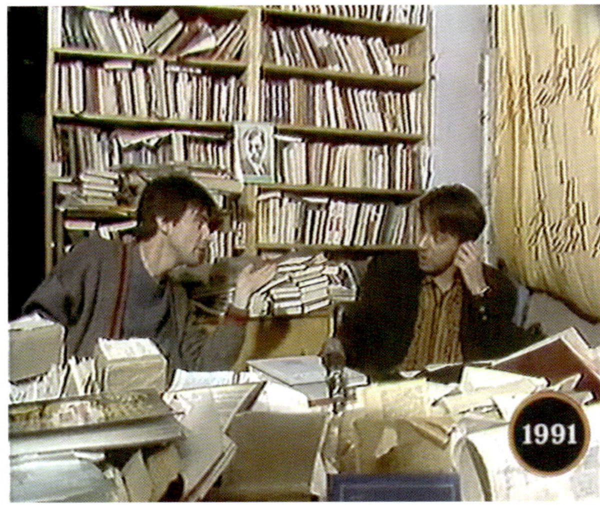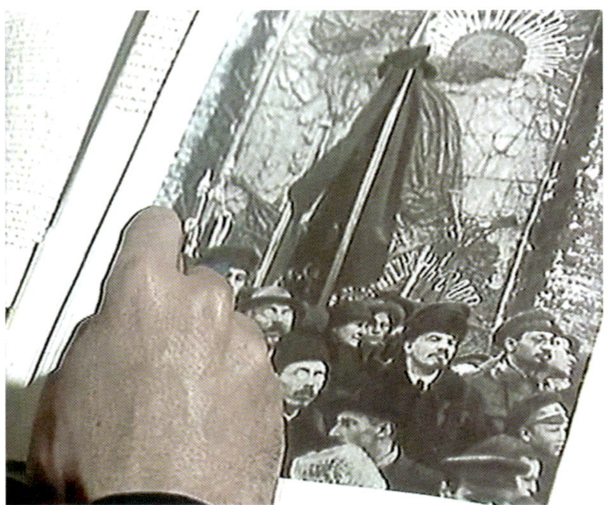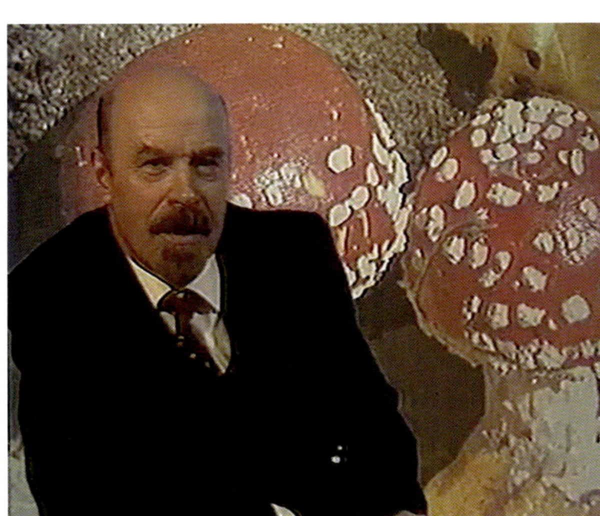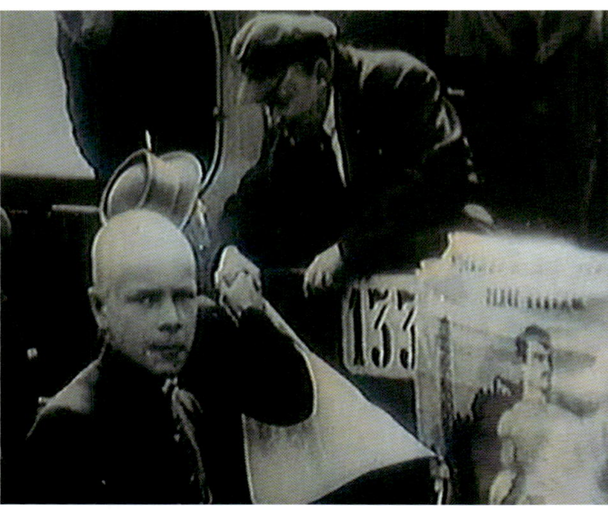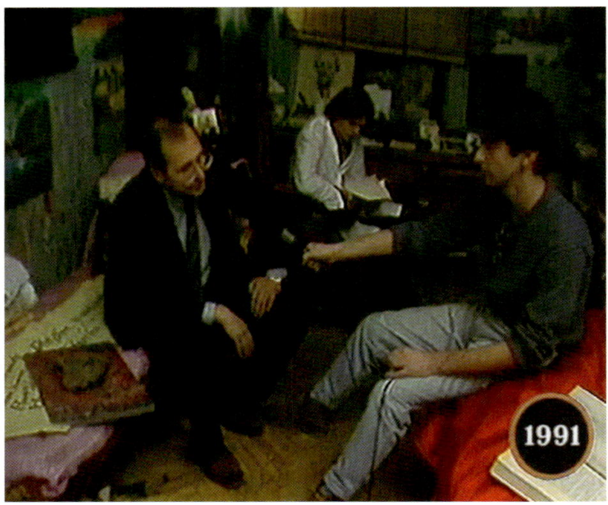

Sergey Kuryokhin and Sergey
Sholokhov, *Lenin — Mushroom*, 1991,
stills from television broadcast.
Archive of Anastasia Kuryokhina

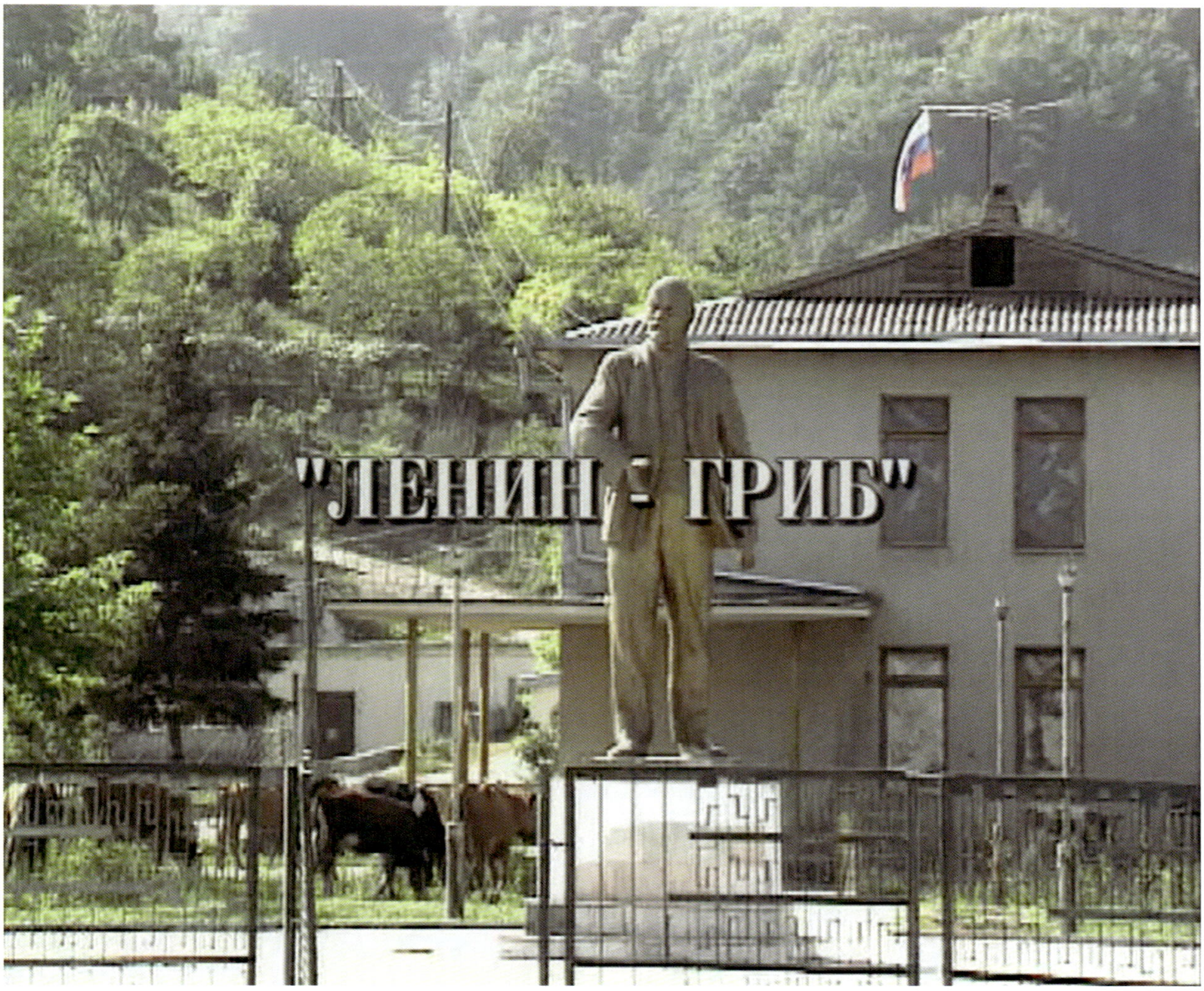

"ЛЕНИН - ГРИБ"

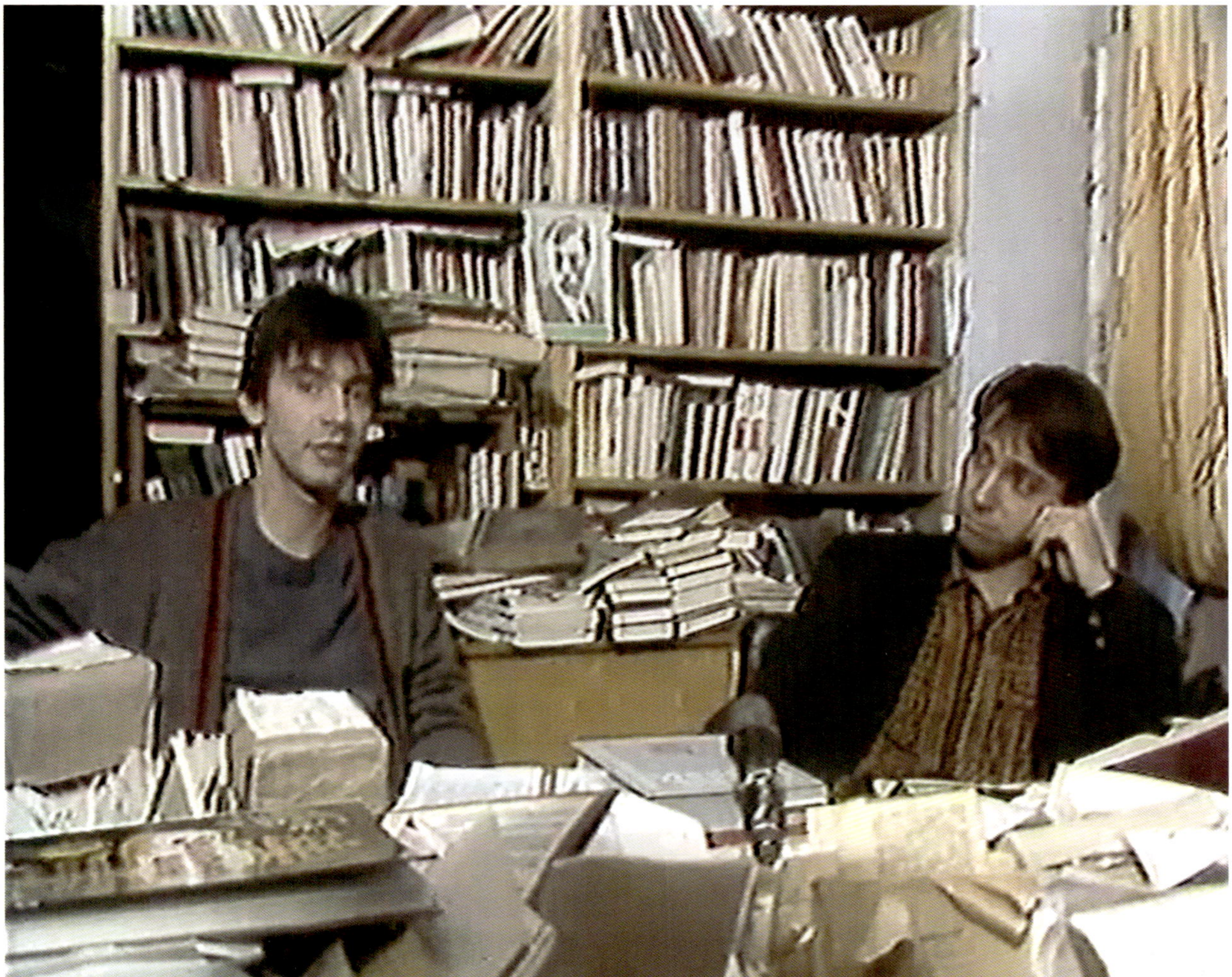

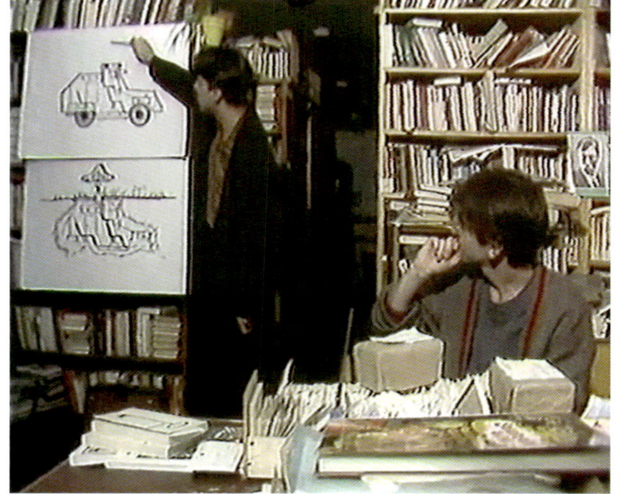
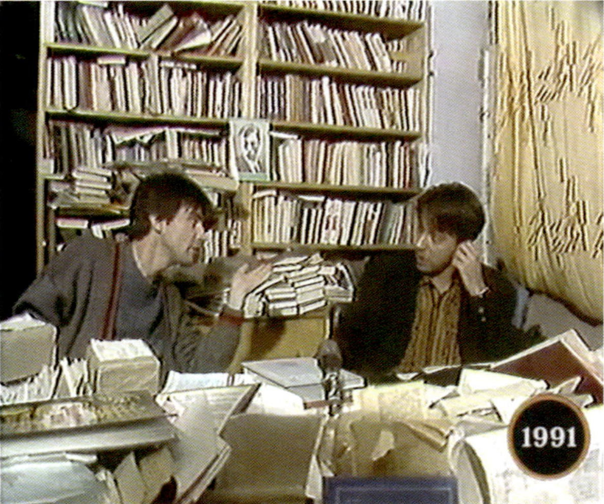
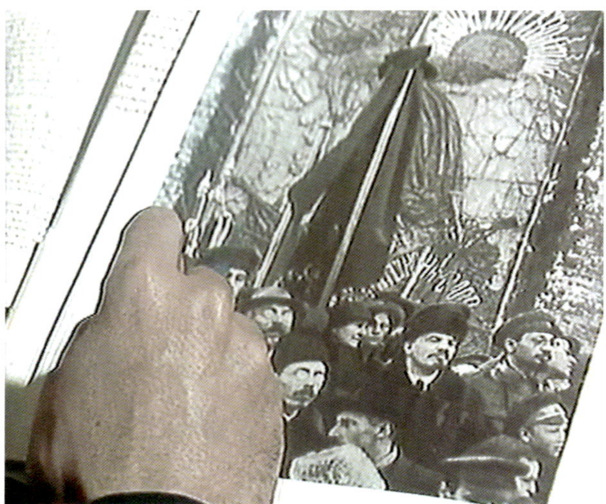
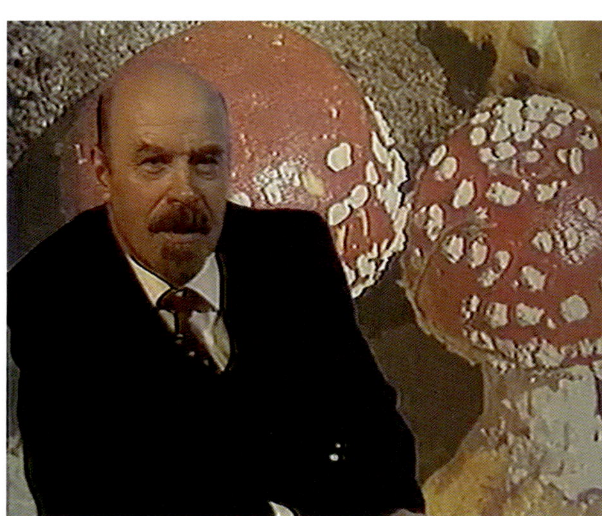
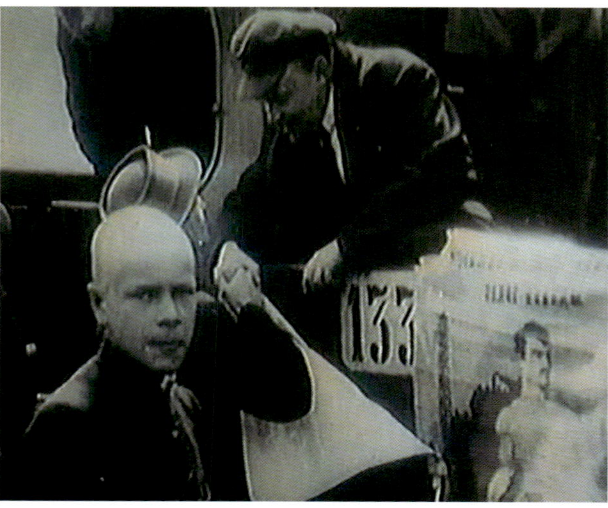
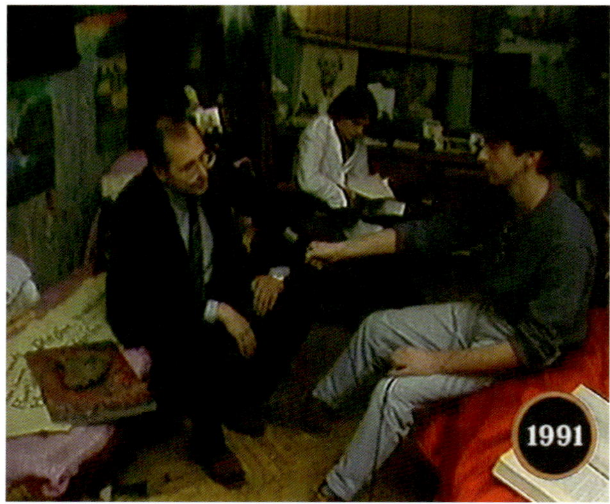

Sergey Kuryokhin and Sergey Sholokhov, *Lenin — Mushroom*, 1991, stills from television broadcast. Archive of Anastasia Kuryokhina

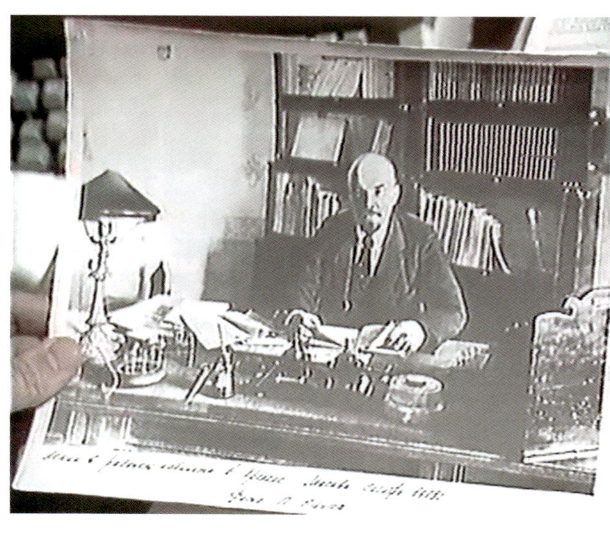

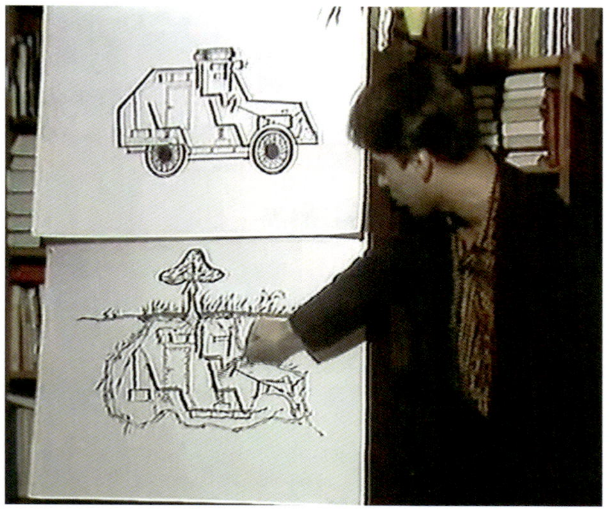

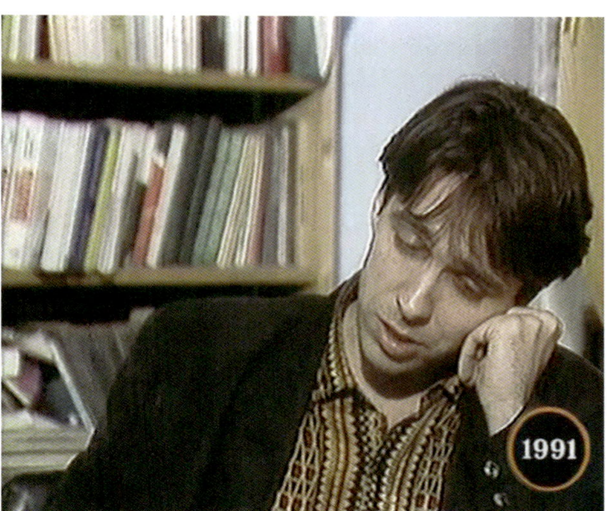

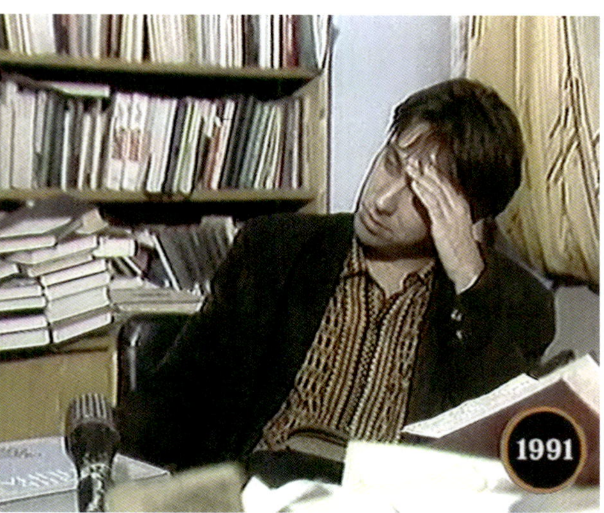

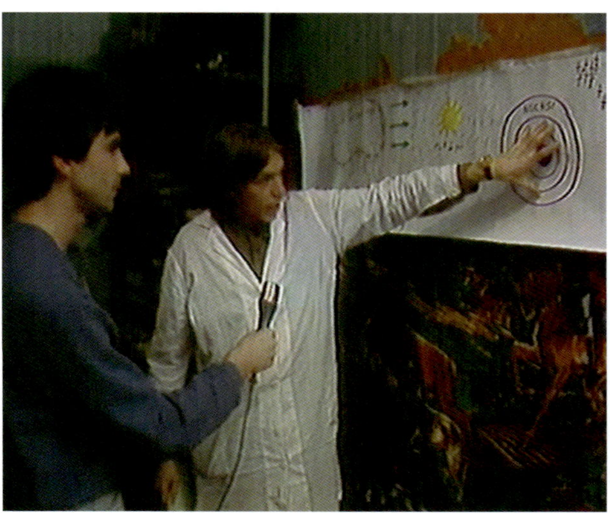

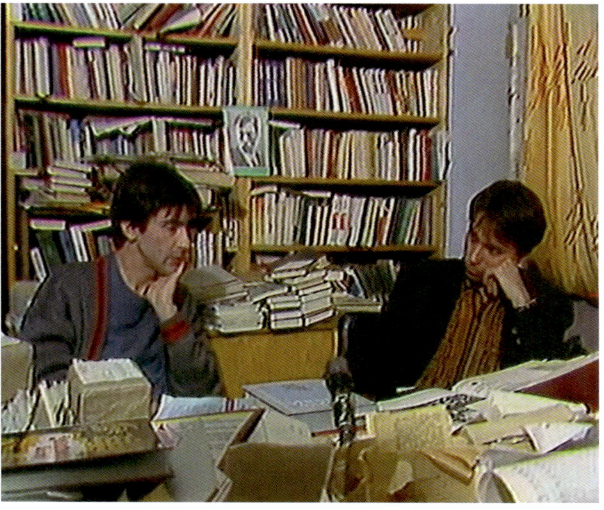

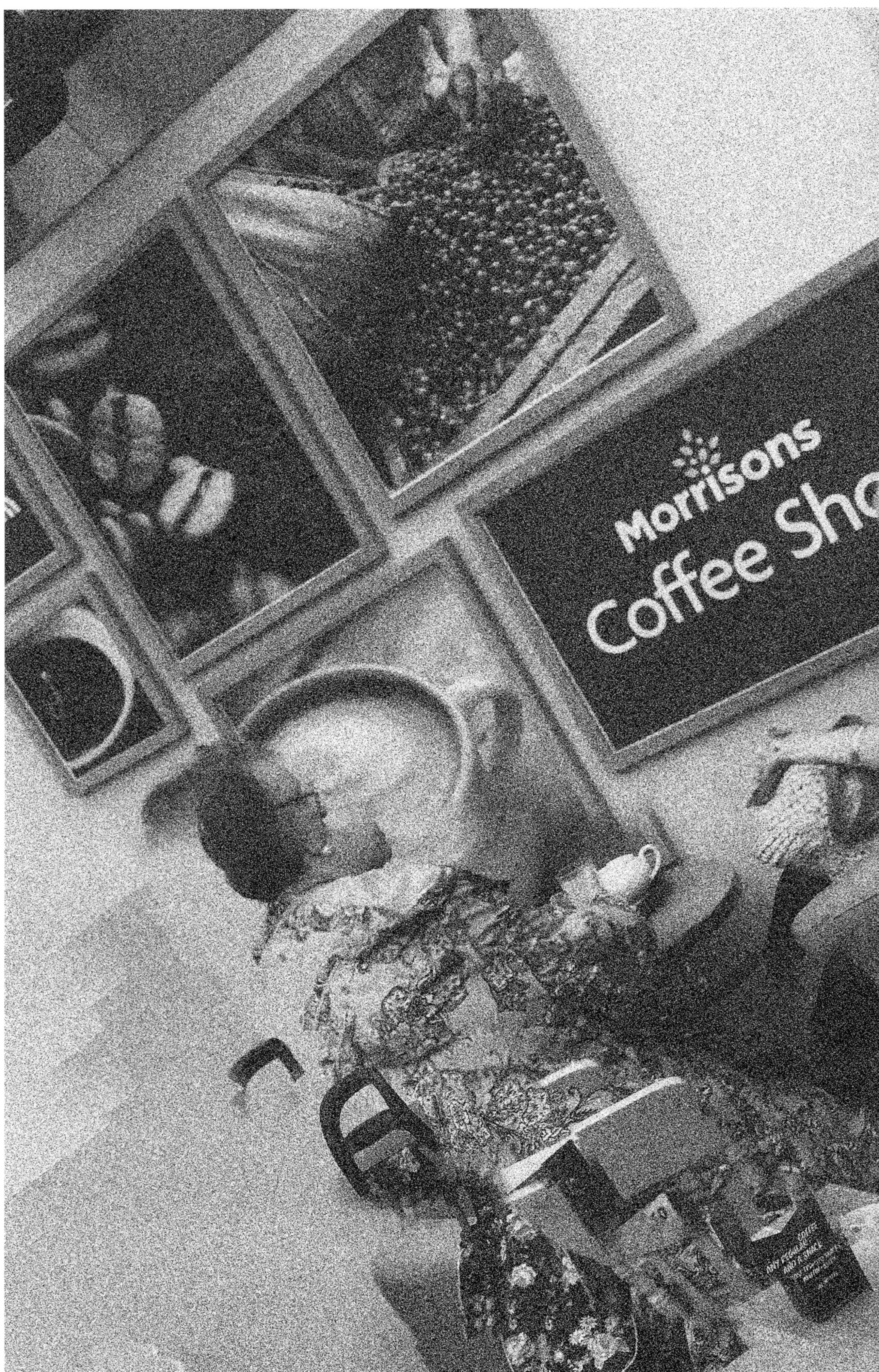
Morrisons
Coffee Sho

FEED THE FIRES, TEND THE STOCK 1973/1981/1994/2021
Laura Grace Ford

City Square. Park Row. Boar Lane.

The air's different, there's heat in it, a rogue Spanish smell. Pine needles and red earth, black tobacco and cardamom.

Trinity shopping centre, a contaminated greenhouse. The escalators are encased in plywood, it's meant to be industrial I suppose, like a club or an art installation, with fluorescent tube lights and zig zag lettering. I'm thinking about the places we went: Phono, Warehouse, Orbit, others I've forgotten the names of. They were dark dens, caverns of dry ice, mirrors and black walls.

Trinity is a circus of chain shops and restaurants, H&M, Primark, shit like that. It's a webbed canopy, an atrium wrapping you in it. A new skittishness pulses in the desperate sloganeering, the swarms of Sale signs. The mall is suspended between the fanfare of its opening and the piecemeal closure of its retail units, there's a shrill defensiveness in the architecture, guards stationed at every level.

A song blares nonchalantly across the desolate cavern, vocals adding syrupy textures to a radically new terrain. In the moment of exception possibilities begin to proliferate, the shopping mall is re-imagined as a social centre, a rave, a cascade of sumptuous bedrooms.

I emerge on Briggate. I remember watching dozens, no, scores, come through here and take the Apple Store. I remember jubilance in the breaching of it, a dark, carnivalesque joy.

My hair's a mess, the heat's flattening it.

I walk through Country Arcade with its iron balustrades and Burmantofts faience. The floors have tiled patterns on them, exploding circles like mandalas. I glance at the window displays, capsules of things I can't afford and feel the judgement spritzing from Reiss and Harvey Nichols. They're just about holding on, these elevated emporia, but I catch the disquiet shimmering in the mineral foundation and neutral eyes of the assistants.

I'd like to go into those air-conditioned rooms, breathe diffuser scents of neroli and grapefruit but I'm in the wrong garb, signalling the wrong code. I feel exposed somehow, maybe I've been drinking too much. I don't like the sheen on my skin, the melting make-up. I pull my cap over my eyes like a visor.

Somewhere between Kirkgate and Vicar Lane a knot of streets. The light is more Granada than West Yorkshire. There's a café, chairs outside. The heat is reordering the architecture, turning it inside out. Porters stagger from kitchens, sprawl in mauve shadows to smoke. I think of the last time we were in this city together, we stopped somewhere, was it here? You'd cut your hair and I imagined the luxuriant heaps spilling on the barber's floor. You looked older then, like you'd shed another life.

The edge of the shopping district is the medieval city boundary. The bricks are searing to touch. Men crouch beneath walls at the cholera grounds. Burley Bar Stone, the corner of the Headrow and Albion Street. Leylands to the east where the Chinese Supermarkets were.

Kirkgate market. I remember one Christmas knockoff Baileys and white chrysanthemums. I was living in Woodhouse then. We came here sometimes, before the coach station or going to Brighouse to see my dad. It was always cold, an excuse to call in at the Brougham Arms with its red bricks, its glowing lantern outside. I liked how they stared when we walked in, the addled, grim-faced punters, the way you eyed them back, daring them to say something. I remember one afternoon it snowed, the coach couldn't leave, and we holed up in a corner with glinting Jameson glasses. We were happy then, marooned in a cabin, conversation unspooling in the glazed tiles and dim yellow light. You were starting a job down south, there was money sloshing around, easy pickings you said.

I walk through the market. The Victorian desire for order is crystallised in the domed glazed roof. Each stall is encased in its own stand, clearly demarcated. A haberdashers, a delicatessen, a florist. It's cleaner than I remember, and lighter.

Balls of wool arranged in pyramids, tubs of pastel-coloured ice cream, spikes of coral gladioli.

Then the 70s market hall: shimmering spills of fabric, kitchen appliances, fake handbags.

A café with orange pendant lights, a smell of popcorn and frankincense. There are booths where you can watch the market through reinforced Perspex. The man behind the counter speaks Harehills with mouldings of Amharic. He appraises me with unexpected fondness, and I wonder if I know him, if we met sometime back then. Maybe if you'd have been here he'd have said something; the two of us together might have jolted a missing piece. I think about halfway houses, hidden meeting rooms, how hard it was then to keep track of everyone.

A couple of blokes are slumped over a Formica table with front room ease. They're in every day I think, eking out sweet coffees, watching the comings and goings through bleary zonked out eyes.

I settle into an alcove, a temporary sanctuary.

Laura Grace Ford, commissioned by Nav Haq

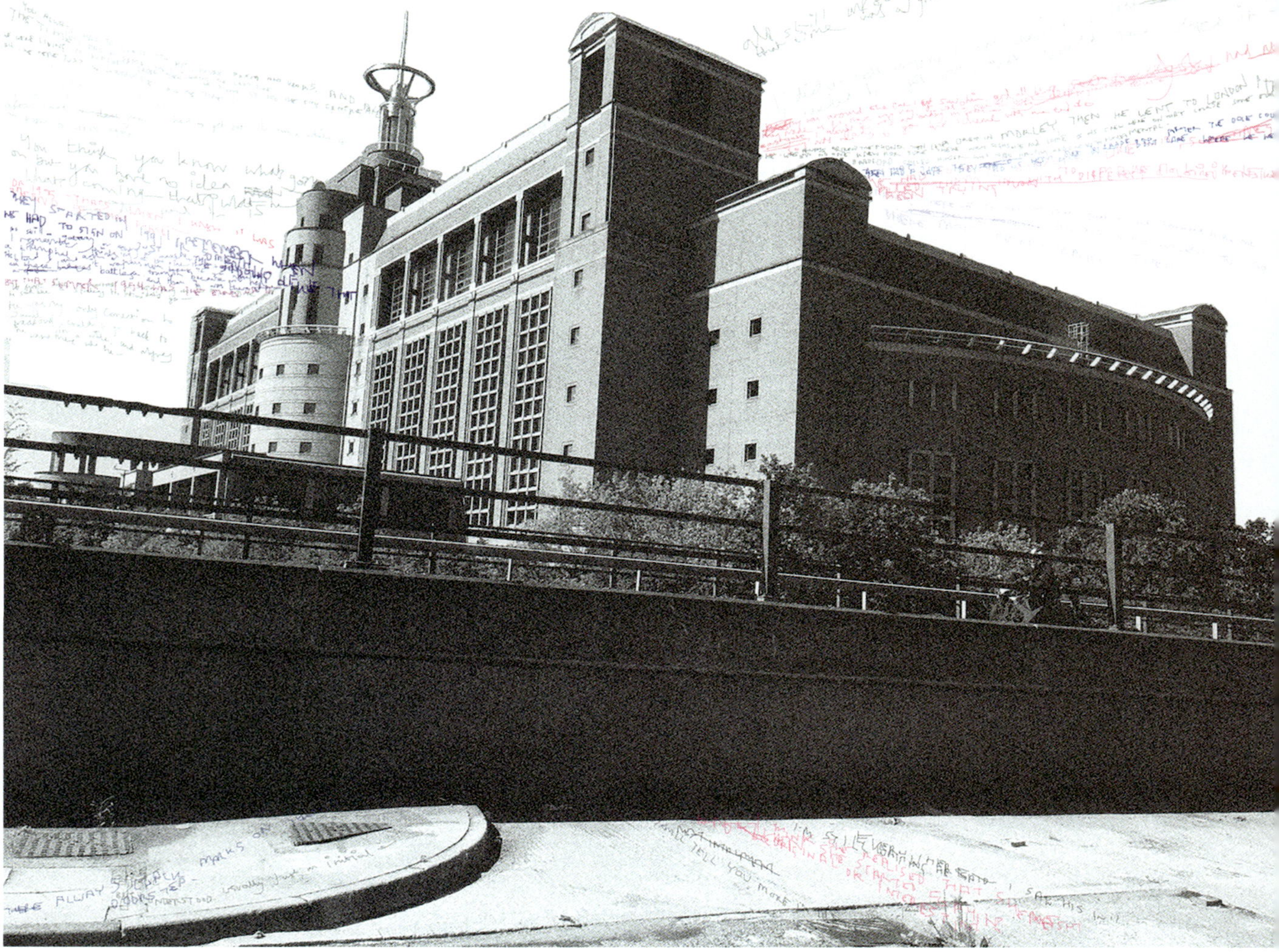

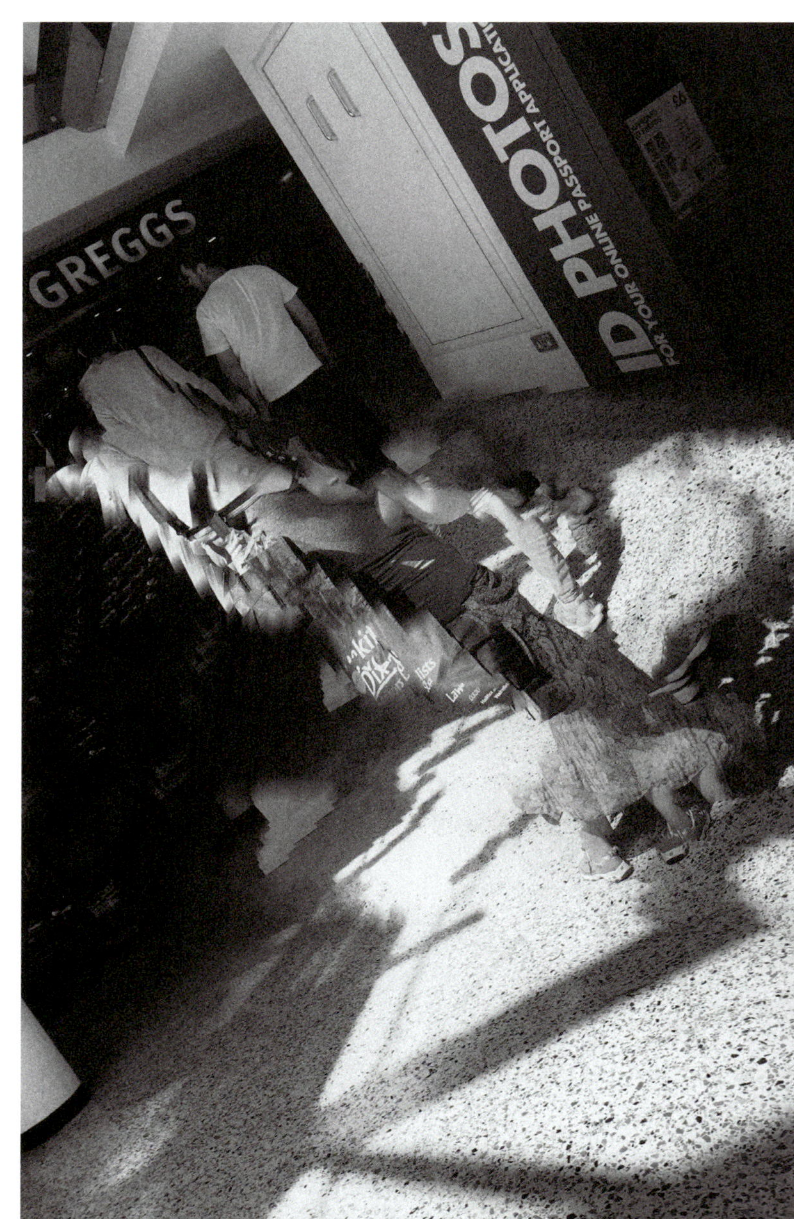
GREGGS
ID PHOTOS
FOR YOUR ONLINE PASSPORT APPLICATION

My phone's buzzing, a cheap burner I got this week. I thumb through texts, directions mostly, encrypted plans for later.

Irish sisters come in with white faces and sombre black clothes. I must be in their corner I realise, between dusty rubber plants and defunct heating appliances; they cast glances, make a show of discomfort as they settle into a diametric booth.

The man brings coffee in a small cup, black like a dilated pupil. There's something tacit in the exchange, an unspoken connection to another place.

I don't stay long, twenty minutes that's all, but something changes, through striated leaves and ketchup bottles I'm tapping into other futures.

*

The market is a maze, a computer game, I go across and down, lose my bearings, feel daft when I see the same faces.

Stalls with second-hand books, birthday cards five for a quid.

Suit jackets, camphor-scented, like they've just come out of storage.

Then the sprawl outside and it starts to unravel, a glitch in the CGI rendering of the brand-new retail development, which is there, braced for the receivers, the chains at the door.

A stall with stolen bikes and heaps of tyres, another with mobiles and chargers. Lads trading, handing stuff over.

A woman with bleached hair and black eyeliner, something familiar about her. She has a dog, it could be an Irish wolfhound, big and rangy with a coat the colour of wire wool. It stands stock still beside me. The woman drags him away, he must have been your dog, she shouts, in another life.

House clearance, old crockery, bric-a-brac, junk. A stink of weed then, green envelope sealing us. Denby coffee cups from the 70s, we had that set, the decades are scored in it, biography in the glazes. I want to repossess the time, undo the mistakes rising in it. I lift one, examine the roundel pattern, the mid-browns and turquoise.

Then I'm jostled a bit and I set it back in the roil of chipped mugs and faulty kettles. I'm trying to stop buying stuff, trying to lose the shoals of memory that swim through it all. I'd like to live in a hotel, I think sometimes, with clean white walls and empty cupboards.

Platform sandals in a heap of trainers and scuffed boots. They're like Yves Saint Laurent ones, spindly and scorching. Sometimes I wear stuff like that, they make me think of you, the eroticism of those times.

I walk through a wall and it's Victoria Gate and the bus station. Last time I was here it was freezing, there was rum in my coffee, there were old people in thin anoraks and black ice, now it's sweltering.

I cross Eastgate where I went on that dole course. I realise the building's been demolished, subsumed into the new department store. I met a crew from Bradford in there, Inder and some of the ADF lot, it was a chance to network, like activists they meant, not LinkedIn. You were away then, but meeting them brought you closer.

This is the boundary, that's why things dissolve, why the council try to shore it up. I recognise the government buildings as fortifications, Quarry House as bastille.

John Lewis homewares, glacial arrangements of candles and ornaments, a white security guard circling. There's never anyone here, it's always chilled to inertia. I'm in a controlled zone, there's a surplus of gear but it's all accounted for, all ordered.

Everything's reduced, you could furnish a house if you had one, kit yourself out with autumn clothes. But it's all wrong, the subdued palette of woolen coats and heavy knitted jumpers are out of kilter. I cast a glance at myself in the mirror, the white denim jacket four sizes too big, the bare legs and white stilettos. The new arcade can't tap into the currents, the ecologies at the edge of the city, the unlicensed and unbound.

The dole office was called Circle House, it had Greek key patterns climbing the walls. The day they refused to let me sign marked the end of a cycle, after that I left for London, watched the pylons and service stations and laybys through a buzz of vodka and lemonade. You'd left Yorkshire years before, the time had passed and I'd been preoccupied, too busy to dwell on you, I suppose things rushed on, a racketing forward momentum, now I see how it moves in and out like the tide.

Boarded up warehouses Phase 2, Victoria Gate.

A traffic island with monkey puzzle trees.

Quarry Hill. The flats were demolished in 1976. I remember the orange street lights, the black arches and windows. It rose like a barrier, on and on like Hadrian's Wall. I must have been three as the motorway slid beneath the city, as I absorbed the image of the estate; my mum was driving, we were coming from Brighouse when it made its indelible mark.

A thicket of buddleia, collapsed plywood boards. A sign saying Assessment Centre. A tang of cortisol and adrenaline from ramps and car doors. Inside are LED lights, a stark reception, staff who won't even look at you.

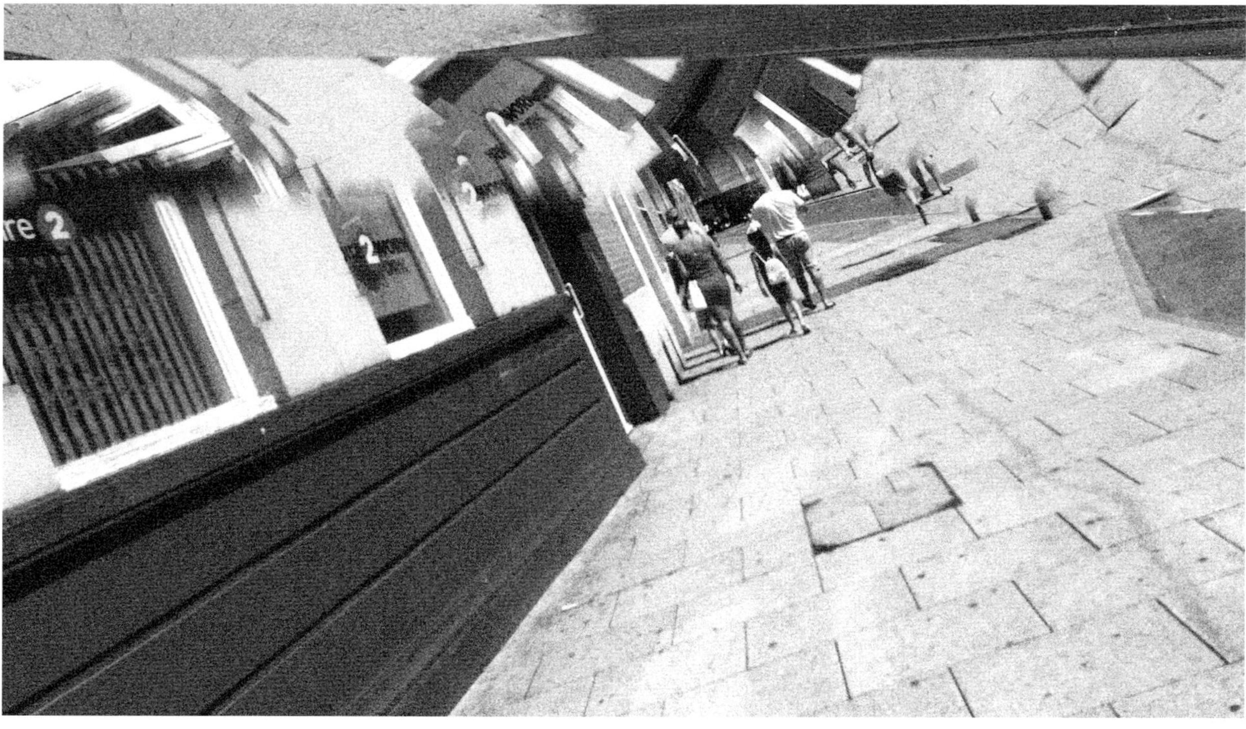

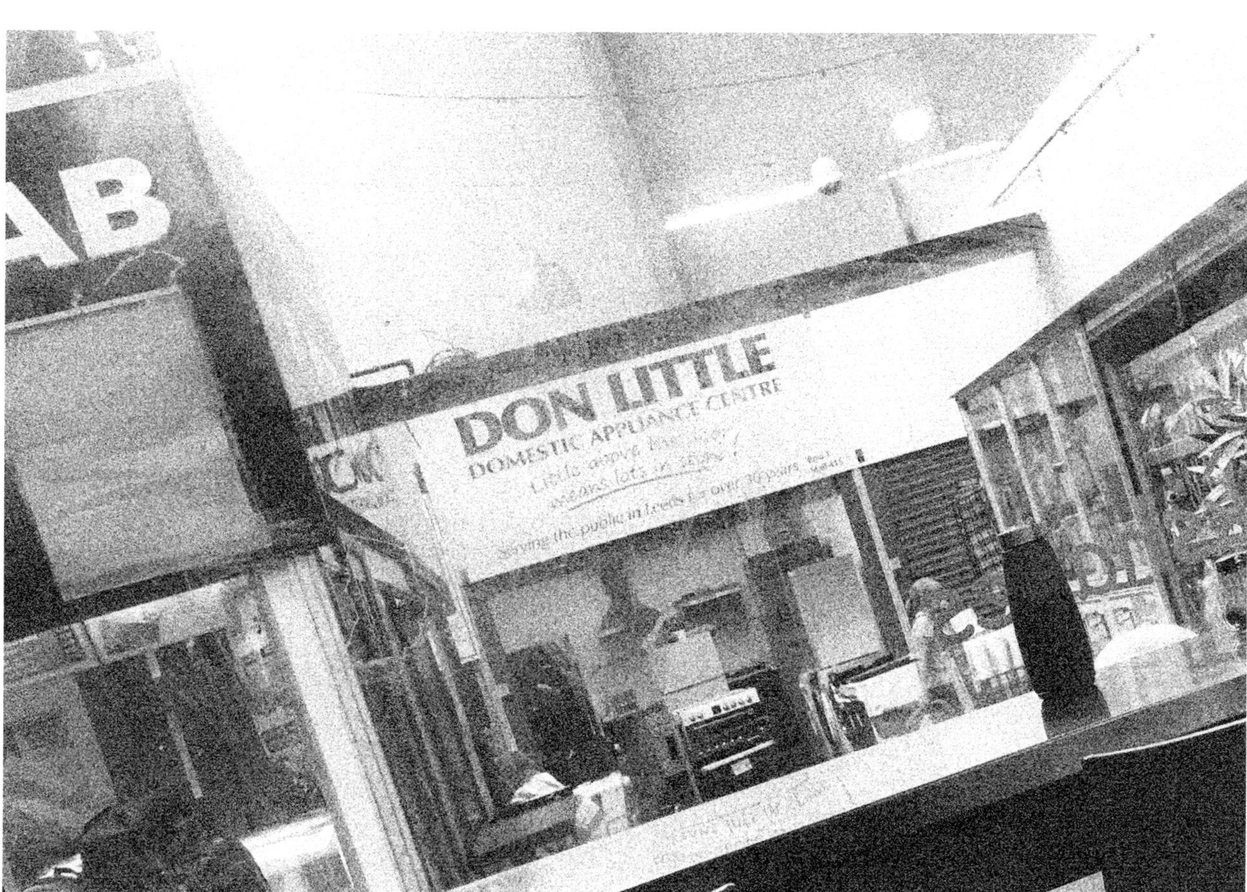
DON LITTLE
DOMESTIC APPLIANCE CENTRE

Footbridge over the A64, site of crossing and conveyance, a new temporality coalescing here. Where is the mediator, the guardian at the gate? Perhaps he's the cab driver dropping them off, or the bloke in the wheelchair saying take good care.

The bridge spans the deep ravine of the motorway. I look for the mosaic patterns, the orange lights. This is the first Leeds, locked and everlasting like ink under the skin.

The other side is Burmantofts, the brickfields and cholera grounds, names rubbed smooth on the ground.

*

I turn back towards the centre. Leeds is an amber mirage, a city wobbling with heat stroke. My stilettos are dusty in the construction lanes, there's grit in my eyes as I step through avenues of stalled towers.

I'm walking up Vicar Lane towards the Merrion Centre. I think there might be some solace there, a reconnection, but they've occluded the brutalism, painted the pillars white.

Morrisons have a café now, it steals around the entrance to the Phono. The door was a portal, you went from brightly lit shopping precinct to dry ice and viscous violet light.

Now, aluminium tables and chairs cling like barnacles or limpets.

I'm craving cool shadows, a swig of something strong. A lot of the pubs have closed now, the city centre has gone quiet, there are no office workers to buoy up lunchtime trade, no rambunctious nights out. Something else has returned to the centre, a system of scavenging and repurposing.

I'm getting the 1970s again, escalators in orange tubes, motionless seconds of tangerine light.

Kirkgate, a temperature drop, warehouses with ferns in fractured brickwork, a bluish haze in the alleys and doorways. Cigarette smoke, kitchen refuse, barbeque sauce.

I've got a couple of hours to kill before I go back up Burmantofts, the burner's been buzzing about a party in an abandoned church near the motorway.

The Brougham Arms is still there, renamed though. The bricks are orange like rust powder or Mars. When I step inside it isn't how I remember; the wooden floorboards are the same, and the panelling round the bar, but there's too much space, too much light coming in. I'm struck by the Harpic fumes from the gents, a chemical assault of cleaning fluids.

This is our table, the one we always gravitated to, there must have been partition walls then because we used to call it a snug, a hidden corner.

The barman serves me in slow languid movements mopping his face with a bar towel. He hands me a half glass, a nice one with a stem, and urges me to enjoy. He's from Kilkenny I think, or Waterford, I should know the difference but I'm out of practice now. They still have the glazed tiles, I'm glad about that, my eyes had fixed on their blemishes as our conversations unwound, locking our words into them, perhaps if I stare hard enough I'll hear them again.

He smiles over, then turns up the jukebox, a song I haven't heard for years, unlocking another vault. The words lag in the topaz light of the bar, a woman singing about leaving her life behind.

A subway with mosaic tiles, yellow constellations beneath a black film. Then the memorial gardens, eruptions of blossom in the half light. London, 1996. We climbed the steps to Glamis Road, then the black expanse of Shadwell Basin. The pub was like a ship run aground in a dim sketch of warehouses. It had walls the colour of nicotine and this song spilling slowly from a knackered speaker. The track, as it decelerated, was bound up with exquisite intimacy, a melancholy eroticism. I'd never heard it that way before, because it was on all the time, sugary trails in the high street, vapid and sentimental, but the faulty wiring was throwing it askance, casting it in a new light. I listened, felt the stone floor keeling; it was like walking under jasmine, the rush of a first kiss.
I remember zinging fruit machines, flashes of unexpected colour. I remember looking at my hands, chipped blue nails, a borstal dot hovering over each metacarpal. The IRA bombing was the start of it, a premonition. The explosion brought the window panes in, rocked the foundations of the building. The bathwater dropped as I stood to watch the cloud rising from Canary Wharf, fragments of glass sticking to my skin. I heard them shouting in the next room, the shock of it, chains of dumb expletives. I remember drying myself off, frantically dressing, it felt like Christmas, a supernatural kind of excitement.

That pub was sliced with cigarette smoke. There were concealed corners, pews that bent out of sight. You couldn't tell who was in when you stepped through the door, you had to adjust to the low light, the ambiguity. There were three of them in a corner, backs pressed to the window. The river was black and tilting, threatening to pull them in. They belonged to a tribe, bomber jackets, combat trousers, shaved heads. They were conspiring you could tell, circles of empty glasses, maps drawn on cigarette packets. You looked up as we passed. You were at the centre, flanked by your adherents, solemn and watchful.
I knew exactly where I'd seen you before, the dots on each metacarpal, the fleeing of that place. I placed both hands over my face, a split-second gesture, and a smile altered you, opened up another lineage, another set of features.

I recognised you, not in an abstract way, although it felt that way sometimes. I mean I'd seen you before. You came the way you remember a dream,

Laura Grace Ford, commissioned by Nav Haq

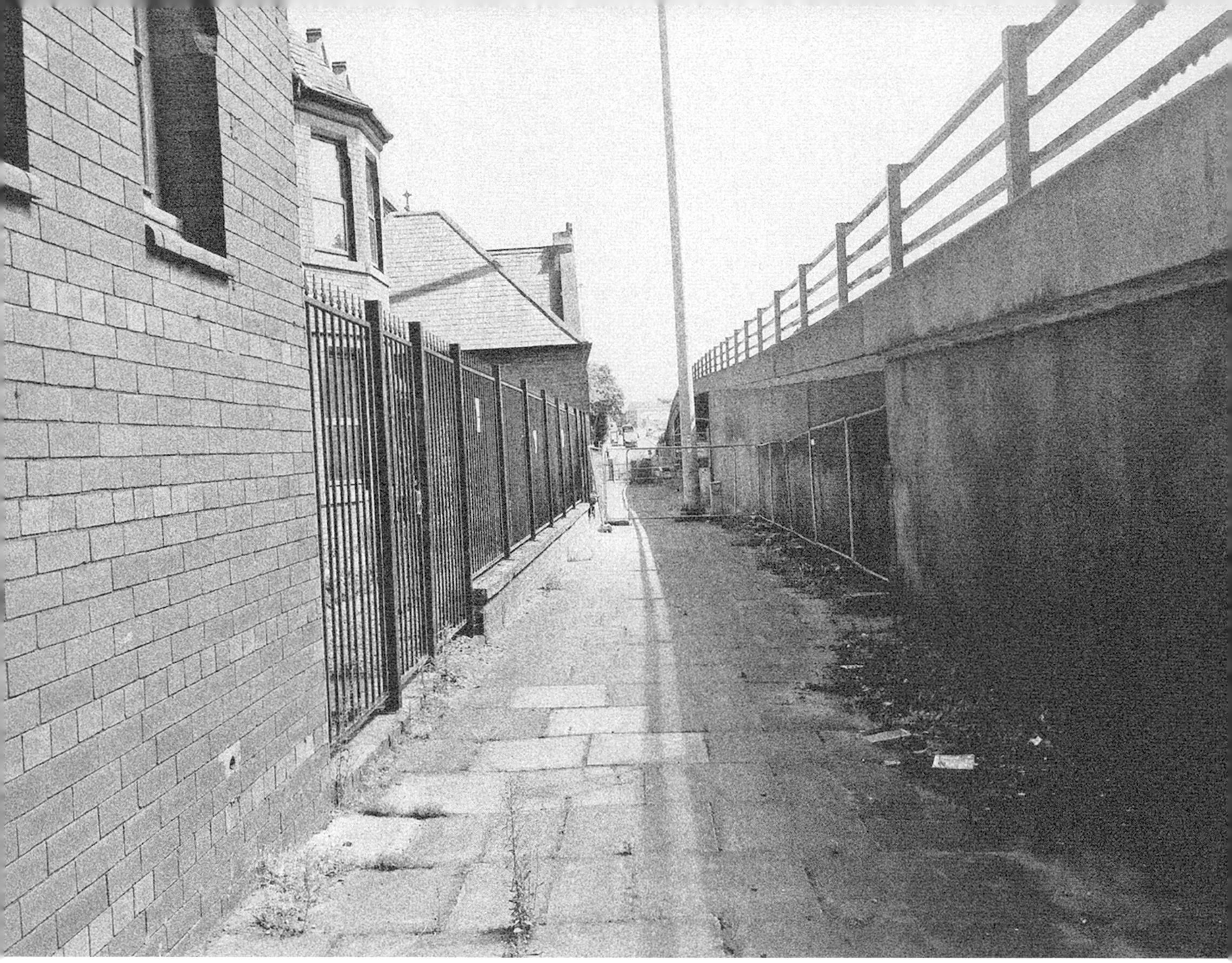

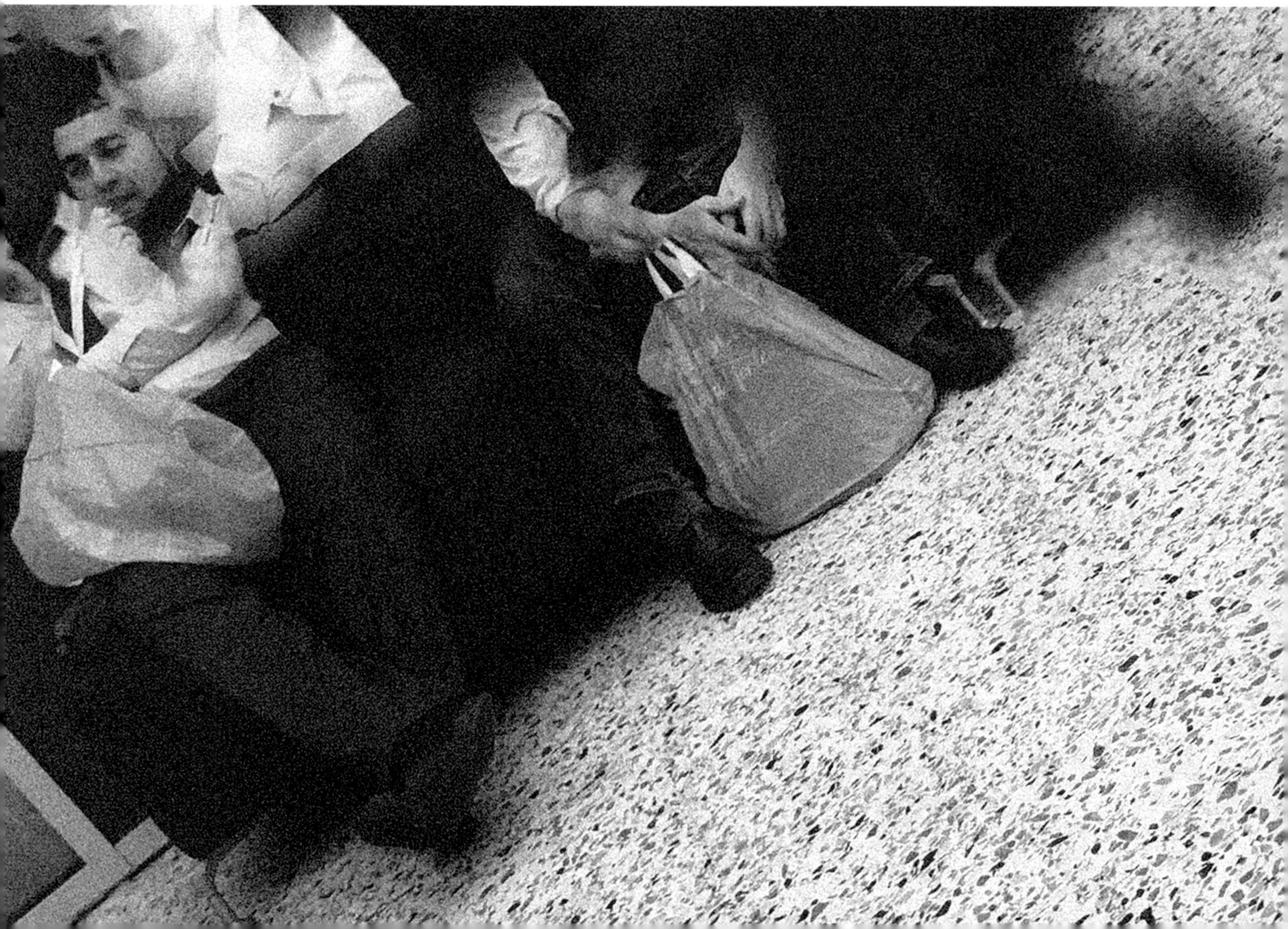

little pieces at first then slow panning sequences: a brutalist precinct, soot blackened buildings. West Yorkshire, we'd met there, in the smoke and darkness of that pub. What was it called? You went down a cobbled street, it was mock-Tudor with red banquettes and a dartboard, the bands were always metal or post-punk.

1989. There were standpipes that year, and the stink of refuse, and scorched drowsy heat.

The bar was prismatic, luminous, we'd have been on strawberries I think, or microdots. I think of that summer as a phase shift, new sonics in the clubs, a force upturning things. It was like getting colour TV for the first time, a saturated palette when all we'd had was dun, khaki and stone.

You were with a crew of punks, I'd seen them in town with their outgrown mohawks and copies of Class War. You were looking over. Your eyes were molten, pools of burnt umber. I remember your hair, cascades of it, so black it was blue, and your shoulders wide like a swimmer's. The span of optics flamed behind you, orange lights casting a glow like the streetlamps they have round here.

I had bleached hair then. My eyes were flicked with kohl. There'd have been a dozen of us, pressed together with crimped hair and black leather and silver bangles. It was the last summer we would dress like that.

I remember the scent of cedarwood, and patchouli. I remember drinking something aniseed flavoured in an alcove next to the cigarette machine and the sound from the stage rippling in envelopes of distortion, it was one of those sessions that went on for days.

You waited, intercepted as I wobbled in my spiked ankle boots to the bar. Your voice was Punjabi Bradford, an accent cooked in Manningham, sensual and hot from that neon hive.

Video shops, black terraces, orange lights.

There was dry ice and black out curtains. It was twenty-six degrees outside and we were sweltering in velvet heat. You took my hands, then fanned out yours, borstal dots on each metacarpal.

That kiss soldered, it made a brand.

I've got a tramadol, some codeine, not much else. I ask the barman for a vodka and lemonade, I haven't had one for years. He drops ice cubes in it, leaves me to the blemishes, the imperfections in the glazed tiles.

The Nokia's shuddering with new messages, a list of locations in spectral sites: Boyles Brickworks, Glassmakers' Arms, St Mary's.

And now, the accent's the same, rising from that hive of terraces and orange street lamps. And your eyes, all that intensity in them, all that sex. The Sun Inn, you say, remember? I feel the heat flare of it, the halo, the name enough to encircle us.

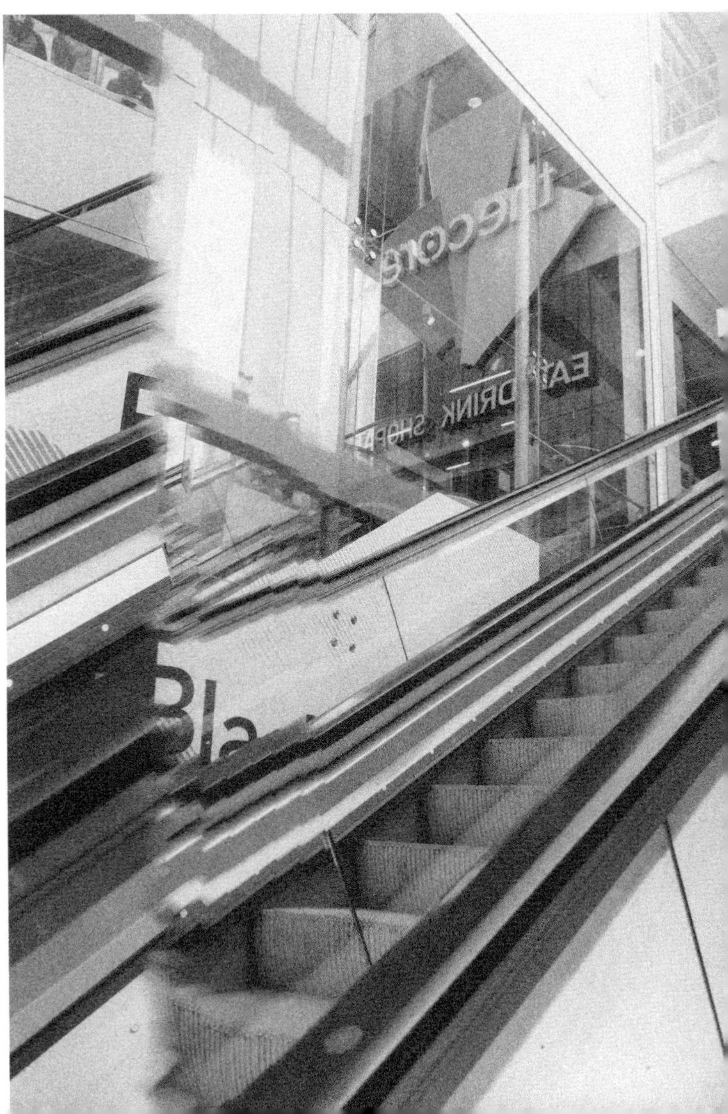

Vladimir Tatlin, Valdis Celms, Lyubov Popova, Hito Steyerl, Netochka Nezvanova, Lygia Pape, Elvia Wilk with Dunne & Raby

Virtual Tower, 'Virtual' Pit: On Potentiality and the Status of Unrealised Art

Amber Husain

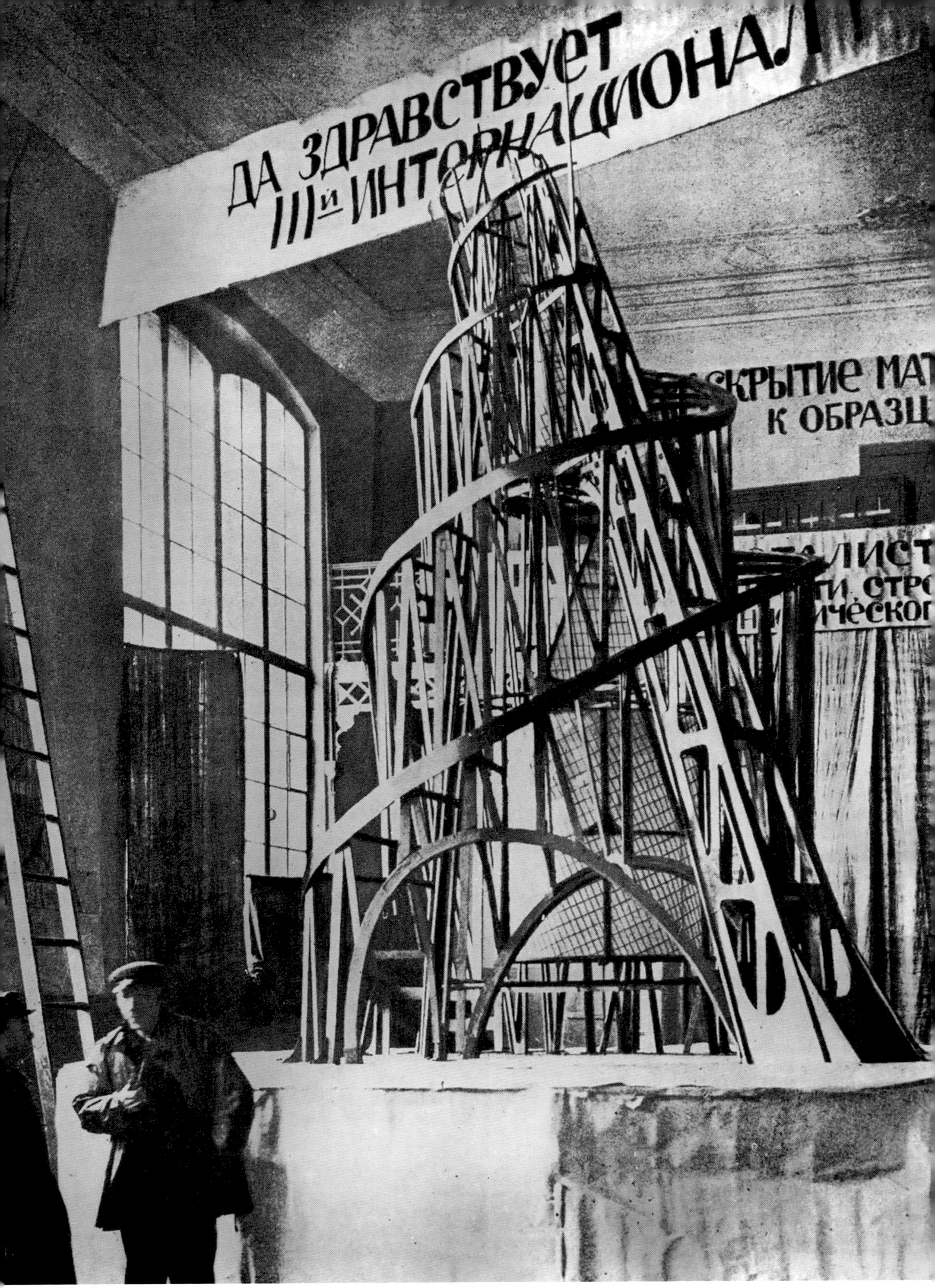

Vladimir Tatlin, *Model of the Monument to the Third International*, 1919, photograph, 1919–1920

In 1976, the Latvian artist Valdis Celms set to work on models for the *Pozitron*, a crystal-disco-ball-like structure imagined as the origin of a sprawling mass of light. Rotating around a central ball, the *Pozitron*'s metallic prisms would refract and reflect both internal and external light sources, bathing the Ukrainian factory for which the structure was designed in various shades of soothing glow. Celms developed four distinct regimes of illumination for the *Pozitron,* each in turn shifting with contingencies of natural light, in a bid to draw sensory lines between weekdays, Sundays, international festivals and state festivals. Detailed plans and drafts were drawn at the factory's request, but years rolled by and the thing was never built. In 2019, it was announced that the 2nd Riga International Biennial of Contemporary Art (RIBOCA2), due to take place from May 2020, would see Celms's neglected project realised at last. By April 2020, with the art world on lockdown in the midst of the Covid-19 pandemic, it was clear that this could not proceed as planned.

What would it mean for a '70s invention, conceived in relation to a Soviet industrial order of which there remain only traces, to be 'realised' as part of a twenty-first-century art show? Which part of Celms's vision, against the shell-like backdrop of contemporary (neo)liberalised Riga, was considered by the artist and organisers compatible with being fulfilled? In modern day Andrejsala, the idea of hypothetically enhancing the sensory experience of factory workers by playing on the rhythms of the social calendar might jar, for instance, with the general liberal consensus that holidays aren't for work. Presented as a 'model', *Pozitron* gestures towards an ideal, but in 2020 would do so by means of a mechanism only tangentially compatible with what that ideal entails. What's more, even in 1976, the work's 'model' status was itself less an earnest statement of intent than a canny means of exhibiting art on otherwise hostile ground. Working in a Cold War dictatorship that rejected the values of artistic abstraction, Celms's designation of the 'design' category to this piece, rather than signalling an expectation of meticulous fulfilment, represented a means of pushing what is now described as an artwork into the space of then-acceptable use- and industry-based endeavour.

According to its own internal logic, the *Pozitron*'s meaning and value is arguably produced without recourse to its purported intention. The aesthetic operations of this kind of kinetic art were, according to Celms himself, to do with the possibilities inherent in a spatial structure.[1] In fact, they might be read as concerned above all with ideas of possibility itself. The kinetic process begins with a static form, the motion of which begins to reveal the potential in that form. Such potential, says Celms, is inherent in the structure itself, the role of motion being one of interpretation. According to this principle, the effect of motion on the structure's shifting manifestation unfurls (in the *Pozitron*'s case through the play of light) a sense of possibility that floods both body and brain. It is such an aesthetic experience, both meditative and emotive, that constitutes the substance of this work – perfected, it would seem, in the function of the 'model' alone. Insofar as the experience of potential is evinced here through witnessing the relationship of motion to structure, a three-dimensional model, or even (in terms of concept) a two-dimensional plan, does much of the aesthetic and conceptual work – work that transcends, in the end, the actualised lighting of a factory floor.

According to the principles of Celms's kinetic process, potential might be best understood as a matter of delicate tension. Stasis, Celms explains, 'is not alien to the kinetic object; on the contrary, stasis plays the role of non-motion within the kinetic object'.[2]

There in that careful phrasing lies the key to an idea that grounds the project in philosophies of power. This 'stasis-as-non-motion' – non-motion as an affirmative state – seems to elevate the *Pozitron*'s powers of exposition towards a proposal that Giorgio Agamben credits with explaining and revealing potential in its truest and most realised form. For Agamben, the power and potential to be or to do involves, indeed requires, the power and potential not to be or do.[3] Thus the *Pozitron*'s potentiality for movement consists in its potentiality not-to-move – its potential, that is, for stasis. Were this potentiality for stasis absent – were the model unable to be still – the *Pozitron*'s potentiality for movement would not be a potentiality at all and merely a matter of the 'actual'. Inasmuch as the model, first in its stasis and then in its moving form, animates these principles of potential, it draws some attention to its own conditions of existence. In 1970s Riga under Soviet dictatorship, the conditions in which an artist grappling with abstract ideas of 'the possible' was able to articulate this project were severely limited. And while the *Pozitron* model appears at a surface level to suggest a horizon – a set of provisional ideals that could then go on to be fulfilled – in fact what it speaks to most of all are the limits of possibility in generalised states of duress. On these terms, if the *Pozitron*'s potential is 'unrealised', that is not because a giant rotating orb never made it through factory doors, but rather because the artist, in actualising his models, had no choice but to position them in terms of 'construction', 'experiment' and 'design'. Agamben would require that artistic mastery retain a trace of resistance in its perfect form. The potentiality attached to the *Pozitron*'s being is lacking in any resistance to the potential (which it lacked) to have taken a different shape.

In attempting to think in terms of pure potentiality, Agamben draws on Aristotle's distinction in his *Metaphysics* between what on the one hand might be called a 'capacity' (*dunamis*), a theoretical kind of possibility, and what on the other is actually able to be realised (*energeia*). Aristotle makes this distinction to affirm that capacities or potentialities exist and persist, even when they cannot or will not be enacted. Perhaps the *Pozitron*'s greatest utopian force resides in its affirmation of just these kinds of potentialities. In its elegant display of movement-as-resistance-to-stagnation, the *Pozitron* subtly points to that which was missing from Soviet-sanctioned art at the time of its own creation: the degree of relative freedom required to enact an ideal. Aristotle's realm of the *dunamis*, the field beyond the actual to which the *Pozitron* points, approximates to the kind of realm that Gilles Deleuze called the 'virtual'. Just as Agamben sees in potentiality an active presence of absences, Deleuze saw in the 'virtual' a set of absences that, rather than awaiting realisation, were themselves completely real.[4] For Deleuze there was more in the vast idea of the 'virtual' than there ever could be in the simple domain of the 'actual'. More, perhaps, in 'virtual' states of art than their realisation in biennials.

But what if the virtual biennial were to become the norm? Does the virtual in its garden sense, which points, in effect, 'online', have any important relationship to the 'virtual' meant by Deleuze?[5] Such a relationship could not be one of equivalence, given that the Deleuzian 'virtuality' is concerned with process rather than any fixed state. But might the process of art's virtualisation, contrary to much common sense, open up a space for encounter with something materially greater than that which can be physically made? From a constructivist point of view (Russian Constructivism forming, indeed, an important part of Celms's conceptual heritage, along with that of others included in RIBOCA2) a work's materiality could certainly exist more meaningfully in relation to potential – Deleuzian 'virtuality'

– than to its physical actualisation. For despite their preoccupation with both matter and abstraction, the Russian Constructivists could be understood as having advocated for an emphasis neither on the 'matter' nor on the underlying 'idea' of an artwork as concerns in and of themselves, but rather on capacities for praxis that might reorient *relationships* to matter in the world – a matter, in itself, of utmost material worth. The First Working Group of Constructivists, whose grand ambition was in 'realising vital acts',[6] were conscious these were not to be mastered in the fields of design, engineering and construction alone, and those such as Boris Arvatov, who insisted on the primacy of material as a precedent for socially purposeful forms, held that command of material presupposed experimentation, 'laboratories' of abstract thought – sites of engagement, above all else, in questions of potentiality.

Can it be any loss, in that case, that Vladimir Tatlin's proposal for the *Monument to the Third International*, all three (lost) incarnations being models, was never intended as something to be rendered 'real'? While the technology to synthesise so dizzying a tower of iron and revolving glass was not remotely within reach of an agrarian 1920s Russia, the work implied an organisational relationship between people (with its communal conference centres and centralised hubs of propaganda), a relationship to politics of space (in its supposed situation at Communism's Muscovite heart) a relationship to the physical world (tilted in perfect parallel with the axis of the Earth) and last, a relationship to the compromised conditions of possibility that worked against all these things. Models of such self-conscious limitation, in the words of Tatlin himself, 'stimulate us to invention in our work of creating a new world, and [...] call upon the producers to exercise control over the forms encountered in our everyday life'.[7]

Can it be any loss, furthermore, that the paintings Lyubov Popova called 'space force constructions' were 'to be regarded only as a series of preparatory experiments'?[8] Or that her contribution to the Third Communist International was also curtailed in the end? Having worked on the sets for a piece of military theatre, titled 'The End of Capital' and destined (at least provisionally) for Moscow's busy streets, what, you could ask, was negated when 'new controls on street activities' called the whole thing off? Not the dream of capital's end itself. Repeatedly suppressed with violent hands, Constructivism's most profound afterlife didn't always manifest in 'realisations'. When Lygia Pape developed Constructivist notions into new sociological and anthropological ideas and forms in '50s and '60s Brazil, most memorable were works, like the strange *Divisor*, that had many more lives than were actualised. First imagined, but never materialised, as a plastic awning for suspension in an exhibition space, hung so that gallery-goers might put their heads through its holes, the artist hoped to induce and critique with the work a kind of embodied alienation. *Divisor*'s first actual staging took place by a Rio favela in 1967. Neighbourhood children, without instruction from the artist, slid onto the sweeping expanse of cloth she had left for them on the ground and poked their heads through its holes. An impromptu performance of sorts was birthed as they chattered away to each other, walking as one sheet. Only after this did the artist ascribe specific parameters to the piece on its renewal in other contexts, and still its possibilities remained continually open. 'There is no work', wrote Pape: 'there is only the unfolding into a thousand routes'.[9]

Perhaps it should come as no surprise, given the traditions of thought from which it emerged, that the *Pozitron* was considered 'realisable', was planned for realisation, without the involvement of its specified industrial site. Or was it that the museum (here the biennial setting) was simply understood as more or less a factory itself? A site, as Hito Steyerl most notably put it, of hyper-production (of images) and exhibition value; a space of confinement and disciplined gazes – a site of organised exploitation?[10] Just as Celms tests out industry's limited powers of wish-fulfilment by projecting his work into the factory, Steyerl posits the museum itself as a site of inherent unfulfillment. A site, that is, of an unfulfilled vision of transparent, 'public' discourse. With its overflow of durational films, blaring at once as nobody listens, woven into a sprawling texture of generalised unintelligibility, the museum, says Steyerl, puts on display its consistent absence of public discourse, making the presence of that absence as public as did Celms with his 'models' in their absence of power to be named as art.

While the museum as represented by Steyerl can hardly be read as intentional or earnest in any reflexive display of unfulfillment, RIBOCA2's re-conception explicitly moved the agenda towards this kind of reflexivity. The biennial's landscape of empty lots and 'wastelands', granaries, a paintball field and various hangars, all of which were earmarked as site-specific backdrops to a series of physical events, instead became the setting for a feature film (constituting the biennial's 'reimagining') that unfolded interactions between finished, unfinished and absent works of art.[11] In its purposeful attention to the question of lack – to that which intervenes both in art's viability and its visibility, the RIBOCA2 film tends towards the engagement of a discourse lacking in the polished museum. As Celms wrote of his kinetic process, motion and structural conditions are not the only relevant factors in the genesis of form. An object's character also depends on 'the source of energy that generates this motion […], the potential uses this source allows and the way in which energy is managed'.[12] So, indeed, does the management of artworks' 'virtualisation' thoroughly shape those artworks' distribution and their meaning. Online museums might frequently be built as variously accessible repositories of virtual simulacra – not much more than thumbnails representing art 'items'. But so might they be built to emphasise the Deleuzian 'virtual' lives of artworks that have not or couldn't be made. The 'virtual' ground of a 'real life' work cannot, says Deleuze, resemble it. The 'virtual' is by definition differentiated in form from that which it might ground. RIBOCA2, always intended as a forum for examining ruptures of modern utopias and Soviet ideals while tending towards counter-hegemonic visions of 'tomorrow', staged its differential re-conception 'somewhere between a ruin and a construction site', in a liminal space that acknowledged both its own situation and 'the limits of our control'.[13] Rather than a stealth, begrudging reconstruction of the works in an awkward and falsely 'complete' online space, the film was a means of drafting in the virtual to engage with the unrealised itself – the virtual as space of potential and therefore a 'virtual' space.

*

The virtual, of course, need not only be a site of utopian 'virtuality', as typified by a phenomenon in early net art that virtualised a vision from the past. In 1848 Fyodor Dostoevsky embarked on a novel which, according to one of his biographers, would have prefigured (Constructivist) concerns with the social value of art, between utilitarian 'goals' and Romantic fancies of autonomy, but the novel in which he would do so was cut off close to inception; *Netochka Nezvanova*, the story of a woman whose name translates as 'Nameless Nobody', only made it as far as its own and its heroine's adolescence. After the author's forced exile to Siberia for collusion in a literary circle whose aim was to unravel the wrongs of autocracy and serfdom with recourse to Western philosophy, the partial novel, not to be returned to, became its own testament to the limits of art and language as means of emancipation. If Dostoevsky meant to speak to the artist's role in the possible, an online materialisation of *Netochka Nezvanova*, in the form of an artist presence identified by that name, would in 1995 become a hallmark for the power of the virtual sphere as a site of malevolent 'virtualities'. Netochka Nezvanova, avatar of avant-garde internet performance, while picking up perversely on Dostoevsky's vision of the artist as an aesthete with a purpose, became as known for her abstract and usable software artworks as she did for aggressive displays of anonymous cyber-domination.

Until around 2002, Netochka Nezvanova put her (lack of a) name to various pieces of widely used software. Although numerous artists and programmers were likely responsible for her output, associated also with other aliases, including antiorp, inte.ger and m2zk!n3nkunzt, she managed to establish a reasonably coherent identity largely through two trademark strategies, one being widespread trolling, the other a knack for proprietary capitalisation. Underlying both was an interest in at once exploiting and exposing online information architectures. Liberal use of largely unintelligible code in relentless mailing-list spam was one basic means of drawing attention to interfaces' internal layers; denial-of-service attacks on websites was another way of showcasing virtual power and vulnerability. Having given the world *Nato.0+55_3d* (1999), one of the first applications with real-time video manipulation capacities, enabling artists to reconstitute video as live performance, Netochka Nezvanova also showed the easy intersection of such internet 'firsts' with functions of monopoly capitalism. Distributing software licenses at whimsical but not insignificant fees, Nezvanova would revoke the access of any who criticised her code in public. Withdrawing licenses or denying already-paid-for software updates, her exercise of power in its fully realised form was a lesson in potentiality-not-to as violence. What's more, it demonstrated the extent to which the virtual economy could be seen as a 'virtual' space of potential for capitalistic exchange minus the basics of accountability.

If Netochka Nezvanova's internet practices floodlight the darker side of virtual art's materiality – the tendency of such art, for all its utopian impulses, to proffer and develop dystopian potentialities too – this testifies, in part, to technology's distance from its surface neutrality. As Nezvanova herself articulated her vision, the internet is formed on a 'panoply of actions and interactions, mutualism, parasitism, mimicry and errors', none of which suggest a neutral and few of which an equitable space.[14] And inasmuch as we *can* understand the virtual to be a space of potentiality, with such virtual artworks as RIBOCA2's revived *Pozitron* working to expose potentiality's dynamics, Netochka Nezvanova pointed to the sense in which the virtual can serve as site of mystification as much as exposure. The characteristic opacity of the code in which she expressed herself, all the while exerting the kinds of tyranny that privileged access to information affords, reveals the truth of the virtual not as a site of dematerialisation, but rather as a site of materiality purposefully obscured. The virtual sphere's tendency towards deliberate obfuscation – protecting the unequal distribution of knowledge and therefore possibility – is precisely the fault that motivates Hito Steyerl's long-term interest in the 'poor image'. The glitchy, scar-ridden digital file that qualifies as 'poor', by drawing attention to its own corrupted code, exposes, for Steyerl, the conditions of its own visibility – the violence that inheres in the distribution of information online.

For Steyerl, any distinction between virtual and material realities is subject to the deepest suspicion. Still, in her art, the virtual is frequently privileged as a means of excavating Deleuze's 'virtual' domain. Her 2015 video installation *The Tower*, for instance, merges CGI and film in a virtual environment from which to consider an unrealised architectural project, spearheaded by Saddam Hussein, that aimed to reconstruct the mythic tower of Babel. Centred on a particular virtual reality graphics company on Ukraine's conflict-riven border with Russia, the three video channels wind through the virtually continuous sites of the eponymous tower, a shooting game and a complex of luxury condos. 'Realisation' is broken down in the context of a world where a metastatic virtual realm is infinitely implicated in what is called the 'real'. 'Immaterial' processes of real estate rendering, online gambling and military simulation, united in relation to this one VR programmer, arc into real-life military conflict and unarguable material dispossession. With *The Tower* Steyerl uses a virtual space to tether hypotheticals to that which they ground, sketching the digital construction of material truths, experiences entangled in 'immaterial' networks that outsource, offshore, exploit and destroy. *The Tower* is neither utopian in the manner of the *Pozitron*, nor a dystopian performance of cyber-tyranny. Rather, it advances a meta-exploration of how virtual art relates to 'virtual' ontology – how the realm of the hypothetical bears on the (mediated) real.

While *The Tower*'s tower graphic is actually based on the Great Mosque of Samarra, the video's reference to Babel as a fulcrum of unrealisation seems far from incidental. Some fifteen years before making *The Tower*, Steyerl had spoken of a Franz Kafka fragment from 1920 in which the writer proposed the idea of digging a *pit* of Babel, rather than the mythic tower. 'Instead of constructing a monumental presence', she noted, 'he suggests the active creation of an absence, which has to be excavated in order to advance things and to be able to progress'.[15] Since the disaster at Babel, according to its mythos, resulted in the loss of a universal language, the implication seems to be that the creation of such a language would require the construction of knowledge 'bottom up'. For while technological means of mass communication might parade pretensions to universality, at least from the aerial perspective signified by a tower, they have in fact concealed those tensions and exclusions that imperfectly 'universal' codes so typically inscribe, and that only a perspective from the ground would ever be able to reveal. Take, for instance, the development of Gottfried Wilhelm Leibniz's universal code at the end of the seventeenth century. As Steyerl points out, his proof of universality leant on a false equation of zeros and ones with (respectively) the interrupted and uninterrupted lines of Chinese hexagrams as found in the *I Ching* – an imposition of correspondence rather than an accurate discovery in dialogue with more first-hand channels of understanding. Netochka Nezvanova reveals something similar in her treatment of digital code, as several of her works showcase the strange and entrancing audiovisual results of translating code from one form into another – code into sound, sound into graphics, graphics into code. That which you'd expect to correspond to something legible often proves harder to fathom, and if *The Tower* attempts to unearth potentialities – plans for building and destruction – that are otherwise sheathed in virtual networks of communication, that which it posits as most unfulfilled is the dream of Babel itself.

As I write, *The Tower* can be seen online, via an independent 'gallery guide', as part of a 'VR' 360° tour of the exhibition 'Life Captured Still' at Thaddeus Ropac in London, providing an alternative channel of access while the gallery itself is closed. Arrows joltily drag the viewer between installations that, given the limitations of this virtual format, are often moments in these videos literally captured still. The purpose of this virtual exhibition in the absence of access to the moving image is somewhat unclear. Pre-dating the gallery's unforeseen closure (which lends the virtual version a kind of 'virtuality' as a shadowy parallel of the exhibition's unrealised run) the virtual tour is predominantly a deadened record of a once-living show. The virtual here intrudes on the work in the interest of little more than its capture as so many units of cultural value, its replacement as so many objects in the kind of contemporary 'museum' that Steyerl aligned with the factory – a container for the production for 'images, jargon, lifestyle and values'.

And yet, if conditions are such that a factory becomes a museum, a museum the set for a biennial-reimagined-as-film, there have arisen artistic inventions that give reason to expect or insist that the film sets of this time might be more than cemeteries of cultural widgets. If the virtualisation of art on the one hand opens onto instances of art's inertia – works entering awkwardly into an order of vacuous commodities while heightening a pretence to immateriality that mystifies that order, the consequence need not be a return to nostalgic veneration of the physical object – the object that is honest, at least, in its relationship to the market. There is scope, it would seem, for virtual art to expose, critique and intervene in the politics of what is materially possible. Such feats of artistic intervention demand an openness and sensitivity to questions of 'virtuality' – that which Deleuze imagined to have greater material significance than what is understood to be 'real', realised, complete. Contra prevailing tendencies in online representation, the virtual can be recruited as a means of manifesting the 'virtual' capacities and limits of artworks that have not been, could not be or will not ever be 'actualised'. Pointing to their own contingency, proposing perhaps utopias, perhaps the violence inherent in non-creation, these artworks attest to what has been revealed about incompatible realities – realities that belong, at once, to the same chaotic world.

1   Valdis Celms, 'The Dialectic of Motion and Stasis in Kinetic Art', *Leonardo*,
        vol.27, no.5, 'Prometheus: Art, Science and Technology in the Former Soviet
        Union', October 1994, pp.387–90.

2   *Ibid.*, pp.389–90.

3   Thus Agamben's influential thesis that the power that grounds the juridical
        order does so by virtue of its power to suspend the law; see *Homo Sacer:
        Sovereign Power and Bare Life*, California: Stanford University Press, 1995.
        It should be noted that in March 2020 Agamben sparked controversy over
        his rash application of this theory to what he deemed to be an 'unmotivated'
        state of exception imposed by the Italian government in response to the
        Covid-19 pandemic. In this case, while Agamben perhaps usefully drew
        attention to the means by which the pandemic was leveraged for the imple-
        mentation of nationalist and authoritarian logics of governance, he was dan-
        gerously incorrect to assume and assert the lack of a legitimate motivating
        force behind any imposition of lockdown measures.

4   Gilles Deleuze, *Difference and Repetition* (trans. Paul Patton), New York:
        Columbia University Press, 1995 [1968].

5   I use quotation marks ('virtual') throughout to distinguish the Deleuzian
        sense of the term from its common meaning.

6   Programme of the First Working Group of Constructivists, March 1921
        (trans. John E. Bowlt).

7   Vladimir Tatlin, 'The Work Ahead of Us' [1920], in John E. Bowlt, *Russian Art
        of the Avant-Garde: Theory and Criticism*, 1902–1934, London: Thames &
        Hudson, 1917, p.207.

8   Lyubov Popova, statement in *5 x 5 = 25* (exh. cat.), Moscow, 1921, p.3.

9   Lygia Pape, 'Divisor. The Skin of All: Smooth, Light Like a Cloud: Loose', in
        Lygia Pape: Magnetized Space (exh. cat.), Madrid: Museo Nacional Centro de
        Arte Reina Sofia, 2011, p.244.

10   Hito Steyerl, 'Is a Museum a Factory?' [2009], in *The Wretched of the
        Screen*, Berlin: Sternberg Press, 2012, pp.60–76.

11   See the RIBOCA2 website, available at https://www.rigabiennial.com/en/
        riboca/riboca-2 (last accessed on 8 July 2020).

12   V. Celms, 'The Dialectic of Motion and Stasis in Kinetic Art', *op. cit.*, p.388.

13   Online announcement, available at https://www.rigabiennial.com/riboca-2
        (last accessed on 21 May 2020).|

14   Netochka Nezvanova, 'The Internet, A Musical Instrument in Perpetual Flux',
        Computer Music Journal, vol.24, no.3, Autumn 2000, p.38.

15   Hito Steyerl, 'The (W)hole of Babel', lecture as part of haus.0, Künstlerhaus
        Stuttgart, 20 January 2000, transcript available at http://www.haussite.net/
        site.html (last accessed on 22 May 2020).

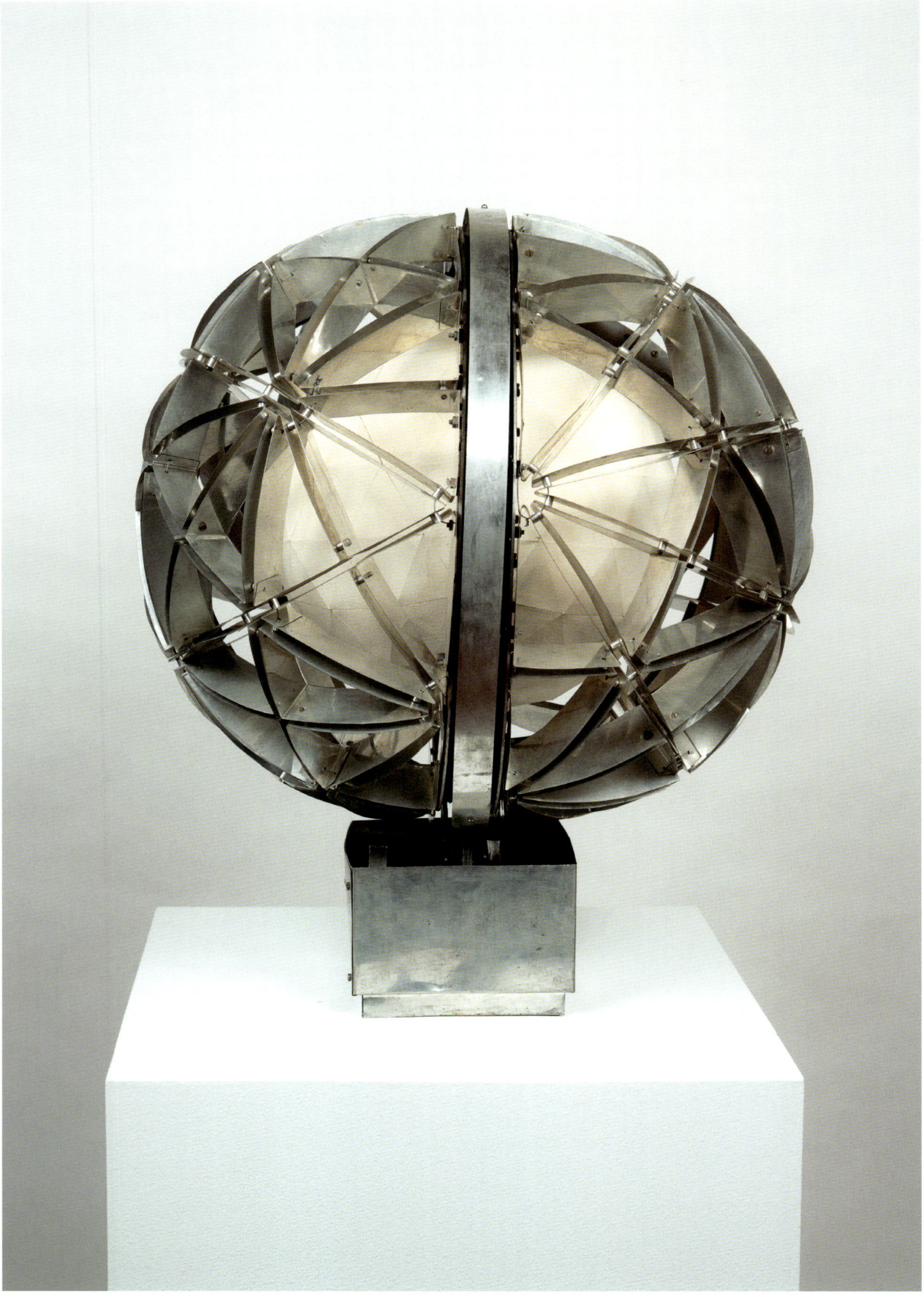

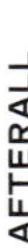

Valdis Celms, *Pozitron*, 1976,
kinetic maquette of steel,
paper and wood, 46 x 37 x 40cm.
Collection Zimmerli Art Museum at
Rutgers University, Norton and Nancy
Dodge Collection of Nonconformist
Art from the Soviet Union.
Photograph: Peter Jacobs

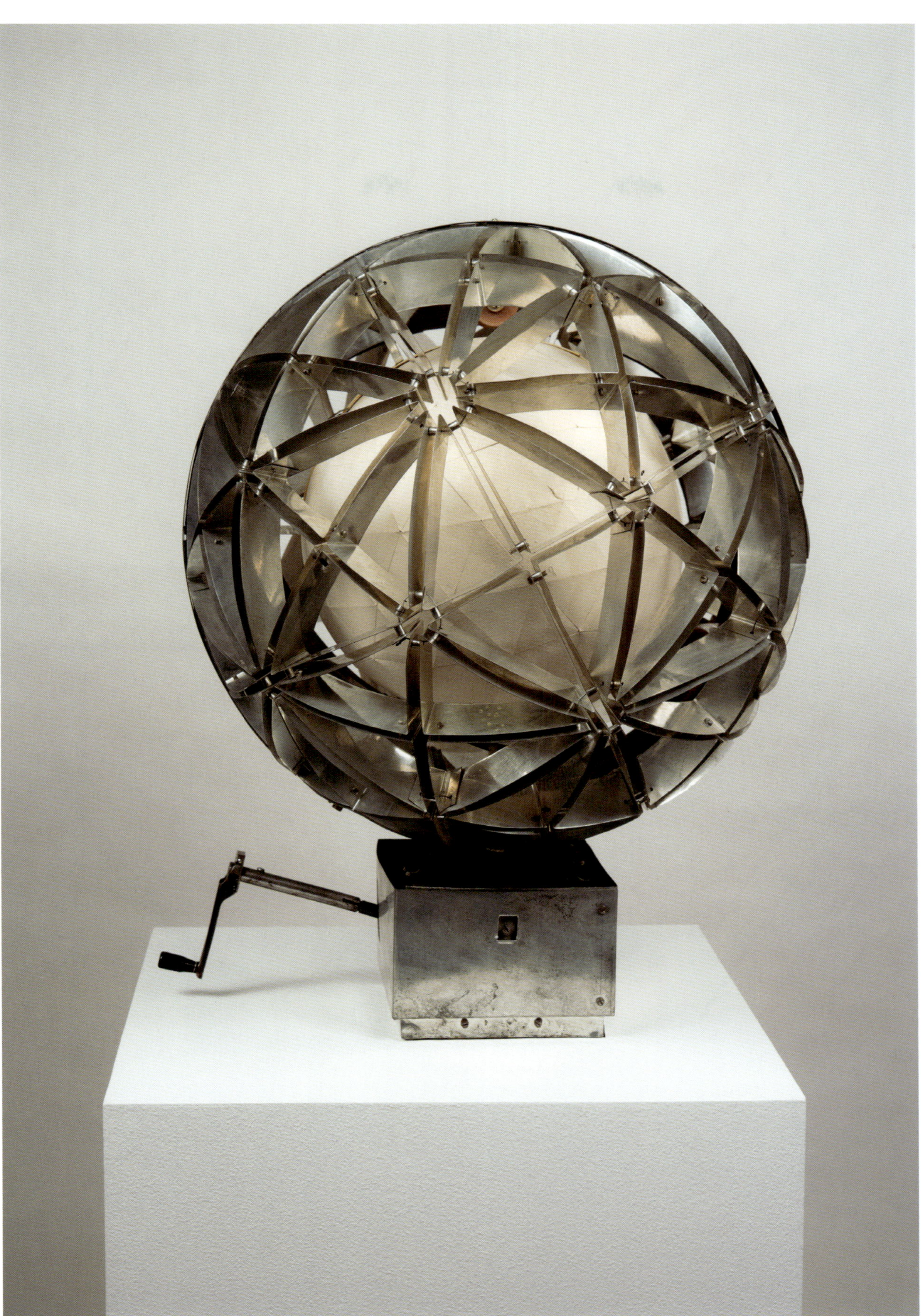

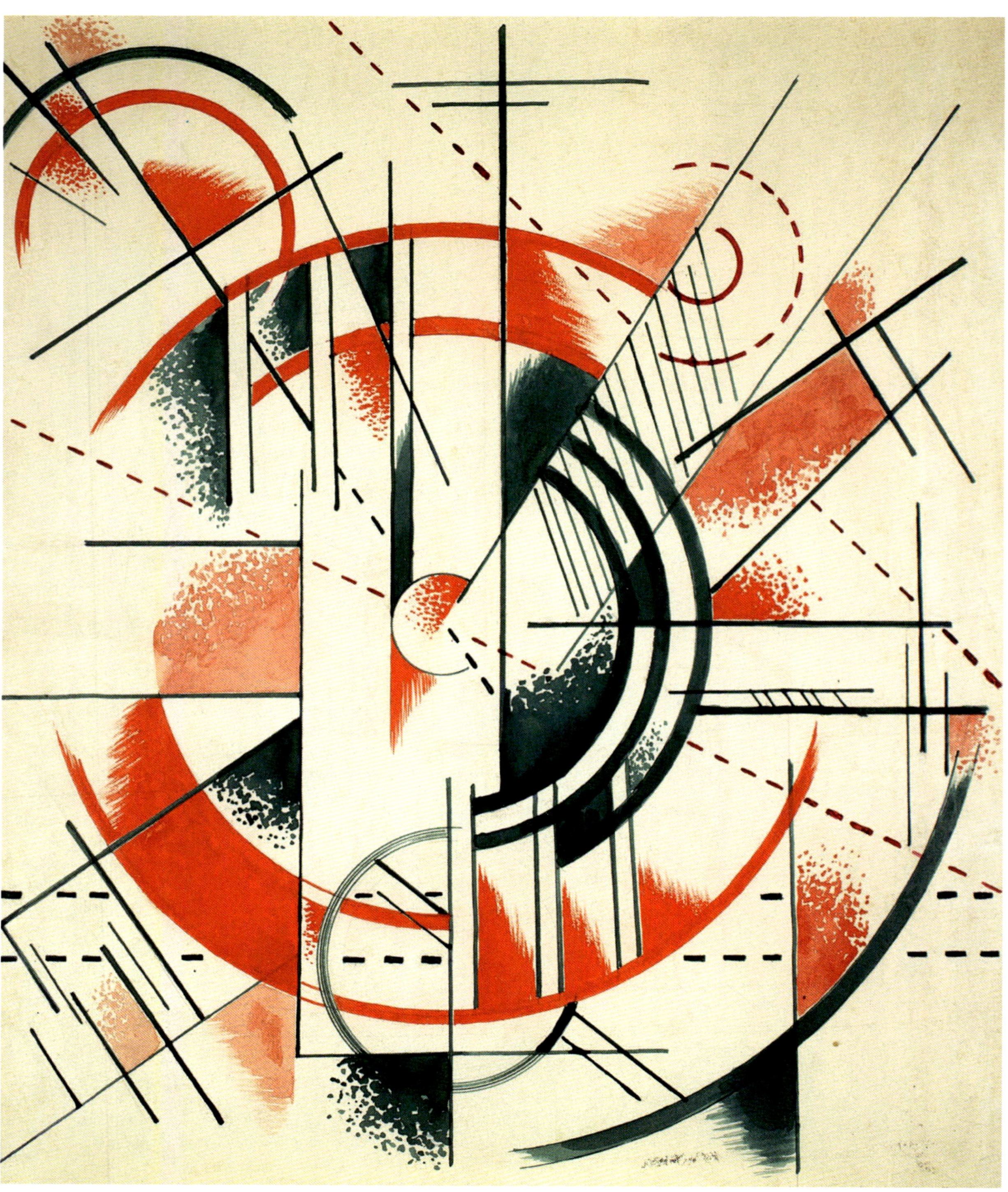

Lyubov Popova, *Space Force Construction*, 1921–22, paper, gouache, graphite pencil, 47.9 x 41cm. State Tretyakov Gallery, Moscow

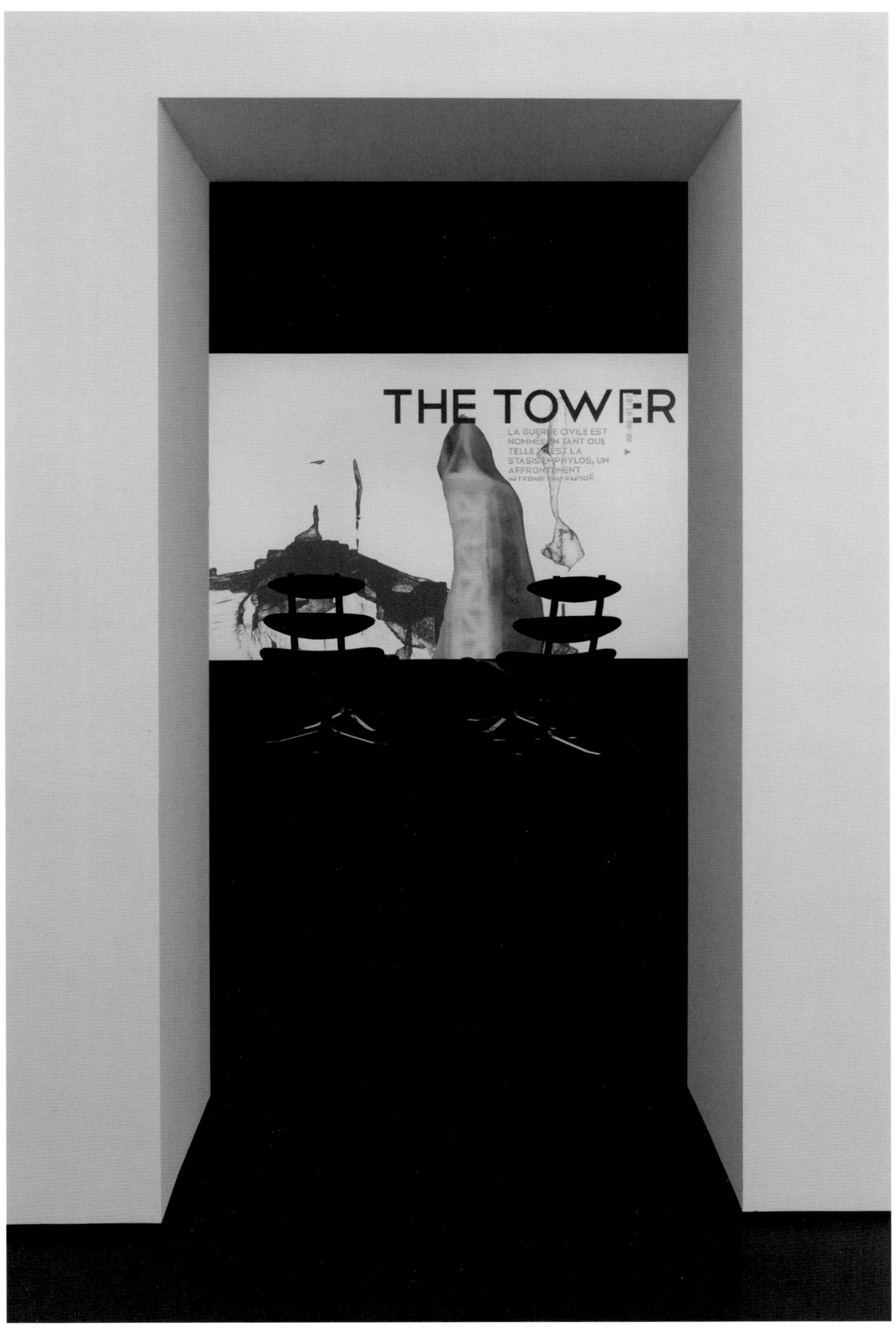

Hito Steyerl, *The Tower*, 3 channel video
installation, 2015 HD video, colour, sound,
6min 55sec. Installation view, Esther
Schipper, Berlin, 2019. Photograph © Andrea
Rossetti. © VG Bild-Kunst, Bonn, 2020.
Courtesy the artist, Andrew Kreps Gallery,
New York and Esther Schipper, Berlin

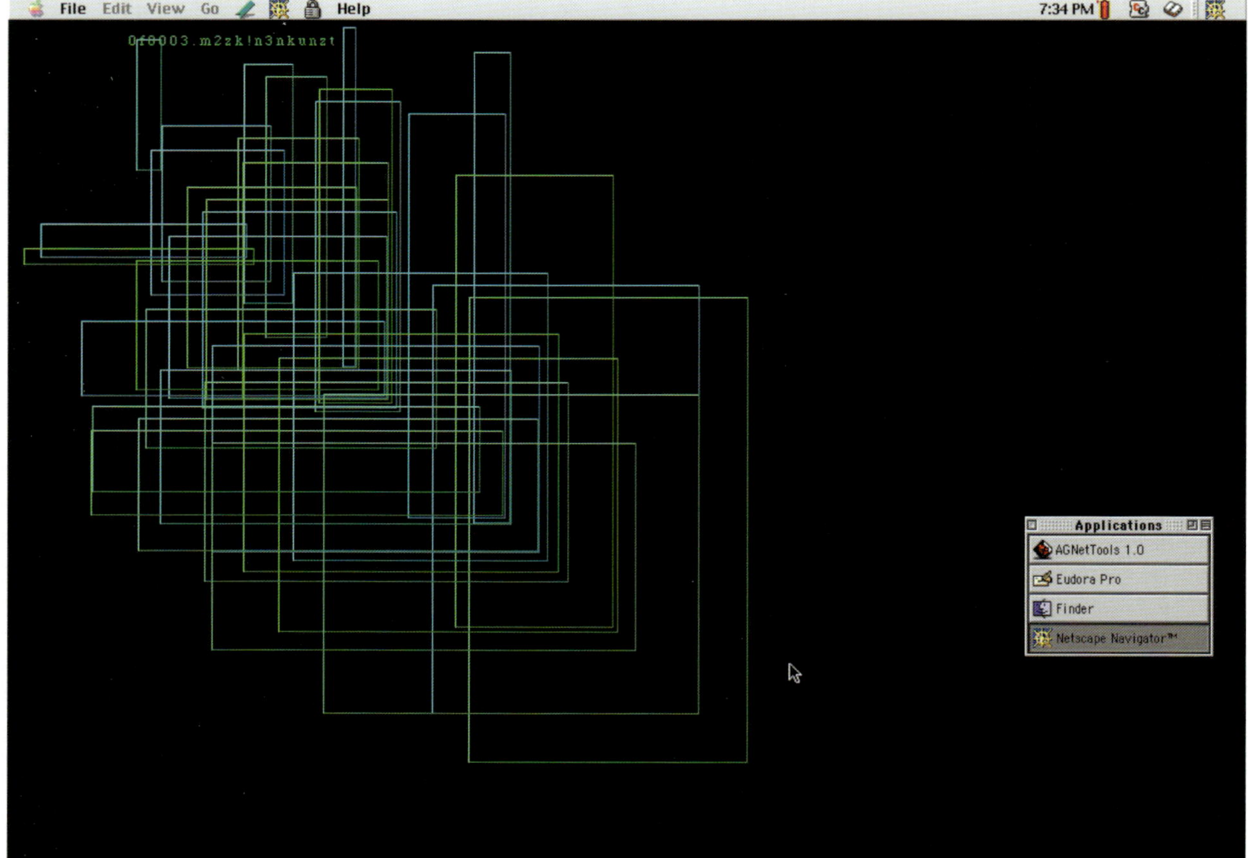
File   Edit   View   Go   Help
7:34 PM
0f0003.m2zk!n3nkunzt
Applications
AGNetTools 1.0
Eudora Pro
Finder
Netscape Navigator™

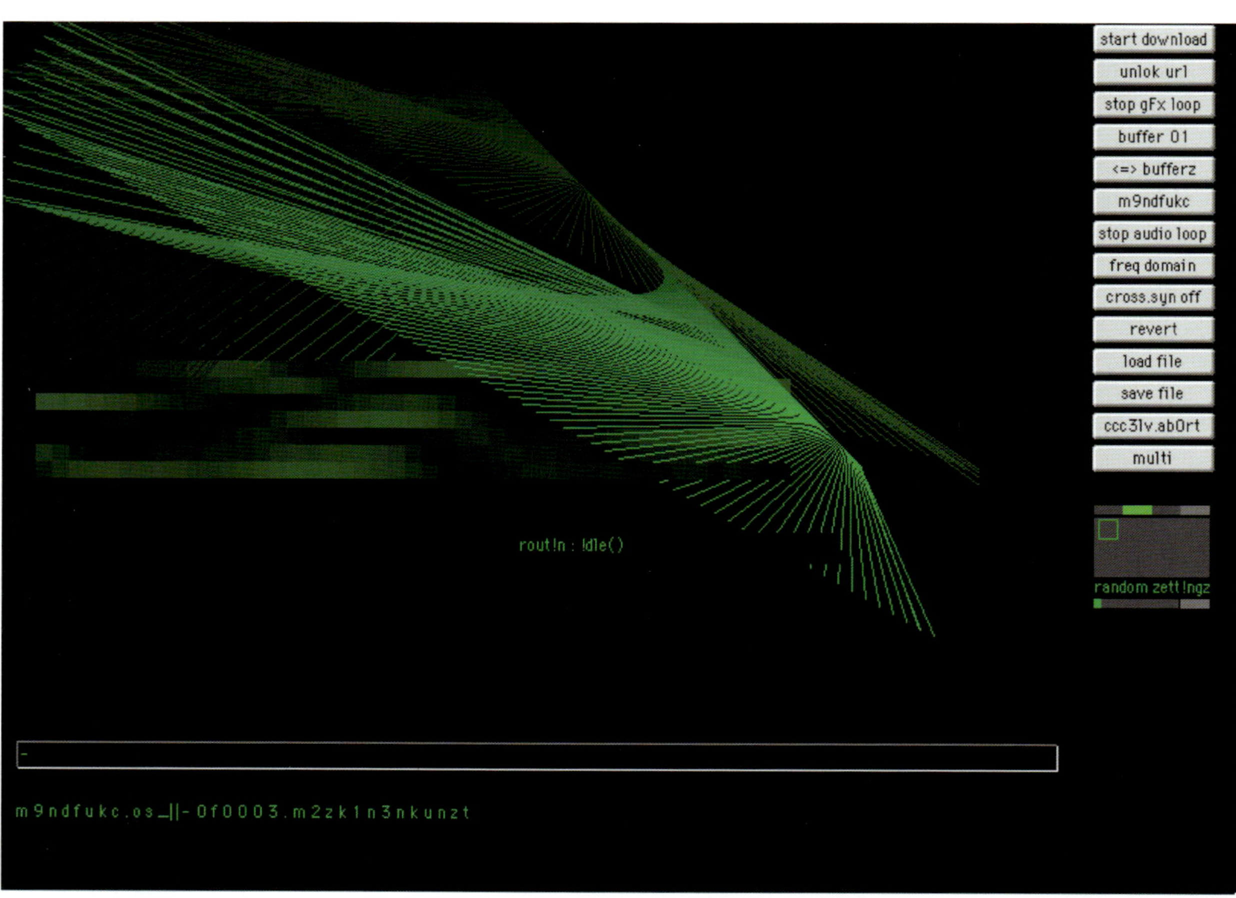
start download
unlok url
stop gFx loop
buffer 01
<=> bufferz
m9ndfukc
stop audio loop
freq domain
cross.syn off
revert
load file
save file
ccc3lv.ab0rt
multi
random zett!ngz
rout!n : !dle()
m9ndfukc.os_||-0f0003.m2zk!n3nkunzt

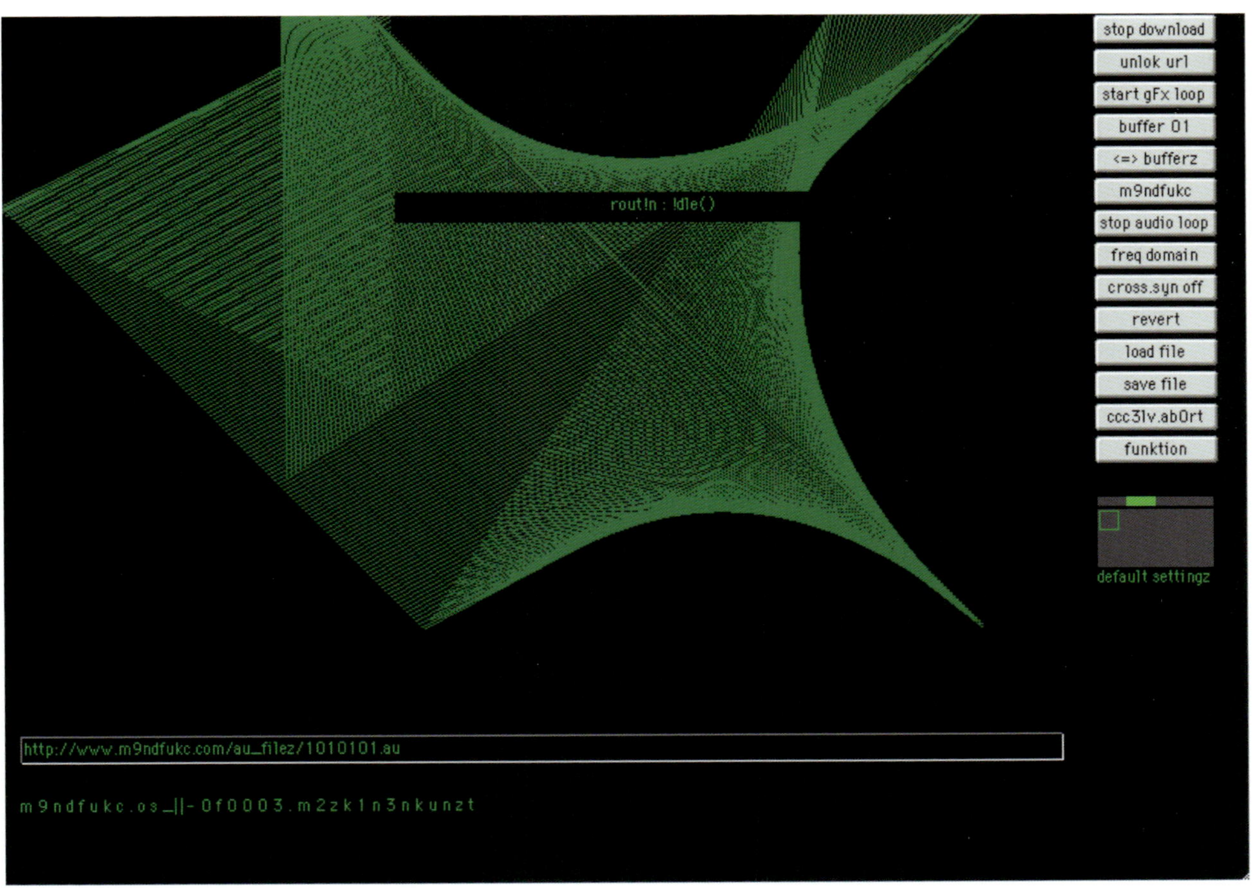

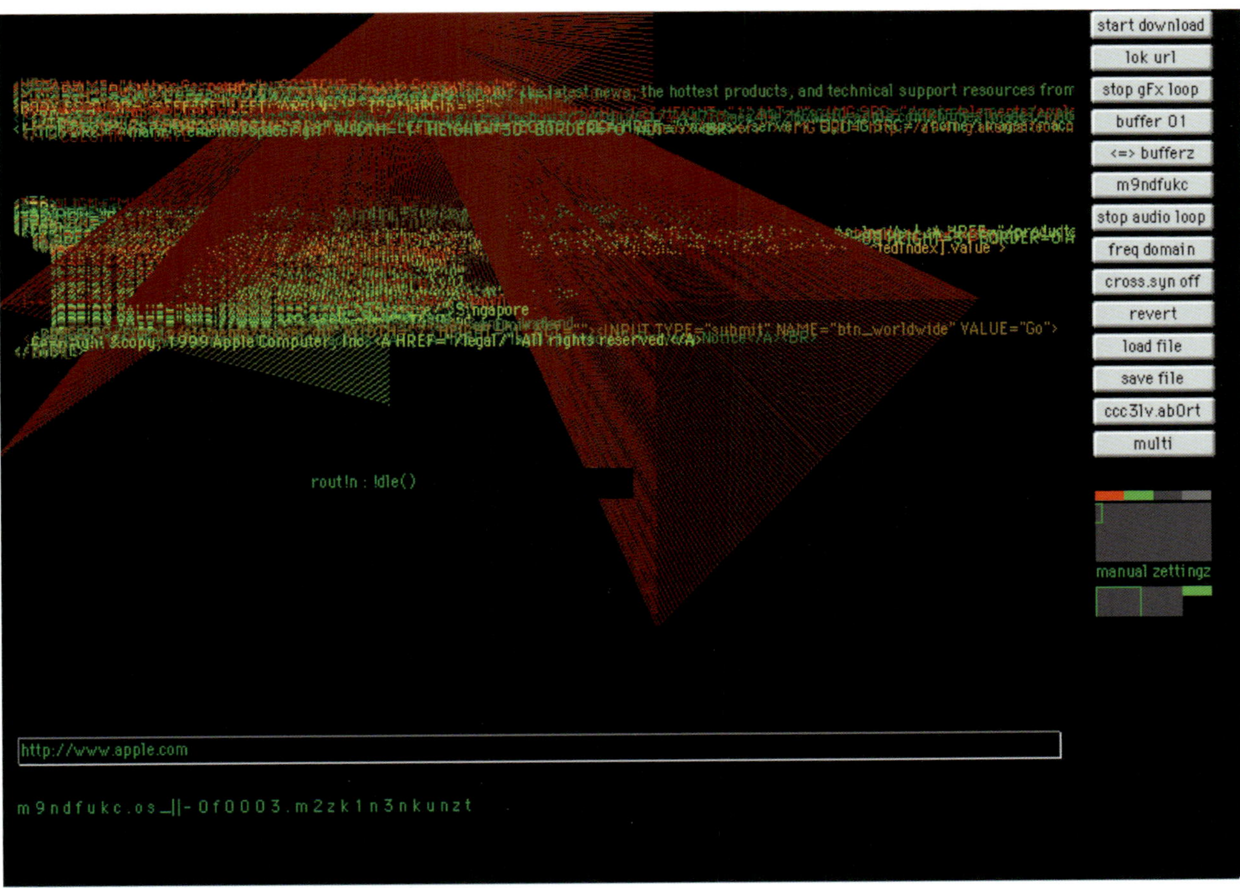

Netochka Nezvanova,
***m9ndfukc.0+99*, 1999.**
Screenshots by Andrew McKenzie

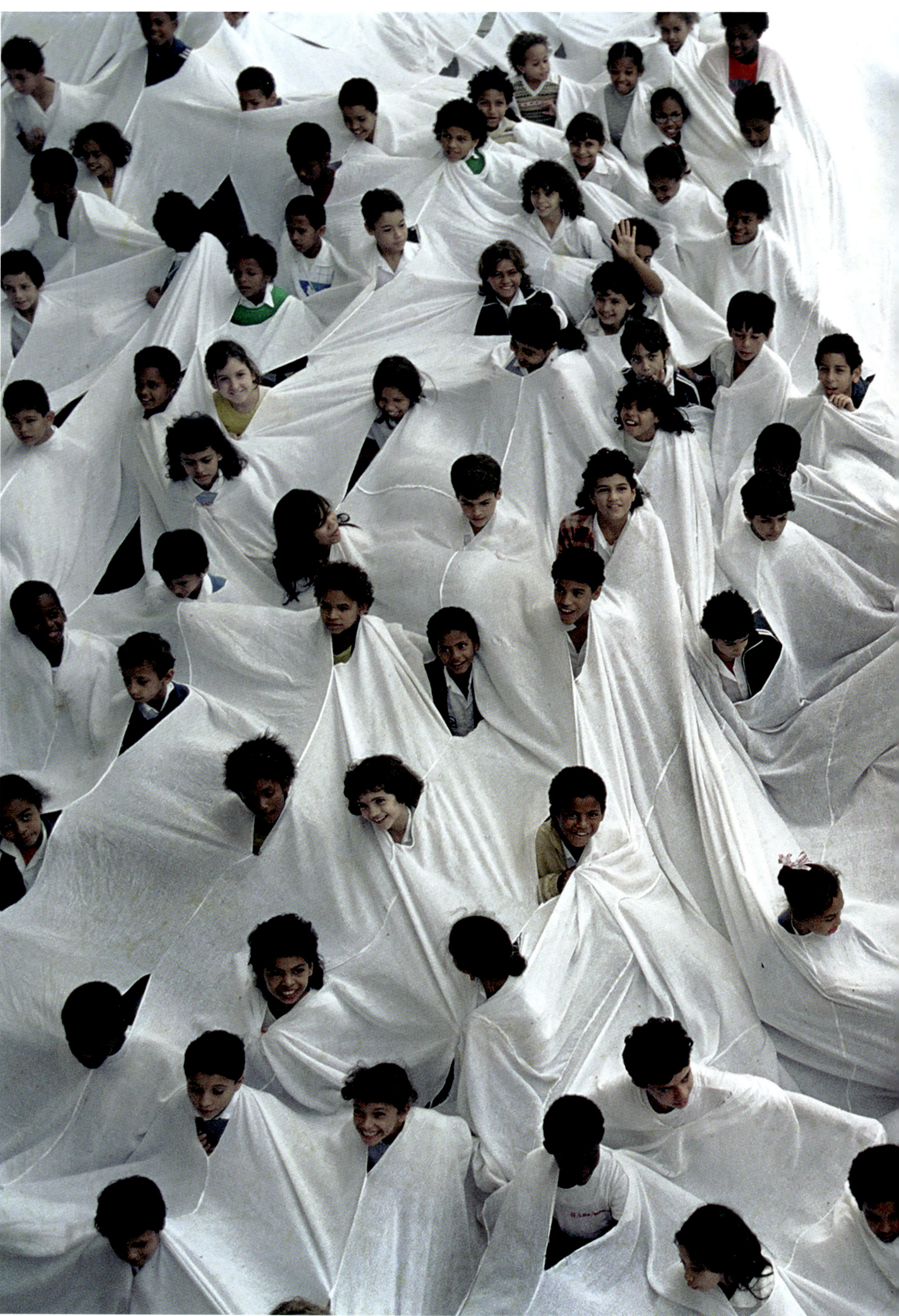

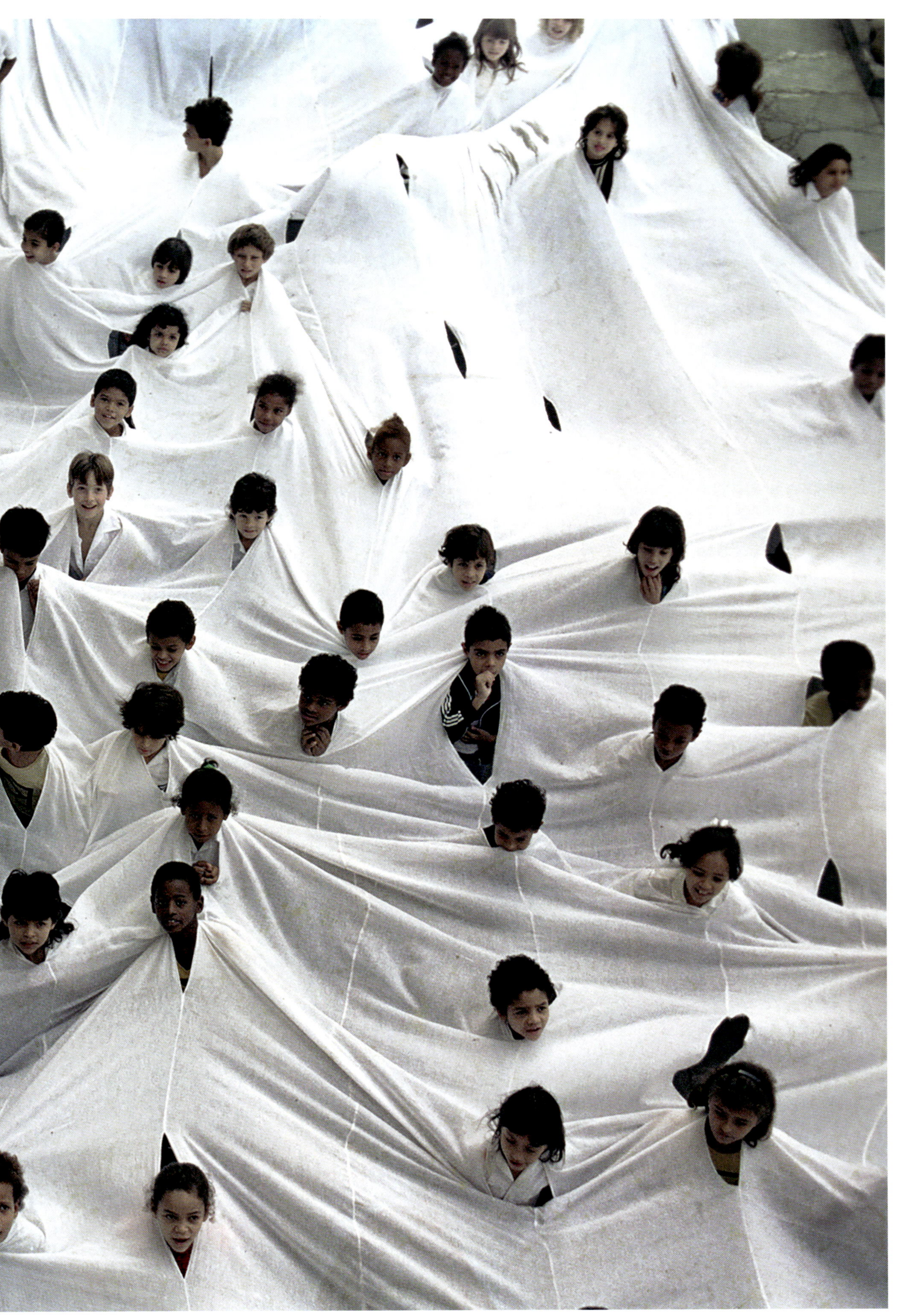

Lygia Pape, *Divisor*, 1967, performance
at MAM, Rio de Janeiro, 1990.
Courtesy Projeto Lygia Pape

UNREALITY
BY DESIGN
Elvia Wilk with
Dunne & Raby

Design is traditionally seen as a realistic and practical field, aiming to land at the intersection of what looks good and what works well. But what does it mean to design aesthetic and functional solutions for 'real' problems in a world where reality itself is all wrong?

For decades the design duo Fiona Raby and Anthony Dunne have been reconsidering the 'realistic' as the basis for design by investigating subjects far outside the field. It's no exaggeration to say that they have shaped a generation of Western design thinking, notably by leading design departments at the Royal College of Art in London and now at The New School in New York. Their landmark 2013 book *Speculative Everything* calls for designers to imagine alternative worlds rather than taking dominant narratives about the future for granted.

Today, objects are often designed as if in a vacuum; designers are asked to ignore the complex social and political ecologies in which they work in favour of fulfilling briefs based on notions of optimisation and efficiency. From benign-seeming ergonomic furniture that keeps workers awake on the job, to more obviously troubling examples like domestic-surveillance – Alexa and the self-driving car – design teams are expected to employ technologies without considering possible unintended effects or questioning the worldviews they reinforce.

Against these mainstream professional tendencies, Dunne & Raby, along with their collaborators and students, offer a gentle but powerful provocation to think differently. In their studio, design objects are treated not as neat and fragmentary solutions, but as catalysts for research and change. Take the *Technological Dreams Series: No.1, Robots*, from 2007, a group of simple-looking household robot prototypes with such character traits as nervousness and neediness – far from the supposedly impersonal and subservient smart fridge or alarm system. In works like these, human interaction is foregrounded. Design becomes ecological and entire systems, institutions and languages become topics for redesign.

Elvia Wilk spoke with Dunne & Raby about their recent work, how the COVID-19 pandemic has affected notions of the future, how the close quarters of 'reality' can be busted open and how 'mindset' may be more important a concept than 'roadmap' when it comes to effecting change.

Within this framework, discussions can reroute from, say, the way design serves the human to what the human is, and what humans might want to become.

EW: A lot of your recent work challenges assumptions about realistic approaches to design. As you beautifully put it, 'the word "unrealistic" often simply means "undesirable" to those in charge'. Reality is a political invention, used to close down the horizon of possibility. Assuming that reality is by design, the question is one of who gets to design it. How can designers resist the imperative to make work compatible with capitalist realism? Among others, your 2019 project *An Archive of Impossible Objects* seems to address this question.

AD & FR: If you are working within, or with industry, there's probably not much designers can do on this front. But if you work in other contexts, such as academic research labs or small studios working mainly with cultural organisations, then there are other possibilities. As you say, in design, a fairly limited notion of what counts as 'real' quickly shuts down thinking about other ways life could be, deeming them unrealistic and void. But maybe this is where to start: to embrace the unreal in constructive ways.

Our ongoing research project *An Archive of Impossible Objects* begins to explore this idea through a collection of actual objects that belong to systems of reality besides our own. Rather than being outside of reality, in the unreal, we think of them as being different kinds of 'real' that remind us how the construction of reality is an ongoing project that has gone through many phases and consists of many variations.

I'm a novelist, so when I think of 'unrealities' I think of storytelling, and how fiction and 'reality' reciprocally influence each other. Lately I have begun to think that this loop between the fictional and the actual is tightening, partly because finance capitalism relies on all sorts of fictions to function: statistics, money, speculative real estate, trend forecasts, fake news. Design fictions have a lot in common with speculative or science-fiction stories in the sense that they can expand or intervene in the set of social and political fictions like these, but there are differences in the way design does so. Could you speak to how design fiction is distinct from, say, science fiction?

Among the many kinds of speculative culture that exist, an interesting issue for us is how speculative forms of design practice can complement work

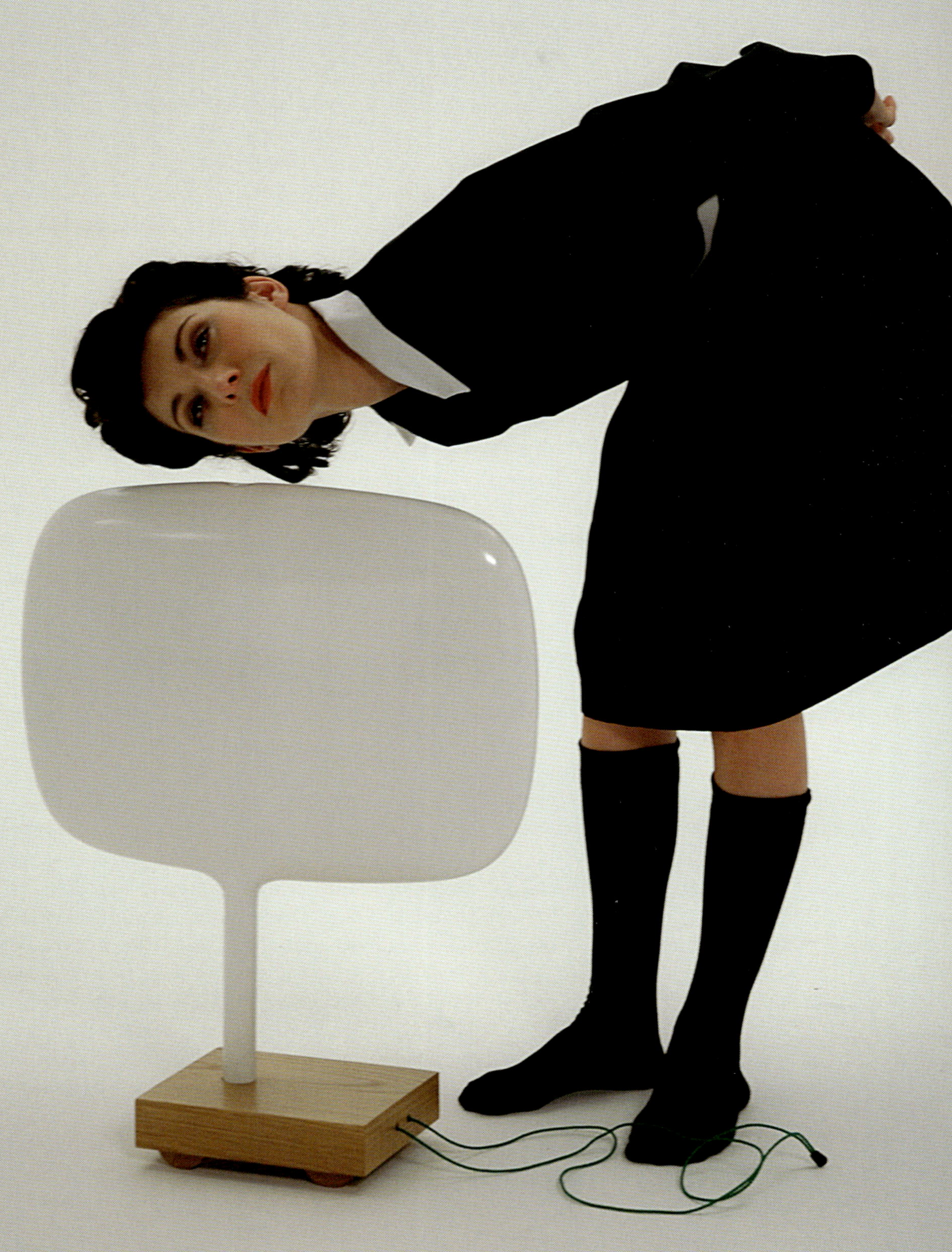

Dunne & Raby, *Technological Dream Series,*
No 1: Robots, 2007.
Commissioned by Kunstmuseen Krefeld.
Photograph: Per Tingleff

being done in other fields. If you want to have a big impact, then film and TV seem more effective – see *Black Mirror*, for example. But one thing design does well in this area, maybe uniquely so, is to bring fragments from imaginary worlds into the space of the viewer, often in a form that echoes existing everyday objects, products and systems.

Unlike architecture or science-fiction cinema where whole cities and worlds can be represented, design materialises only small parts of fictional worlds. Maybe this fragmentary approach creates more room for the viewer to imagine the world such objects belong to for themselves. So perhaps another quality design brings to the conversation is a more suggestive and open-ended approach. But compared to literature and even architecture, where speculative forms of thought have existed for centuries, it's still early days for design.

All of us are currently living in New York, where first the pandemic and now the national uprising have redefined – redesigned? – daily life. I find it curious that the news often presents these events in terms of immediate design challenges: How can office spaces and apartments be reorganised to reduce contagion? How can masks and protective equipment be 3D-printed? Or even, how can city budgets be 'redesigned' so public services can be properly funded? Yet this goal-oriented, solutionist approach distracts us from asking questions about the systems that brought us here in the first place.

In one of your texts, you frame this exact conundrum in a series of questions:

> **What if teaching student designers to frame every issue, no matter how complex, as a problem to be solved squanders valuable creative and imaginative energy on the unachievable? What if design education's focus on 'making stuff real' perpetuates everything that is wrong with current reality, ensuring that all possible futures are merely extrapolations of a dysfunctional present?**[1]

With this in mind, how can designers operate as problem-solvers and also undermine the notion of problem solving?

This is something we really struggle with: the idea that design, without any grounding in economics, politics or even social theory, can solve massively complex problems that many other disciplines have been grappling with for decades. It diverts so much creative energy away from the things design can actually do.

To work in this space, designers need to collaborate more with people from fields like economics, law or political science and draw on very different kinds of disciplinary imaginations and knowledge, in order to go beyond critique and analysis to generate new ideas and possibilities. Again, not as solutions, but to expand our collective imaginative horizons and to challenge what people think is currently possible, or impossible. One thing design does do well is to give tangible form to different ideas, beliefs, and ways of seeing and making sense of the world – materialising ideas using the stuff of everyday life in ways that inspire and energise people.

The other day it was announced that Darrick Hamilton will be rejoining The New School and setting up the Institute for the Study of Race, Stratification and Political Economy, which is very exciting news. One of the ideas he is a leading advocate for is 'baby bonds' as a way of confronting wealth inequality: 'The idea is for the federal government to establish a trust at birth for every child ranging from 1,000 upwards to 50,000 dollars. The accounts could be used when the child reaches adulthood as a capital foundation to finance higher education, start a business, or purchase a home.' Is this design? Probably not in the way we usually think about design, but it is a form of policy design that begins to a reimagine a broken and dysfunctional economic system.

By now the word 'speculative' has become a buzzword in design and other fields. Your incredibly comprehensive and now canonical 2013 book *Speculative Everything* both reclaims the term's potential and pokes a bit of fun at its ubiquity. I love the hyperbole of the title, which opens the door to wild thinking but also recognises limitations when such thinking gets labelled or commodified as a movement, moment or product. As you write in the book, the only kind of commercially sanctioned 'speculation' is the kind that functions as an industry media stunt, or as technofuturist propaganda. How have you managed to reappropriate the notion of the speculative time and again for designers who want to operate outside of this instrumentalised sphere?

We may have lost this time! When we hear the term speculative design today, it is usually far removed from what we imagined. In design, it has moved closer to classic future forecasting approaches, where trends are predicted, and away from, or actively opposed to, many of the qualities that make speculation

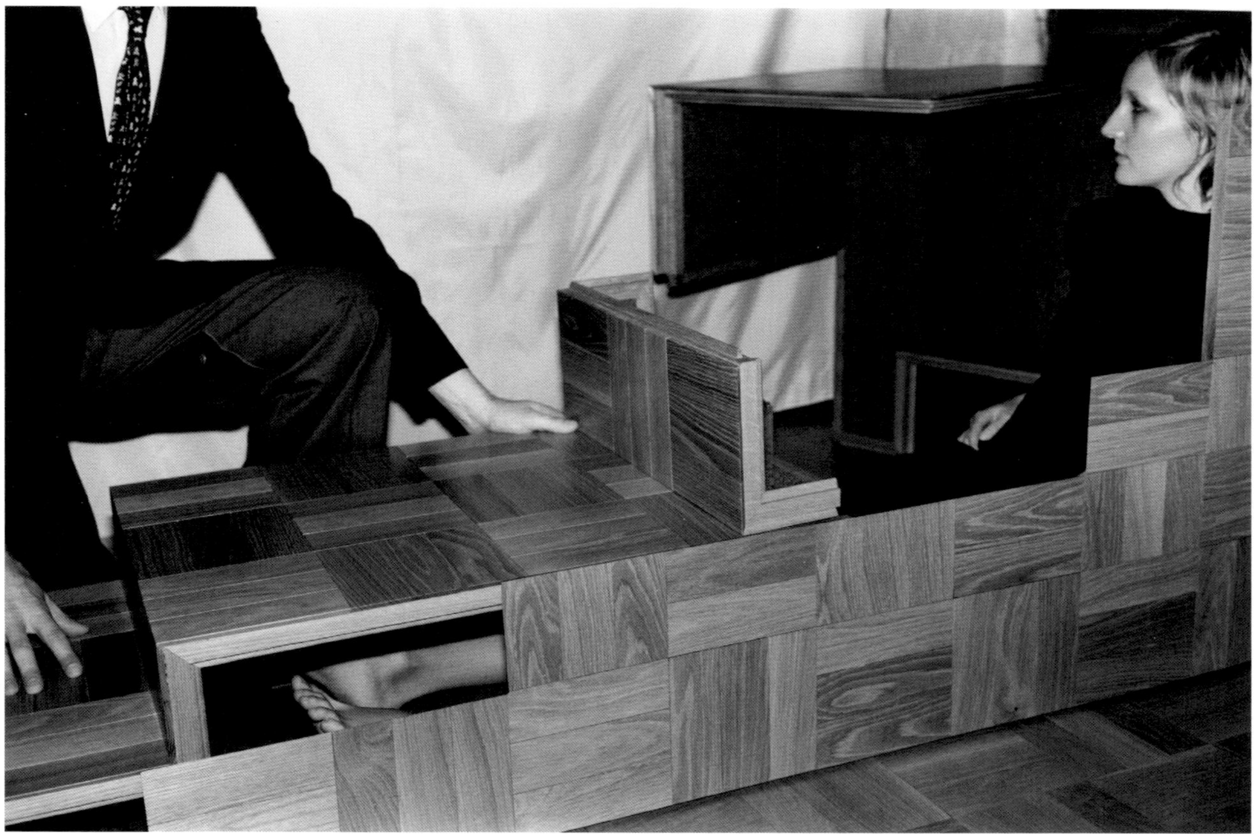

Elvia Wilk, commissioned by Amber Husain

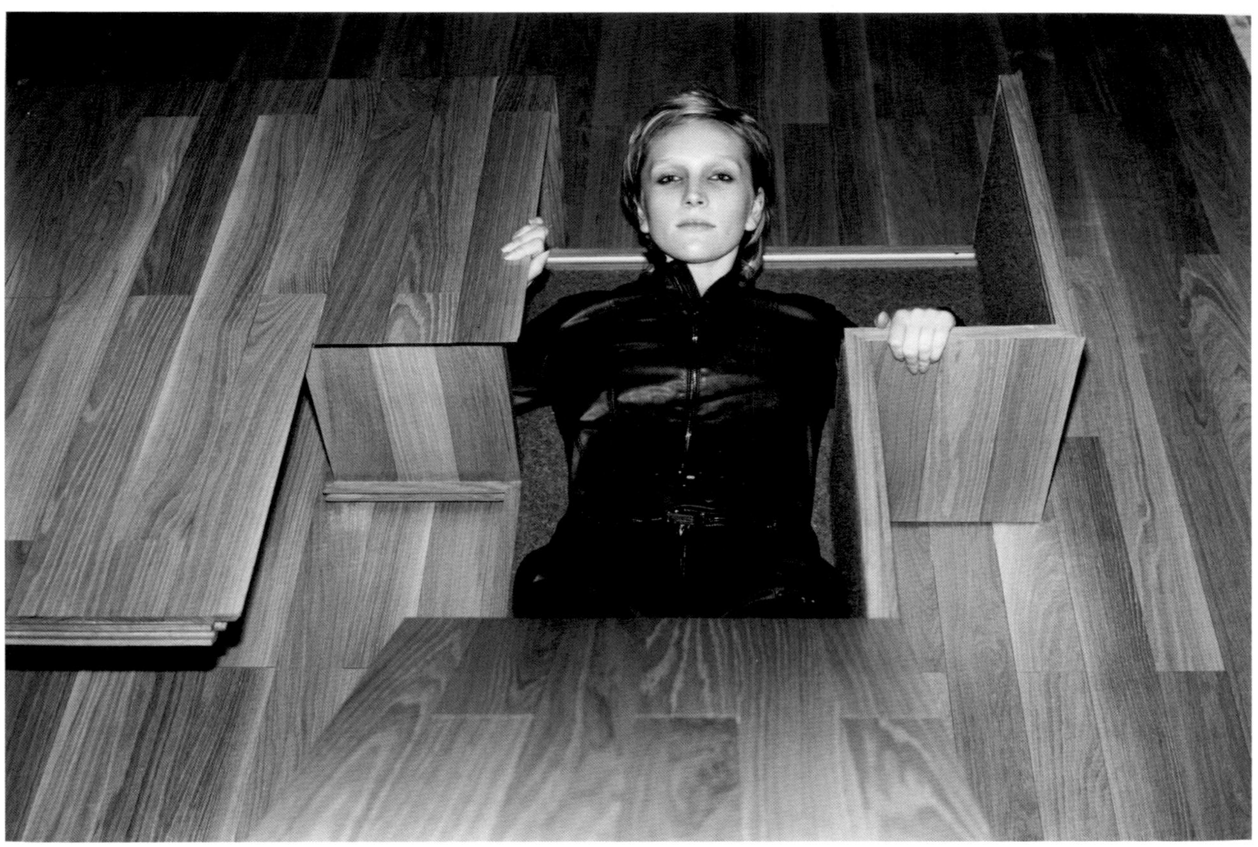

Dunne & Raby, *Designs for Fragile Personalities in Anxious Times*, 2004–05.
Photograph: Jason Evans

Unlike architecture or science-fiction cinema where whole cities and worlds can be represented, design materialises only small parts of fictional worlds.

…utopia's value lies in it being an impossible but useful guide, rather than a concrete destination that can be reached.

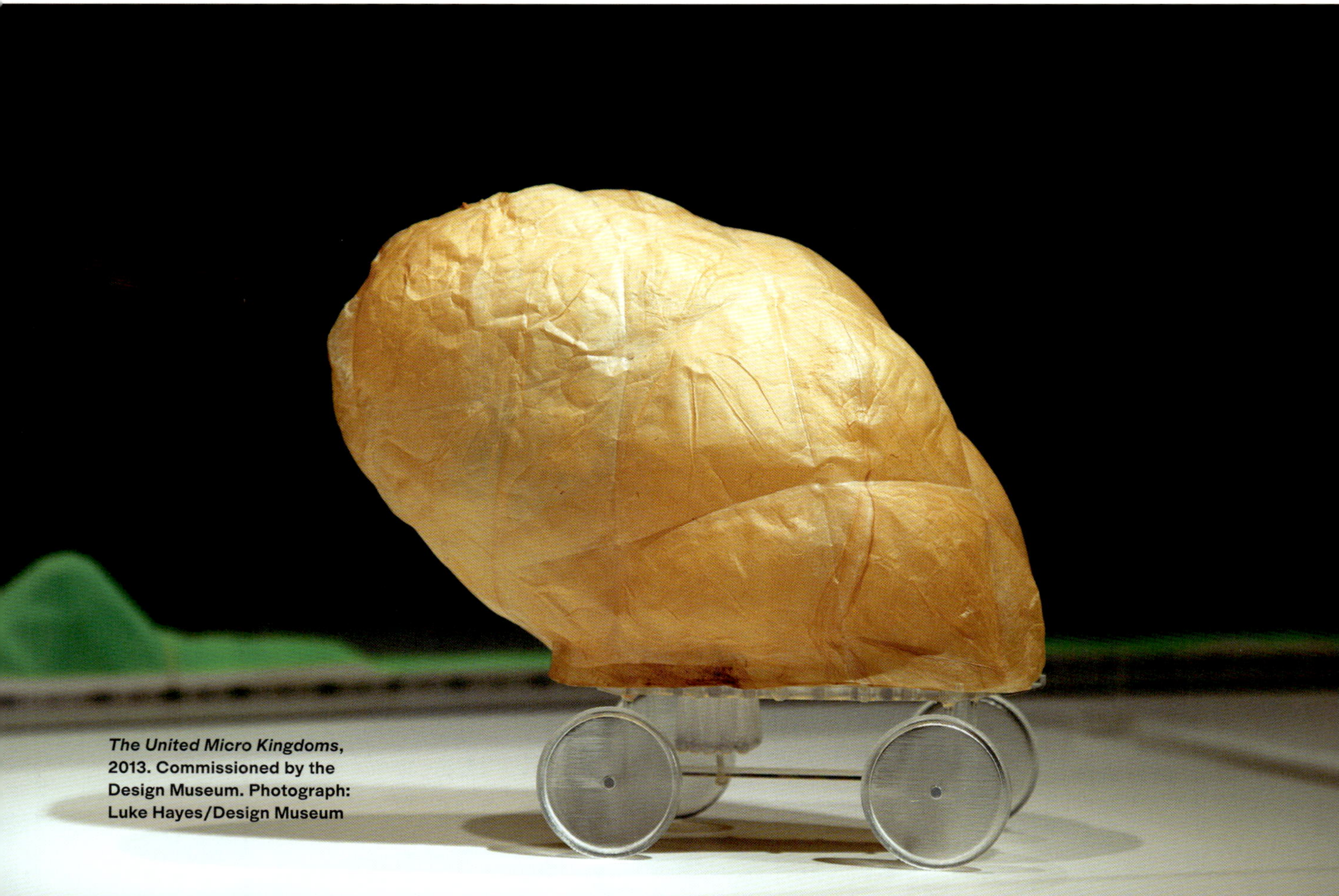

The United Micro Kingdoms, 2013. Commissioned by the Design Museum. Photograph: Luke Hayes/Design Museum

interesting for us – ambiguity, open-endedness, aesthetic experimentation, abstraction, poetics.

Still, it is good to see different variations evolving in response to different contexts and needs. And despite the 'hype' phenomenon, a lot has been achieved. One of our aims was to try to expand what counted as a design project within an educational setting, and that is happening. Speculative design has played a part in this by creating a space where designers are given a little more license to challenge prevailing realities, not as solutions, but as prompts for further imagining, or tools for thinking with. Whether it is called speculative design, conceptual design, discursive design or something else doesn't really matter as long as there continues to be room in design for speculative thought in its many varied forms.

I find thinking about the future, any future, exceedingly difficult in 2020. But even long before the pandemic, using the future as a horizon for imagining alternate scenarios often backfired. 'Classical futurism' intrinsically focusses on plausibility and predictiveness – partly because the future has been colonised by profit, the language of predictive finance and commercial conjecture. (For this reason I always say that my novel is set in an alternate reality rather than in a future moment.) But do we have to give up on the future because it doesn't currently belong to us and we might not have a language for it?

We agree, futures can be quite limiting as a way of thinking about how the world could be otherwise. Maybe the pandemic will open up a space for wilder futures, more like Quentin Meillassoux's Extro-Science Fiction, H. G. Wells's 'domesticating the impossible' (hypothesis), or Darko Suvin's Cognitive Estrangement, rather than trying to tie speculations or alternative realities too closely to existing ones through overly cautious extrapolations.

Maybe the pandemic will also put an end to 'the future' as a dominant framing device for design speculations about the not-here and not-now, and we will begin to see bolder, more radical and genuinely alternative modes of being, being explored. Not as goals to move towards, but as prompts and catalysts for further imagining, to tease the currently unknown and even unthinkable into existence as a set of ideas and possibilities. We're firm believers in the idea that a utopia's value lies in its being an impossible but useful guide, rather than a concrete destination that can be reached.

To reframe that question explicitly in terms of contemporary events: many are calling for change that until now was dismissed as entirely unrealistic. For instance, the total abolition of the police. It is exceedingly hard to draw a roadmap from here to there, but if we stop trying to predict what is going to happen and just work in that direction, I think it is possible to adopt an abolitionist *mindset* today. By accepting or speculating on an alternate reality in the here and now, maybe we can live differently already. I wonder whether you could speak to the difference between 'roadmap' and 'mindset' when it comes to speculative practice?

That's quite a subtle and important distinction for us. For many designers, the focus is on roadmaps, but we find this too prescriptive unless it is done through some kind of genuinely democratic process, which is increasingly unlikely. Trying to focus on how to develop new mindsets or ways of seeing the world is far more valuable and something that has been neglected in design as attention has shifted to changing the world out there without paying attention to the worlds inside us, in our minds, meaning not much actually changes at a deeper level. If we could develop new ways of seeing the world, designing from that position might help a very different world begin to take shape.

I'd like to ask about your approach to pedagogy, since you've been incredibly influential on legions of design students. You've set up hubs for interdisciplinary thinking, for instance, in Design Interactions at London's Royal College of Art, and now with the Designed Realities Lab at The New School in New York. From sitting in on some of the discussions at The New School, I got a sense of how expansive these courses can be, but I was impressed that design-focussed issues were continually brought to the fore. So, when anthropologists, architects, writers and many others are part of the learning process, what makes a design-led education? What specific questions do designers need to ask that others might not? Does it even matter what we call it, as long as students are equipped to think critically as well as aesthetically and sensorially?

Design brings a propositional stance to learning by constructing some idea about how things could be different, then exploring it, testing it and interrogating it through experiments, readings, conversations and so on. It's almost like a hypothesis but a lot less scientific and driven more by intuition, assisted by reason. It starts with an idea about how things could be different, which serves as a device for thinking through, and with – a sort of vehicle for exploring ideas.

We're finding students from non-art and non-design disciplines enjoy this way of working too,

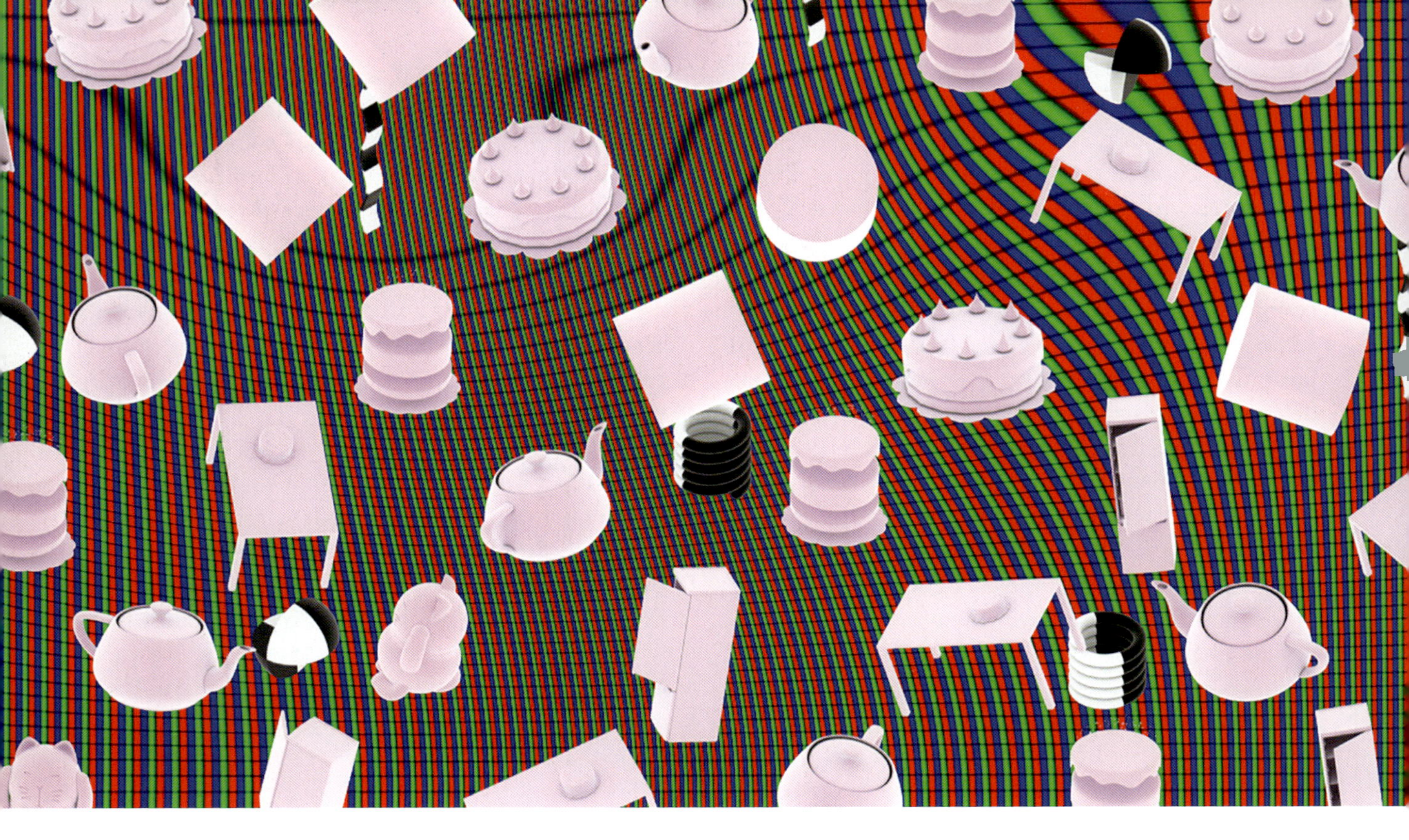

and find it helpful for their ongoing research. One project that opened our eyes to ways that social scientists could use speculative thinking was by an anthropology student with a background in law, who redesigned a constitution to help her think about what constitutions mean today. To explore the idea, she decided to design a constitution for a nation that decides to phase out human life over a hundred-year period. This foregrounded issues such as intergenerational legitimacy, how constitutions belong to the time they were conceived in and how they suggest a trajectory of perfectability. It was a thought experiment rather than a design proposal. It also made us aware of a wider category of 'objects' that includes legal and financial instruments, and how they can be used as vehicles to explore other ways society might be constituted or organised.

We're not sure what you would call this. It is design, but on a fairly abstract level. It is done by people without a design background, but they do have a solid grounding in a discipline. They are not solving problems or telling people how to live, but exploring an idea, or topic, or issue, and as you say, it is being done in a way that equips the student to think critically as well as aesthetically and sensorially, and maybe socially too.

On the other hand, designers in our classes are letting go of a solutionist framework, or 'speculative solutionism' as we call it, and are beginning to use their design projects to explore ideas. Julia Szagdaj recently developed a lovely project about accents and their social role by redesigning the US anthem to be more accent-*ful* rather than accent-*less*. Each line was reconstructed using sounds from other spoken languages as well as musical motifs. It's really beautifully crafted and evokes a very different reality from the one we are all currently experiencing – one where difference unifies rather than isolates.

Is one of your goals to contextualise design choices within current society, so that aesthetics becomes tied to politics?

We're trying to let politics surface in their projects, but not in an overt way, or as a form of activism or propaganda, more as an awareness that design, along with its aesthetics, is always political, and always needs to be taken into consideration. Despite the many claims being made for design as some kind of panacea, it has its limitations and sometimes doing things as a citizen can be more effective; or for those seriously committed to genuine political change, participating in local councils or politics. Although it can of course take many years, or even a lifetime, it is possible to bring about change through politics. Design works differently and needs to regain some humbleness.

Do your students tend to go on to work as designers?

Our students go on to do a variety of things. Some work in industry, but usually in the research divisions – where it is possible to initiate change – rather than at the product end; others set up their own studios often working with NGOs and cultural

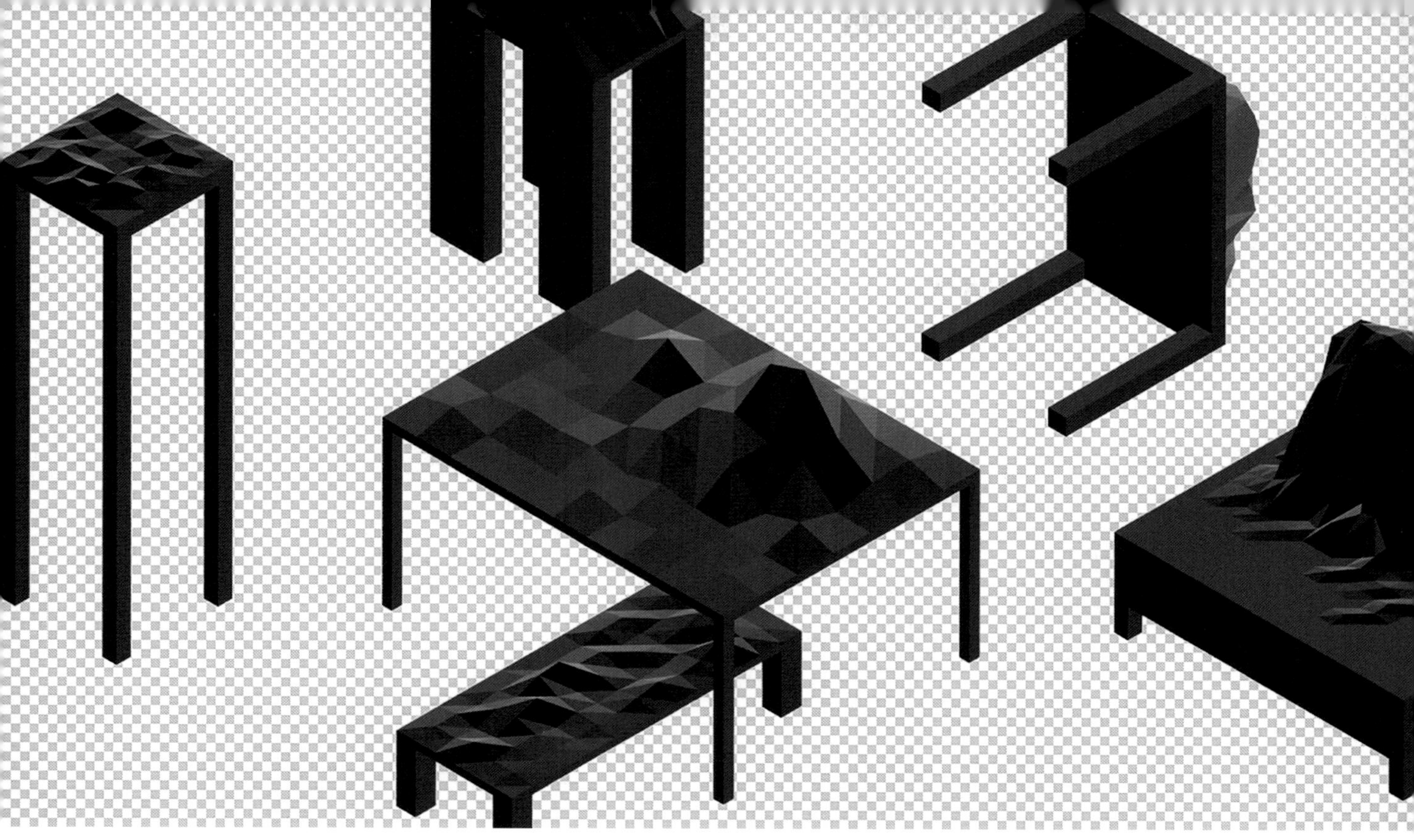

organisations; some return to education as teachers experimenting with pedagogy; while others become researchers working in an academic setting to explore different possibilities for design itself. It's all about trying to change the environment around you, both intellectually and materially, working in a focused way at a scale you can actually affect.

One part of the *Archive of Impossible Objects* questions the globe as our default representation of the planet (*Realists of a Larger Reality: Globes*, 2019). You built other possible globes – cuboid, toroid, boloid – to represent the Earth, the implication being that there are many ways for us to imagine our planet besides the literal, 'accurate' one (which is of course full of inaccuracies). I'm not sure how to articulate this, but I have been asking myself whether the pandemic is giving us a new 'Whole Earth' moment – that visual and imaginative epiphany when people first saw the 'Blue Marble' shot from space in 1972 – but an epiphany about our cellular interconnectivity and individual vulnerability. What sort of globe do you think the pandemic looks like?

That's really interesting. It's too soon for us to suggest one, but we recently saw a globe table by the artist duo Langlands & Bell. The globe is blank except for flight paths, maybe that's a little literal, but it also reflects how the virus spread so quickly around the world, uniting us in our shared struggle against it.

I'm currently a fellow at the 'Transformations of the Human' programme at the Berggruen

Institute, an independent think tank in Los Angeles, which you were also involved in during its first year. The project, led by Tobias Rees, aims to bring the sciences and the humanities together to rethink the Enlightenment assumption about what makes us human, removing disciplinary divisions in the process. One goal is to bring forward the ways that technological development is fundamentally informed by assumptions about what the human is (above nature but other than machine), and vice versa: the way that the human gets defined by assumptions underlying technology (i.e., that our minds are comparable to advanced computers). Designers have a large role to play here, because they deal with both 'practical' or empirical construction and human interaction. Does the fundamental question of what makes us human inevitably come up in the design process, even when not explicitly?

When we worked as researchers in the Computer Related Design Studio at the Royal College of Art in the 1990s, we spent a lot a time thinking about the idea of a 'human' that computer scientists and engineers used when developing interfaces for computers, and how they in turn shape us, as humans. 'User-centred' design was anything but.

Later, in the mid-2000s we did a project with Michael Anastassiades called *Designs for Fragile Personalities in Uncertain Times*, based on a shared frustration with the limited or narrow model of a 'person' most designers worked with, or designed for, at that time, especially in the tech industry.

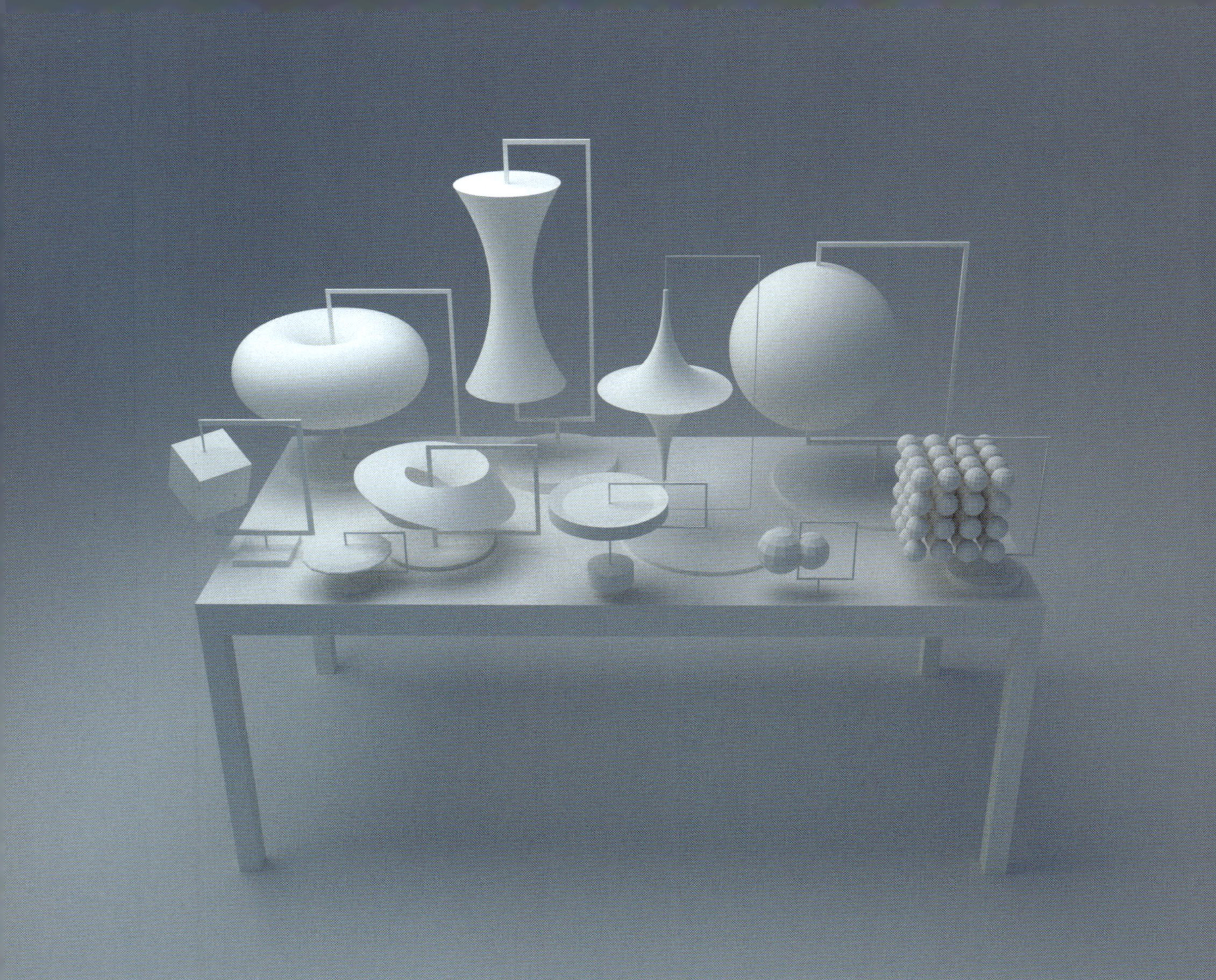

We proposed a range of products for a more complex, troubled and contradictory person, based on irrational needs and impulses, treating them as equal to more rational needs. The products look quite calm, but the idea of the human they embody is hopefully a little more realistic, although many people would probably disagree! Three of the pieces were variations on what we called 'Hideaway Furniture', for people who were afraid of being abducted. The pieces were designed in a way that undermined their own effectiveness, more like placebos than solutions.

In another more recent project from 2013, *United Micro Kingdoms*, we designed a number of vehicles for four fictional groups of people based on different combinations of technology and worldview. We were interested in the idea that you can't start and end with technology, because you need to consider underlying worldviews as well. People's ways of seeing the world, rather than the specific technologies developed according to them, are what is often problematic. There's plenty of knowledge on how to develop new technologies, but how do you develop new worldviews? In fact, this was one of our motivations for joining The New School, where as designers we can work with social scientists, writers and philosophers with a lot more knowledge in this area than we have.

Design certainly has to do more than 'humanise' technology by, say, adding human figures into a rendering, doing surveys on how people feel, trying to give self-driving cars 'ethical' decision-making capacity, making surveillance capitalism more 'accurate' by expanding a data set or making robots that can appear to empathise. Maybe instead we need to question the hierarchy between humans, the natural world and technological tools, and learn to see ourselves as imbricated in a feedback process with the ecological and technological world. Design doesn't exist in a vacuum.

We completely agree with this. We enjoy spending time wandering in the back country, where you very quickly develop a new awareness of where humans sit in the hierarchy of the natural world once you step away from the technologies we have become so dependent on. You really do feel like a visitor entering a landscape shaped by non-human dynamics and priorities. And of course, there is an expectation that you will minimise your impact on

asking. Mayors and local governments are setting up commissions. Crowds of young people gather around statues demanding removal or radical transformation, often proposing creative ways to reveal the past evil deeds of the individuals the monuments caricature. Unpleasant angry characters from the fringes of right-wing politics mill around these same monuments threatening violence to those who might add text or posters, or who simply climb upon a monument to add a mocking article of clothing or some other sign of 'disrespect'. Heritage protectors in full uniform stand guard. The British prime minister, channelling Donald Trump, goes on Twitter to defend the heritage value of aesthetically shoddy statues of murderous slave traders. Trump himself orders that disgraced, and recently felled monuments to confederate leaders immediately be 'cleaned and reinstalled'.

In a crazed rodomontade, delivered in front of Mount Rushmore and sounding every inch like a Soviet leader at the height of their powers, he announced the creation of a new 'National Garden of American Heroes', a collection of 'lifelike or realistic representations […], not abstract or modernist', with an obvious eye to his own reincarnation in stone and bronze, small hands and all. At times like these, you would be forgiven for thinking that monuments are defended and protected with more vigour and rigour than citizens. But that's the thing about monuments. They lie, or rather stand sleeping until the political stakes are impossible to ignore. Then it's all Pygmalion.

Take Churchill (again). Bring up the racism and we are told that he was 'a man of his time'. To which we might well ask, is it the men of 'their time' that we should be celebrating, rather than the events and histories, involving women and men, black and white, that were not of their time, that confirmed and recognised that time is often out of joint? These events and the people who participated in them, imagine a *different* time, a better time. Thomas Carlyle and his Great Man theory bequeathed an epidemic of monuments of *men of their time* in public places, an epidemic that sought to drown out memories of repression, theft, enslavement, degradation and so on, as well as all the human struggles against these very wretched things. James Baldwin says somewhere, that for a black woman or man, even the Statue of Liberty is a joke. So when people say: 'but he was a man of his time', are they not giving up on all those who were decidedly not of their own time? Aren't these sleights of hand how racism lives? As Wallace Stevens wrote: 'It is hard to think of a thing more out of time than nobility. Looked at plainly it seems false and dead and ugly. To look at it at all makes us realise sharply that in our present, in the presence of our reality, the past looks false and is, therefore, dead and is, therefore, ugly.'

'Everyone', writes Charles W. Hedrick Jr., 'stumbles among the detritus of their lives, remembering some things, remembering that they have forgotten others.' Therefore all history is 'a writing over, an erasure'. Monuments of 'great men' are no different; they repress and contain the complicated, contradictory even aggressive erasures of 'their time'. Churchill's monument in London's Parliament Square is banally ordinary in this respect: it 'celebrates' a man who argued that Africans and Asians were primitives and needed permanent colonial rule; who thought 'Aryan stock [was] bound to triumph' and proposed forced sterilisation to ensure this victory; who detested Indians because he felt they 'bred like rabbits'; who professed hatred for people 'with slit eyes and pig tails' because he abhorred their looks and thought they smelt bad (amongst other things). Should we be surprised then, that with Black Lives Matter, the monument's 'job' (Georges Bataille) has gone into reverse and it is now compelled to reveal all of this? It's as if this disruptive ambition was always already embedded in the statue's very unveiling, just waiting to be revealed and written in/on stone (or bronze). To paraphrase a line from Jean Cocteau's poem 'Le Paquet Rouge' (1958) (itself already a paraphrase of something Picasso wrote in a letter to Marius de Zayas), a monument is a lie that can always tell the truth. A disgraced monument then, is a palimpsest. Its job? To erase uncomfortable, often vicious stories, but, by virtue of this fact, to be a witness to that very erasure, a reminder of a necessary future correction, of what eventually needs to be done. Writing, as some did 'Churchill was a Racist' on the monument's plinth was simply an attempt to dishonour Churchill's memory in this respect, not to destroy it. But if the statue came down, would that even be enough? And is it, against its own worst intentions, a work of art? Robbed of its public plinth should the monument be museum-bound? So *what is to be done?*

Just before Laura and I made our film *Disgraced Monuments,* and while the monuments of Eastern Europe and Russia were crashing down, I wrote the following text, asking the same question: 'What is to be Done?'

WHAT IS TO BE DONE?, 1990

Revolutions, rebellions, uprisings, even terrorisms: each gives to public works a particular visibility, one that as Robert Musil has noted, is often denied them at other times.

> The most striking feature of monuments is that you do not notice them. There is nothing in the world as invisible as monuments. Like a drop of water on an oil-skin, attention runs down them without stopping for a moment... We cannot say that we do not notice them; we should say that they de-notice us, they withdraw from our senses.[2]

This invisibility is a sign of a silent interpellation, of a subtle but nevertheless pervasive marking-out of the public realm in which a dominant authority's concept of history, and its heroics, is accordingly installed. After all, is it not always an authority that installs or permits the installation of 'public' works of art? If monuments remain silent, they only 'de-notice us' insofar as they become part of the architectonic and semantic landscape.

When there is a crisis in the realm of the social – a revolution or political uprising – the symbolic realm, of which public art is part, becomes the subject of a certain re-evaluation. The visibility that inaugurates such an attack is a prerequisite for any attempt to reinterpret and intervene within this area of the symbolic realm. Clearly, this impulse is part of a general attack on the continued presence of the signs of an ancien régime. It is confirmation also that in moments of 'madness', publics will treat monuments and public works of art as if they were the actual leaders themselves. In a 27 May 1871 report on the destruction of the Vendôme Column, for instance, the *Illustrated London News* gave this account of what happened after the column was felled:

> Three orators of the commune stood at different points in the ruin and made speeches. They treated the statue [of Napoleon] as the Emperor itself, spitting on his face, while members of the national guard hit his nose with rifles.[3]

The Hungarian crowds in Budapest in 1956, may have felt that they were literally attacking Stalin himself as they smashed a statue of him, each crack of the hammer on metal and stone producing at once a delicious and murderous pleasure. Angry and rebellious publics quite rightly desire to have a say (albeit sometimes through simple acts of negation) in the semiotics of 'their' public space. Insofar as they are acting on that desire, attempts to remove and smash certain works of art are as much a part of the project of a public art as the discrete objects themselves.

Two forms of negation need to be distinguished, two different orchestrations, if you like, of a mass iconoclasm with respect to the revolutionary and post-revolutionary moment. On the one hand, are seemingly spontaneous actions of various publics as they vent their anger and frustration on the visible signs of power of an ancien régime. Stalin's desecration in Budapest can be understood in this context, as can the defacement of the statue of Felix Dzerzhinsky by students in Warsaw.[4] On the other hand, are planned removals of the art and images of the old political regime, where 'revolutionary' governments order their destruction. In Poland today, the Solidarity government has been overseeing such a programme of removal and destruction. The Lenin statue in Romania was also removed by state order.

We can speculate that the iconoclasm of art's orderly removal by an authority embodies more of a respect for the image than does a public's spontaneous destruction. Stalin's boots remained as the container for the Hungarian flag in 1956; In Leningrad in 1918, the inscriptions on many statues were altered to reflect the revolutionary moment. That such appropriations and semiotic disruptions can occur suggests that there is more than one possible future for the public work of art 'after the fall' of the ancien régime.

Such iconoclasms can unwittingly, and against their own best intentions, display an immense respect for the image. And further, through an act of destruction, the power of the image, the power of public statuary to control and define the public realm may paradoxically be confirmed. An inevitable consequence of such respect might be the erection of yet more permanent statues and monuments, their 'contents' differing perhaps, but their formal precision remaining much the same. The question of respect (for the image), and how it is invested very differently in the two forms of removal (as well as destruction/modification) that I have proposed, leads very directly to a critical consideration of the various arguments that are often made for the retention and conservation of problematic or discredited public monuments and other works of art. These are arguments that are predicated on an assumption that a work's meaning can change; the semantic charge of a work from the past will be different once it has been re-appraised and displaced according to the symbolic reorganisation of the post-revolutionary state. But how is that reappraisal and displacement accomplished? It is, as I suggested above, primarily because that possibility is already contained within the work from the start, because the work will never be the simple representation of its subject, no matter how important or trivial the latter may be.

The axis of visibility-invisibility is the determinant field across which the public work of art exacts its different meanings. The monument covers up crimes against the public insofar as it is able temporarily to 'smother' the possibility of remembering specific histories in terms of the violence that engendered them; it instead commemorates a history or event in terms of a pernicious heroism or nationalism. But at the same time, the monument exists as a perpetual marker, a reminder of those very crimes. It waves a red flag, so to speak, on the site of its repressions. And when the symbolic order is thrown into crisis-revolution or terrorism, the public monument's semantic charge shifts and the work becomes less heroic in form and begins to take on the characteristics of a scar, literally a permanent monument to the original crime(s). This may be as good a reason as any for the retention of at least some works, certainly worked on, transformed and annotated differently, perhaps even displaced somewhat after the demise of the regimes responsible for their erection. That is the argument, for instance, of Samir al-Khalil, in his proposal for a possible future for *The Victory Monument* in Baghdad after Saddam Hussein is overthrown or dies.[5]

Georges Bataille had much to say about this idea of the repression of social life by monuments. He wrote more specifically about architecture, but in the following quote, we can also detect the figure of the stone or bronze statue: standing upright and phallic, pretending to guard the public space when in actual fact, it both constitutes that space and simultaneously demands that we forget by what means the latter's publicity is obtained.

> The ideal soul of society, that which has the authority to command and prohibit, is expressed in architectural compositions properly speaking. Great monuments are erected like dikes, opposing the logic and majesty of authority against all disturbing elements... it is obvious in fact, that social monuments inspire social prudence and even real fear. The taking of the Bastille is symbolic of this state of things: it is hard to explain this crowd movement other than by the animosity of the people against the monuments that are their real masters.[6]

A public monument, which, like architecture is to some extent the image of the social order, guarantees, even imposes that very order. Far from expressing the soul of society, monuments then, to paraphrase Denis Hollier, smother society, stop it from breathing.

REVOLUTION
'Revolutionary' and immediately 'post-revolutionary' societies have been forced to deal with representations of their pre-revolutionary histories, articulated through public art. In France, there were fierce debates over what was to happen to the public works of the Royalist regime following the revolution of 1789. Attempts were made to determine to what extent particular monuments represented the ideology of the past, and to therefore apportion a punishment commensurate with the degree of a work's culpability. Works of art were forced to stand trial. As was the case with all other mock trials in post-revolutionary France during the period of 'the terror', the works were often executed, destroyed before they ever had a chance to account for themselves. Angry crowds may indeed have felt they were robbed.

Some revolutionaries argued that the old monuments and other works of art should be used as the building materials for new 'revolutionary' works. This indeed was the idea that originally motivated the looting and destruction of the Royal Tombs at St. Denis when it was agreed that all the works contained there should be used in the construction of a symbolic mountain in honour of Marat and Le Peletier. Other projects of this nature involved saving some works, or at least parts of them, so that their recognisable form could be reintegrated within new allegorical projects. J.P.B. Le Brun, for instance, argued that Angler's statues of Louis III, his wife and son, should be saved so that they could be overturned at the feet of David's project for *The Colossus of the People Sovereign*. He also suggested that the left foot of the statue of Louis IV from the Place Vendôme be saved in order to '[c]onserve the proportions of these monuments, which, when placed beside the French People, will show the smallness of the monuments to those that they regarded as the greatest'.[7]

Others, arguing against the continued existence, in any form, of any traces of the old art and public monuments, participated in an orgy of destruction, knocking down and breaking every work that offended their revolutionary sensibilities. In this rampage, they were supported by successive legislatures and officials. A Parisian police officer of the time noted that he had heard: 'complaints on all sides that the eyes of patriots were offended by the different monuments built by despotism in the time of slavery, monuments that should certainly not exist under the reign of liberty and equality'.[8] When it was detailed in the legislative assembly that the people were destroying bronze statues of Henry IV, Louis XII, Louis XIV and Louis XV, the assembly simply encouraged these actions by declaring that 'it is the manifest will of the people that no monument continue to exist that recalls the reign of tyranny... the statues in public squares in Paris will be taken away and statues in honour of liberty will replace them'.[9] Into this mire of debate and unpredictable action stepped the Abbé Grégoire. Anthony Vidler has presented Grégoire's project of redeeming and saving works. In the brief summary that follows I have borrowed from Vidler's published texts on this subject.

Grégoire was a supporter of the revolution but one who argued for the conservation of old works of art and public monuments, on the grounds that they were: 'transforming the symbols of oppression into permanent reminders of tyranny, forcing them to become a kind of permanent pillory'.[10] By using a rhetoric that he knew would be warmly received by the revolutionary assembly, Grégoire began to formulate a notion of what he called 'cultural vandalism', a kind of thoughtless and destructive behaviour that was to be understood as distinct from, even contrary to, correct or corrective revolutionary behaviour. That is to say, Grégoire believed that once these objects were no longer smothering a public history, they might then take their place in a museum of art and antiquity. Such a museum could serve, simultaneously, the nation's need for nationalism, didacticism and moral improvement. Grégoire was beginning to articulate a sense of the discontinuity that overdetermines the symbolic realm and how that discontinuity would always already be part of any monument's history. It is a discontinuity that ultimately inscribes within the work a built-in obsolescence; and it is this built-in obsolescence that will finally allow the work to be rescued by a museum where it will take its place in the national history of a country, its patrimony of (im)permanence. Indeed, many have noted that for the museum to really begin to exist, it needed 'vandalism': the museum fed off the fragments left behind by, and saved from, cultural vandalism.

V.I. LENIN

All over Eastern Europe, every day for some months, cities have been overseeing the removal of busts, statues, bas reliefs and pictures of Lenin. These are images that are hated by many, hated because they are understood and perceived as synecdoches for equally despised communist regimes. Perhaps the removal of these massive monuments is not totally incommensurate with some of Lenin's original ideas, particularly his concept of a revolutionary public art. The Lenin of 1917–18, the Lenin of 'On the Monuments of the Republic',[11] would probably not have approved of the erection, in the first place, of the bronze statues in his so called 'honour'. Insofar as Lenin's ideal might be relevant to debates today, I want to briefly examine his relationship to the question of public art as it emerged during the immediate months after the October Revolution.

By the time of the 1917 revolution, Lenin had already insisted that art under socialism should no longer serve the elite of society, 'those 10,000 suffering from boredom and obesity; it will rather serve the tens of millions of labouring people, the flower of the country, its future'.[12] In order to further this aim, Lenin proposed what he called *A Monumental Propaganda*. This was to be a so-called 'people's' art, one that would become part of everyday life, assisting in the ideological shaping of a new revolutionary mass consciousness. Lenin argued that this Monumental Propaganda should be produced through the posing and installation of slogans and other 'quickly executed forms'. Even more important to Lenin: 'the statues – be they bust or bas reliefs of figures and groups',[13] were not to be made of marble, bronze or granite, but on the contrary, were to be extremely modest in their production, and should take advantage of cheap and readily available materials such as plaster. Above all, Lenin wrote, 'Let everything be temporary.'[14] And with these words addressed to Bolshevik Soviet People's Commissar Anatoly Lunacharsky, Lenin announced the beginning of a massive project (much of it centred around May Day celebrations) to install dozens of plaster statues and busts, each one celebrating a revolutionary figure or event. Very few of these works survived more than a few months, and almost none remain in any form today, as Lenin and the artists involved must have anticipated. Some of the works were crudely executed, others crudely conceptualised, while others were extremely radical insofar as they challenged the whole notion of permanence with regard to public monuments and statuary.[15]

Particularly interesting is Nikolai Kolli's *The Red Wedge Cleaving the White Block* (1918). In this work, Kolli seems to parody and question the whole historical project of the permanent public monument, a monument that relies on the height and unassailability of a stone plinth from which it towers over the publics that move within its domain. The plinth is also the site of the official inscription, of the command to respect kings and dictators. In plaster form, what Kolli is splitting open, is the very support system of all monuments. It seems to suggest the absurdity, within the revolutionary context, of erecting yet another bronze statue on the physical supports of historically inscribed tyranny. If the revolution did produce its fair share of 'cultural vandalism', it is also the case that many at the time thought that this exercise of destruction was not only unnecessary, but actually counter-revolutionary. As the poet, playwright and literary critic Aleksandr Blok put it at the time: 'Even while destroying we are still the slaves of our former world: the violation of tradition itself is part of the same tradition.'[16] Not quite the Abbé Grégoire, and perhaps not sharing his archivist's imperative for conservation, but nevertheless, Blok's demand, his perception is part and parcel of a more complex and interesting approach to the art of the past. Moreover, it is an approach which I believe is not at all contrary to Lenin's own desire that contemporary public works be temporary.

MILITARY METAL

Many of our monuments and public works of art are made from metal. Metal is cold to touch. This is a metaphor that on closer inspection constantly envelops the description of leaders, now bronze cast or engraved in metal, unimpeachable in their authority. It is a metaphor that quite literally formalises the close association of metal figures with the cold terror they can always summon up. The text of terror, its cold economy is embodied, figured in the surplus of the king's image of authority. Which is to say, we do not need to see it in order to see it. Metal will always remind us of this absence. Here is Pascal:

> The custom of seeing kings accompanied by guards, drums, officers and all those things that bend the machine toward respect and terror causes their face to imprint on their subject's respect and terror, even when they appear by themselves, because one does not separate in thought the persons from their retinues with which they are ordinarily seen.[17]

Not only does metal statuary have metaphoric resonances with terror, which allow us to recall unwittingly the invisible retinues of power, but in the very production of bronze figures – their forging and moulding – there is an inextricable link with the very economy of the military machine. Traditionally, bronze is the material of guns and cannons, and we should not be the least bit surprised that the latter have often been made by melting down uprooted and destroyed public statues.[18] Guns can be made from melted statuary, but, equally public statuary can be produced from melted guns. The Vendôme Column, erected by Napoleon to commemorate the French victory at Austerlitz,[19] was covered with 425 bronze plaques moulded in bas relief, which displayed some of the incidents of the Austrian campaign. The bronze, which weighed close to two million pounds, was obtained by melting down 1200 captured Austrian cannons. In 1871 the column was destroyed during the Paris Commune (at the suggestion of Gustave Courbet), and while the masonry was quickly broken up and taken away by onlookers as souvenirs, the National Guard kept a protective eye on the bronze plaques – plaques which, of course, would be extremely valuable if and when they were returned to their military form.

I would like to think of Lenin's demand for temporariness, his proscription on the use of bronze, as in some sense an intervention within this economy of military terror. Plaster will only crumble and therefore prove useless in the manufacture of instruments of war (a crucial exigency, one imagines, for a country surrounded by hostile forces just ready to turn any existing metal against the revolution, and in this context, Kolli's work would seem to have a particularly materialist resonance). Its use in the public sphere recalls the military economy of statuary at the same time as it disrupts it. It asks us to think less about the permanence of the structure – its apparent right to exist forever – and rather more about any particular work's contingent meaning, how, for instance, that work imposes itself in a very contradictory way. After all, as I suggested earlier, permanent monuments are often born of terror and force – they are literally imposed, and occupy spaces like an invading army – and it is not the least bit surprising that their eventual demise should reduplicate that terror, both in the act of destruction itself and in the recycling of the works into yet further instruments for terror and subjection.

There are many other examples of plaster monuments being used to address the question of military terror. Perhaps the most famous one was the *Liberty Statue* erected in Tiananmen Square in China. Students not only created a symbol that in its temporariness called attention to the spontaneous and changing nature of their revolution, but they also made an ironic and critical commentary on the tradition of the public monument itself. It was, recalling Lenin, 'modest' and 'quickly executed', and importantly it also appeared to be from the wrong tradition – a 'statue of liberty' being so closely associated with a hostile power. Indeed, when the army finally stormed the square, one of the first things it did was smash the statue of liberty.[20]

IMPERMANENCE

Perhaps a truly public art would be one that allowed different publics to make their (temporary) marks on what Bataille has called the fascist organisation of public life. These works might then attempt to give air to what the statist installations have worked so hard and effectively to smother. The paradox is that as soon as these works become permanent, they tend to become the very objects that they were intended to intervene against. This is perhaps why we need to reinvent each work, each public, in order to make the art answerable to successive publics. This reinvention, though, would ask of us something both more ambitious and subtler than the simple negation that destruction implies.

The statues and other public monuments that had, until very recently, occupied the streets and civic squares of Eastern Europe, were the remainders of a project which had defied Lenin's own understanding of public art. 'Let everything be temporary' he demanded. Yet it took the citizens of Bucharest and elsewhere some 30 years before they had the right to remove the clumsy bronze statue of Lenin that had imposed itself upon the city and its publics.[21]

Against this motif of permanence and metal, of coldness and terror, I would argue that it might be more useful, at least for the moment, to take up Lenin's demand for temporariness. On the one hand, permanence and durability are at odds with the mutability and entirely arbitrary constitution of art's publics. On the other hand, the work of research, historiography and connoisseurship will continue nevertheless: through records, photographs, texts, witness accounts, sometimes even the actual objects, the impermanent monuments will survive. As the early street art of the Russian Revolution demonstrates, permanent bronze works they may not be, but the record of their interventions, what Gregoire might have called their inevitable didactic presence, lives on.

CODA

Recent events have drawn attention to an important area that is integral to any discussion on the idea of public art, but one that I hardly touched on in my 1990 paper. Above all, there is the question of difference. The history of racism has been central to the recent protests and has, at last, drawn the attention of the world to long-standing attempts by local communities to have public monuments of figures associated with racism removed (for instance, the Confederate statues in the Southern United States and Edward Colston in Bristol). Finally, I would like to envisage a project in which the colonial history of Europe, including how much of Europe's wealth was and still is today dependent on the murderous slave trade, would be traced simply through a mapping of its celebratory monuments: where they have been placed and how and when they have been were removed. Such a project would be a point of intersection at which art, history and politics might inform each other.

13 JULY 2020

This morning I cycled again through Parliament and Trafalgar Squares. It was a busy day for the monuments, perhaps their busiest day in years in terms of attention. A thousand or more aggressive far right-wing men, mainly in their fifties and sixties, had assembled to 'defend' them. I filmed a few of the right-wingers, with their 'white lives matter', and 'proud loyalist' T-shirts, as they gathered around the newly minted *Boxed Churchill*. They were trying to explain their 'position' to an elderly black man who had bravely turned up to protest the men's presence. 'Don't worry', I heard the obvious leader of this little group of angry white men say, 'We are not going to hurt *you*.' The people they wanted to hurt, however, didn't turn up, so in the end they drank a lot and urinated on the monuments, even on *Boxed Churchill*, now baptised or christened by fascist fools. Then they fought each other and the police.

14 JULY 2020

Overnight the artist Marc Quinn, aided by a large crew of construction workers and an industrial crane, installed a resin and steel monument to the Black British activist Jen Reid upon the denuded plinth recently occupied by the slave trader Edward Colston. Revolutionary intervention or artistic prestidigitation? Certainly Quinn seems to have out-Banksy-ed Banksy, the latter now fuming, presumably incognito in the bank cave, over an opportunity missed, and on his 'own' turf no less. But the thing about monuments is that their vicissitudes are strange and unpredictable. One thing we know for sure is that if they are perceived by some as acts of love, gifts to subjects, then they are gifts that are heavy in more ways than one. Here we might usefully recall one of Jacque Lacan's definitions of love as trying to give something you don't have to someone who doesn't want it.

1. This original paper was based on a talk given for the symposium Art Creating Society organized by Stephen Willats at the Museum of Modern Art, Oxford (now Modern Art Oxford) in June 1990. Thanks to Laura Mulvey for suggested edits and much useful discussion. Also, to my daughter Olivia Gagnon for edit suggestions.
   For the exhibition that accompanied the symposium, I installed in the streets of Oxford a 1/3 scale plaster model of a statue of Lenin removed from its pedestal in Bucharest. Thanks to Jeff Brandt for research and building assistance.
2. Robert Musil, quoted in Marina Warner in *Monuments. and Maidens*, London: Picador, 1987.
3. *The Illustrated London News* (27 May 1871).
4. Dzerzhinsky, a Polish citizen who was the founder of the Soviet secret police, was monumentalised in metal in what used to be called Dzerzhinsky Square (Now called Bank Square). In a celebrated incident, students climbed up the statue and painted its hands red. The Government later ordered the removal of the statue.
5. The Victory Arch in Baghdad consists of a pair of 20-metre arms that hold two swords that cross over Victory Square some 45 metres in the air. The arms are bronze cast. from the actual arms of President Saddam Hussein. Hussein's fists emerge from two heaps of helmets, each helmet from a dead Iranian soldier, with bullet-holes that are stained with the blood of exploding heads. Samir al-Khalil has suggested that the monument be retained so that it can stand as a reminder of the fear and tyranny brought on by the megalomania of Hussein. al-Khalil reminds us that the West was far too hasty in their destruction of fascist public art after the fall of the Third Reich. See *Rear Window: The Architecture of Fear* [documentary film], dir. Samir al-Khalil, England Channel 4.

6.   Georges Bataille, 'Architecture', *Documents*, no.2, May 1929 (OC 1:171). As quoted in Denis Hollier, *Against Architecture: The Writings of Georges Bataille*, Cambridge: MIT Press, 1989. After quoting this passage from Bataille, Hollier suggests that we only have to look at contemporary 'government ideas' on monumentality to realise that Bataille was not jumping to conclusions. Hollier finds this example in *Le Monde* in May 1973 from the then Minister of Cultural Affairs, Maurice Druon: I am convinced that one of the reasons for what we certainly must call urban decadence results from the absence in our cities of temples, palaces, statues, or anything that represents the superior facilities of human beings: faith, thought and will. An urban civilisation's vitality is measured perhaps by the prestigious monuments it is capable of erecting.

7.   See Claudette Houlde (ed.), *Images of the French Revolution*, Quebec: Musée Du Quebec, 1989.

8.   Daniel Hermant, 'Destructions et vandalisme pendant la Révolution française', *Annales: Economies, Sociétés, Civilisations*, vol. 33, no. 4, 1978, quoted in Anthony Vidler, 'Monuments Parlants', *Art and Text*, Melbourne, Winter 1989.

9.   Cl. Houlde, *Images of the French Revolution, op. cit.*

10.   See A. Vidler, 'Monuments Parlants', *op. cit.*, and A. Vidler, *The Writing of the Walls: Architectural Theory in the Late Enlightenment*, Princeton: Princeton Architectural Press, 1987.

11.   V. I. Lenin, 'On the Monuments of the Republic' (12 April,1918), *On Literature and Art,* Moscow: Progress Publishers, 1967.

12.   V .I. Lenin, *Complete Collected Works*, vol. 12.

13.   A.V. Lunacharsky, 'Lenin o Monumental anoi propogande', *Lenin i izobrazitelnoe iskusstvo*, Moscow: 1977, quoted in Vladimir Tolstoy, 'Art Born of the October Revolution', *Street Art of the Revolution*, London: Thames & Hudson, 1990.

14.   A.V. Lunacharsky, 'Lenin o Monumental anoi propogande', *op. cit.*

15.   In the essay 'On the Monuments of the Republic', Lenin does in fact 'order' that those 'monuments erected in honour of tsars and their minions and which have no historical or artistic value are to be removed from the squares and streets and stored up or used for utilitarian purposes'. He did, however, order that such a program of adjudication and removal should be done under the auspices of a special commission made up of the People's Commissars for Education and Property of the Republic and the chief of the Fine Arts department of the Commissariat for Education. Together they were to work with the Art Collegium of Moscow and Petrograd. This does suggest that Lenin was sympathetic to the idea that politicians alone would be unable to decide which works were of 'merit', etc., and that he felt it necessary for 'experts' to be consulted. Despite, for example, the fact that many hundreds of religious icons were destroyed, it is still the case that Lenin's approach to the art of the past was significantly more sophisticated than either the legislators of the French Revolution and many of the current 'post-communist' governments in eastern Europe. An exception would seem to be the Czech government of Václav Havel, who suggested that many of the socialist realist monuments should be placed, undamaged, in a forest so that 'nature' would grow around and over them.

16. Block's sensibility has, by and large, been lacking in present day Eastern Europe. However, there have been exceptions. For instance, there is a group in eastern Germany called 'The Monuments of the DDR Committee' who have been arguing that none of the old public works should be torn down or destroyed precipitously. They have insisted that there be generous public consultation and that the artists of the works (if still alive) should be included in any discussion concerning the future fate of the works.

17. Blaise Pascal, 'Les Provinciales', *Oeuvres*, Paris: Galllmard, 1950. Quoted in Louis Marin, *Portrait of the King*, London: Macmillan Press, 1988.

18. Invading armies as well as revolutionary armies have historically used the metal from statuary to help in the production of weapons. When the Germans were invading the Soviet Union, they actually melted down Statues of the 'Czar and his minions' that still remained to manufacture of guns for the campaign.

19. Interestingly enough, the Vendôme Column was built on the spot where a statue to Louis the IV had been destroyed by the revolutionaries in 1792. The original statue of Napoleon was placed on top of the column in 1810. In 1814, the Bourbons were restored and the statue was taken down. Twenty or thirty years later, under King Louis Phillipe, another statue of Napoleon was placed there, this time representing the Emperor standing on a heap of cannon balls. Napoleon III had this statue removed and instead replaced it with a reproduction of the original statue of Napoleon in Roman costume and crowned with a laurel wreath.

20. As reported in the *South China Morning Post* (31 August 1966). As many have pointed out, as the tanks entered the square, the students stood in front of their 'statue' and sang 'The Internationale'. For a brief moment, then the Statue of Liberty became something else, its meaning in the context of socialist students who had built a replica of it, was transformed. As Lou Reed has aptly put it, the inscription on the Statue of Liberty should read: 'Give me your tired, your hungry, your poor, and I'll piss on them.' Lou Reed, 'Dirty Boulevard' *New York*, Sire Records, 1989.

21. The statue was built by the Romanian artist Boris Caragea in 1960. Caragea's design was selected after a national competition. But as anyone familiar with statues of Lenin in the Soviet Union knows, his design was simply a replica of one of the standard poses used to depict Lenin.

Mark Bradford,
Dancing in the Street, 2019,
video, 2min, 50 sec.
© Mark Bradford.
Courtesy the artist and
Hauser & Wirth New York

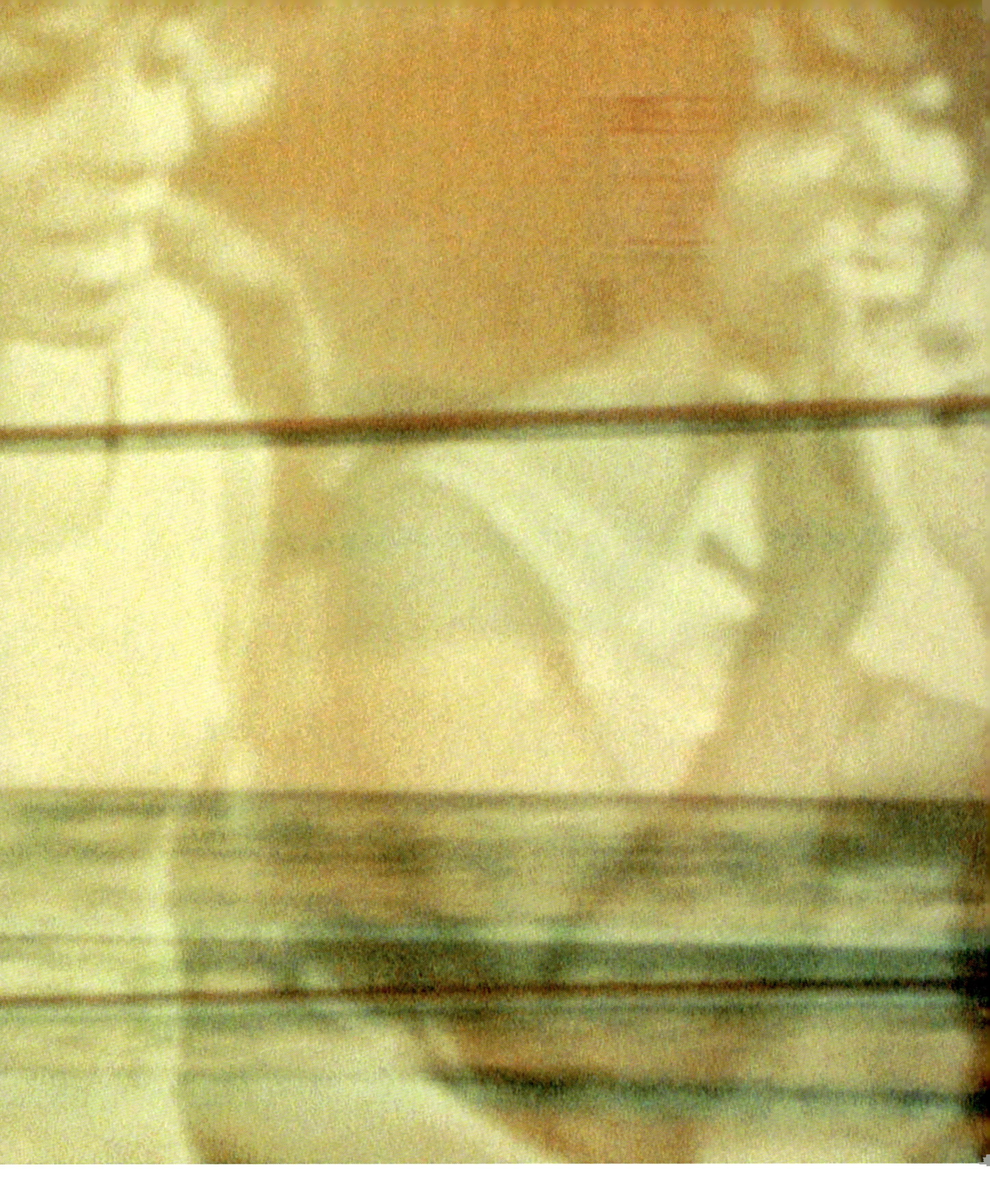

Ed Ruscha, *The End*, 1991,
acrylic on canvas, 177.8 x 284.5cm.
© Ed Ruscha.
Courtesy the artist and
Gagosian, Venice, CA

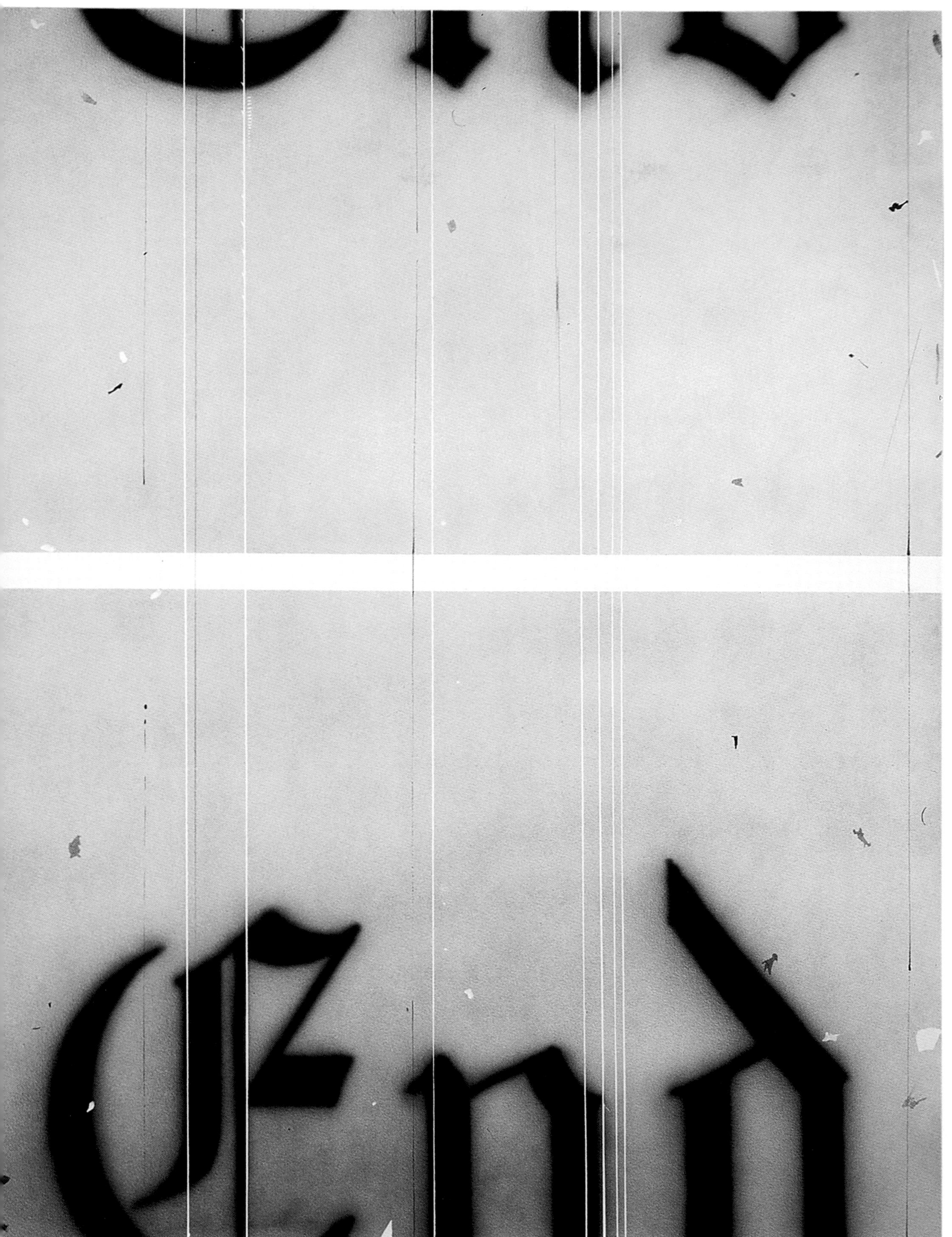
End

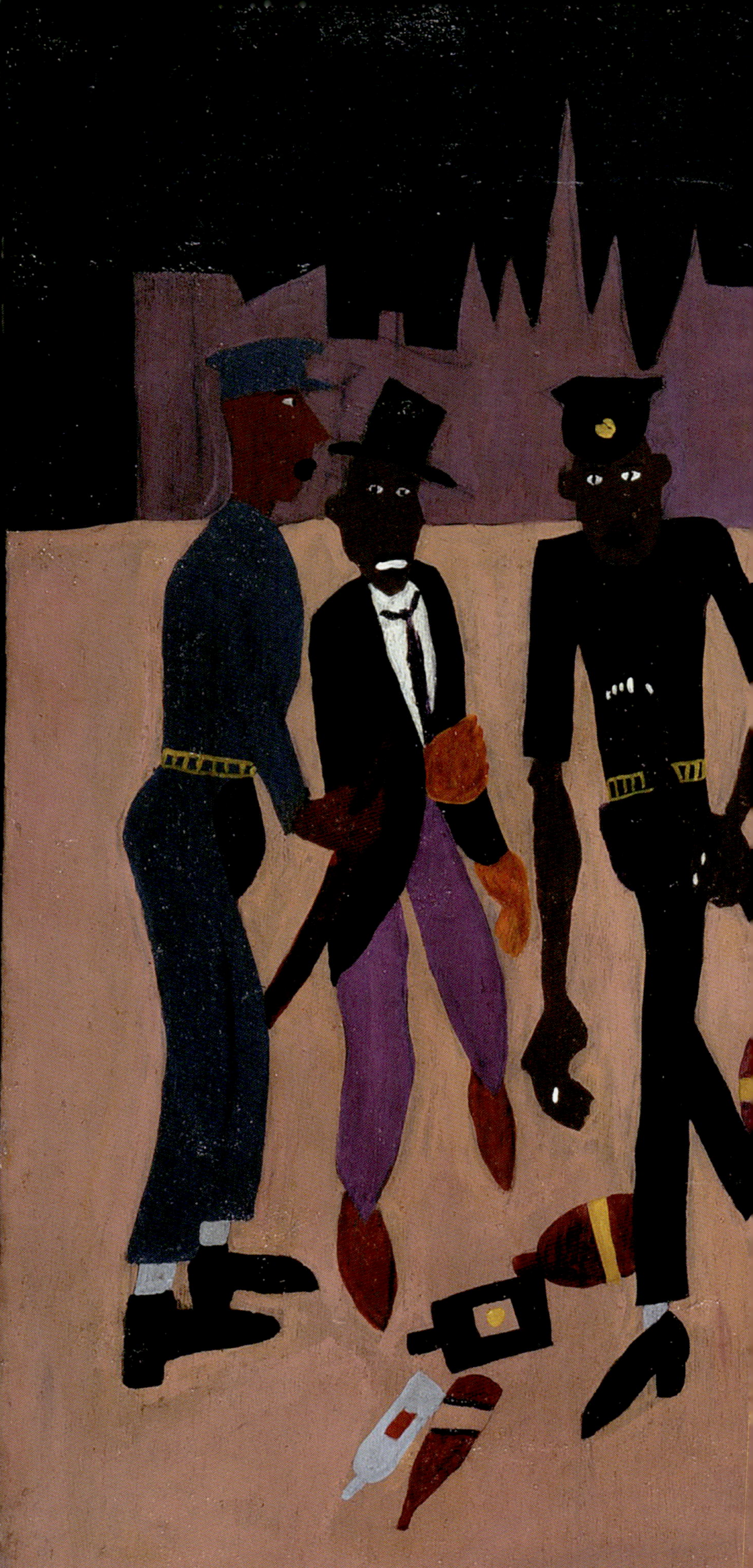

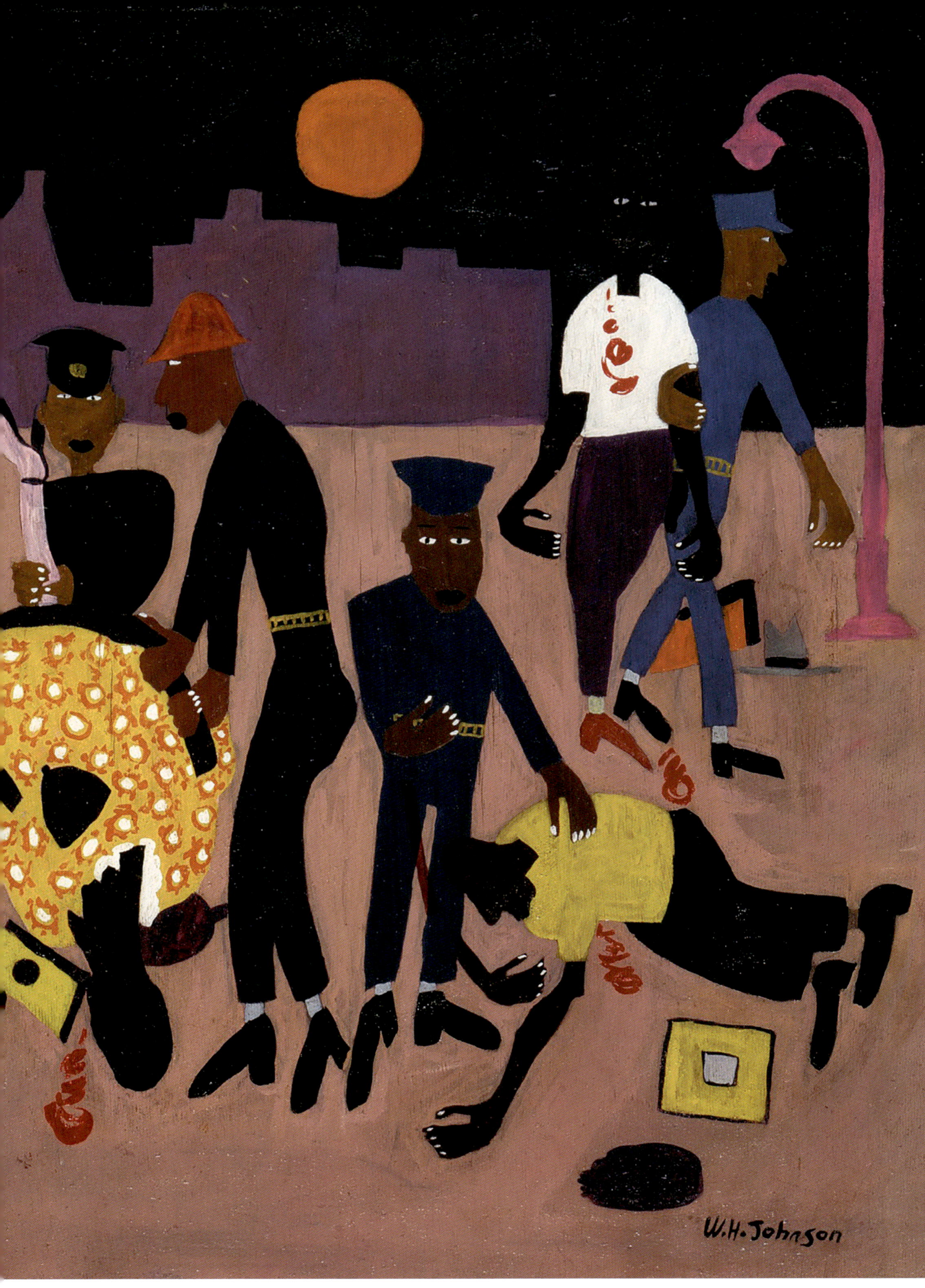

William H. Johnson, *Moon over Harlem*,
c. 1943, oil on plywood,
Smithsonian American Art Museum, Washington, D.C.

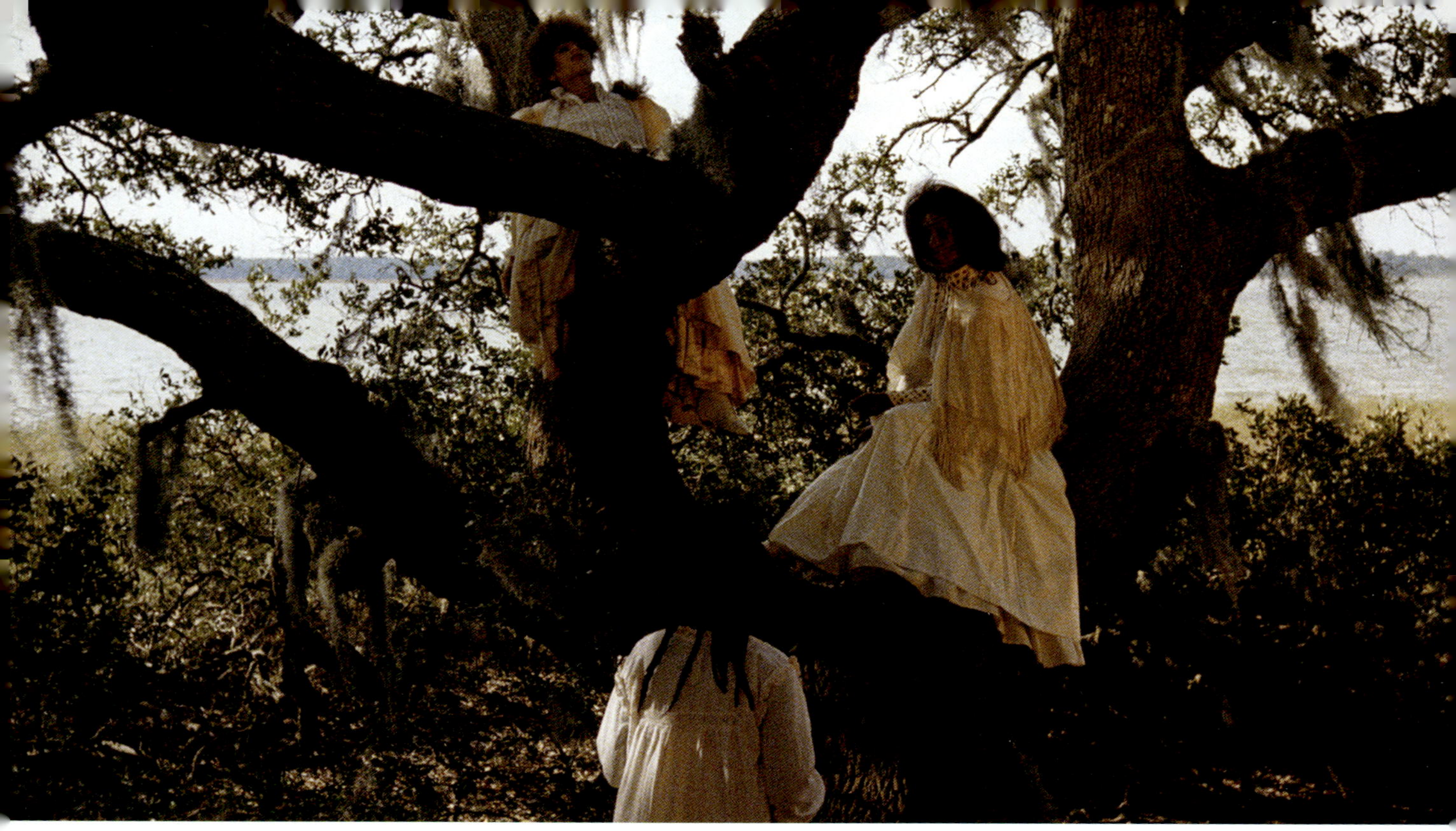

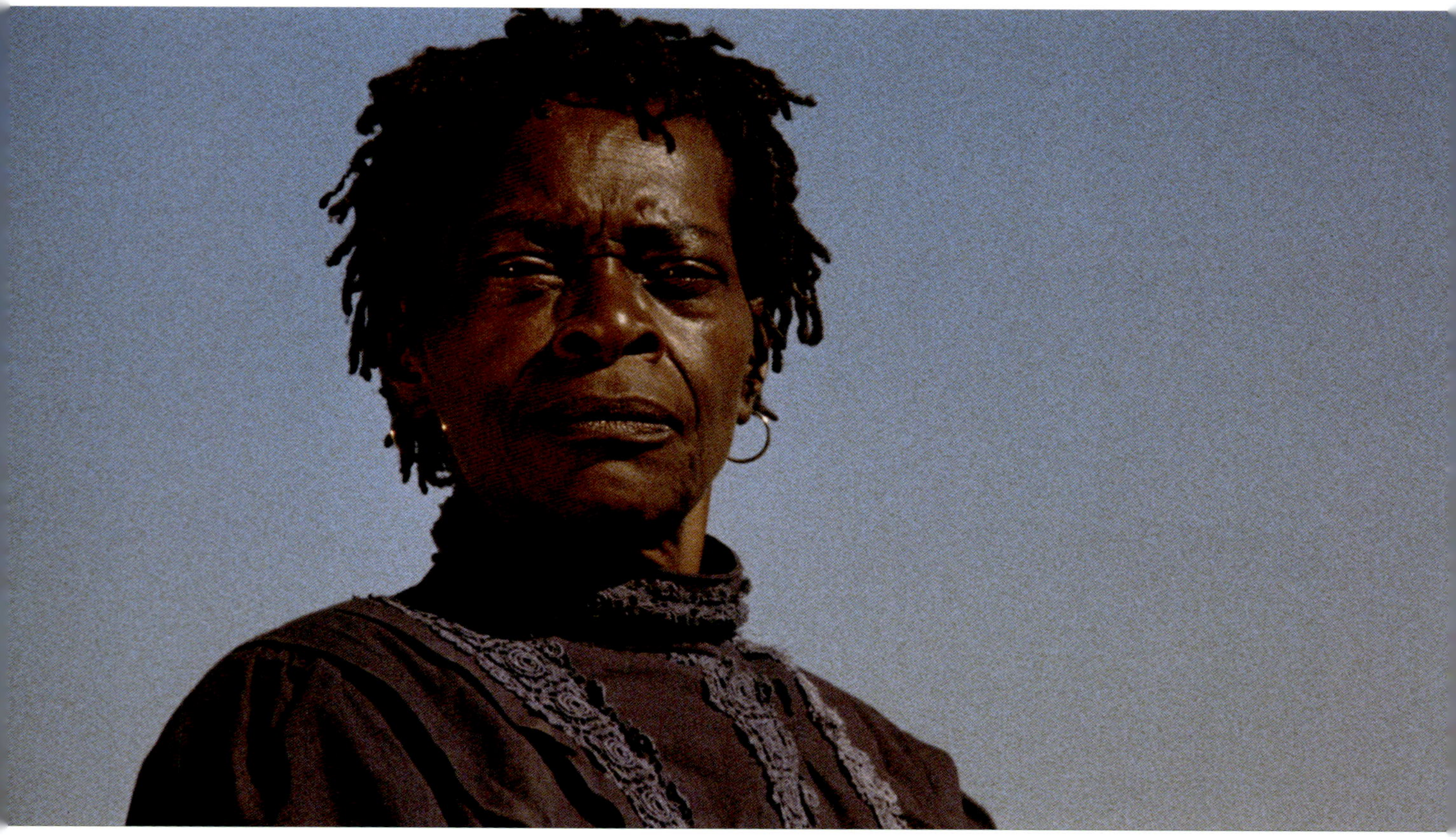

Julie Dash, *Daughters of the Dust*,
1991, film, colour 112min.
Courtesy Cohen Film Collection

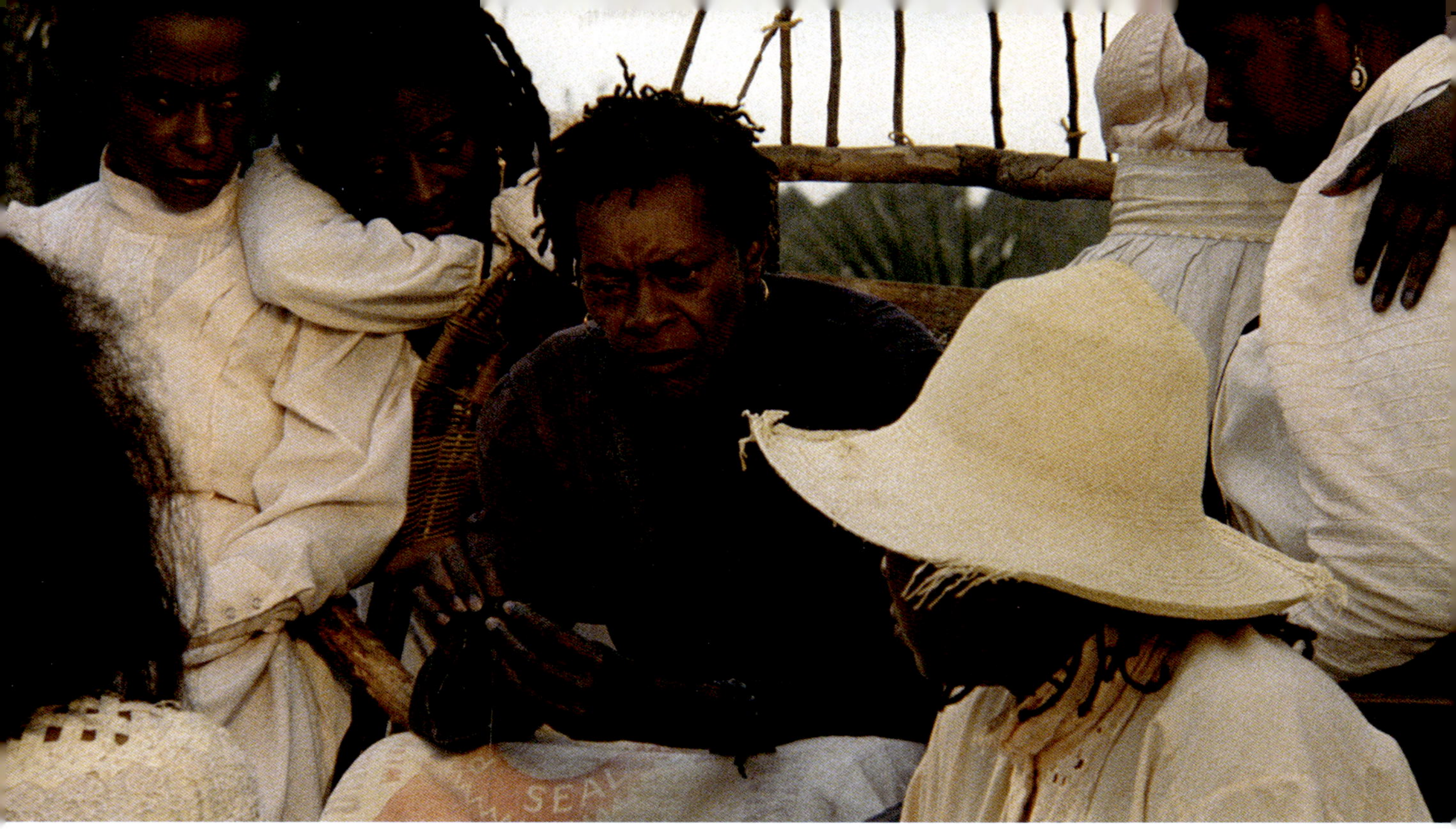

AFTERALL

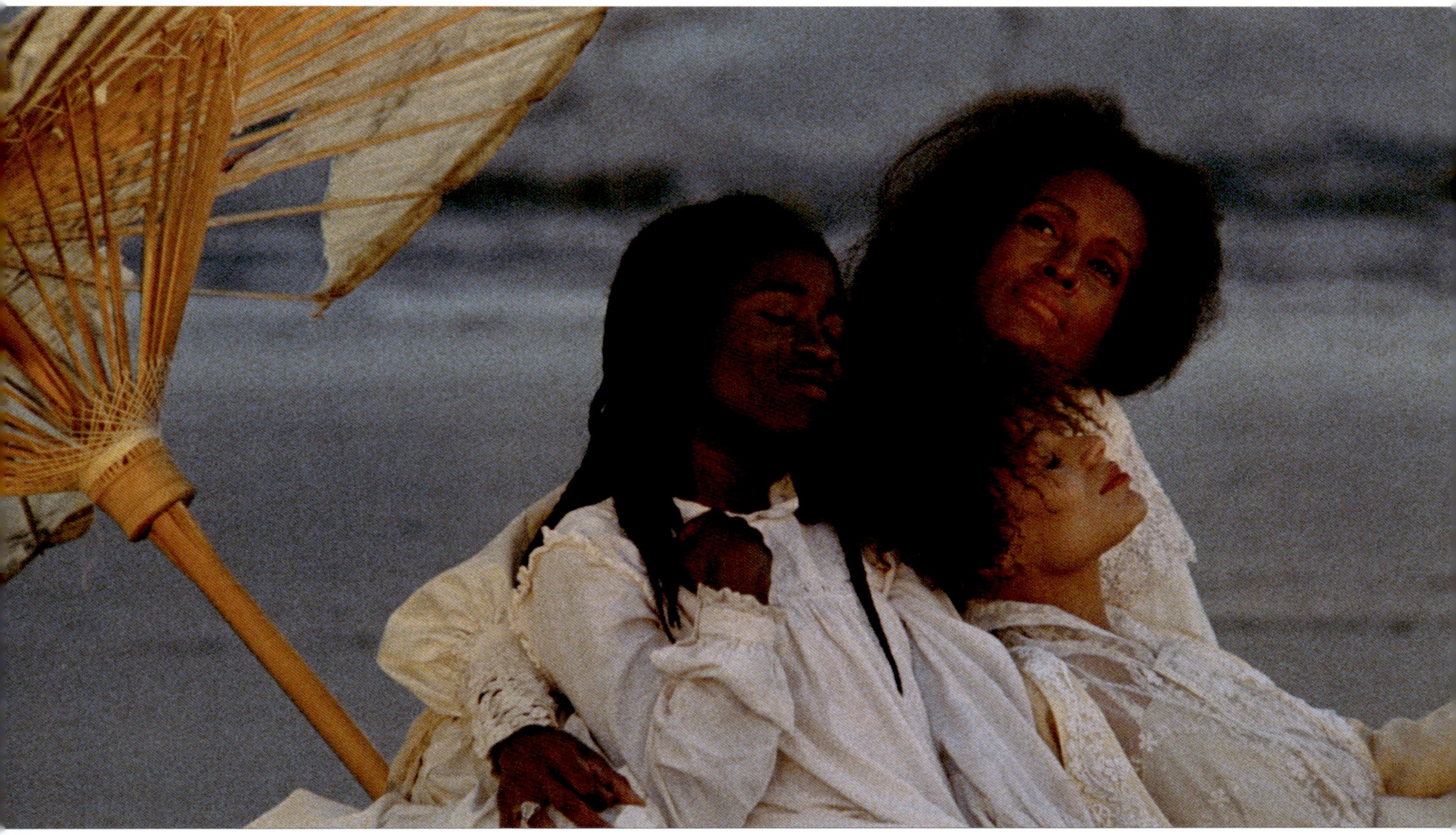

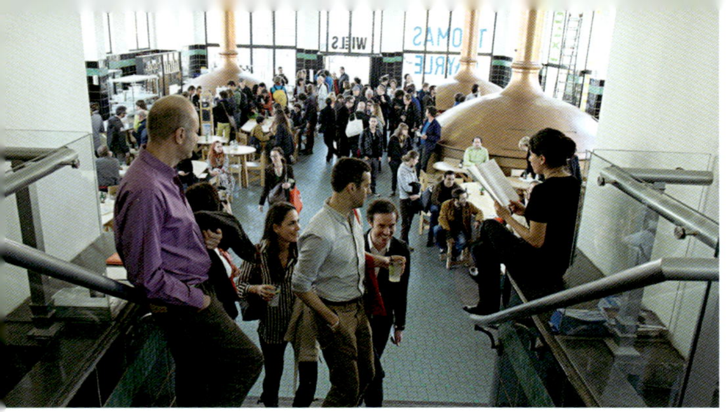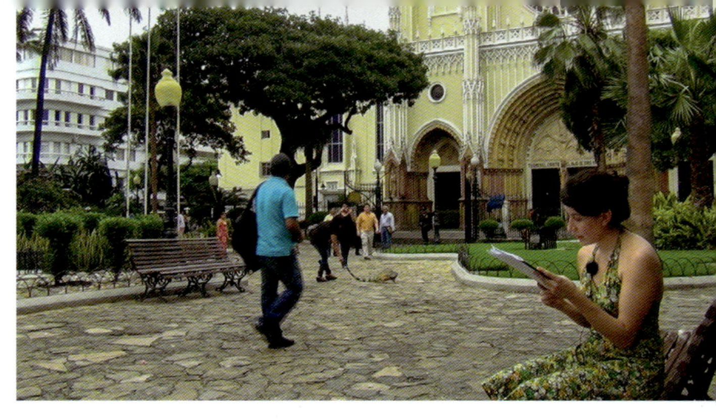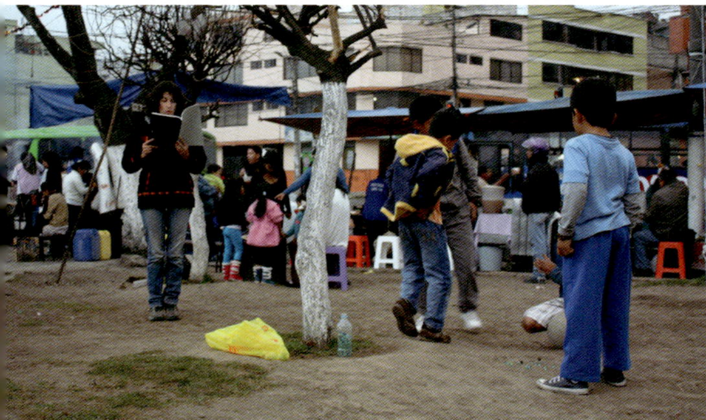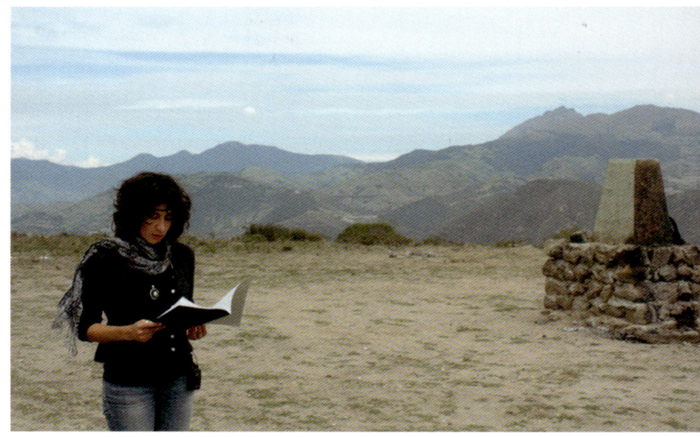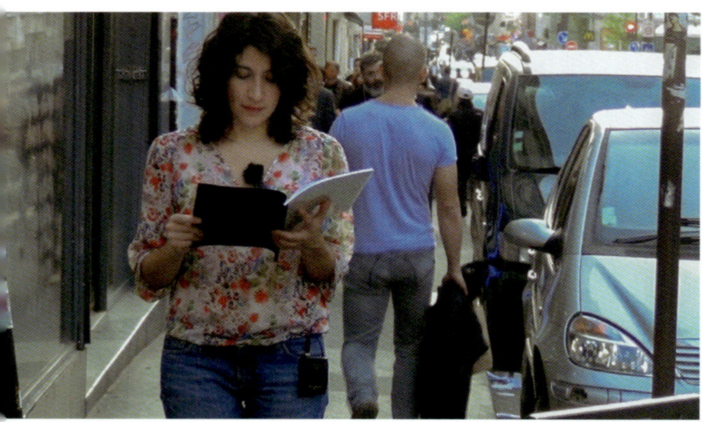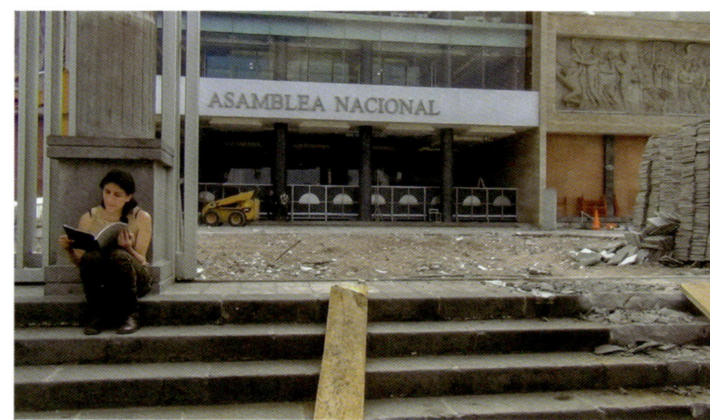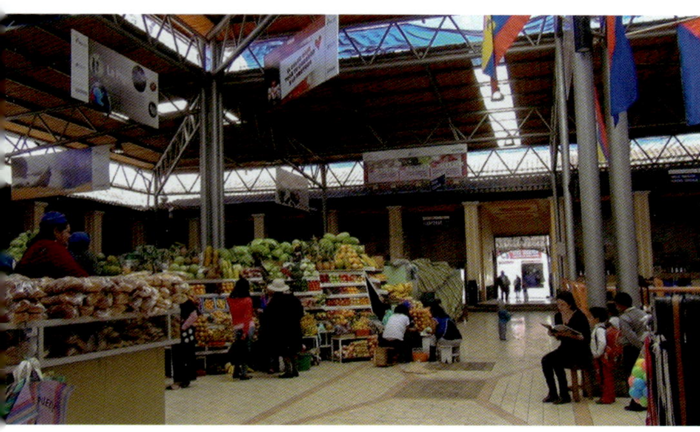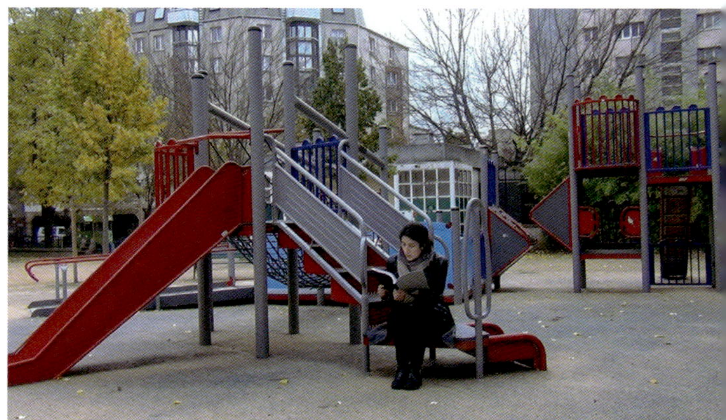

Estefanía Peñafiel Loaiza,
Compte à rebours,
2005–2013, video, 78hr.
Courtesy the artist

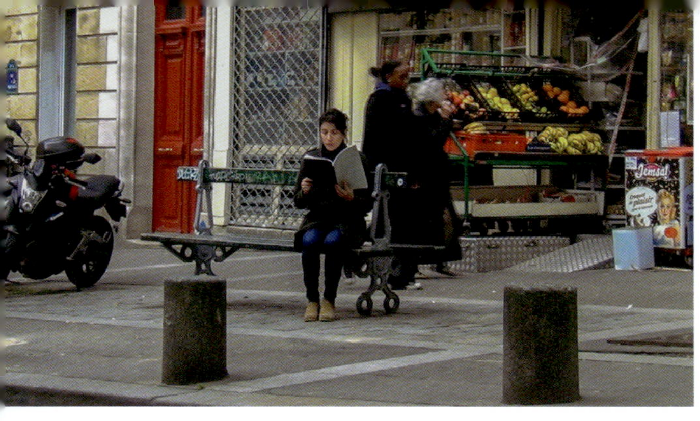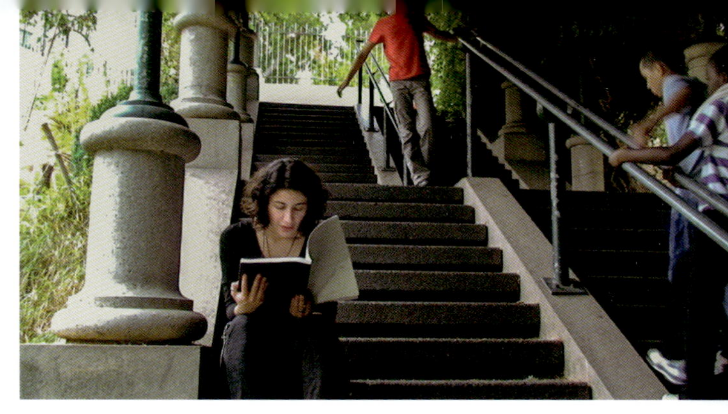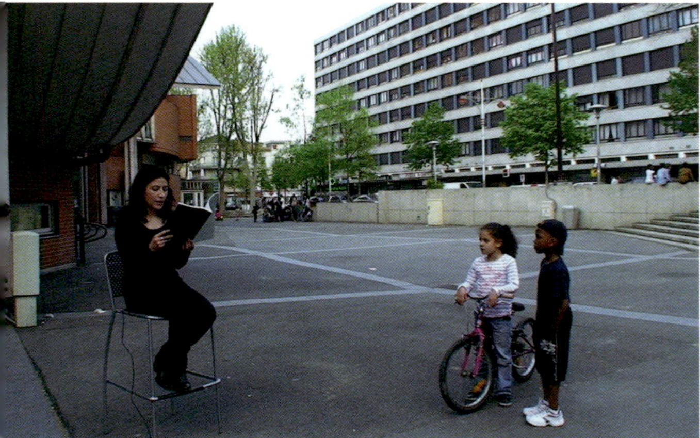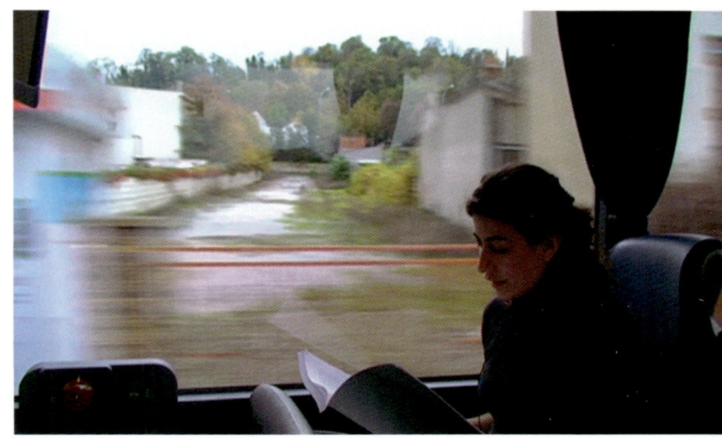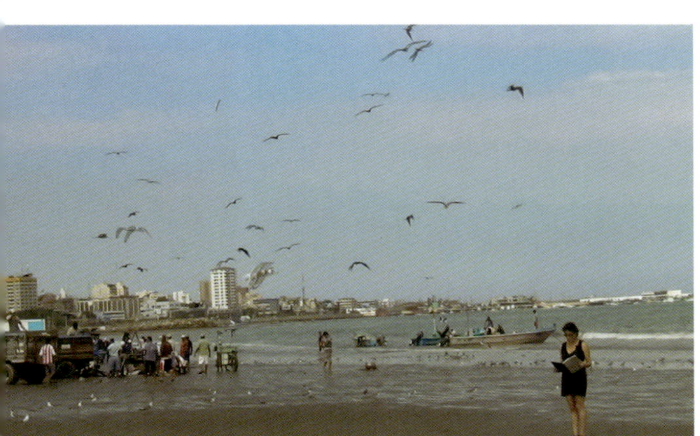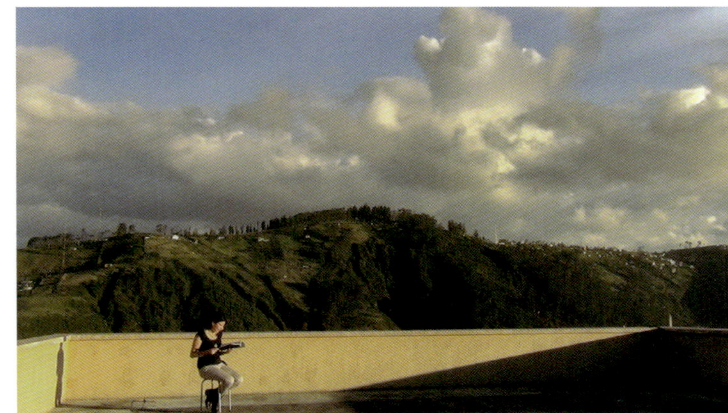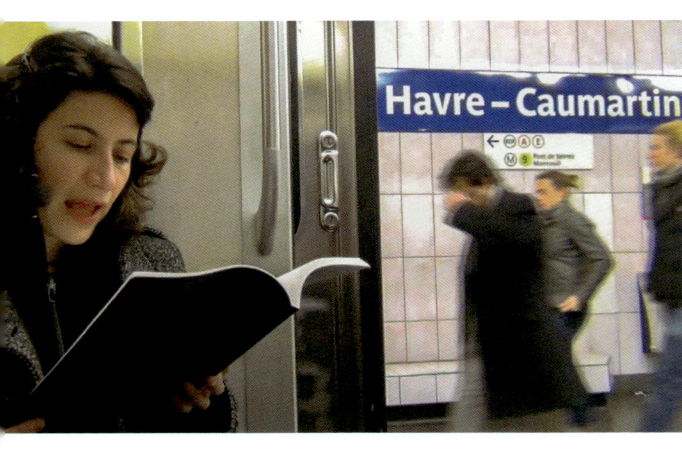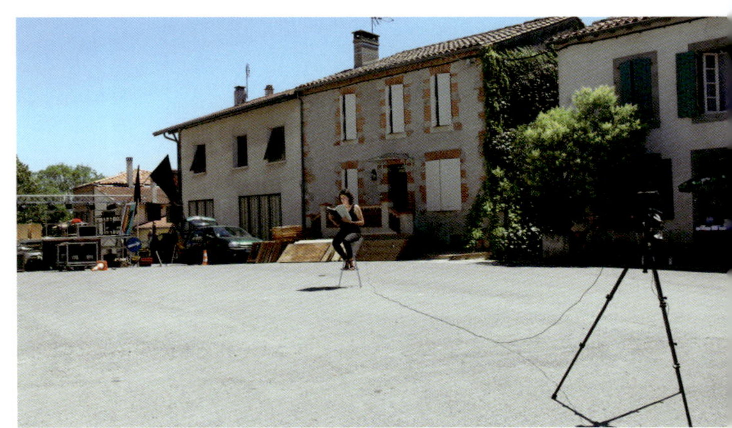
Havre – Caumartin

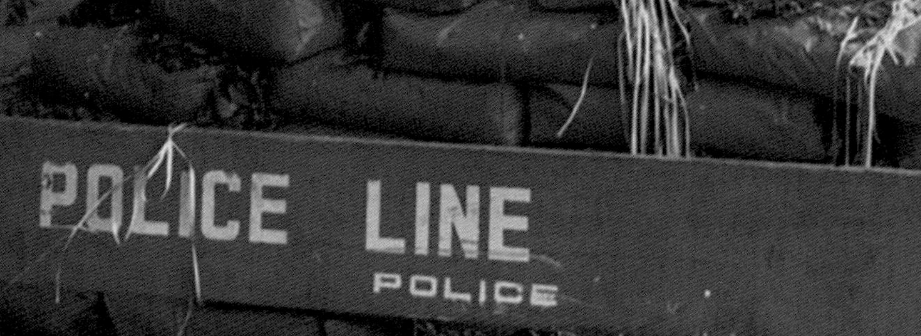

POLICE LINE
POLICE
POLICE DEPT.
POLI
NET WT.

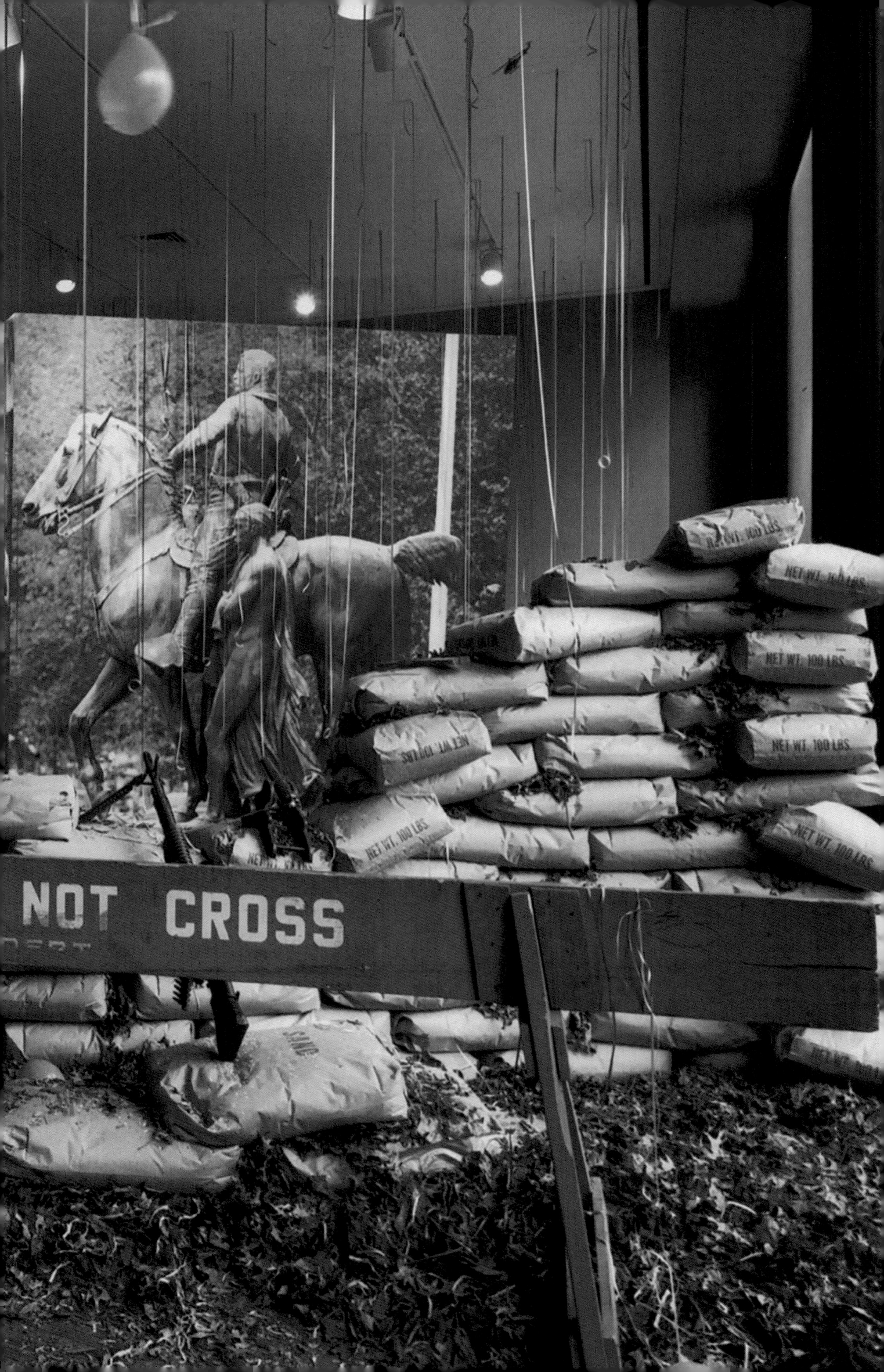

NOT CROSS
NET WT. 100 LBS.

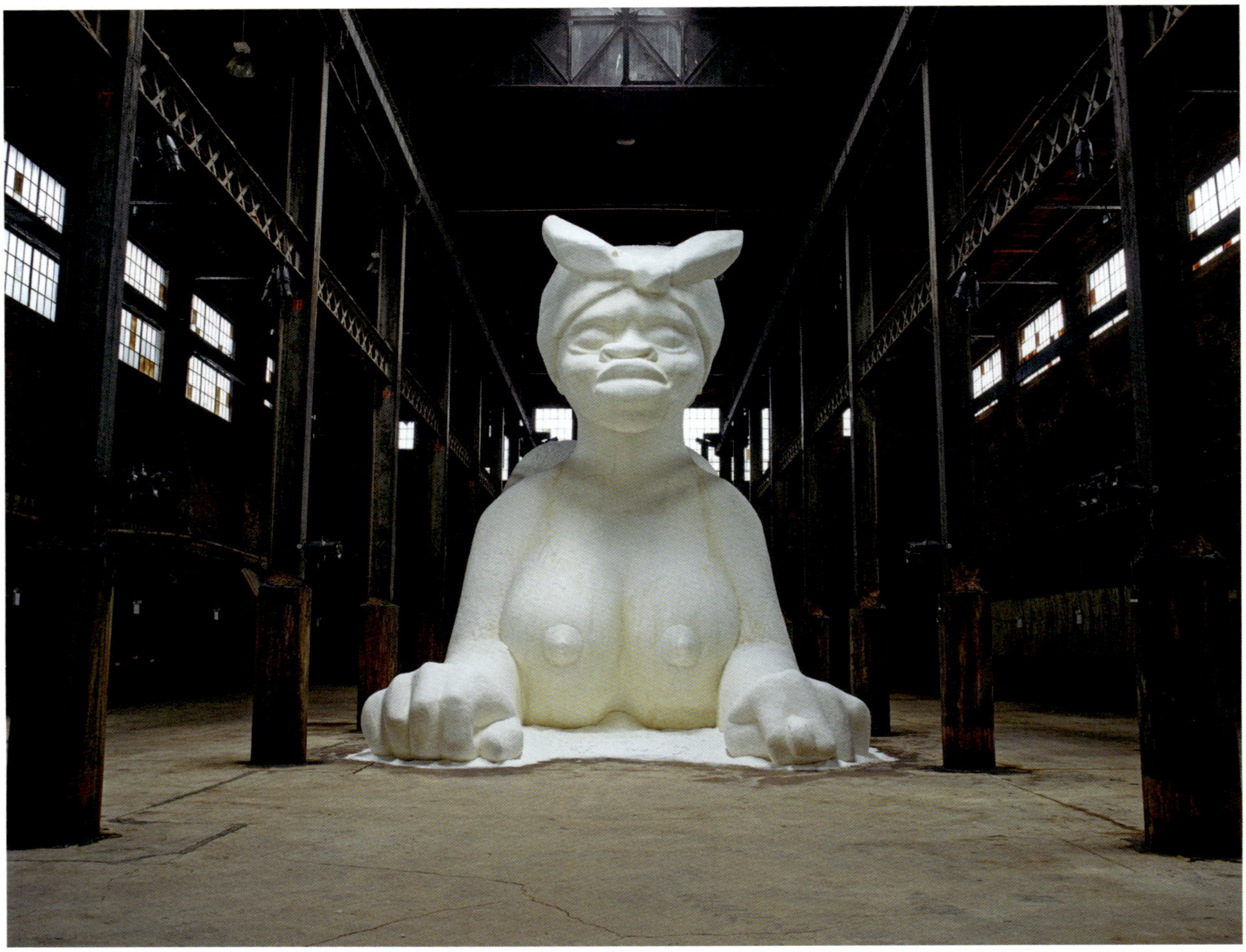

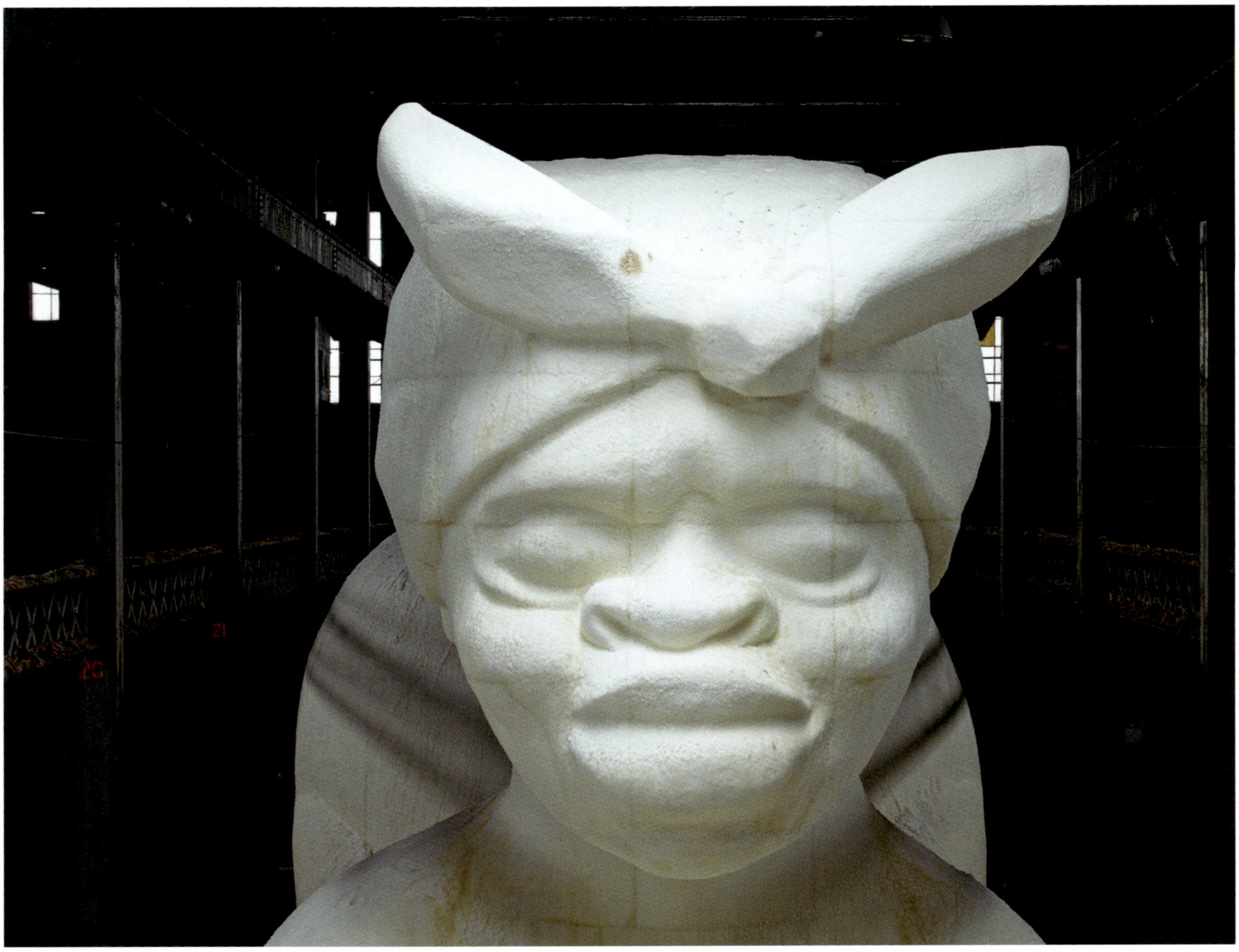

Previous: David Hammons, *Public Enemy*, 1991.
Courtesy the Museum of Modern Art Archives,
New York/SCALA, Venice.
Photograph by Mali Olatunji

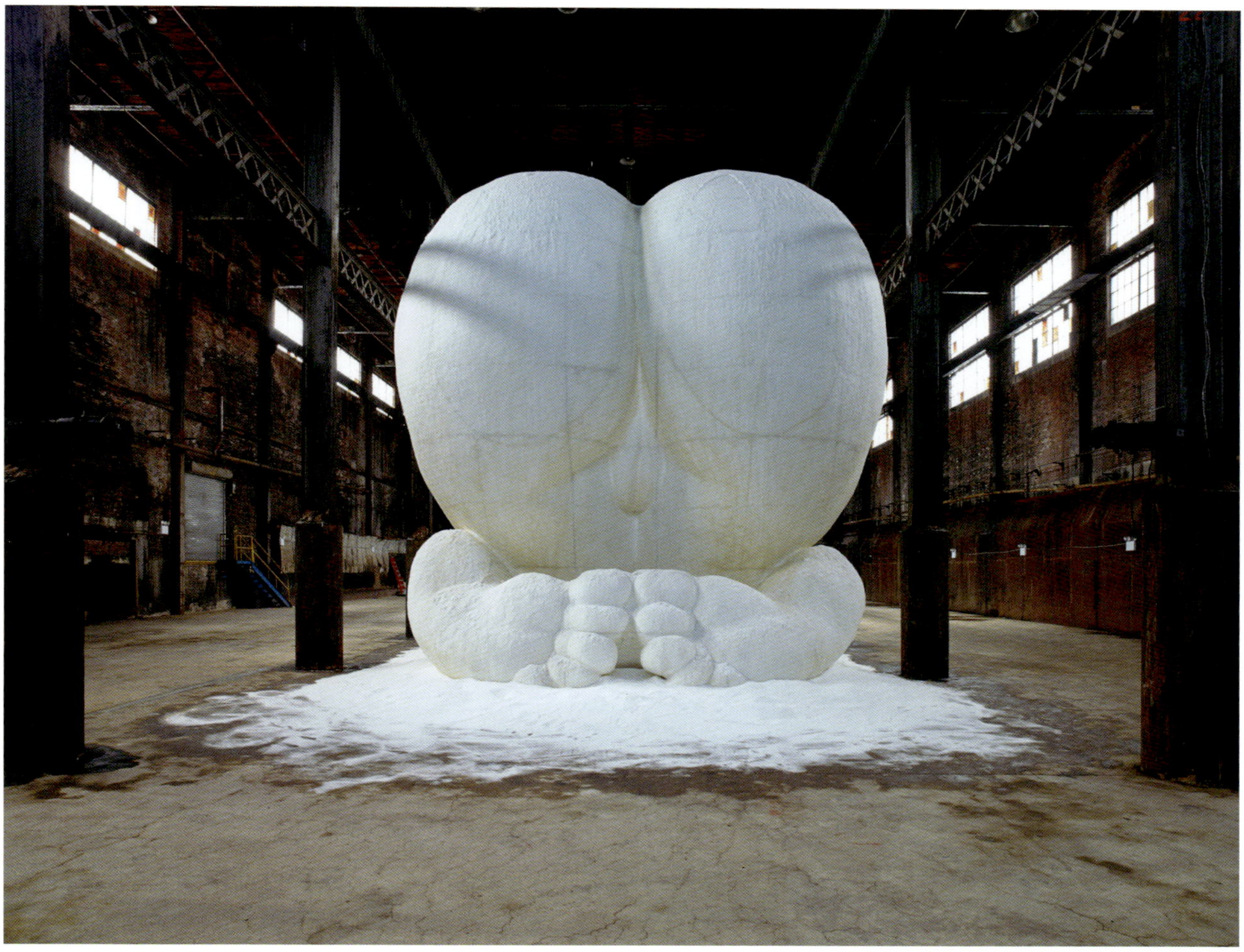

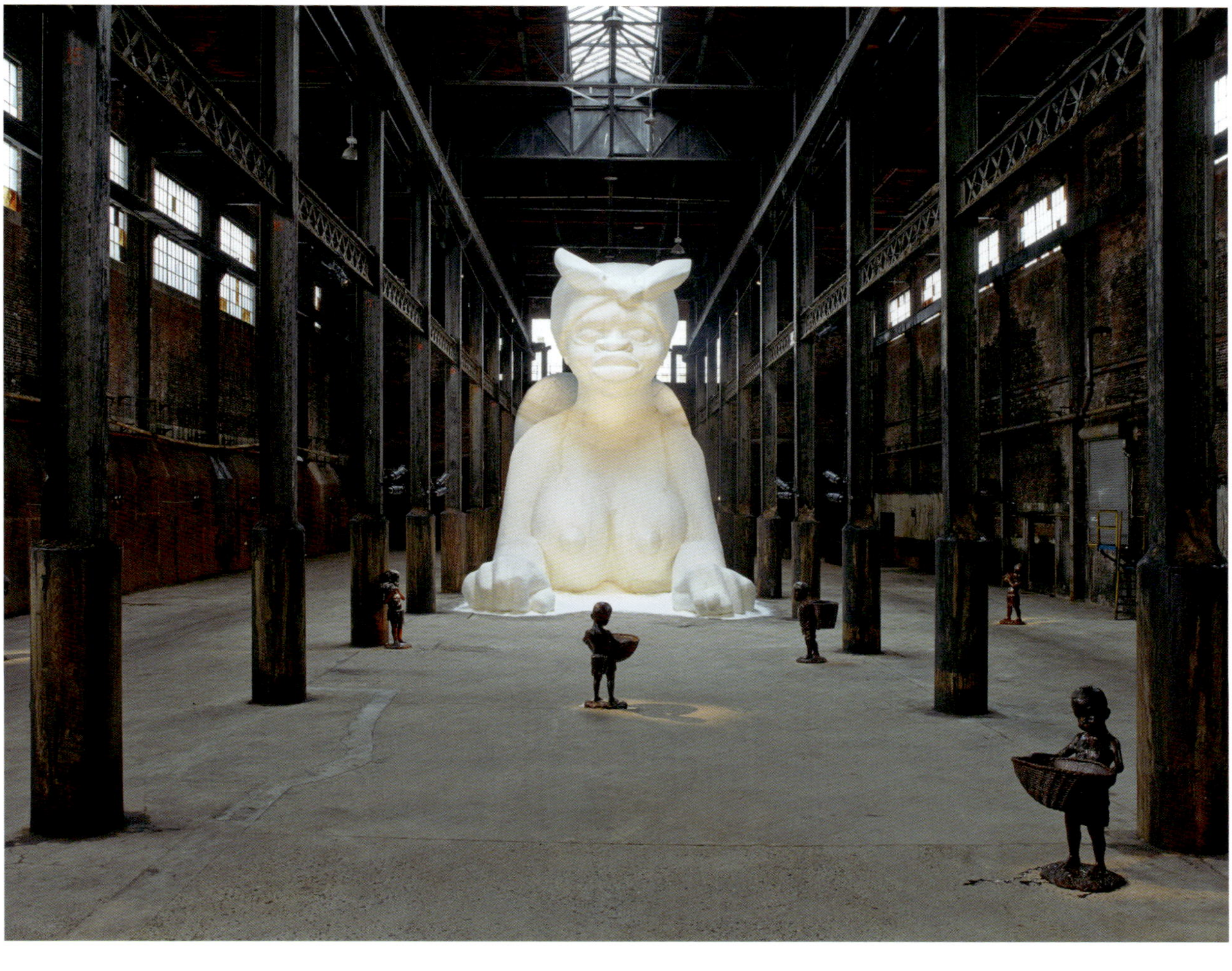

Kara Walker, *A Subtlety, or the Marvelous Sugar Baby, an Homage to the unpaid and overworked Artisans who have refined our Sweet tastes from the cane fields to the Kitchens of the New World on the Occasion of the demolition of the Domino Sugar Refining Plant*, 2014, polystyrene foam, sugar, c.10.8 x 7.9 x 23m. © 2014 Kara Walker. Photograph: Jason Wyche

Stan VanDerBeek, The Colloquy of Mobiles, Pratchaya Phinthong, Sung Tieu, Chloé Delarue/TAFAA, Dana Liljegren on Ndary Lô, Vuth Lyno on the White Building

Re-purpose and Remake

Adeena Mey

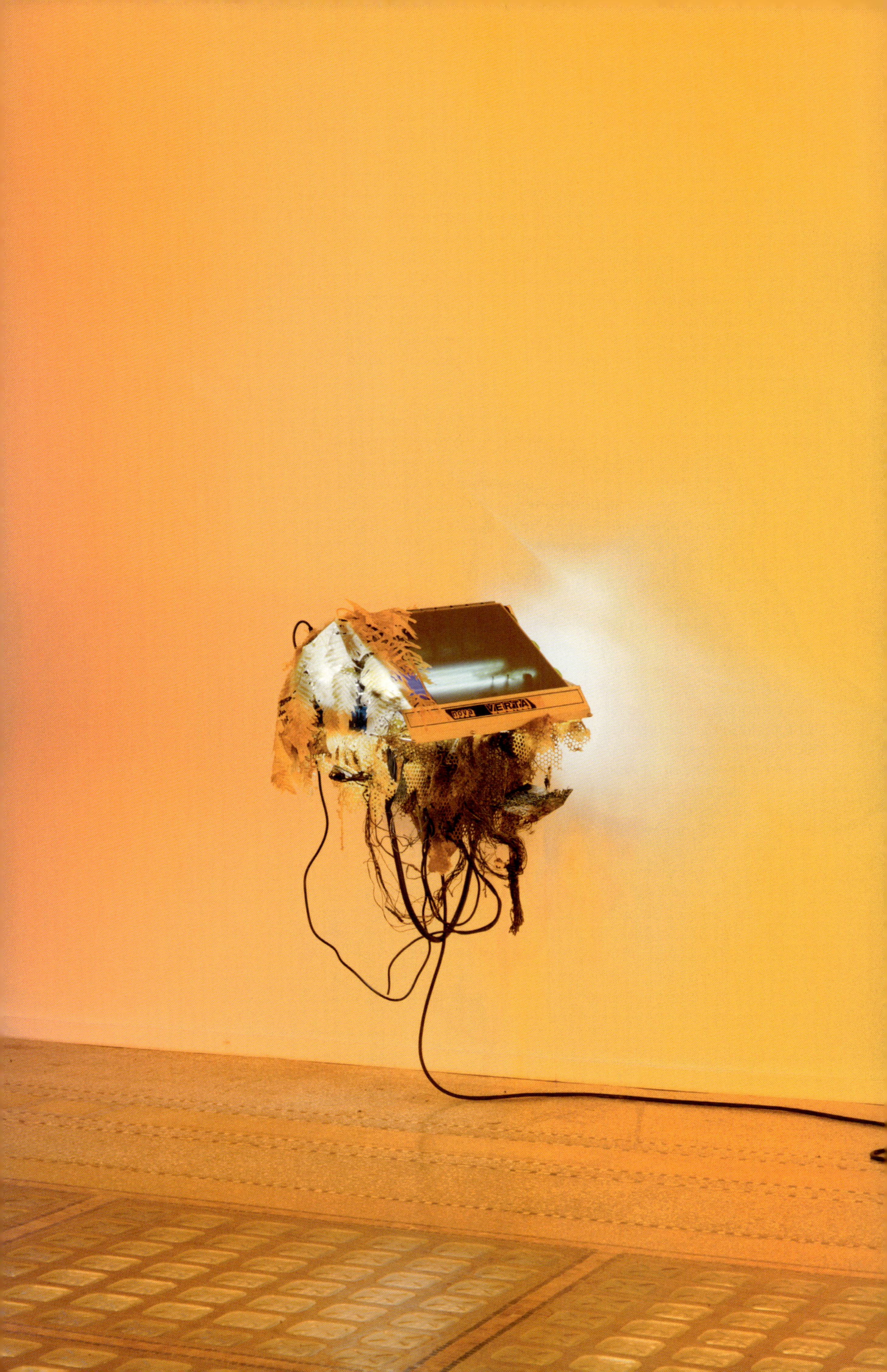

nova VERTA

By the 1970s, television had penetrated most homes in America, Europe and Japan. New forms of information circulation ushered in an age of new media that included telecommunications, telematics and cybernetic feedback. In parallel to this rapid spread, TV became a prime vector for the diffusion of violence. In *Violence Sonata* (1970), media artist and experimental film-maker Stan VanDerBeek uses TV as means by which violence impregnates the collective body to reflect on that same violence. The work, which involves video and live performance in a studio setting, intervenes in this violence that the artist described as 'the digestive act of our inability to communicate'. 'Man's frustration at not being able to communicate with words leads him to violence', said VanDerBeek. 'Centuries of words have meant centuries of violence. We must explore all other ways to communicate if we hope to live non-violent lives.'[1] To that end, the artist appropriated and expanded TV's material apparatus to render it a site for the articulation of a language – informational and aesthetic – beyond words.

Aired on channels 2 and 44 of Boston's WGBH TV on 12 January 1970 from 9 to 10pm, VanDerBeek defined *Violence Sonata* as 'TV as an "information concert"; TV as a "sensory experience"; TV as a form of "pre-fab theatre"; TV as a psycho-drama and feedback'.[2] Already known for his experimental animation work and as a pioneer of Expanded Cinema – a term he coined – VanDerBeek was no stranger to forays into mass media and technology, having previously collaborated with computer scientist Ken Knowlton at Bell Labs, working with his BEFLIX ('Bell Flicks') computer language.[3] This work led to the series *Poemfield* (1966–71), bringing together experimental film, visual poetry and programming 'conceived for use in VanDerBeek's multi-screen installations and performances as well as for single channel projection'.[4] The search for a new formal language through novel technologies was entwined here with the exploration of the different social forms of installations, performances and screenings. And with *Violence Sonata*, this search could be taken to the level of what the artist referred to as the 'city's communal nervous system'.[5] Structured in three parts – man; man-to-man; man-to-woman – *Violence Sonata* unfolded on a TV studio set with an audience of about 300 people, 35mm film and slide projections, several TV monitors and a group of performers staging live actions (happening, drama, soap opera) in response to the real-time TV transmission. These two simultaneous live broadcasts, which included footage from newsreels, political events, sports, performances and animated collages by VanDerBeek, were processed by the artist using a range of techniques afforded by the WGBH equipment: image juxtapositions, fades, distortions and transitions that resulted in a large-scale intermedia, multisensory, multi-temporal, collage/theatre piece, all via mass communication.

The ambition behind the work was that it foster a non-violent culture, predicated on notions of audience participation and the reuse of materials, performing cybernetic feedback – the regulation, that is, of the production and circulation of information in the Boston area. The area is here conceived as a kind of 'nervous system' organised and regulated through retroactions. The audience could respond to the studio during the broadcast by telephone to which performers would react. In this 'pre-fab theatre', the video tapes, slides and films that would 'become the sets needed for the theatre' were also intended to be reused by other local TV channels and theatres 'for interpretation and adaptation of the central premise', triggering reflexivity around issues of violence.[6]

Bearing in mind the kind of techno-utopianism of much early media art, to which VanDerBeek was not immune, *Violence Sonata* was nonetheless compellingly cognisant of a context marked by the emergence of 'real-time' and the parallel development of a fragmented social body, as well as of telematics and networked cultures. In this regard, it is also prescient today, and offers tools that, following the artist's own wish, can be reused, adapted and reoriented in other contexts and towards different ends. In TV VanDerBeek seemed to have seen a *pharmakon* (both poison and cure, according to Plato) for an increasingly violent society; he offered a techno-pharmacological apparatus to a public that had become atomised behind their monitors. The artist saw *Violence Sonata* as part of his concept of Expanded Cinema, or a 'culture-intercom', made up of audio-visual centres for the production, storage and distribution of information.[7]

In the spirit of the 'information concert', the works gathered here pay homage to *Violence Sonata* and exist as the result of, or engage with, repurposing, reuse, recombination or re-creation in the face of the changing futurity that stems from the current crisis. As VanDerBeek concluded in a long-ago project proposal: 'THE FUTURE IS NOT WHAT IS USED TO BE.'[8] Proceeding through montage, free but concrete associations, and heterological connections, this constellation of meta-stabilising objects adopt the logic of the remainder, the non-original, questioning *how* the future is not what it used to be.

In his recent essay 'One Hundred Years of Crisis', Yuk Hui makes the claim that an optimistic politics is grounded in concrete processes (of solidarity, of technical objects). With regards to the current crisis – immunological in its nature – the philosopher writes that a 'True co-immunity' needs to be articulated that 'is not abstract solidarity, but rather departs from a concrete solidarity whose co-immunity should ground the next wave of globalization (if there is one)'.[9] Unlike the abstract imagination of the Futurists on the one hand, and the 'cancellation of the future' by neoliberalism discussed by theorists Franco 'Bifo' Berardi and Mark Fisher on the other, one might look at 'biographies of objects' and their concrete modes of individuation.[10] What do operations such as repurposing, reuse, recombination or recreation tell us about our relationship to temporality and futurity? Artworks and other cultural artefacts produced as non-originals or unfolding from remains – reproduced, recast or resampled – speak to a non-linear conception of time. Untying themselves from the finality to which they were once assigned, they generate bifurcations and are reinscribed in different, perhaps unexpected, time-axes suggesting, perhaps, how to reinhabit the world differently.

✳✳✳

Created by cybernetician Gordon Pask, the *Colloquy of Mobiles* was first presented as part of *Cybernetic Serendipity* curated by Jasia Reichardt at the Institute of Contemporary Arts (ICA) in London in 1968. Bringing together the work of 43 composers, artists and poets, as well as 87 engineers, doctors, computer systems designers and philosophers, without distinguishing these from each other, Reichardt conceptualised the exhibition as 'the exploration and demonstration of connexions between creativity and technology (and cybernetics in particular)'.[11] It was also conceived to investigate 'the links between scientific or mathematical approaches, intuitions, and the more irrational and oblique urges associated with the making of music, art and poetry'.[12] One of the 'cybernetic devices as works of art' included in the show, Pask's *Colloquy of Mobiles* articulated a specific take on the analogy between the nature of cybernetic and artistic artefacts

Chloé Delarue, *TAFAA–SOPORIIS #2*, 2019. Exhibition view 'TAFAA - ACID RAVE,' Musée des beaux-arts, La Chaux-de-Fonds. Photograph: Florimond Dupont. Courtesy the artist

through his notion of 'aesthetically potent environments'.[13] Pask's observation of social environments was characterised, he wrote, by the search for 'social communication, conversation and other modes of partially co-operative interaction', which 'represent an essentially human and an inherently pleasurable mode of activity'. Pask saw aesthetic potency in 'environments designed to encourage or foster the type of interaction which is (by hypothesis) pleasurable'.[14] The *Colloquy of Mobiles* was one such realised environment.

The installation of five mobiles hung from a ceiling was intended to advance possibilities of 'artistic communication' and predicated on furthering (re)activity and participation – male and female robots or electro-magnetic beings engaged in a complex and open-ended game of mating in which they activated lights and sounds corresponding to movements of 'cooperation' and states of 'satisfaction'. Pask defined it as 'a group of objects, the individual mobiles that engage in discourse, that compete, co-operate and learn about one another'.[15] The installation was also designed to enable interaction with humans, who could 'enter the environment and participate; possibly modifying the mode of communication as a result'.[16] Despite its binary conception of gender, the work represented a remarkable apparatus and early experimentation with forms of non-organic organisation, life and communication between machines and between machines and humans.

Since 2018, cybernetician (and Pask's former student) Paul Pangaro and designer Thomas J. McLeish have been working on an exact replica of the *Colloquy of Mobiles*, exhibited for the first time in 2020.[17] Instead of the electro-mechanical computer device that enabled the various interactions, the 2018 *Colloquy of Mobiles* uses 'modern digital software, sensors, and motors'.[18] Pangaro and McLeish's media archaeological reconstruction of this synthetically, dynamically and actively produced machine-man social environment is intended to 'change how we feel about going home to voice interfaces such as Siri and Alexa, Cortana and Google Home, and how we experience living among smart machines'.[19] In this regard, the replica intervenes in the present technological teleology fuelled by artificial intelligence and the drive towards systematic automation, re-actualising Pask's project of cybernetics – described by sociologist of science Andrew Pickering as 'thematiz[ing], the unpredictable liveliness of the world, and processes of open-ended becoming' – through a replica.[20]

***

Also a replica, the third work in this selection engages with the origins of humanity and its mediation through (his-)tory telling. For his solo exhibition at Chisenhale Gallery in London in 2013, Thai artist Pratchaya Phinthong exhibited an exact copy of the Broken Hill skull, the first human fossil found in Africa.[21] Aged at an estimated 299,000 years, the skull was discovered in Zambia in 1921 and is a remnant of a male *Homo heidelbergensis* – a species from 700,000 to 150,000 years ago, believed to be 'the last common ancestor of our species *H. sapiens* evolving in Africa, and *Homo neanderthalensis* (the Neanderthals) which evolved in Eurasia'.[22] Taken the same year by the mining company who had been excavating that site to the Natural History Museum, the skull has since 2015 been permanently exhibited in the institution's Human Evolution gallery. Moreover, it is considered a highly significant piece in furthering the understanding of human evolution.

Close to when Phinthong conducted research for dOCUMENTA(13) around flies in Africa that provoked 'sleeping sickness', his friend, the film-maker Jakrawal Nilthamrong, told him about a peculiar object held at the Lusaka National Museum that appeared to be a replica.[23] This reproduction is on view as part of the permanent archaeology collection; the museum's website presents it as 'one of the most fascinating exhibits'.[24] Addressing art's function as a mediator for the voice of others through artefacts often remade or displaced, Phinthong's specific interest in the Broken Hill skull was in its being revealed as a fake by the museum's guide, which nevertheless enabled a certain narration of history, in particular the importance of discoveries made in Zambia. At Chisenhale, Phinthong exhibited the replica in exchange for a similar artefact found on the internet, while in the Lusaka National Museum, museum guide Kamfwa Chishala gave tours and explained the complex history of the skull and how it had informed the many interpretations of the development of the *Homo heidelbergensis* and *Homo sapiens*. A strange coincidence – at the time of his show at Chisenhale, not only could Phinthong see the original skull for the first time, but it was also the first instance of the object's being put on public display, of the two Broken Hills skulls existing in the same city. And as Phinthong notes, both 'came from the same place'.[25]

In a 2013 article, archaeologist Francis B. Musonda exposed detailed evidence of the circumstances and colonial mechanics in which the skull was 'donated' to the Natural History Museum, triggering what has since then been a movement advocating for its repatriation to Zambia.[26] The skull is at a crossroads, its future being potentially its place of origin, and the study of our origins based on the Broken Hill skull will likely be carried over from Zambia rather than London. As for the replica, however, there seems to be no plan.

✳✳✳

In *Memory Dispute* (2017) by Sung Tieu, the question of repurposing and remaking is addressed through two forms of violence in Vietnam: the destruction of its biodiversity wreaked by chemical Agent Orange during the Vietnam War; and the use of acid fluid in skin-whitening treatments. The moving-image work juxtaposes footage of the forest, the river and a monk looking after a temple around Bạch Mã, with close-ups of a young man undergoing skin-whitening. Bạch Mã was heavily bombed by the Americans and the artist was interested in examining how it had 'recovered or whether [one] can still find traces of its harm'. What the artist found most 'mysterious about nature', she said, is how one 'can never fully understand the cause and effects' of one's action on it. While 'on the surface the landscape ha[d] grown back', she observed that 'the soil might have been altered in ways we cannot fully grasp'.[27] It is filmed in black and white, with an atmospheric soundtrack that translates the various intensities of the images. The soundscape produces contrasting levels of proximity to protagonists, or immersion and detachment with the filmed environment, through found and field recordings (environmental sounds or voices from a quiet protest), compositions and electronically altered sounds.

Similar to the sound, outdoor scenes also provide contrast between those shot in nature and those filmed inside in the sanitised context of the skin-whitening session. Reconstructing the situation chronologically, through close-ups, one progressively witnesses the application of a fluid – illegal and bought on black markets – on a man's arms and torso. The gloved hands of a beautician apply the harmful – even fatal – desired product with a brush, eventually allowing the patient to tear off the darker layers of his skin, the object of self-scorn. Two topical questions in contemporary Vietnam are addressed: a traumatic past that seems ever distant from the present, recovered by nature's almost miraculous powers of self-recovery; and the harmfulness of a practice fed by a desire for body normativity, arguably inherited from the colonial past. *Memory Dispute* seems to posit the impossibility of addressing history from a frontal perspective – the recovered landscape parallels an irrecoverable past – the Bạch Mã sequences have a kind of spectral aesthetics. In a similar manner, the danger potentially suffered by the young man is rendered in formal gestures, avoiding any commentary. However, these two questions within the film – of trauma born of colonialism and of nature's recovery – are traversed by the question of toxicity, bringing together land and body as sites of violence, and hence as sites to be cared for and with the potential for reconstruction.

***

Since 2015, under the acronym TAFAA, Chloé Delarue has been developing work that combines sculpture and installation that embodies technological hallucinations. As the generic title of her 'simulated machine bodies' suggests, *Toward A Fully Automated Appearance* addresses the issue of automation and its consequences: artificial intelligence and the limits of human agency, the datafication of the world and cybernetics.[28] The initial experience with one or other version of *TAFAA* is that of its spatial deployment and, above all, its materiality, the latter generating movement between what is perceptible and intelligible by individuals who encounter the work. *TAFAA* is based on a regime of materialities, the different combinations and variations of which are the vectors of the movement between genericity (expressed by the invariant element of the name 'TAFAA') and its multiple individuations (expressed by a subtitle, for example *TAFAA-LAGUNA* or *TAFAA-OVERDRIVE SIMULATION ROOM*). *TAFAA* makes recurrent use of certain materials: latex, for example, with which the artist often moulds objects or surfaces, giving the work an organic appearance, in the form of mouldings that are spread out or hanging in tatters. The effect of this process of translation or transfer is one of doubling, of simulation, or the ghostly presence of organs from the ruins of the 'already ancient future before it occurs', to quote Chloé Delarue. One of the speculative scenarios conceived by the artist is that of a near future when data centres have ceased to function – a hypothesis bizarrely confirmed in reality by the flooding of bitcoin farms in China, leaving endless lengths of wrecked computer racks. Operating as an archaeology of this horizon made of debris, *TAFAA* integrates metal frames, carcasses and hardware – the remains of an infrastructure decimated by entropy and the artificialisation of the planet by capital. Among the array of complex references instilled in *TAFAA*, the psychiatric phenomenon Capgras' Syndrome offers a striking parallel with the work of Chloé Delarue. In a 1923 article, psychiatrist Joseph Capgras described a form of delirium in which the patient believes that their relatives, or even themselves, have been replaced by look-alikes, most of whom have bad intentions.[29] In a similar way, *TAFAA* is the material projection of the double created in a delirium by the planetary cybernetic organism; a relic, in the form of a hand-crafted simulation, of the hallucination resulting from the artificialisation of the globe through techno-capitalist machines.

This constellation of artworks weaves a trajectory between art, cybernetics, human bodies and remains, natural and machine-made environments, and draws connections between Asia, Africa and the West. In addition to the works discussed above, discussions on the life of the White Building in Phnom Penh and on the strategies of repurposing materials by the Senegalese artist Ndary Lô are included in this section. These works take repurposing, reusing and remaking in yet further directions.

1   Stan VanDerBeek, quoted in Gerald O'Grady, 'Stan VanDerBeek's "Violence Sonata" Realized In and On Channels 2 and 4, WGBH-TV, Boston January 12, 1970', unpublished typescript, Stan VanDerBeek Archive, p.3.

2   S. VanDerBeek, 'A Rough Outline of the "Violence Sonata" Concept for TV', 15 November 1969, unpublished typescript, Stan VanDerBeek Archive, p.2.

3   See S. VanDerBeek, 'Culture: Intercom and Expanded Cinema: A Proposal and Manifesto', *Film Culture*, no.40, Spring 1966, pp.15–18.

4   Chelsea Spengemann, 'New Restorations from the Stan VanDerBeek Archive', LUX [website], 6 February 2020, available at https://lux.org.uk/writing/new-res torations-from-the-stan-VanDerBeek-archive (last accessed on 5 October 2020).

5   S. VanDerBeek, quoted in Gerald O'Grady, 'Stan VanDerBeek's "Violence Sonata"', *op. cit.*, p.3.

6   S. VanDerBeek , 'A Rough Outline of the "Violence Sonata" Concept for TV', *op. cit.*, p.1, 'untitled (SV Description)', unpublished typescript, Stan VanDerBeek Archive.

7   S. VanDerBeek, 'Culture: Intercom and Expanded Cinema. A Proposal and Manifesto', *op. cit.*, p.16.

8   S. VanDerBeek , 'A Rough Outline of the "Violence Sonata" Concept for TV', *op. cit.*, p.2.

9   Yuk Hui, 'One Hundred Years of Crisis', *e-flux journal*, no.108, April 2020, available at https://www.e-flux.com/journal/108/326411/one-hundred-years-of-crisis/ (last accessed on 5 October 2020).

10   On the notion of 'biography of objects', see Lorraine Daston (ed.), *Biographies of Scientific Objects*, Chicago: University of Chicago Press, 2000.

11   Jasia Reichardt, 'Cybernetics, art and ideas', in J. Reichardt (ed.), *Cybernetics, Art and Ideas*, London: Studio Vista, 1971, p.11.

12   *Ibid.*

13   Gordon Pask, 'A comment, a case history and a plan', in J. Reichardt, *Cybernetics, Art and Ideas, op. cit.*, p.76.

14   *Ibid.*

15   G. Pask, 'The colloquy of mobiles ', in J. Reichardt (ed.), *Cybernetic Serendipity: The Computer and the Arts*, London: Studio International, 1968, p.34.

16   G. Pask, 'A comment, a case history and a plan ', *op. cit.*, p.88.

17   The replica was included in 'Neurones. Les intelligences simulées', Centre Pompidou, Paris, 26 March – 20 April 2020. It is now part of the permanent collection of the ZKM Karlsruhe.

18   Paul Pangaro, 'Remaking Pask's COLLOQUY OF MOBILES', Design & Conversa- tion [website], 14 January 2018, available at https://pangaro.com/design conversation/2018/01/remaking-pasks-colloquy-of-mobiles/ (last accessed on 7 October 2020).

19   *Ibid.*

20   Andrew Pickering, 'Cybernetics and the Mangle: Ashby, Beer and Pask', *Social Studies of Science*, vol.32, no.3, June 2002, p.430.

21   Pratchaya Phinthong, 'Broken Hill', Chisenhale Gallery, London, 6 July–1 September 2013.

22   Chris Stringer quoted in Josh Davis, 'Dating the Broken Hill skull: Homo heidelber- gensis was younger than we thought', National History Museum, [website], 1 April 2020, available at https://www.nhm.ac.uk/discover/news/2020/april/dat ing-the-broken-hill-skull--homo-heidelbergensis.html (last accessed on 7 October 2020).

23   Katie Guggenheim, 'Chisenhale Interviews: Pratchaya Phinthong' (exh. pamphlet), July 2013, available at https://chisenhale.org.uk/wp-content/up loads/Chisenhale_Interviews_Pratchaya__Phinthong-1.pdf (last accessed on 7 October 2020).

24   See National Museum Board Zambia [website], https://www.museumszambia. org/lusaka-museum-exhibitions-programs/permanent-exhibition-archaeology (last accessed on 7 October 2020).

25   K. Guggenheim, 'Chisenhale Interviews: Pratchaya Phinthong', *op. cit.*

26   Francis B. Musonda, 'Decolonising the Broken Hill Skull: Cultural Loss and a Pathway to Zambian Archaeological Sovereignty', *African Archaeological Review,* vol.30, no.2, June 2013.

27   Email conversation with the artist, 11 June 2020.

28   This term was coined by curator Sabine Rusterholz Petko who wrote about the artist for a group show titled *Me, Inc.*, Rotwand Gallery, Zürich, 2016. See her short text on the artist at the gallery website: http:// rotwandgallery.com/exhibi tions/ group-show-16 (last accessed on 7 October 2020).

29   Joseph Capgras and Jean Reboul-Lachaux, 'L'illusion des "sosies" dans un délire systématisé chronique (The Illusion of "Doubles" in a Chronic Systemi Delirium)', *Bulletin de la Société clinique de médecine mentale*, 1923, no.11, pp.6–16.

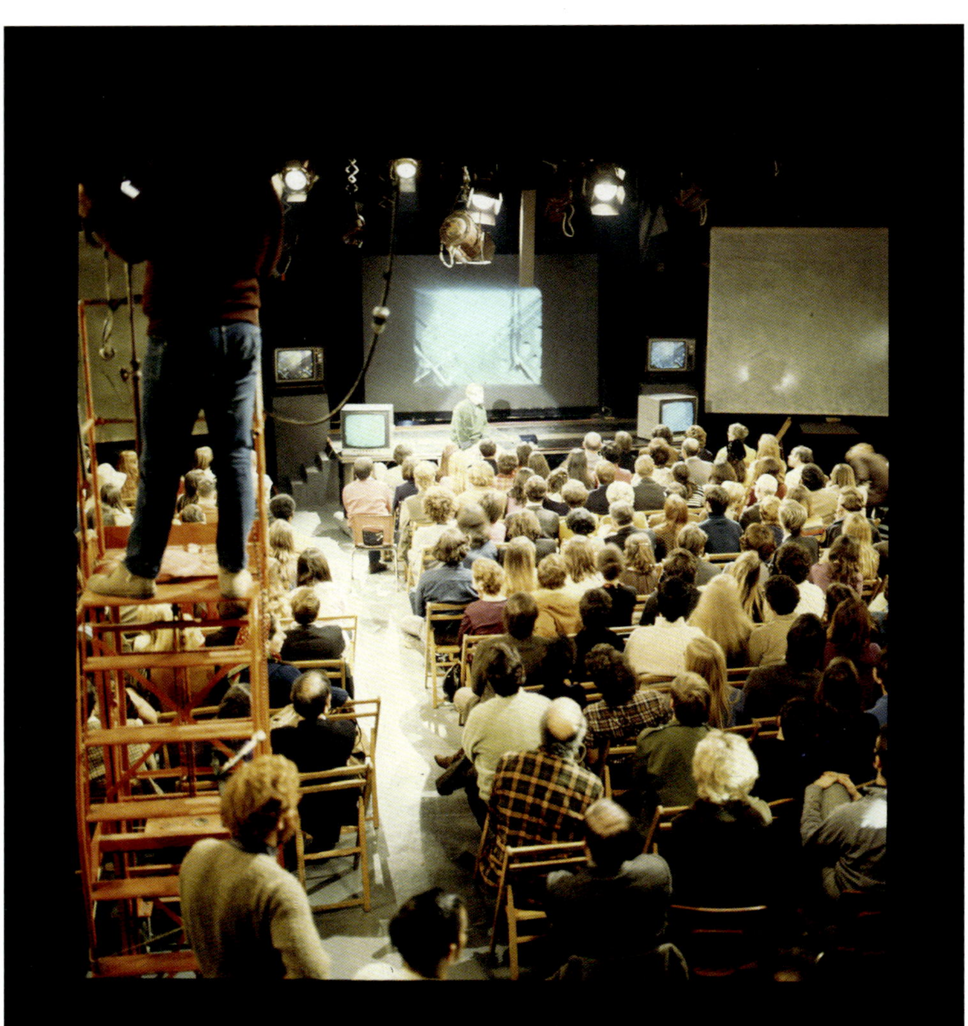

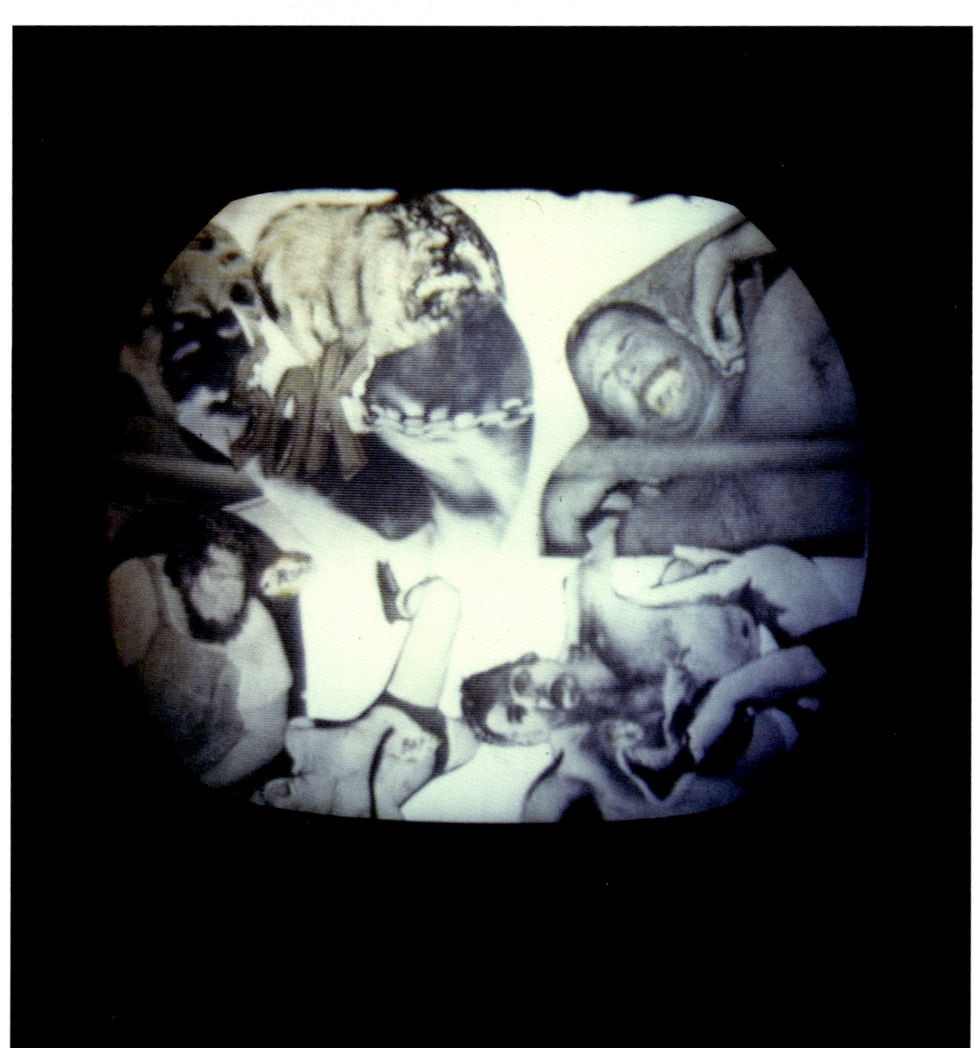

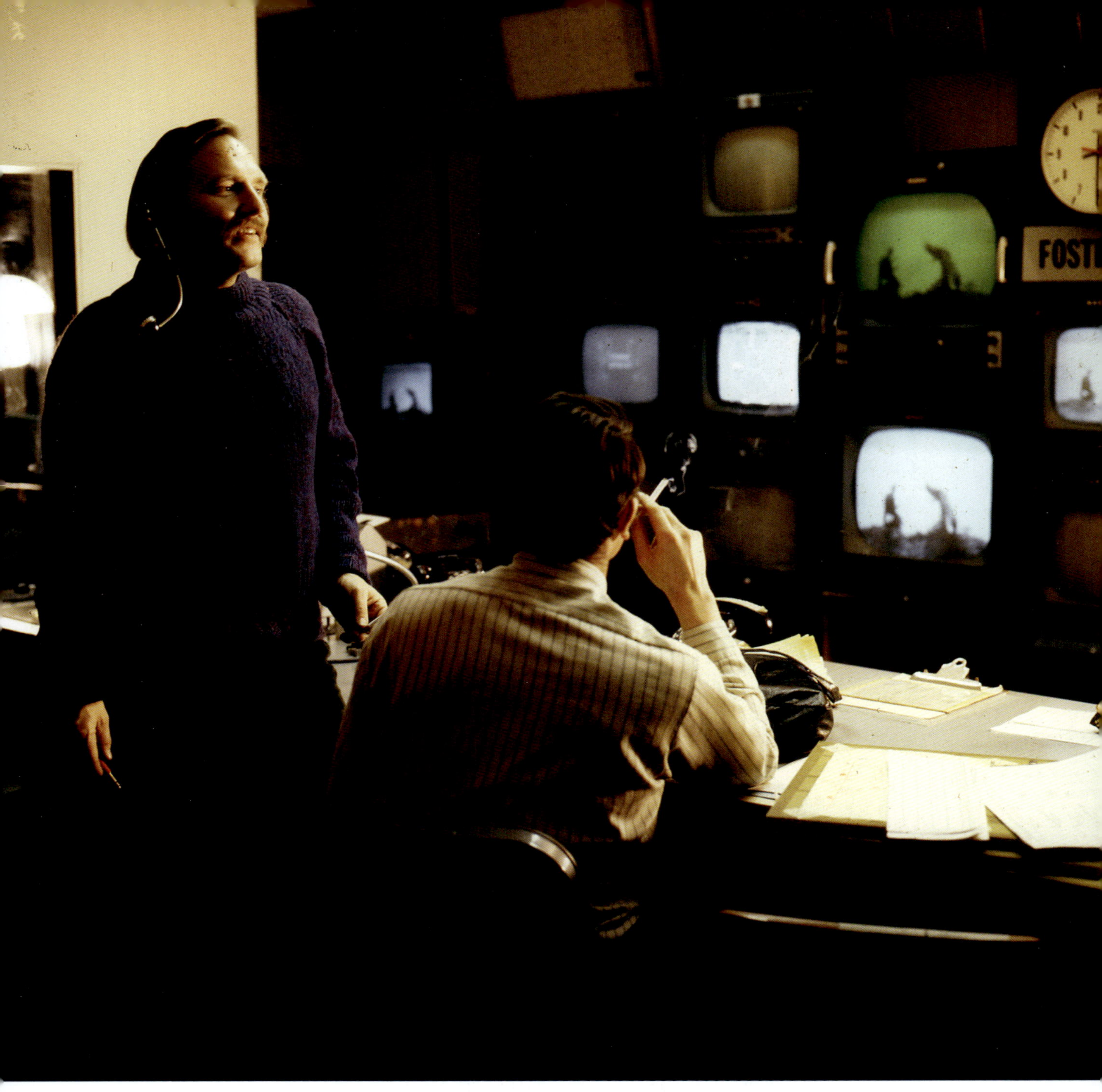

Stan VanDerBeek, *Violence Sonata*, **1970.**
Courtesy StanVanDerBeek Estate

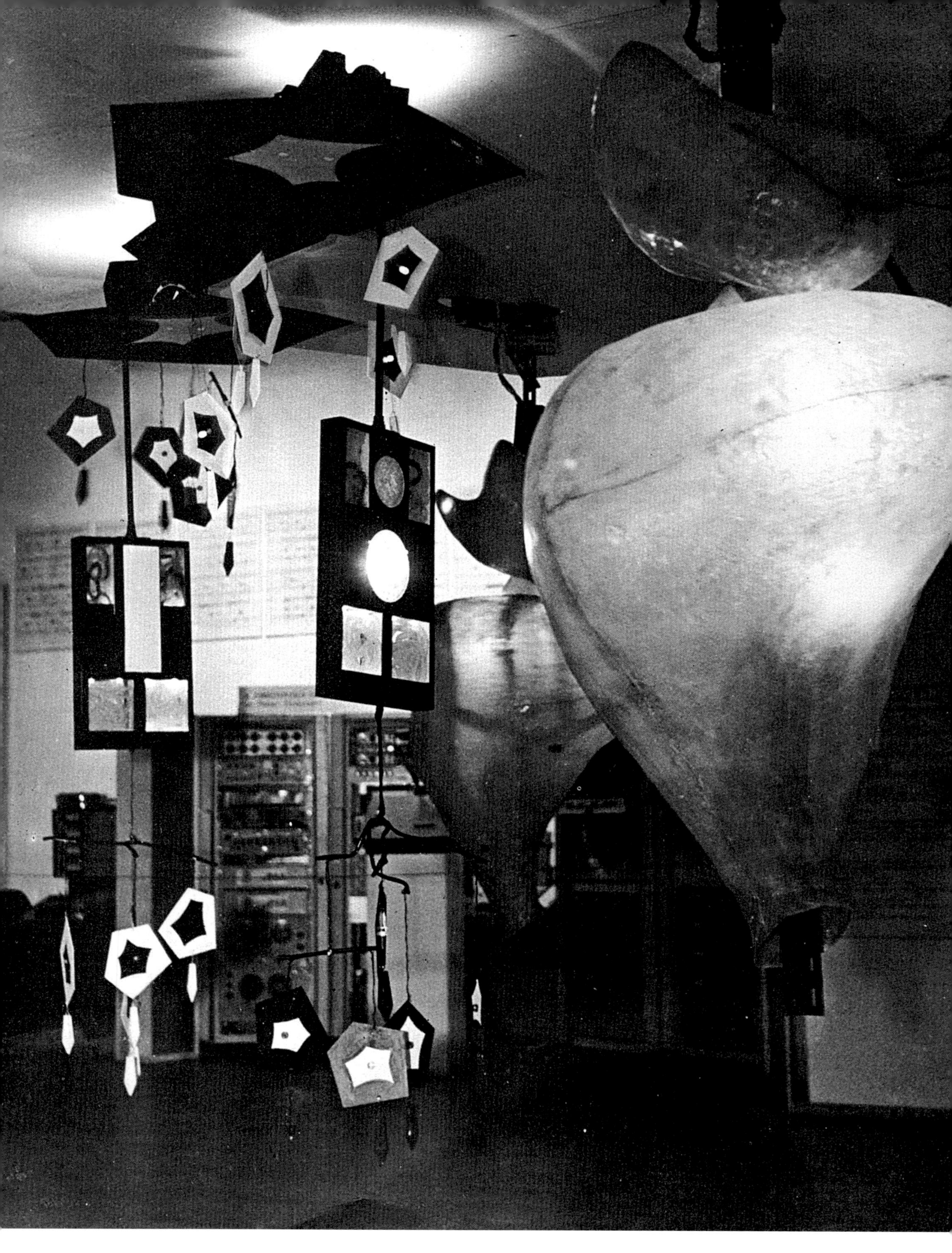

Gordon Pask, *The Colloquy of Mobiles*, 1968.
© Cybernetic Serendipity, Institute for
Contemporary Arts, London.
Courtesy Jasia Reichardt

Gordon Pask, *The Colloquy of Mobiles*, 2018,
reconstruction by Paul Pangaro and TJ McLeish.
Courtesy Paul Pangaro and TJ McLeish

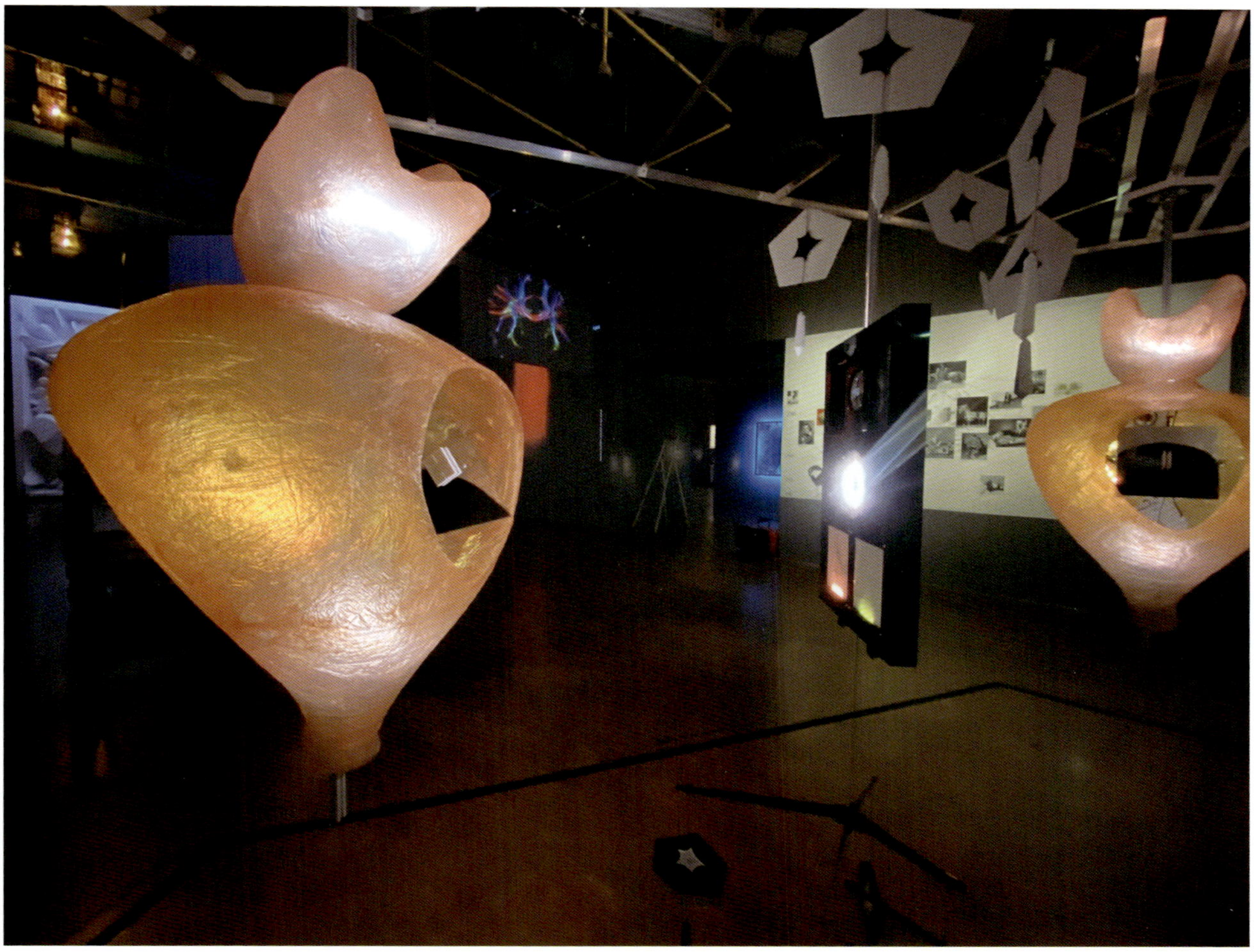

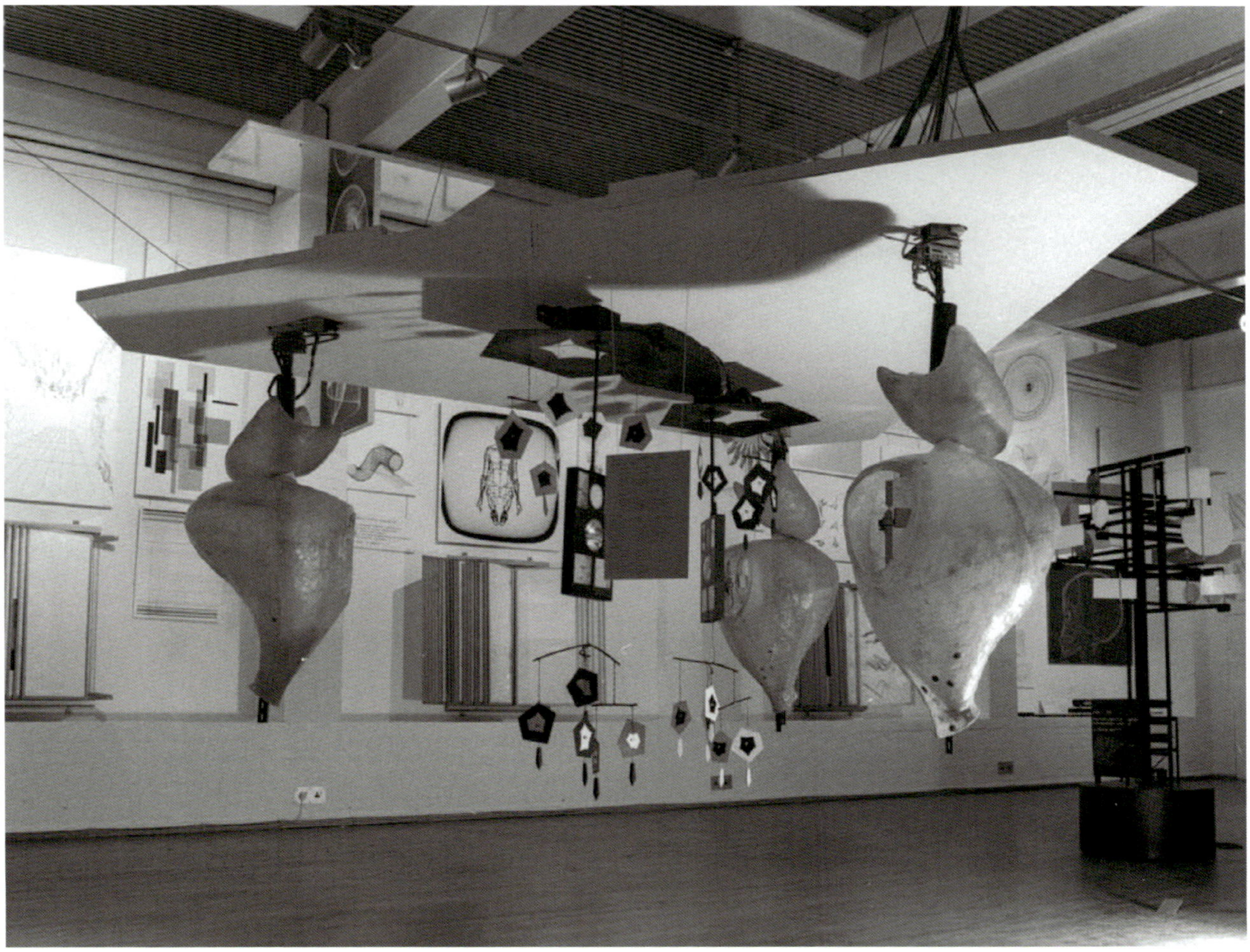

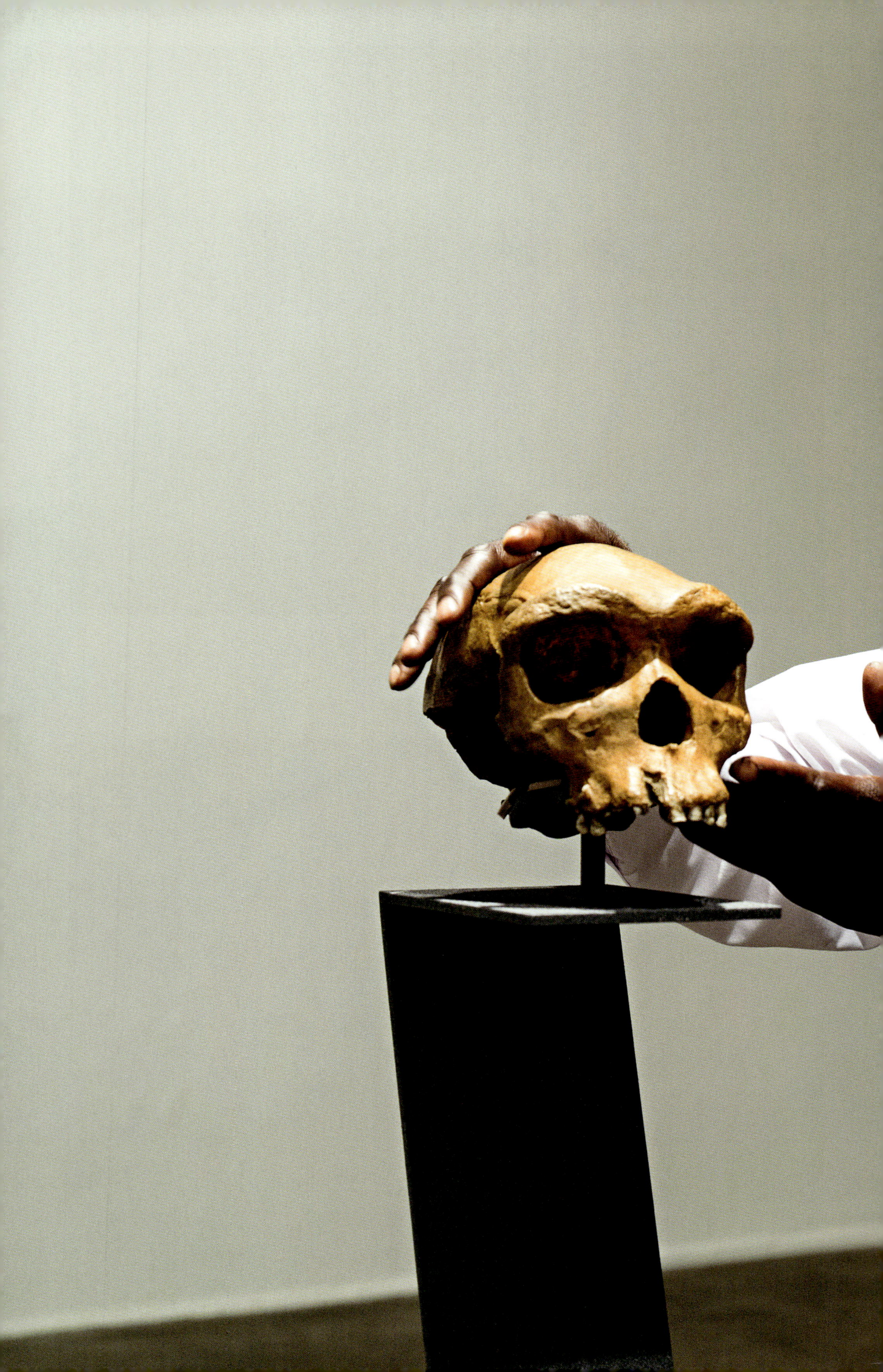

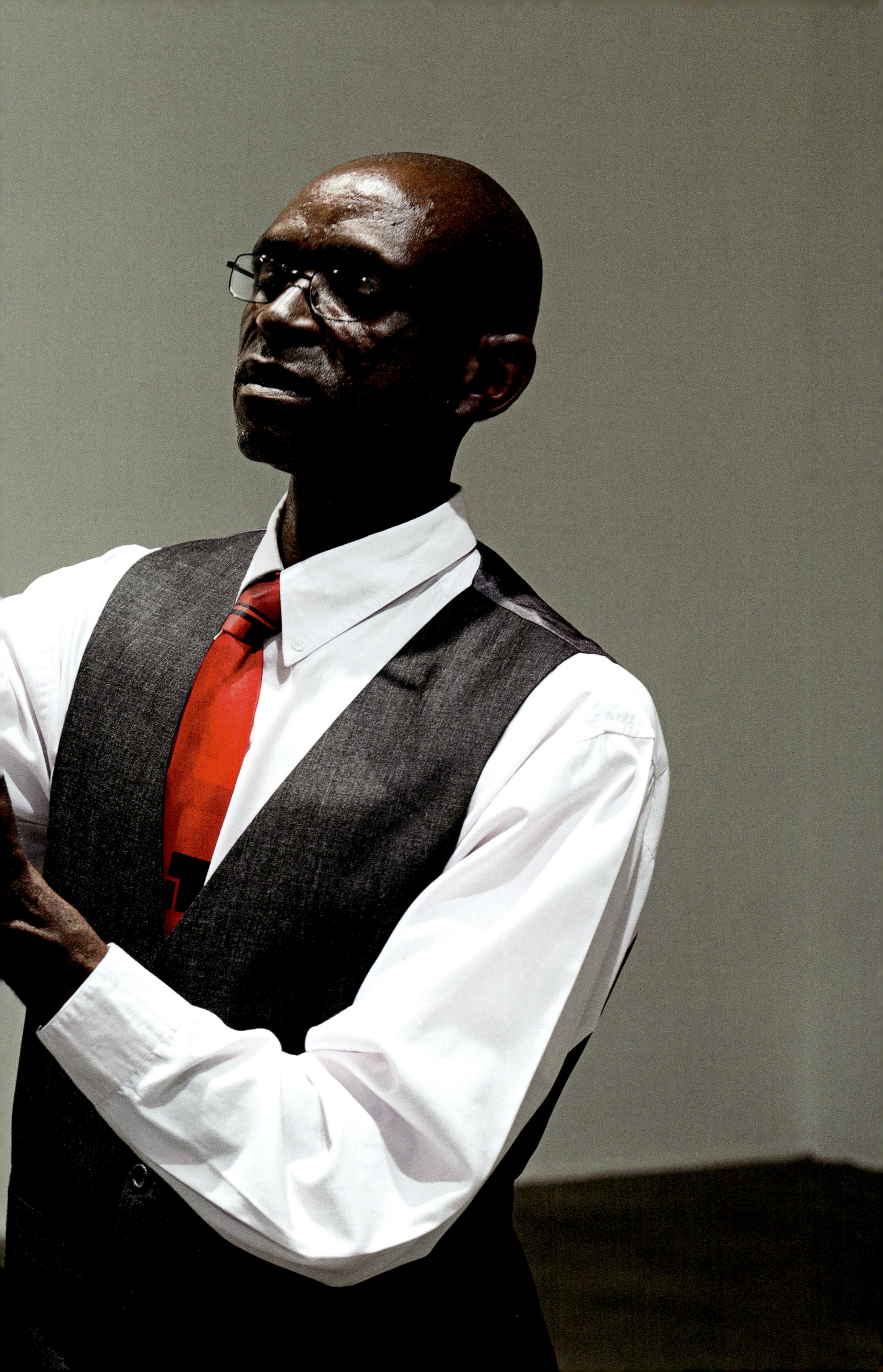

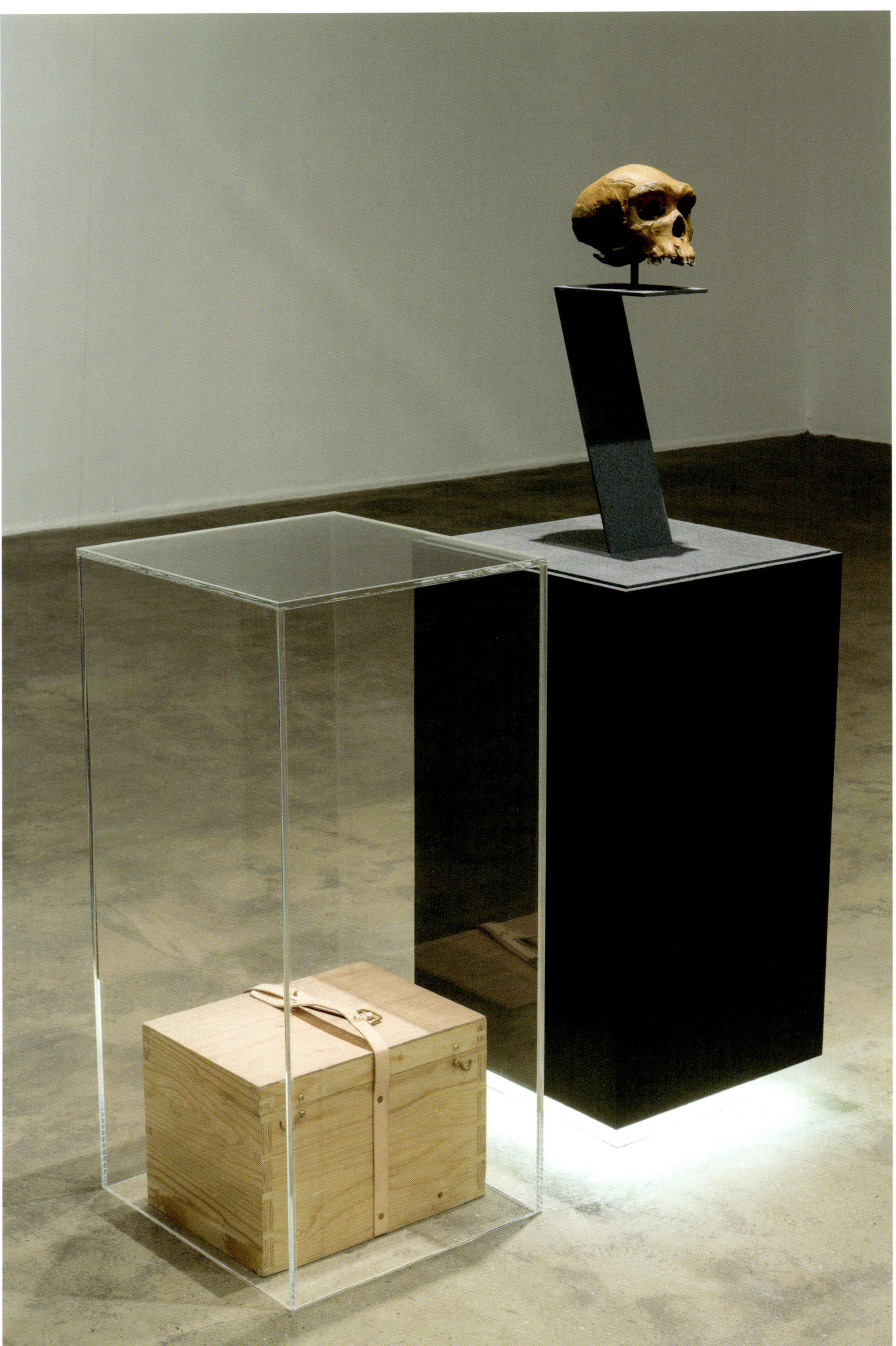

Pratchaya Phinthong, *Broken Hill*, 2013.
Commissioned by Chisenhale Gallery.
Photograph: Mark Blower.
Courtesy Chisenhale Gallery

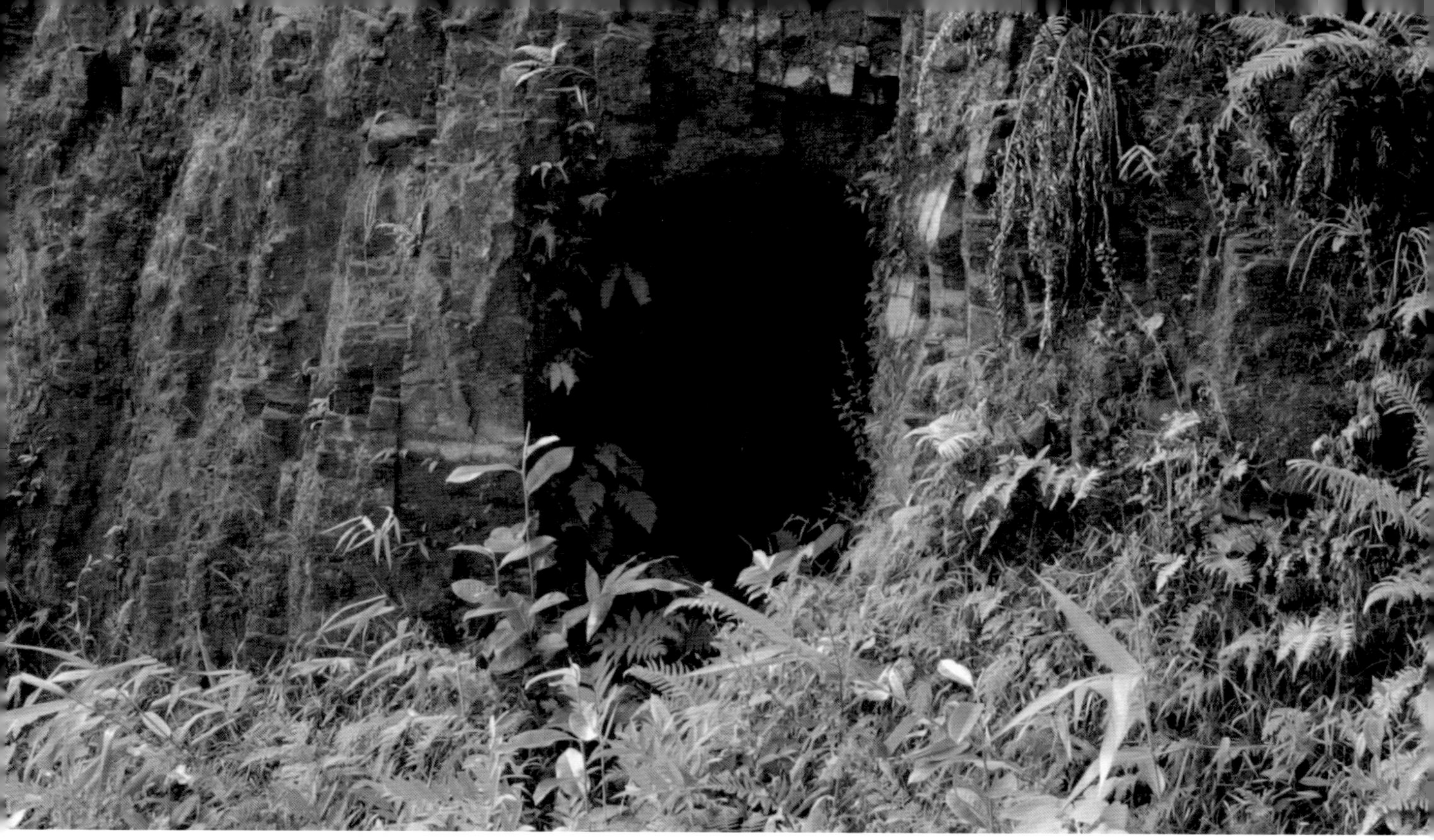

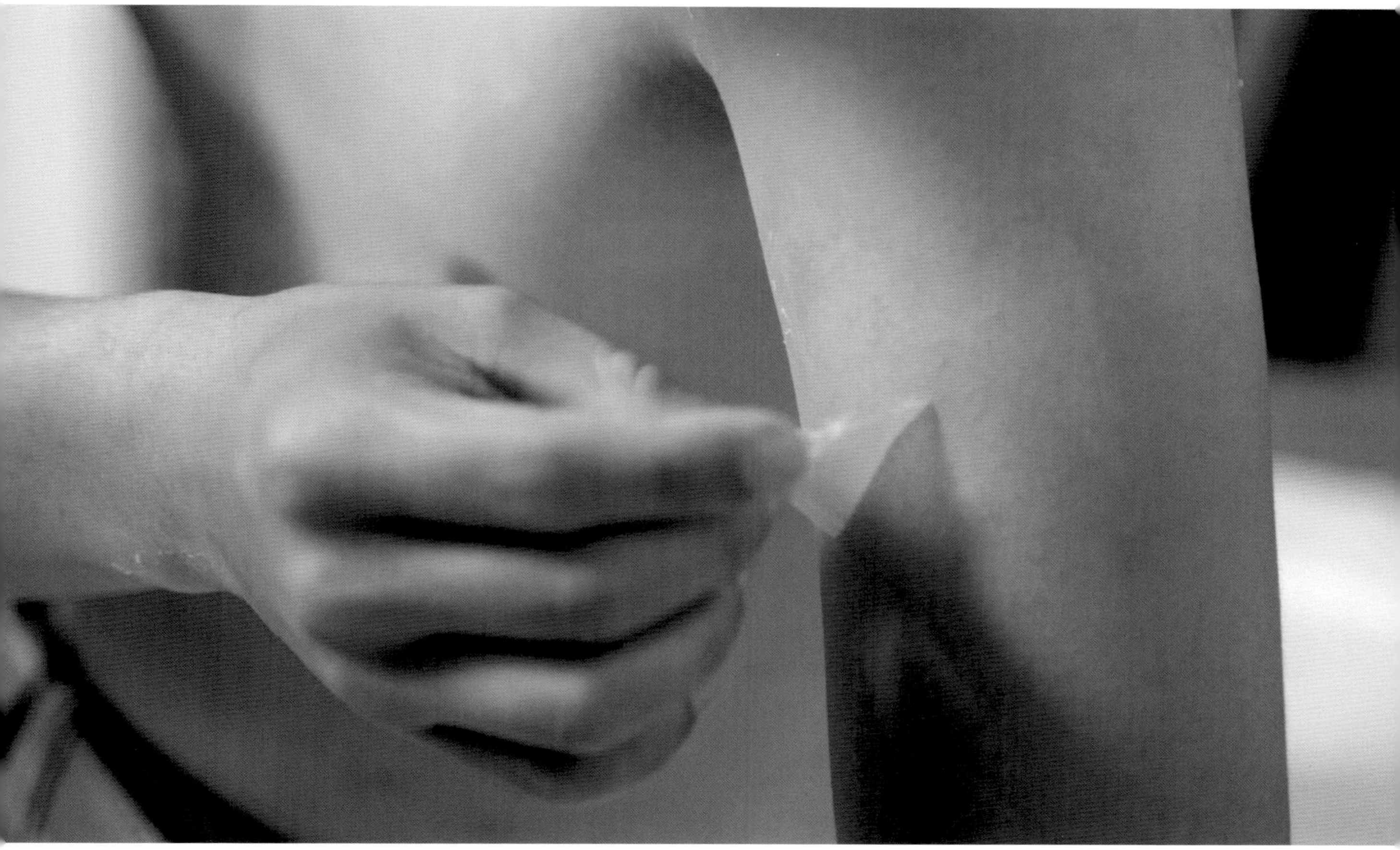

Sung Tieu, *Memory Dispute*,
2017, video.
Courtesy of the artist and
Emalin, London

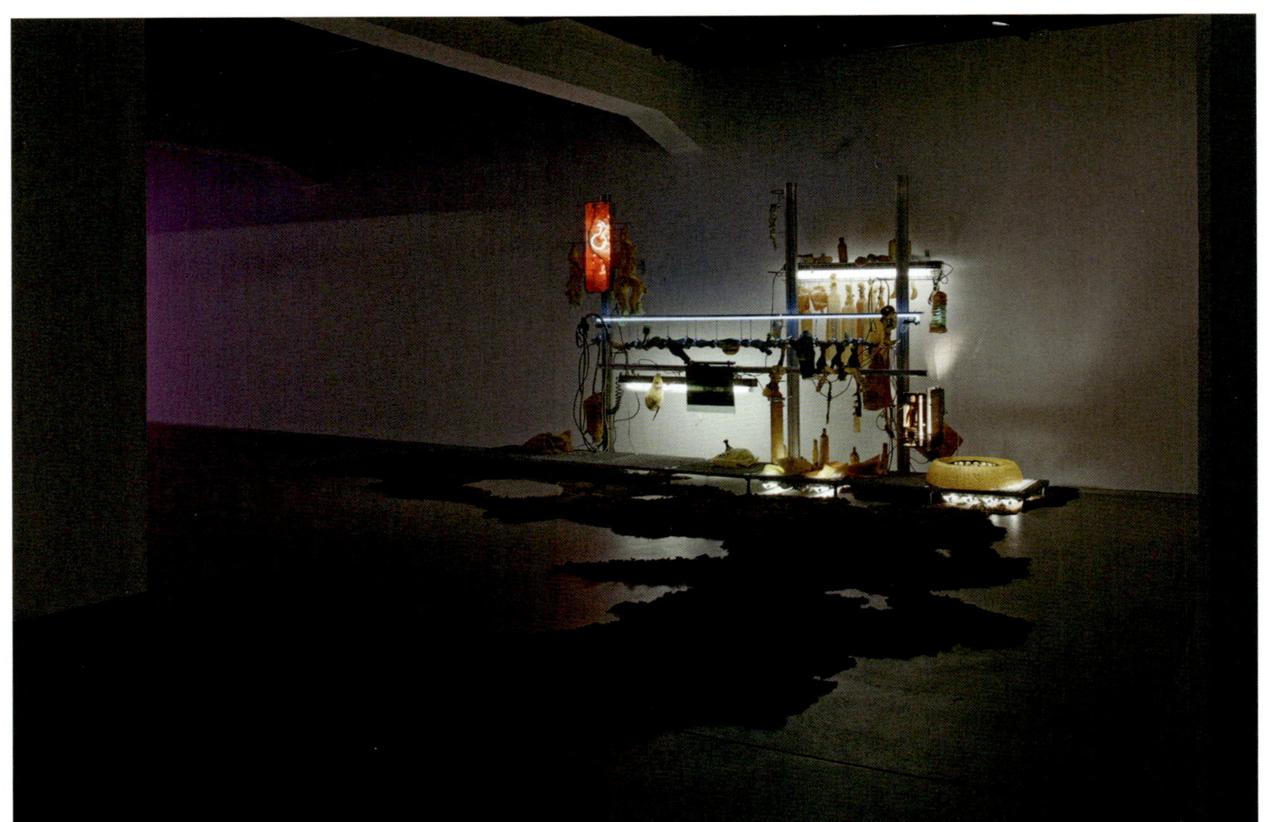

Chloé Delarue, *TAFAA–HIVE*, 2018.
Exhibition view 'Future Love.
Desire and Kinship in Hypernature,'
Haus der elektronischen Künste, Basel.
Photograph: Florimond Dupont.
Courtesy the artist

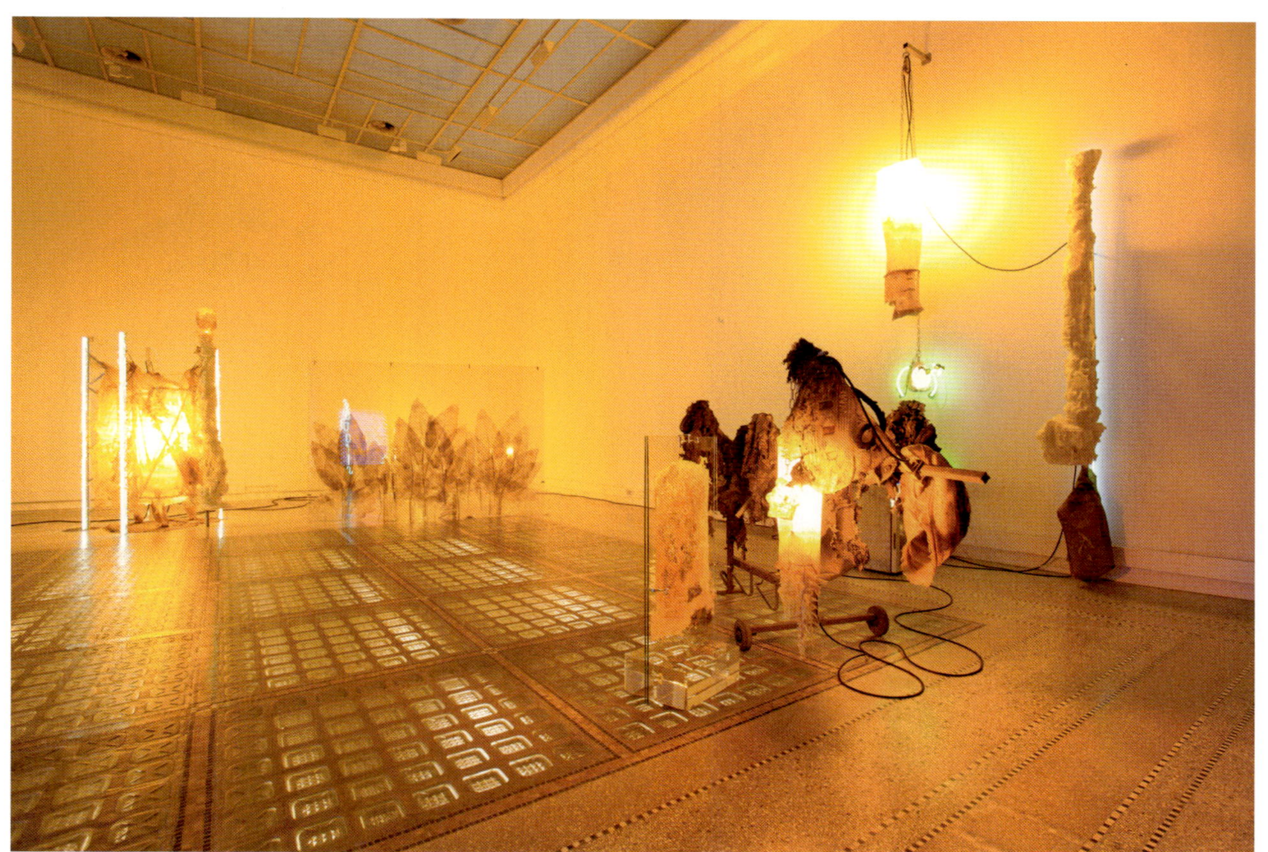

Chloé Delarue, *TAFAA–ACID RAVE*, 2019.
Exhibition view 'TAFAA - ACID RAVE,'
Musée des beaux-art La Chaux-de-Fonds.
Photograph: Florimond Dupont.
Courtesy the artist

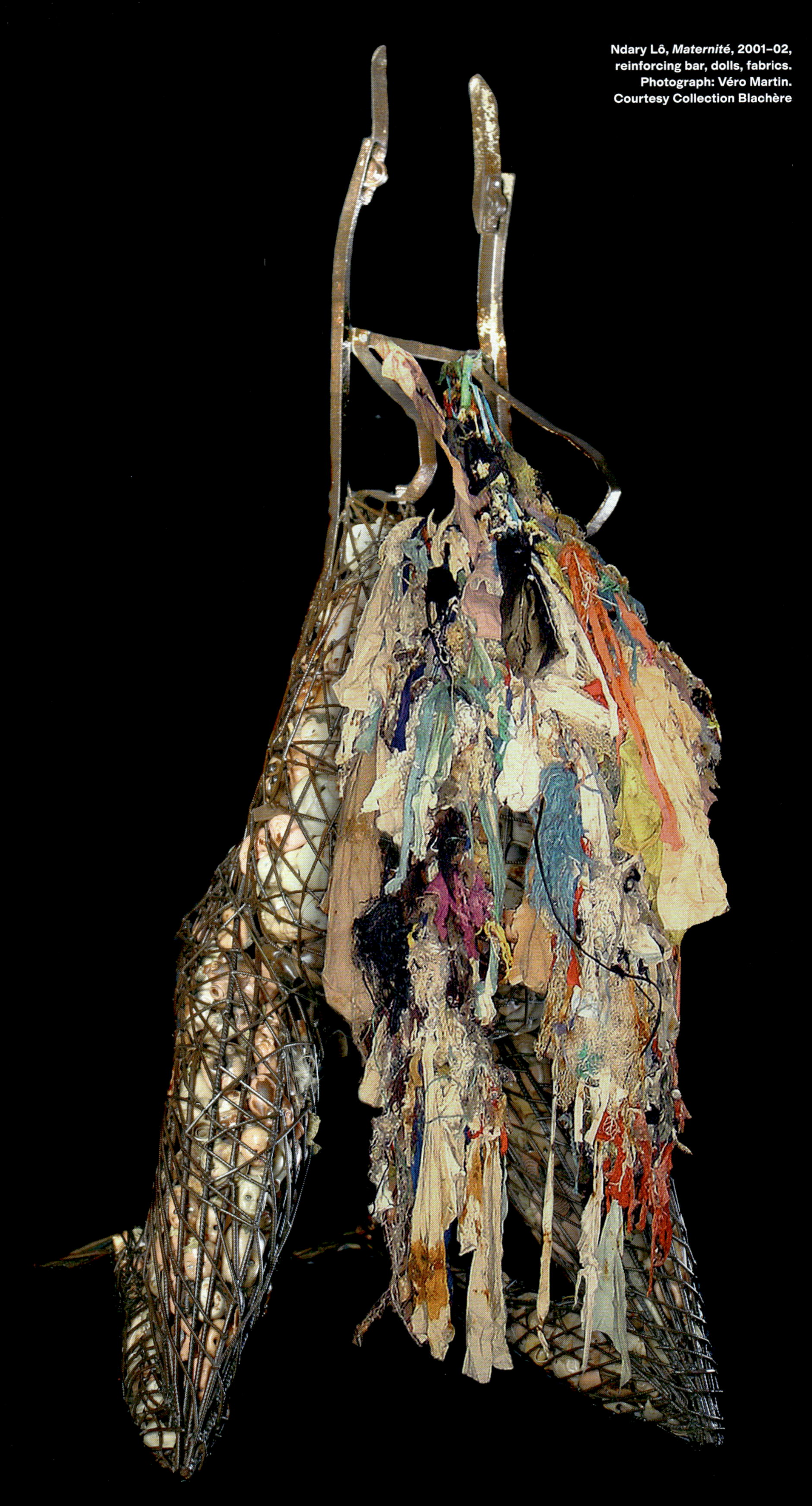

Ndary Lô, *Maternité*, 2001–02,
reinforcing bar, dolls, fabrics.
Photograph: Véro Martin.
Courtesy Collection Blachère

WASTE NOT: NDARY LÔ, RÉCUPÉRATION, AND THE LIVES OF THINGS
Dana Liljegren

For nearly 30 years, the concept of artistic *récupération*, broadly defined as the reclamation and reuse of existing materials, has been attached to much of the contemporary art to come out of Senegal, situated on the western cusp of Africa's Sahelian region. Despite the pervasiveness of related practices around the globe – seen in the work of Vik Muniz (Brazil, b.1961), Subodh Gupta (India, b.1964) and Khalil Chishtee (Pakistan, b.1964), to name only a few – and despite unsurprising comparisons to the Duchampian readymade – *récupération* in Senegal bears a specific and politicised history, the early postcolonial manifestations of which can be traced back to the 1970s. Existing accounts of this practice within the capital city of Dakar tend to locate the term's emergence around the early 1990s; however, even before *récupération* was named as such, the strategy of reinventing found objects for art and performance was often a tactical feature in the overtly activist work of the Laboratoire Agit'Art, a collective founded in Dakar in 1974.[1] In gestures of resistance and refusal, the artists of the Laboratoire frequently eschewed European oil paints and prepared canvases in favour of versatile materials reclaimed from the immediate environment, privileging local resources over imported commodities.

One of the most prominent and celebrated Senegalese *récupérateurs* to arrive during the 1990s is the late Ndary Lô (1961–2017), whose sculptures and installations feature a carefully curated array of supports including reclaimed rebar, old horseshoes, repurposed commercial objects (dolls, shoes, defunct electronics) and organic items such as bones and gourds. Through compositions that range from figurative to abstract, Lô's work offers commentary and reflection on spirituality, humanity and the ecological intertwining of people and things.

In conversation with art historian Joanna Grabski – one of only a small cadre of scholars to undertake an analysis of *récupération* for English readership – Lô described an aspect of his personal philosophy: 'Objects have multiple lives… The first life is as a material, before being transformed into an object…The second life is the manufactured product, the object itself… The third life is when the object is discarded.'[2] Adopting the term *Daptaïsme* to describe his approach to both artistic creation and harmonious living, Lô seemingly understood his practice as inextricably linked to notions of existence and coexistence alike. '*Daptaïsme*, which comes from the verb to adapt, is to create with what is found in one's environment,' he explained. 'This approach also embodies respect and tolerance towards other cultures, towards the other, quite simply.'[3] Consider these perspectives in relation to the theorisation posited by Michael Thompson, for whom the category of rubbish – 'a valueless and timeless limbo' – represents the state through which objects pass in in their transformation from transient to durable; Lô's view, by comparison, less concerned with economic notions of value, suggests an understanding of objects as moving through states of reincarnation or metaphysical transformation.[4] Philosopher François Dagognet, perhaps an even more apt interlocutor to place in dialogue with the artist, mobilised the concept of *réhabilitation* – an apropos companion to *récupération* – to propose an understanding of how artists in particular convert and reintegrate material that has been cast out as undesirable.[5] Consumer society tends to prefer that which is shiny and new, perceived as untouched and untainted; but the histories that visibly inhabit a found object may be productively activated in the hands of the artist.

For the large-scale sculpture *Maternité* (2001-02), representing an abstracted female figure, Lô used recovered rebar for the outer frame, and incorporated the disembodied heads of plastic dolls to flesh out, so to speak, the hollows of the work. The visual effect of these combined objects is uncanny: the rotund body of the female figure visualises the protective states of pregnancy and motherhood; yet the cage-like enclosure of the figure's torso (fittingly described by author Adramé Diagne as an 'iron matrix'), crowded with bulbous, subtly smiling faces, evokes a visceral sense of claustrophobia or entrapment.[6] The grouping of countless faces, fragmented and showing marks of disuse and dislocation, suggests rampant growth or accumulation, almost parasitic in nature. The maternal figure is anonymous in her facelessness, while the dolls' bodiless features seem to stare out at us, sometimes with only one remaining eye alongside an empty socket. They prompt contemplation of the various identities of those to whom they once belonged: Who cherished these objects, and later neglected or relinquished them? How many individuals or distinct locations did they each encounter before Lô brought them together in this new artistic context? Through these objects, the work speaks of love and loss, in the forms of parental sacrifice and childhood innocence. It speaks of cyclical processes and progressions, referencing the biological and psychological arcs of birth, growth and death, while also pointing to the circuitous processes of globalised consumerism from which the objects were themselves ultimately retrieved by the artist. 'I find material and gather it', Lô explained. 'I walk around collecting … the fruit of my environment. This act embodies the attitude and feeling of movement.'[7] This artistic engagement with peripatetic movement can be seen not only in the acts of searching and gathering, but also in the traces of circulation that Lô's collected objects bear.

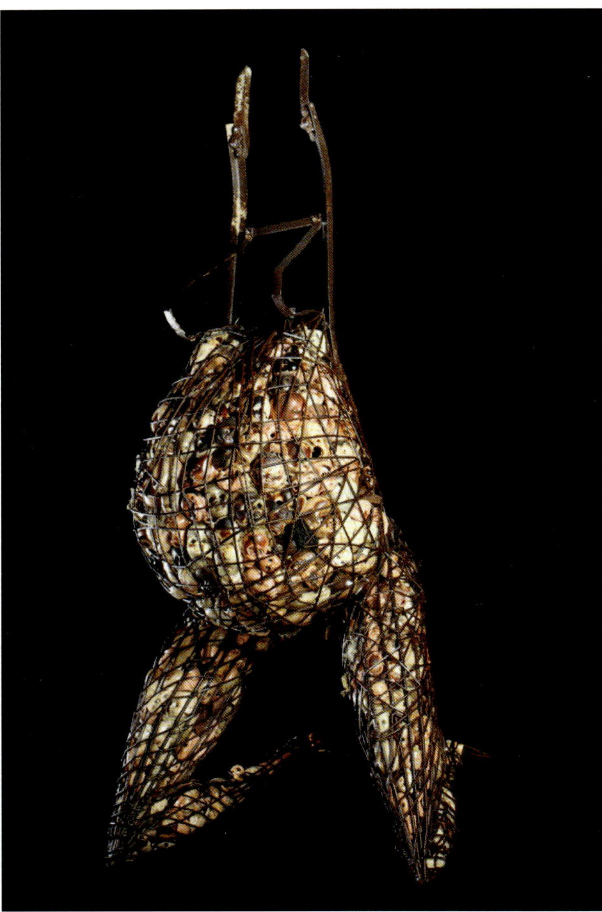

Ndary Lô, *Maternité*, 2001–02, reinforcing bar, dolls, fabrics. Photograph: Véro Martin. Courtesy Collection Blachère

The presumed trajectories of these materials and their various implications and significations, while indispensable to a reading of Lô's practice, are of course only part of his work's rich and layered message. The haunting assemblage of *Maternité* reveals an artistic contemplation of creation itself, and of the ways in which creative processes are constantly cycling throughout time.[8] We can perceive a sense of this temporal movement in one of the most prevalent motifs of Lô's oeuvre: the image of the walking man,

the *marcheur*, a visual trope that is threaded through the artist's body of work from the 1990s until the end of his life. Frequently compared to the skeletal constructions of Alberto Giacometti (1901–66), Lô's tall, slender forms occupy space through a sense of vitality rather than volume, suggesting ambulatory rhythm and forward movement through their spry linearity. The formal similarity between Lô's and Giacometti's figures is notable; but to read Lô's work as decidedly hinging upon that of his Swiss predecessor would be reductive, even pseudo-morphological. Giacometti's emaciated, elongated bodies are often interpreted as representations of post-War trauma, alienation and Surrealistic nihilism, their craggy silhouettes reflecting the artist's aggressive sculpting and reworking. Lô's *marcheurs*, meanwhile, often shaped quite literally by the artist's use of longitudinal iron rods or crescent-shaped horseshoes, impart a sense of engaging dynamism and efficiency – not just through their particular economy of resources, but also by their posture of intent striding and striving. Describing his first voyage to Europe in 1996, Lô emphasised his experience of movement within and around cities there: 'Throughout the subway, in the streets, I found people walking quickly, energetically… in Africa one never seems to be in a rush. I told myself that this is perhaps one of the secrets of the development of Europe. As soon as I returned to Senegal, I wanted to make figures and set them in motion.'[9] Lô's

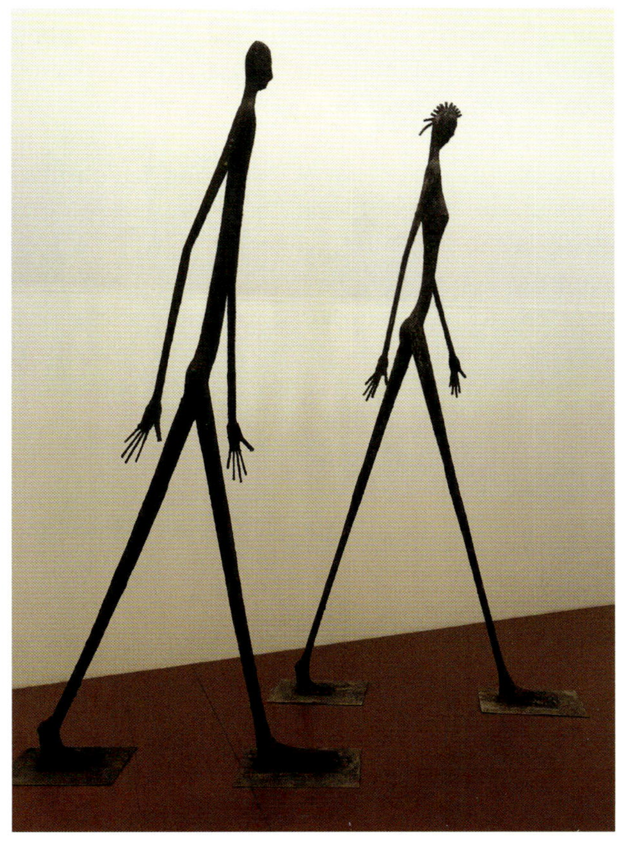

Exhibition view, 'Exposition de sculpture : hommage à Ndary Lô, retrospective', Dak'Art/ L'heure rouge, 2018. Photograph: Dana Liljegren

statement on the perceived connection between energetic motility and European productivity provides worthy insight into this particular artistic motivation. While the idea of European success without qualification is undeniably problematic – it must be acknowledged that this growth has been linked to and dependent upon exploitation of the so-called Global South – we might interpret the artist's words here as a reclamation and poeticisation of his own productive encounter with and experience of motion and migration.

For Lô, iron's structural sturdiness and simultaneous susceptibility to the elements render it a particularly meaningful material for his work.[10] One of his sculptures, for example, when installed outside, may outlive many of its beholders, but not escape the corrosive effects of Dakar's ocean air. The material's intrinsic mutability and responsiveness to nature, rather than seen as deficiencies to work around, become features through which to illustrate and explore an intellectual interest in relentless change, the passage of time and forces of the environment that are larger than ourselves.

The strategy of *récupération* and the critical discourse surrounding it are, necessarily, often preoccupied with issues of art's materiality, its corporeality and the physical realities that contribute to its conditions of production. Part of what makes Ndary Lô's oeuvre remarkable, however, is his recognition of, and his desire to realise, a certain kind of synchronicity between the spiritual and the material. A practising Muslim, Lô acknowledged the potential for contradiction between the tenets of his faith and his investigations as a figurative artist, but described the Qur'an itself as instrumental to his practice: 'I need that inspiration to make a sculpture. I created an immense figure open to the sky, open to the world, open to God. He is in prayer, arms raised, addressing heaven, but I wanted the prayer to be universal. God knows', he said. 'I don't have to explain.'[11]

1   The Laboratoire Agit'Art was founded by the artist Issa Samb, the film-maker Djibril Diop Mambéty, the painter and performance artist El Hadji Sy and the playwright Youssoupha Dione. El Hadii Sy is documented as having experimented with recycled materials as early as 1975. See Clémentine Deliss and Yvette Mutumba et al., *El Hadji Sy: Painting, Performance, Politics*, Zürich: Diaphanes, 2015, p.398.

2   Ndary Lô, quoted in Joanna Grabski, *Art World City: The Creative Economy of Artists and Urban Life in Dakar*, Bloomington, IN: Indiana University Press, 2017, p.161. Additional English-language scholarship featuring or referencing Senegalese *récupération* can be found in the writing of Joshua Cohen, Mamadou Diouf, Thomas Filllitz, Elizabeth Harney, Susan Kart, and Ugochukwu-Smooth Nzewi and Sophia Powers.

3   Ndary Lô, quoted in Marion Brousse, *A La Rencontre des Artistes Contemporains du Mali, du Burkina Faso et du Sénégal*, unpublished thesis, Université Paris I Panthéon-Sorbonne, UFR Arts Plastiques et Sciences de l'art, October 2002, p.90, available at https://douniala.com/wp-content/uploads/2018/10/Memoirembrousse.pdf (last accessed on 28 July 2020). Unless otherwise stated, all translations are the author's.

4   Michael Thompson, *Rubbish Theory: The Creation and Destruction of Value: New Edition*, London: Pluto Press, 2017, p.10. Thompson's book, originally published in 1979, proposes that objects and materials exist within and between states of transience (in which things decrease, over time, towards a value of zero) and durability (in which things' value increases towards pricelessness), and are affected by human activities of consumption and production.

5   See Jacqueline Amphoux, 'François Dagognet, Des détritus, des déchets, de l'abject: Une philosophie écologique', *Autres Temps. Cahiers d'éthique sociale et politique*, no.59, 1998, p.113.

6   See Adramé Diagne, 'Échos et correspondances', in *Ndary Lô: Verticales*, Villeneuve d'Ascq: Périplans éditions, 2004. Diagne refers here to *Échographie* (1998–99) and *L'incompris* (1999), works by Lô that are formally and thematically related to *Maternité*, describing the iron lattice-like structure of the figure's womb as a 'matrice de fer'.

7   Ndary Lô, quoted in Joanna Grabski, 'Urban Claims and Visual Sources in the Making of Dakar's Art World City', *Art Journal*, vol.68, no.1, Spring 2009, p.11.

8   For additional interpretations of Lô's artistic exploration of creation, see Sylvain Sankalé, 'Où allons-nous?', in *Ndary Lô: Verticales*, op. cit., p.29.

9   Ndary Lô, quoted in Yacouba Konaté, 'Afrique ! Lève-toi et marche', *Ndary Lô: Verticales*, op.cit., pp.7–8.

10 See Sylvain Sankalé, 'Où allons-nous?', in *Ndary Lô: Verticales*, op. cit., p.29. Sankalé writes: 'It is the humble rebar rod, without which there could be no sustainable structure, but which left in the open quickly completes its life cycle, which [the artist] prefers.'

11 N. Lô, quoted in M. Brousse, *A La Rencontre des Artistes Contemporains du Mali, du Burkina Faso et du Sénégal*, op. cit., p.91.

THE WHITE BUILDING: BUILDING A COMMUNITY, A CITY AND ART
Vuth Lyno

After gaining Independence from France in 1953, Cambodia went through an unprecedented process of urbanisation and modernisation. Many housing projects were constructed in Phnom Penh in response to the burgeoning urban population. Among those were the Municipal Apartments, one of the first experiments in multi-storey, modernist, apartment-style housing in Cambodia designed by Cambodian architect Lu Ban Hap with Ukraine-born French engineer Vladimir Bodiansky. The structure was conceived along similar lines to the Carrières Centrales Housing Project (1953) in Casablanca, Morocco, designed by Bodiansky and others under the aegis of ATBAT-Afrique.[1] The Municipal Apartments, later known as the White Building – in a precarious condition until its demolition – primarily housed municipal staff and then gradually cultural workers and low-to-mid income families who were seeking to own new homes in the face-changing city.

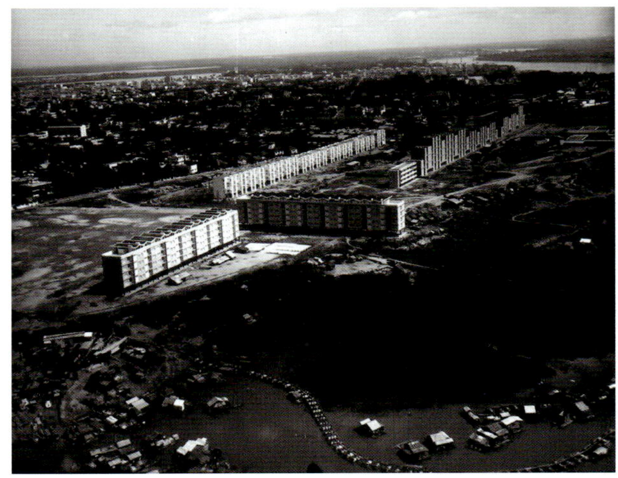

Aerial view of the Bassac River Front with the inner city of Phnom Penh in the background, c. 1960. Courtesy Vann Molyvann Collection

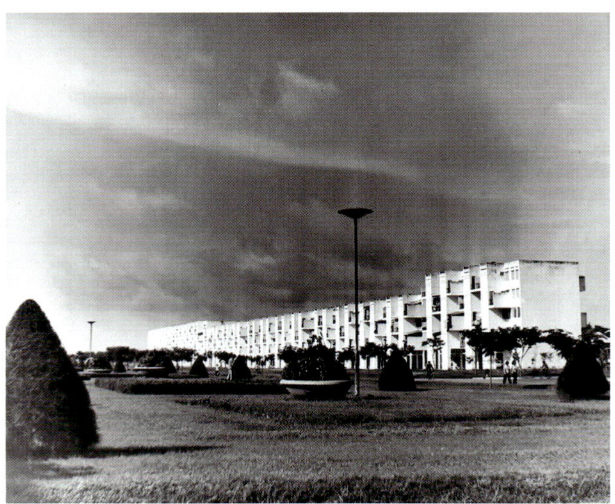

Municipal Apartments, also known as the White Building, ca. 1960. Courtesy Vann Molyvann Collection

The White Building was in fact part of a larger project called Front du Bassac or Bassac River Front, a public and cultural complex built on reclaimed land along the Bassac River. It comprised several social housing structures, a National Theatre, the Sangkum Reastr Niyum Exhibition Hall, and recreational parks. Altogether, the district represented a new vision of independent Cambodia: a pro-public and pro-culture regime, under the leadership of Norodom Sihanouk and his political movement, the *Sangkum Reastr Niyum* or 'People's Socialist Community'. Strategically located to the east of the Independence Monument along Preah Sihanouk Boulevard, the Bassac River Front emerged from the river's waters and was the first part of the city to be illuminated each day by the sunrise. A new future of Cambodia was born. A future that was an effect of the Independence and symbolised by the 'boulevard of Norodom Sihanouk'. By transforming nature (the river) into a built environment for cultural infrastructure, the Bassac River Front offered a vision for connecting art with the public, translated into a physical space.

After the fall of the Khmer Rouge regime (1975–79), surviving artists were the first residents to come and live in the White Building while resuming work at the nearby National Theatre. The neighbourhood grew again as an artist village. Until 2010, it housed a vibrant community of more than 2500 residents, including different generations of artists, craftspeople, cultural workers, civil servants, street vendors and migrants from the countryside. Over the

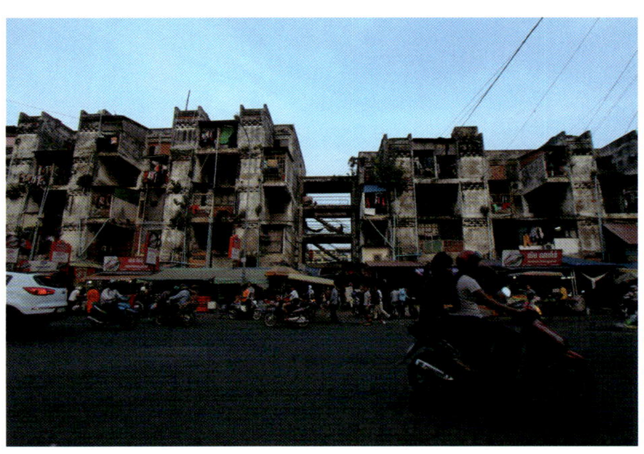

The White Building in 2015, prior to demolition in September 2017. Photograph: Sok Chanrado

years, the residents had altered and adapted the structure to accommodate more spaces for their practical housing and living needs. The White Building had become a vibrant, creative and self-sufficient micro-city in itself, encompassing market stalls, restaurants, cafés, salons, entertainment houses and a community school. It was an extraordinary model of what an urban architectural block could be: an infrastructure that (even if unintentionally) allowed rooms for the residents to further transform and repurpose their space into an organically growing and lively neighbourhood.

In awareness of the White Building's dense historical and contemporary context, the Stiev Selapak ('Art Rebels') arts collective, of which I myself was a part, decided in 2010 to start Sa Sa Art Projects from an apartment inside this neighbourhood. We wanted to revisit the 1960s vision of building a society through public culture, experimentation and transformation of the built environment. We committed to experimental art practices grounded in interaction with everyday, ordinary people and artists from the White Building community, while fostering dialogue with audiences and artists from the city and beyond. We were interested in how art and community can transform each other. We wanted to explore, learn and share contemporary art by experimenting with different modes of engagement other than exhibitions; these included art classes, workshops, residencies, events and collaborations.

The process of making and presenting artworks and events at the White Building was the premise for building a transformative dialogue among the residents, visiting and resident artists, and Sa Sa Art Projects. Previously restricted to the interior space, our events began to happen throughout the neighbourhood. Local students and artists would negotiate with residents to transform their places into ones in which people could experience art. For example, a café was converted into a community cinema screening different kinds of moving image works (including short video documentaries, contemporary video art, educational animation and award-winning feature films) ; the street and the building's rooftop became platforms for traditional and contemporary performances; and a residence's exterior wall was transformed into a living installation of photographs where the residents collected their pictures over time. These kinds of short-lived events produced experiences and conversations rather than tangible outcomes or products. In this case, art enriched the community relationship and, in turn, allowed the community to challenge and alter the art itself. Art was infused into the fabric of everyday life, either becoming a part of life or temporarily disrupting and transmuting it, highlighting the neighbourhood's resourcefulness.

Sa Sa Art Projects operated as a mechanism for catalysing locally driven initiatives by the residents and students. By facilitating relationships between the students, residents and artists through artistic activities, we strived to produce a form of agency among community members. For example, in the *Snit Snaal* (2012) project, twenty young students collectively decided how to present their works in various media, including choosing a title and locations throughout the block.[2] Though intended as a one-night event, the students restaged it the following evening. Through this process of organisation and presentation, the young students involved in *Snit Snaal* not only developed a sense of their own agencies, but also gained organisational and negotiation skills, and performed a democratic exercise at a micro-level by producing a collective consensus. The same year, Sa Sa artist-in-residence Masaru Iwai did a project consisting of cleaning a staircase in the White Building, with the support of some local youths. The event started with the artist and the teens doing the cleaning. Then, one by one, the residents began to join in to clean their respective floors. The next weekend, the residents in the next block of the building collectively self-organised and cleaned their own staircases.

After Iwai's project, many more self-organised and collaborative campaigns of cleaning,

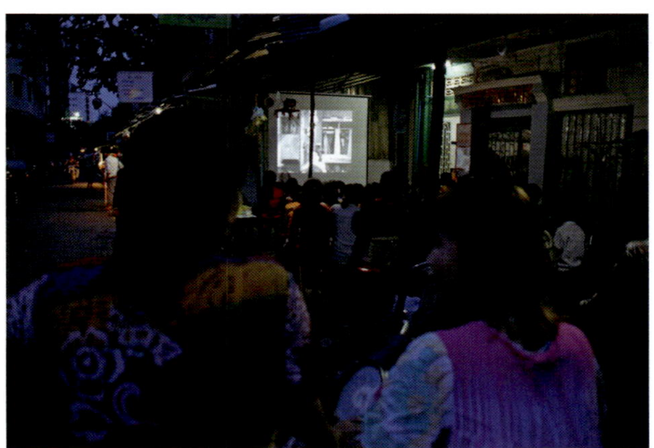

A street-side coffee shop turned a community theatre at the White Building with film screenings for residents as part of Sa Sa Art Projects' monthly village cinema programme, 2016. Courtesy Sa Sa Art Projects

repainting and renovating the open staircases, internal corridors and rooftops took place over the years. These transformed both the face of the building and the pride of the residents. While each of these events alone appeared small and trivial, they gradually accumulated and became a necessary part of the White Building community's advocacy in appealing against regular threats from the Phnom Penh Municipality, who condemned the structure as dilapidated and unsafe. By working on the sanitary and infrastructural condition of the building through communal action, these contagious artistic activities had become an effective means for the youth and older residents to mobilise and exercise their citizenship, and to reassert ownership of their community's future.

The residents' self-organised advocacy against the municipality, supported by various cleaning and renovation campaigns, has helped in the resistance of gentrification processes for some time. In October 2016, however, the city and a private Japanese development firm announced an eighty million US dollar onsite development. On 15 July 2017, the last of around 500 households were moved out of the White Building, and demolition started the following week. Two years later, it was confirmed that the nearby casino had bought the area from the Japanese developer. The loss of the White Building is a loss of part of Cambodia's architectural, social and cultural history and a significant loss of a unique community and organic urban fabric. The White Building was a remarkable example of adaptable urban development and a creative city. Built by an architect, it was only a structure. But it was made inhabitable, lively and meaningful by and for its residents. This should be the way we build our city.

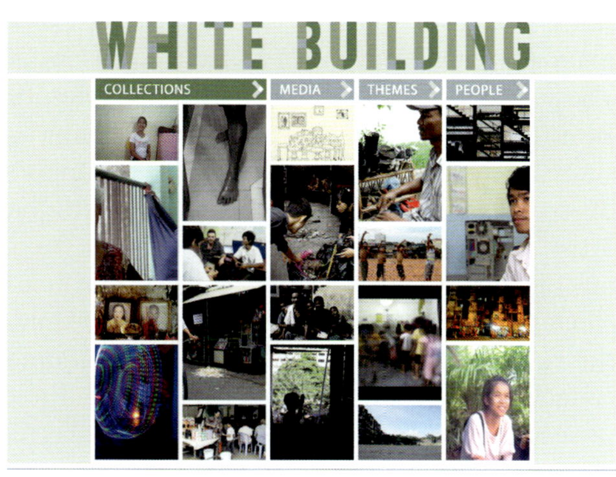

Produced by Sa Sa Art Projects and Big Stories, the White Building Archive (whitebuilding.org) collected audiovisual works produced by students, artists and White Building residents.
Courtesy Sa Sa Art Projects and Big Stories Co

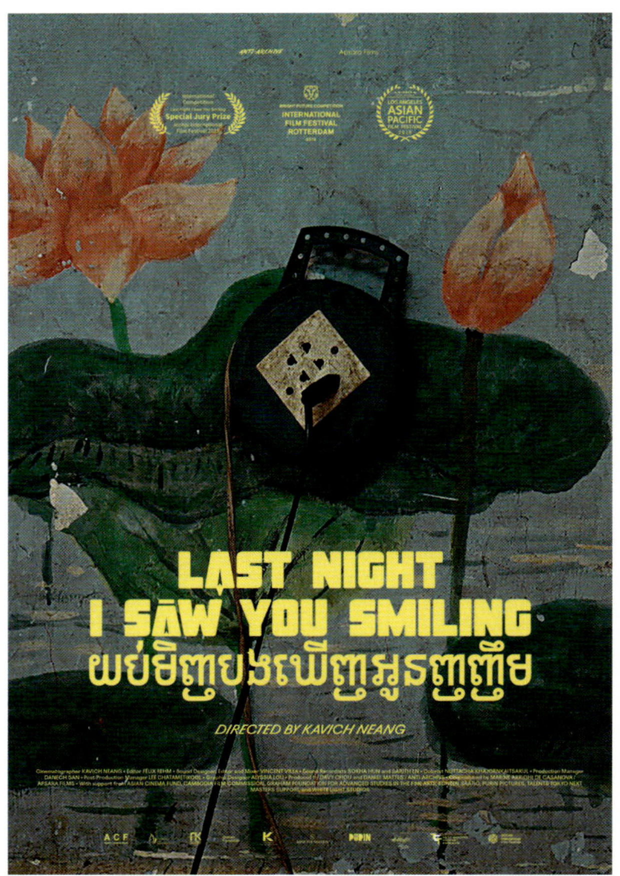

Film poster of *Last Night I Saw You Smiling* by Kavich Neang, 2019. Courtesy Anti-Archive

Despite the erasure of this part of Phnom Penh's urbanity and life, the spirit and knowledge of the White Building community continue. These manifest in various forms, from a digital archive to films and art projects. For example, Sa Sa Art Projects and the Australian media organisation Big Stories produced the White Building Archive, which gathers visual and audio materials produced by art and media students and residents from the White Building.[3] The archive also collects selected materials from projects created collaboratively by Cambodian and visiting artists from the neighbourhood. Through a collection of micro-stories, the archive reflects the recent experience of this vibrant community. Former resident and film-maker Kavich Neang recently produced the video documentary *Last Night I Saw You Smiling* (2019). The film recorded the last moments of the lives in the White Building, following some families, including the film-maker's father, as they packed their belongings and moved out before the building's demolition. Neang is currently working on a new feature film titled *White Building* to be released in 2021.

Architect and urban researcher Pen Sereypagna, along with a group of architectural students and graduates, has produced rich interdisciplinary research mapping a genealogy of the White

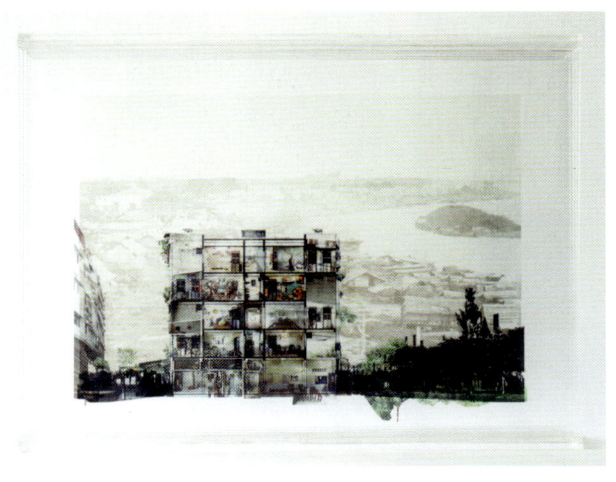

Pen Sereypagna and Genealogy of Bassac, *Transparency of Time*, 2019, vinyl sticker on Plexiglas, 29.7 x 42 x 3.7cm.
Courtesy the artist

Building and of the Bassac area. Through archival and ethnographic studies, the project produced various visualisations of the changing structure, of the urban form and community fabric of the White Building over time. In this case, the recent past converses with history – the resident-adapted place-making complementing the architect-designed built-environment, serving as a model and idea for building a living city.

I myself collected more than one hundred spirit houses from the White Building residents as the families were moving out and transformed them into an architectural installation of shrines. Informed by animism and Buddhism, these different forms of domestic shrines are a mixture of Cambodian, Chinese and Vietnamese cultures. Each family regularly prayed to the spirit houses, telling their worries, hopes and dreams and asking for wishes. So, these spirit houses performed the role of memory banks and witnesses of what happened to the families in the neighbourhood. They were the spirits (in various senses) of the White Building community. These spirit houses were the embodiments of many intersecting dimensions: architectural and urban history, stories of families and community building, the practice of spirituality, and memories of a remarkable, resilient neighbourhood. The installation is supported by a scaffolding-like structure made of recycled windows and door grids from various second-hand shops in Phnom Penh. Hence the stories and memories of the White Building are presented by way of its foundation, through the skeleton of the city and its history.

After seven years operating from the White Building, Sa Sa Art Projects moved into a new home in 2017. The new space is situated in a quiet yet central residential neighbourhood, about 2 kilometres from the White Building. While we lost the majority of our former audience, the new space provides a new opportunity to review and clarify our direction and path. Our goal has become clearer: to facilitate a growing, healthy and critically conscious art community that is actively engaged in the experience of art and in creative conversation, and well connected within Asia. Built on the experience of the White Building, we expanded our art education programme and engagement with a growing community of art students, graduates and early art practitioners through classes, exhibitions, residencies and collaborative projects.

Although the White Building was demolished and its former community dispersed, its spirit endures as a living history, creative memory and as the seeds of inspiration for new thinkers and creators.

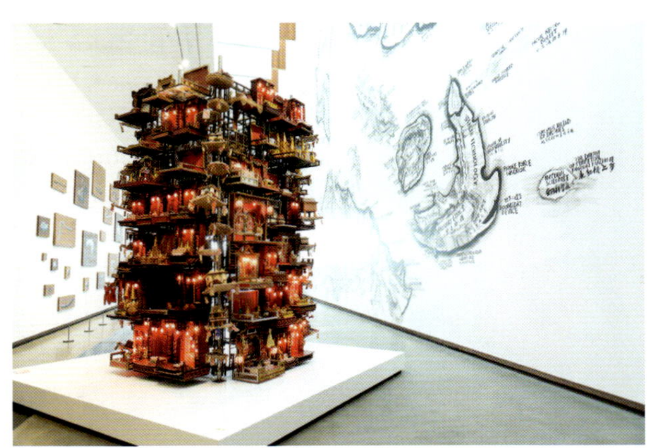

Vuth Lyno, *House – Spirit*, 2018, spirit houses, steel, door and window frames, 2 x 2 x 4m. Installation view, 9th Asia Pacific Triennial of Contemporary Art, QAGOMA, Brisbane, 2018–19. Collection of Queensland Art Gallery | Gallery of Modern Art. Photograph: Natasha Harth

1   ATBAT-Afrique was the African branch of ATBAT (Atelier des bâtisseurs, 'builders' workshop'), a research group founded by Bodiansky with architects Georges Candilis, Le Corbusier, André Wogencky, Marcel Py and Jacques Lefèbvre. The Carrières Centrales was a project by French urban planner Michel Écochard, with Bodiansky, Candilis and architects Shadrach Woods and Henry Piot.

2   *Snit Snaal* translates as 'loveable, friendly, and close'; to *snit* with someone is to love wholeheartedly and trust completely, see Vuth Lyno, 'Knowledge Sharing and Learning Together: Alternative Art Engagement From *Stiev Selapak* and *Sa Sa Art Projects*', Udaya, Journal of Khmer Studies, no.12, 2014, p.267.

3   The archive website is available at whitebuilding. org (last accessed on 28 July 2020).

Francisco Goya, Sacred Cave of Kamukuwaká, Dorothea Tanning, Marguerite Humeau, Morehshin Allahyari, Julian Charrière, Larissa Sansour and Søren Lind

Sleep of Reason: An Atlas of the Philosophical Imaginary

Dehlia Hannah, Ala Roushan, Nadim Samman, Charles Stankievech

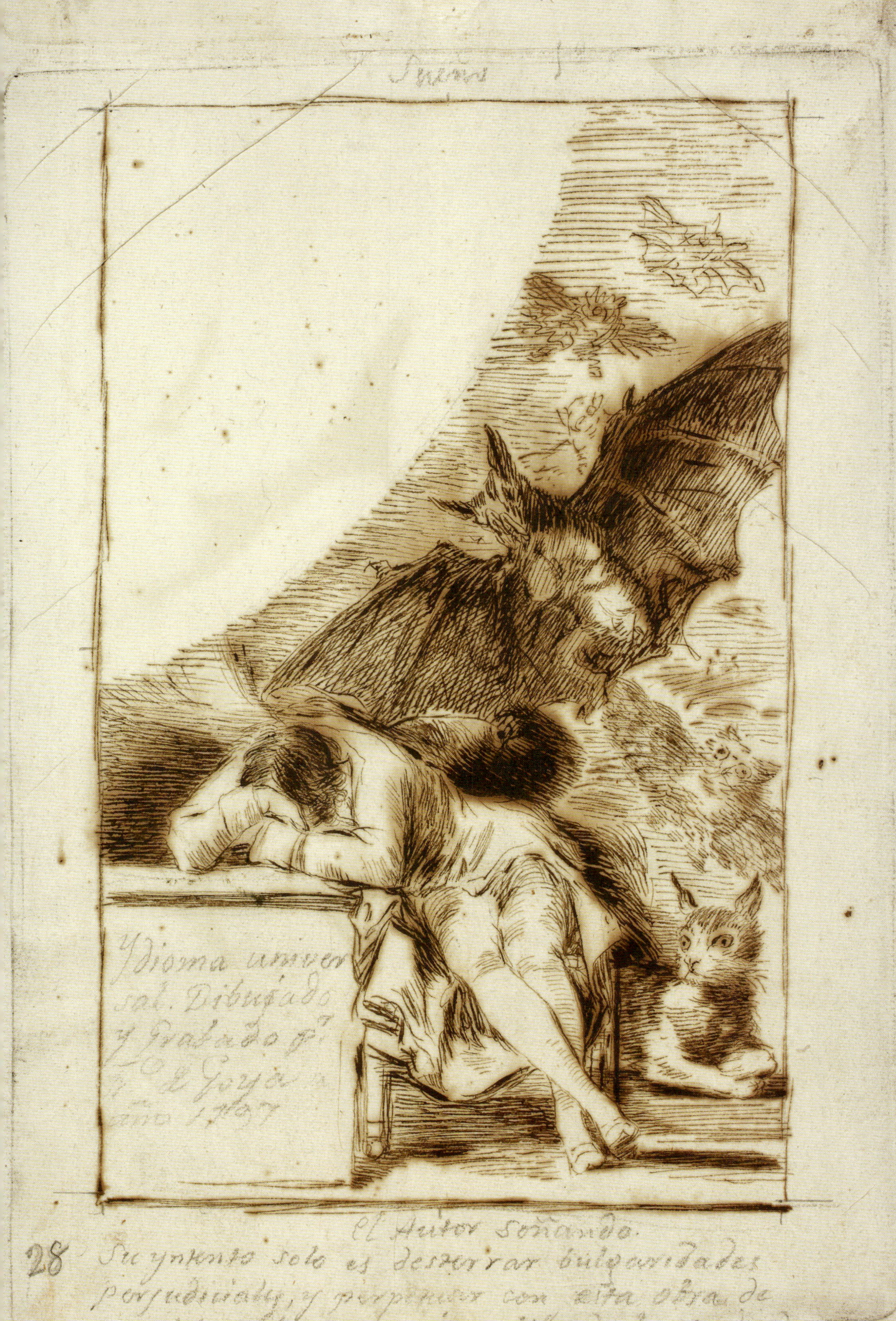

Sueño
Ydioma univer
sal. Dibujado
y grabado p.r
d Goya
año 1797
El Autor soñando.
28 Su yntento solo es desterrar bulgaridades
perjudiciales, y perpetuar con esta obra de
caprichos, el testimonio solido de la verdad.

> . . . after all the will has some say in any decision of whether an individual is to remain independent or become only an integral part of a common personality. It's hard to imagine what basic objection there could be to a marriage à *quatre*. But when the state tries to keep even unsuccessful trial marriages together by force, then, in so doing, it impedes the possibility of marriage itself, which might be helped by means of new and possibly more successful experiments.
>
> *Athenaeum Fragments*[1]

Echoing a time two hundred years ago, humans have once again taken shelter to protect themselves from particles spreading across the globe. In the past, the contaminated air erupted from a volcano in Indonesia that resulted in a global shift in weather. During this period, a group of four writers communing together indoors explored imaginary scenarios – the most popular we know of today as *Frankenstein* (1816–18) by Mary Shelley. Such thinking, in an interior space and away from the sublime, indulges new types of imagination, giving rise to forms of thought that are monstrous.

Moments when humans have been forced into domestic spaces can be identified as long ago as prehistoric times when humans found protection in caves. With a temporary boundary established against the unknown – both the darkness outside and the underworld – our ancestors created rituals and art that attempted to make sense of the world and generate solidarity in their community. In a world rapidly changing and increasingly unknowable – as though experienced from a cave, under siege, in quarantine – a sense of the mental protection from the outside world triggers the imagination. In altered states, we hallucinate and dream ever more of monstrous beasts and places – black swans that don't fit within a clearly established order.

Instead of writing individual literary fictions, the four authors of the following text have attempted the beginning of an atlas of the monstrous throughout philosophical history. Here, we turn to a rhetorical style of the same period that brings together art and philosophy as favourited by the Jena Romantics (c. 1795–1802). While today science fiction (with its stock footage of creatures) is the lingua franca of contemporary critique, we look to a past of critical thinking. In particular, our collaboration *à quatre* has produced the following text in the spirit of the collectively written Jena Romantic journal *Athenaeum.* The result is a reading against the grain of philosophy, with an eye on its imaginary places, inhabited by imaginary creatures, and arguments that might or might not apply to alternative worlds, other clearings in the woods, other caves, other rivers, other islands.

What happens when an island or otherwise isolated ecological niche becomes inhabited by a very small population of creatures who go on to proliferate and mutate, such as in the Galapagos? Does it then become the only place in the world where that particular varietal can exist? Is philosophy not full of turtles, bats, cats, demons and particular species whose survival depends on the rationale of a very narrow philosophical niche? What justifies the assumption that a creature, or a stone dreamed by a philosopher – one which obeys its own peculiar laws, has its own special implications and its own conditions of possibility – exists anywhere else in the universe?

To read philosophy through these imaginary creatures and places – as a collection – whose existence is uncontested only in their radical particularity is to read philosophy upside down. For in philosophy particular imaginaries are always offered as exemplars, illustrations, or applications of some general if not universal rule. But if we take them to have an existence of their own that does not rest on their universalisability, then we find ourselves living in a very strange world indeed. What we offer as a claim is that, in fact, these imaginaries are real and we do live among them regardless of whether they hold philosophical water. If we allow ourselves to inhabit and explore them, and read them as images, rather than as derivatives or additions to philosophy, they might disclose their own implications and secretions.

SLEEP

Francisco Goya's famous print contends that 'the sleep of reason produces monsters'. The implication, of course, is that such an outcome must be avoided. One surmises that André Breton's question 'When will we have sleeping philosophers?' sought the opposite. Though separated by a century and their respective artistic *programma*, both men are bedfellows in their belief that slumber *demonstrates* a rift in being. This idea has an ancient lineage, running back to Ionia: 'One ought not to act and speak like people asleep', according to Heraclitus. For the awake have 'one common world, but when asleep each person turns to a private one'.[2] What Peter Sloterdijk calls the 'pathos-filled equation of waking and thinking' is at issue here. The ones who are awake find little rest. On the other hand, those who do not awaken to the realm of the shared (*koinon*) 'remain in their private world, their dream idiocy, as if they had some special knowledge (*idían phrónesin*)'.[3] Thus, sleep puts the stupor in stupidity and, moreover, the *idios* (the private) in idiocy. But there is more: though living, the sleeper 'touches the dead'.[4] With this turn of the screw, the zombie, contemporary monster *du jour*, is more readily understood.

HEDGEHOG

'A fragment, like a miniature work of art, has to be entirely isolated from the surrounding world and be complete in itself like a hedgehog' reads a cryptic *Athenaeum Fragment*.[5] Follow the hedgehog in its wanderings and the fragment becomes a puzzle piece: in one moment, immersed in the world, in another, a world unto itself. As it moves across its larger environment, relaxed, spines pointed outward in every direction, it bristles with references and associations. But when startled, it lies down and curls itself inwards, becoming self-contained, inscrutable. Philosophy is littered with such miniature works of art, images embedded in texts, which, when poked and prodded, withdraw into themselves to safety. Some contain entire *Gesamtkunstwerken*, universes that threaten to swallow up the arguments that they were devised to illustrate. Isolation, for the fragment, as for the hedgehog, remains a problematic ideal. Drawn together for warmth yet repelled by the prick of their quills, the hedgehog becomes a parable of group psychology for Arthur Schopenhauer, and later, for Sigmund Freud, who kept a sculpture of one on his desk.

WALNUT

'O God,' quoth the Great Dane, 'I could be bounded in a nutshell and count myself a king of infinite space, were it not that I have bad dreams.'[6] Nut dreaming is not inherently bad. Indeed, according to philosopher of science Gaston Bachelard, it has a special quality. Such oneirism goes 'into the walnut's every wrinkle'. There is a kind of exquisite, expanding pleasure to be found within such reverie, 'becoming familiar with the oiliness of its two halves', and endless detail to be savoured. The sovereignty of this becoming familiar may even incorporate 'the masochism of the interior prickles on the shell's underside'.[7] Kafka supplies the example: enclosure in a nut can be dreamt well.

OWL

'The owl of Minerva begins its flight only with the onset of dusk.'[8] Both Minerva, protector of philosophers and poets, and her owl, with its special sight, see *more* than most – deeper into obscurity. Historical

Francisco de Goya y Lucientes, *Universal Language: The Author dreaming*, 1797. Black chalk, pencil, iron gall ink on laid paper. © Photographic Archive, Museo Nacional del Prado, Madrid

thought, born in the rear-view mirror, only unfolds as the light wanes. As Hegel has been taken to claim, a way of life is sufficiently mature to contemplate its own passing. But the night is an image, too, and – more to the point – so is twilight. The latter cannot be taken as a throwaway token, for it equips Hegel's successors (including Hölderlin and Nietzsche) with a dramatic frame.[9] The twilight owl of *Elements of the Philosophy of Right* is, according to George Shapiro, one of 'a few striking figurative passages' that the late Hegel would paint as extrinsic 'to the central structures of his major texts'. But its lyrical force indicates otherwise. Indeed, it appears that the mature philosopher 'may never have peacefully *aufgehoben* the young man who believed in 1796 that philosophy, in order to resume its original role as educator of mankind, must become aesthetic, mythological, and poetic'.[10]

AVIARY

There is an aviary in the mind of each man – Socrates informs the credulous Theatetus – that contains a great variety of birds. Some flock together in groups, others fly solo, 'anywhere and everywhere'. These birds are kinds of knowledge. When we were children the aviary was empty. To have learned or discovered is to have 'detained' the thing that is the subject of knowledge, rendering it unto this enclosure. However, Theatetus is warned, 'possession of knowledge is not the same as having or using it'. Sometimes, when a man wishes to 'capture a certain sort of knowledge out of the general store' (a number, for example) he mistakenly grabs the wrong one. Which is to say, 'when he thought eleven to be twelve, he got hold of the ringdove which he had in his mind, when he wanted the pigeon'.[11]

SIMORGH

In *The Conference of Birds,* the twelfth-century Persian Sufi poet-philosopher Farid ud-Din Attar, recounts a flock in search of a transcendental leader.[12] Gathered together, they chose the legendary Simorgh, a bird beyond birds, enlightened, other worldly, with expansive wings and an intellectual mind. Convinced by their decision, the birds set off on a journey in search of their future, elusive leader. They travel through seven valleys, and at each valley shed a different vice. Faced with difficult challenges (internally and externally), one by one many of the birds drop out, unable to complete the difficult journey. Eventually only thirty birds reach the land of Simorgh, but instead of finding their mythical leader, all they see is their own reflection in the lake. At that moment, they realise a metamorphosis has occurred; it becomes evident that the leader they sought to find is the evolution of their own consciousness, a misrecognition that Simorgh is an external entity rather than emergent from within. *Si* literally translates to 'thirty' and *Morgh* to 'bird'. They were always Simorgh, awakened by a journey that bound them as a collective, becoming an intelligent swarm. Arriving at the destination of self-awareness – and most importantly, doing so as a collective body – allows for the interpolation of a kind of joint spirit and expands on the contemporary notion of a post-human and artificial intelligence as a network. Specifically, this intelligence is an emergent condition of multifarious bodies. Avoiding the typical poetic strategy of creating a mythical chimera as a symbolic creature, Attar's Simorgh never exists, but functions more as a philosophical imaginary among animals.

BAT

We do not primarily perceive the world by way of sonar, or echolocation, though we know this is how bats do it. So, what is it like to be a bat? In lieu of an answer, Thomas Nagel observes that the question itself requires the essential belief 'that there is something *that it is like* to be a bat'. Moreover, as his subsequent argument famously maintains, there is no good reason 'to suppose that it is subjectively like anything we can experience or imagine'. In the bone-dry tone of analytic philosophy, this 'creates difficulties for the notion of what it is like to be a bat'.[13] The implications of this problem are wide. It points to the idea that consciousness is based on embodiment, and that not only is it impossible to know what it is like to be a bat, but that the same goes for a cat, or an angel, an alien or an AI… or even, to some extent, another human as each person senses and processes the world differently through their body.

PLATYPUS
'In an attempt at least to update the bestiary, I have introduced the platypus as the hero of my book […] The platypus accompanied me step by step even where I don't mention it, and I took the trouble to supply it with philosophical credentials by immediately finding it a relation with the unicorn, which, like bachelors, can never be absent from any reflections on language […]. I explain why the platypus is not horrible, but prodigious and providential, if we are to put a theory of knowledge to the test. By the way, given the platypus's very early appearance in the development of the species, I insinuate that it was not made from the pieces of other animals, but that the other animals were made from pieces of the platypus.'[14]

CEPHALOPOD
As we descend into the darkness of the deep ocean, we also descend into an unknown region we know less about than our solar system. Stories abound of sea monsters lurking at the ends of the earth, on the blank spots on maps and 20,000 leagues beneath our breath. Taking different forms, one creature perennially appears in philosophers' thought as an Other: the cephalopod. A taxonomic class collecting octopus, squid, cuttlefish and nautilus, cephalopods share a shapeshifting potential that not only provides them with camouflage and sophisticated signalling in the wild, but also provides us with a malleable monster for our phobias and phantasies. Contemporary philosopher of science Peter Godfrey-Smith has instrumentalised the octopus as a foil for human consciousness in order to determine the baseline for self-awareness. In examining the octopus, one of *homo sapiens*'s evolutionary kin, with a comparably large optical nervous system, Godfrey-Smith fleshes out the levels of feedback loops that distinguish consciousness from self-consciousness.[15] Previously, in the twentieth century, phenomenologist Vilém Flusser imaginatively wrote about an elusive species of cephalopod: the *Vampyroteuthis Infernalis* (at the time of this writing the existence of the species was suspect and almost considered mythological). For Flusser the intention was less about sketching out a realistic description of a biological creature and more about the creation of a monster that disrupted taxonomies and disciplinary boundaries. In an early example of philosophical writing that wove science and fiction together, he imagined expeditions to the depths of the sea to explore the relations between the human and non-human, scientists and artists: 'Whether manned by psychologists, cultural critics, geneticists, molecular biologists, or neurophysiologists, each of these differently equipped vessels will begin to encounter one another soon after they have submerged below the surface. Down below, all superficial categories converge and intertwine to the extent that it seems pointless to insist upon clear disciplinary boundaries.'[16] More recently, feminist and multispecies philosopher Donna J. Haraway has cycled from cyborg to dog to Cthulhu in finding interlocutors for her theories. For Haraway, Cthulhu, an ancient, alien octopus-like monster from H.P. Lovecraft's American Gothic science fiction, functions as antagonist to our human-centric era often referred to as the Anthropocene. Rather than suggesting a critical take that focuses on the human, a Cthulhucene, in Haraway's terms decentres the human and creates a

multispecies network of relations: 'the chthonic ones are not confined to a Vanished past. They are a buzzing, stinging, sucking swarm now, and human beings are not in a separate compost pile. We are humus, not Homo, not anthropos; we are compost, not posthuman.'[17] Poly-perverse cephalopods with their orgies, drag performances and psychedelic dreaming have fascinated philosophers in the past and will continue to tempt them as rising waters encroach our shores.

LEVIATHAN

In an inverted twist à la *lettre* a postmodern Hegel, Thomas Hobbes poetically named his social contract masterpiece *Leviathan* (1651). An ancient Hebrew monster from the deep sea, the name etymologically deracinates into 'connect' and 'serpent', possibly to describe its vast size and shifting form. Originally, in its mythological and religious context, the monster metaphorically represented chaos and evil forces to be overcome, but within Hobbes' revolutionary political theory, *Leviathan* came to represent the social body made up of individual citizens united together under an absolute sovereign that collectively possesses an insurmountable power to overcome the original state of nature: 'the war of all against all'.[18]

ANGEL

'Seventeenth-century epistemology aspired to the viewpoint of angels; nineteenth-century objectivity aspired to the self-discipline of saints.'[19] Mapping the development of objectivity that guided mid-nineteenth-century sciences, Lorraine Daston and Peter Galison argue that while Kant sought knowledge valid for angels in their incorporeal existence, thinkers of later periods attempted to define epistemology as rigorously embodied. Walter Benjamin, famously inspired by artist Paul Klee at the start of World War II, expressed the modern melancholy of a transcendental view outside of historical causation as the viewpoint of an angel without agency:

> A Klee painting named 'Angelus Novus' shows an angel looking as though he is about to move away from something he is fixedly contemplating. His eyes are staring, his mouth is open, his wings are spread. This is how one pictures the angel of history. His face is turned toward the past. Where we perceive a chain of events, he sees one single catastrophe which keeps piling wreckage and hurls it in front of his feet. The angel would like to stay, awaken the dead, and make whole what has been smashed. But a storm is blowing in from Paradise; it has got caught in his wings with such a violence that the angel can no longer close them. The storm irresistibly propels him into the future to which his back is turned, while the pile of debris before him grows skyward. This storm is what we call progress.[20]

GHOST

'One must also underscore the instant immediacy with which, as Marx would like at least to believe or make us believe, mysticism, magic, and the ghost would disappear: they *will vanish* (indicative), they will dissipate in truth, according to him, as if by magic, as they had come, at the very second in which one will (would) see the end of market production. Assuming even, along with Marx, that the latter will ever have a possible end. Marx does indeed say: 'as soon as,' *sobald*, and as always he is speaking of a disappearance to come of the ghost, the fetish, and religion as cloudy apparitions. Everything is veiled in mist, everything is enveloped in clouds (*umnebelt*), beginning with truth. Clouds on a cold night, landscape or setting of *Hamlet* upon the apparition of the ghost ("It is past midnight, bitterly cold, and dark except for the faint light of the stars").'[21]

CLOUDS

One searches the history of philosophy in vain for a cloud that plays host to philosophical argument rather than casting its shadow over reason's ground. In contrast to caves, rivers, clearings, and earthquakes, clouds are notoriously evanescent and changeable, transforming themselves upon closer inspection. They are dark mirrors of the mind's own susceptibility to projection, of philosophy's perpetual pareidolia of causes and patterns within the noumenal chaos of the universe. Just as they might obstruct the astronomer's view of the stars, clouds connote bad weather for thinking. In Aristophanes' *The Clouds* (423 B.C.), a comedic chorus of rain clouds temp young novice philosophers, disciples of Socrates, to 'worthless arguments' and worse – trickery, lies, and seductive oratory. Burping thunder and farting lightning, they play the prototypical role of antagonists to philosophy. Thinking *with* clouds necessitates searching out the oversights and disavowals in philosophy. It is such a problematic atmospheric figure that alerts Luce Irigaray to the 'forgetting of air' in favour of ground in the philosophy of Martin Heidegger.[22] '*I opened my eyes and saw the cloud. And saw that nothing was perceptible unless I was held at a distance from it by an almost palpable density.*'[23] In the philosophy of Gaston Bachelard one discovers the virtues of clouds for the poetic thought:

> The whole world can be brought to life by the command of a hypnotic gaze. But with clouds the task is grandiose and easy at the same time. In this globular mass, everything rolls on just as you please. Mountains glide, avalanches fall and then regain their composure; monsters swell up and devour each other; the whole universe is governed by the will and by the imagination of the dreamer.[24]

It should come as no surprise that clouds serve as exemplars in the logical study of vagueness – and at the same time bedevil climate modelers who seek to predict the course of anthropogenic climate warming. They play a central role in moderating the earth's temperature, trapping heat beneath them and at the same time cooling the ground below by reflecting the sun's rays.

BLACK SUN

Albrecht Dürer's *Melencolia* (1514) depicts the early modern challenge to imagine the monsters of *terra nullius*. Breaking away from the fantasy of religious and mythological monsters, the new scientific paradigm demanded the imagination of new forms of monsters, which continued to play an important function as societal projections of the unknown, only now within empirical and rational systems. The modern self in formation was struck with a horror of the void rather than the terror of Hades. And while the Copernican Revolution expanded our understanding of the solar system, the dark recesses of the mind itself became more and more a mystery. Julia Kristeva sees in Dürer's masterpiece – and the subsequent musing upon the work by nineteenth-century poet Gérard de Nerval, which focused on the 'black sun' in the background – as a potent metaphor for the malaise of melancholy: 'Beyond its alchemical scope, the "Black Sun" metaphor fully sums up the blinding force of the despondent mood – an excruciating, lucid affect asserts the inevitability of death, which is the death of the loved one and of the self that identifies with the former (the poet is "bereft" of the "star").' The Black Sun, for Kristeva, delineates one of the crucial sicknesses of the modern subject, the psyche struggling not with the loss of a shooting star, but rather 'against dark asymbolism'.[25] A nineteenth-century metaphor, the Black Sun's poetic power manifested one of the paradoxes of light as a blinding dark star. In the twentieth century these paradoxes became clearer, fostering a scientific iteration of the metaphor. Specifically, the black hole is a sun so massive its own light cannot escape it, yet we feel the abyss of its gravitational forces. With this updated concept, contemporary Lebanese philosopher, Jalal Toufic, places the black hole at the core of his philosophical system of 'radical enclosure'.[26] In a seminal text on Black Aesthetics, Fred Moten, likewise with poetic and paradoxical power, refers to black holes as 'that utopic commonunderground of this dystopia'.[27] In the twenty-first century, black holes with their event-horizons have updated and imagined the function that lost islands held in previous centuries.

LOST ISLAND
Imagine an island than which no greater can be conceived. Does this island exist in the world, rather than only in the mind? Volcano-peaked, palm-fringed, teaming with life and abundant in fresh water, and as yet unclaimed – the only thing better would be for it to be real. 'It is more excellent to exist in reality and not in the mind alone, for this reason it must exist.'[28] If this all sounds too good to be true, the medieval monk Gaunilo of Marmoutiers argued, it is all the more so as a proof of the existence of God. In his *Reply on Behalf of the Fool* – in which Gaunilo offers the perfect island as an analogical refutation of St. Anselm's proof of the existence of God, which takes exactly the same form – Gaunilo demonstrates that the argument is capable of proving the existence of anything and is thus absurd. And yet, as St. Anselm replies, it matters *what* one seeks to prove the existence of. In the case of gods, as of islands, existence need not be a predicate in order to motivate belief and an enduring search. Of the many lost islands of philosophy, on which fictive societies are founded and sailors stranded, the question of plausibility necessarily arises.

DONKEY
As an absurdist rhetorical quip, Mullah Nasruddin would ask: 'My friend, who are you going to believe? Me or the donkey?'[29] A thirteenth-century philosopher and satirist, Nasruddin is often recalled as riding his donkey backwards... or was he riding forward as the donkey walked backwards? Riddles and tales ridicule and tip the balance of knowledge and wisdom, questioning and confusing the very structure of our reality. The donkey, as both the simple fool and the fool's fool, exemplifies all that we take for granted in our assumptions of certainty. A century later in France, the donkey reappears to satirise John Buridan's moral determinism. In this scenario, when relying solely on rational decision making, a paralysis occurs when faced with two equally valid options. Metaphorically, the donkey starves to death because it cannot decide between two equally appealing options for what to eat. Such dilemmas of action have plagued philosophers from Aristotle to Jacques Lacan, the latter proposing as counter-intuitively as Nasruddin: 'Les non-dupes errent.'[30]

INVISIBLE HAND
'[The rich] consume little more than the poor, and in spite of their natural selfishness and rapacity [...] they divide with the poor the produce of all their improvements. They are led by an invisible hand to make nearly the same distribution of the necessaries of life, which would have been made, had the earth been divided into equal portions among all its inhabitants, and thus without intending it, without knowing it, advance the interest of the society, and afford means to the multiplication of the species.'[31]

RING OF GYGES
The Ring of Gyges is a mythical magical artifact, mentioned by Plato in the second book of the *Republic*, that grants its owner the power to become invisible at will. Through the story of the ring, Plato considers whether an intelligent person would choose to act

justly if they suffered no reputational damage. The tale is described by the character of Glaucon, who asks whether any man can be so virtuous that he would resist the temptation of killing, robbing, raping or generally doing injustice to whomever he pleased if he could do so without the fear of detection. The issue's contemporary accoutrement is a mask, or (in its multifarious sense) a screen, with respect to online anonymity. Notwithstanding millennia of discussion, the morality and politics of this topic have only become more fraught in this post-digital world. Herein, assertions of a 'right to disappear' and data protection gain traction, just as encryption tools and botnets offer bad actors new opportunities to cause harm.

GRIFFIN
Two thousand years ago, Scythian miners worked the Gobi Desert for gold. Relying on travellers' tales, Greek authors reported that in the scorching heat the miners battled not only the blazing sun, but also the mighty griffin: a fierce half-eagle, half-lion hybrid that guarded fantastic treasures of gold. In 2000, classical folklorist Adrienne Mayor argued that the many similarities between *Protoceratops* dinosaur fossils and griffins indicate that the fossils may have influenced descriptions of the mythic creature.[32] A beak, just like a griffin. Four legs, just like a griffin. The thin, bony frill of *Protoceratops* fossils often breaks off, leaving behind small stumps, which may have been interpreted as griffin ears. The elongated shoulder blades of *Protoceratops* may explain why griffins are commonly said to have wings.

CAVE
As we move ahead in time, we paradoxically can look further back in time. The understandings of cave art have radically changed over the last hundred years as better techniques and more diverse archaeological sites have been unearthed. Beyond these spaces functioning as hermetic time capsules, caves resonate with a deep psychology concerned with origins. Whether we intellectually associate our origin with the home of our palaeolithic ancestors or phenomenologically associate a cavern with our mother's womb, the space of the cave holds a deep place in the imagination. Typically, research into caves and their ancient artifacts is the domain of archaeologists and anthropologists, but in the middle of the twentieth century, French philosopher Georges Bataille wrote the text for the first colour reproductions of the then newly discovered cave paintings at Lascaux. Rejecting earlier theories that cave paintings were fearful scratches against the void or magical images for hunting, Bataille argued the images were sophisticated remnants of rituals that established a complex social order, all while developing self-consciousness in the species he refers to as '*Homo Ludens* (Man who plays, plays above all the admirable game of art).'[33] Not surprisingly, Bataille's fascination with the ancient flickering deep in the cave (captured artificially with flash photography) came at a time of rising suspicion of the Enlightenment project (*à la* Frankfurt School). In the aftermath of World War II, the path of reason that first took form in the depths of Plato's cave, moving towards the 'light', unfortunately ended in the blinding brilliance of Hiroshima and the Holocaust. Confidence was shaken in the idea that progress reliant on 'reason' constituted a steady march forward. Instead of fleeing from the cave, such recesses into the earth provided new insights into who we were and thus who we are. Instead of imagining the cave as a dungeon, the cave can become the pilgrimage site for the shaman, a place of refuge and introspection for the artist, far from the dazzling spectacle of society.

LABYRINTH
'To think is not to get out of the cave; it is not to replace the uncertainty of the shadow by the clear-cut outlines of things themselves, the

flame's flickering glow by the light of the Sun. To think is to enter the Labyrinth; more exactly, it is to make be and appear a Labyrinth.'[34]

NORTH-WEST PASSAGE

Philosopher and writer Michele Serres imagined 'The Northwest Passage' – a mythically elusive shipping route through the Canadian Arctic waters – as a geographical metaphor for the difficult connection between the humanities and the sciences. Unlike the islands of Atlantis or Utopia (or other forgotten or unmarked places on the map), The North-West Passage, for Serres, was less a lost place and more a dynamic journey that denied static representation and repetition. From the shifting ice flow and constantly changing landmarks to the extremes of darkness and the blinding glimmers, Serres found in the paradoxical descriptions of the passage apt metaphors for the challenges one must go through in a search for the connection between two worlds. Once a naval officer himself, Serres took the experiences of his personal voyages and allegorically mapped them to The North-West Passage to impress upon the reader:

> . . . that the passage is rare and narrow. It is not secured in its great width as by a flat sea without reef, as by a running strait. From human sciences to exact sciences, or inversely, the path does not cross a homogeneous and empty space. The metaphor of this extraordinarily complicated archipelago of the Canadian Far North, most often encumbered with ice, is correct. Most often, the passage is closed, either by land, or by ice, or also because we get lost. And if the passage is open, it is along a difficult path to predict.[35]

Such a description was a meta-metaphor, describing the difficulty even of the method of analogy itself, which must be traversed anew each time it is encountered. Among Serres's attempted journeys through metaphor, one could list many other monsters: the Parasite, Noise, Harlequin, Hermes, Angel, Quasi-Crystal – each its own island in the archipelago of The North-West Passage.

ISLAND

> We have now not merely explored the territory of pure understanding, and carefully surveyed every part of it, but have also measured its extent, as assigned to everything its rightful place. This domain is an island, enclosed by nature itself within unalterable limits. It is the land of truth – enchanting name! – a surrounded by a wide and stormy ocean, the native home of illusion, where many a fog bank and many a swiftly melting iceberg give the deceptive appearance of farther shores, deluding the adventurous seafarer ever anew with empty hopes, and engaging him in enterprises which he can never abandon and yet is unable to carry to completion.[36]

In a surprising passage in the *Critique of Pure Reason*, a philosophical study in the limits of knowledge, Kant proffers an evocative image of the mind itself as an island shrouded in mist and surrounded by seductive seas. Blurring the island's shoreline, fog obscures the horizons of thought, tempting the mind to overstep its bounds and mistake vague understanding for well-grounded knowledge. Through this analogy, the philosophical imperative to survey the island – to correctly discern what can be known from its highest vantage point, who inhabits it, and by what right we can rest upon it – echoes an anxious colonial disposition of entitlement. A thick fog doubles as a projection screen for latent desires and unchecked assumptions. Thus, as Michèle Le Doeuff argues, Kant's island embeds an implicit castration of reason upon the shores of the reality principle.[37] Where the horizon is obscured, one ought not only to peer more intently into the mist, but also find compensatory pleasure in the sure footing of the ground beneath one's feet.

DUST
Dust to Dust, Ashes to Ashes. Our lives begin and end in the quotidian materiality of dust. It comes as no surprise that one of the oldest philosophical models of reality aligns with our everyday observation of particles on the verge of invisibility. Constantly moving, in swirls and drifts, dust became knowingly or perhaps unknowingly the model for the abstract theories of the ancient Atomists. In one poetic image, such a theory of the physical universe appeased its own paradoxes, intuitively accounting for both material determinism *and* free will. As Gaston Bachelard observed, 'The entire set of departures from usual laws, when manifested in the aerial play of dust, is precisely what makes its intuition so appropriate. The speck of dust, in particular, departs from the general law of gravity. For a truly primal intuition, need it be noted, it floats in a *void*; it follows its fancy. Of course, it responds to puffs, but with what freedom! It illustrates the *clinamen*.'[38] Much like the current debate around whether light is a particle or a wave, dust lingers on the threshold of order and chaos, destruction and immutability. Dust's power resides in never being singular. As an infinitely amorphous body it manifests as dust-devils, shifting dunes, rapid prototypes and layers of time. A timeless foe – older than the grim reaper, conquer of *Ozymandias* – dust is the endgame of one's destruction while being indestructible itself.[39]

METEORITE
We can excavate meteorite fragments from the early narratives of several religious traditions: Aztecs pointing to the sky as the source of their weapons, Ancient Greeks worshiping meteorites in temples, the Wormwood falling star in the Apocalypse, Jacob sleeping on a stone that opens to heaven and Muhammad placing the Black Stone at Mecca. An aerolith's power was directly witnessed in their explosive impact. Maintained as heavenly objects up until the early nineteenth century, their role in philosophy is more tortuous. The first recorded meteorite fall was in China c. 500 BCE by Confucius, relatively concurrent with Anaxagoras – one of the first philosophers to argue for a 'scientific' understanding of the world. A proto-scientist, the pre-Socratic thinker discussed the extraterrestrial origin of meteorites alongside accurate speculation of the topography of the moon.[40] Under the heretical threat of atheism, he declared the sun was an ignited rock. Meteorites are of course astral bodies captured by the earth's gravity, which light up the sky through the friction caused by entering the atmosphere. More poetically aeroliths have been referred to as 'falling stars', marking their arrivals as important events by a variety of witnesses; more speculatively, exo-rocks have been posited as the source for the seeding of life on our young planet or inversely as the trigger of a mass extinction event of the past and possibly our future. Philosopher and literary critic Maurice Blanchot has reflected on the nature of disaster (*désastre*), linking the term etymologically to the Italian sixteenth-century term *disastro*, meaning 'ill-starred event' or literally as the negation of the Latin term *astrum*: 'If disaster means being separated from the star (if it means the decline which characterizes disorientation when the link with fortune from on high is cut), then it indicates a fall beneath disastrous necessity.'[41] The falling star is a disaster; the fall of man from disorientation is the disaster. Rock fragments. Textual fragments.

LIGHTNING
'Lightning is an energizing play of a desiring field. Its tortuous path is an enlivening exploration of possible connections. Not a trail from the heavens to the ground but an electrifying yearning for connection

Dehlia Hannah, Ala Roushan, Nadim Samman, Charles Stankievech

that precedes this and that, here and there, now and then. Lightning is a striking phenomenon. It jolts our memories, flashing images on the retina of our mind's eye. Lightning arouses a sense of the primordial, enlivening questions of origin and materialization. It conjures haunting cultural images of the summoning of life through its energizing effects, perhaps most memorable in the classic films *Der Golem* (1920) and *Frankenstein* (1931). And it brings to mind credible (if not uncontroversial) scientific explanations of the electrifying origins of life: nature's fury shocking primordial ooze to life, an energizing jump start. Lightning, it seems, has always danced on the razor's edge between science and imagination.'[42]

EARTHQUAKE

> Her appearance would necessarily bring on, if not revolution – for the bastion was supposed to be immutable – at least harrowing explosions. At times it is in the fissure caused by an earthquake, through that radical mutation of things brought on by a material upheaval when every structure is for a moment thrown off balance and an ephemeral wildness sweeps order away, that the poet slips something by, for a brief span, of woman.[43]

Reappropriating the mythological monsters of Medusa and the abyss, Hélène Cixous likens woman's explosive power to that of an earthquake, creating new space in the deadly and darkness. In contrast to Jean-Paul Sartre, who anthropomorphically (we could say phallogocentrically) defined earthquakes as negative, Cixous laughs with Medusa upon the thought that woman is a 'dark continent.' Instead woman is a storm without lack that flows, disrupting the landscape with a new energy. As Nietszche prophesied in *Thus Spoke Zarathurtra*:

> He who hath grown wise concerning old origins, lo, he will at last seek after the fountains of the future and new origins.–
> O my brethren, not long will it be until *new peoples* shall arise and new fountains shall rush down into new depths.
> For the earthquake – it choketh up many wells, it causeth much languishing: but it bringeth also to light inner powers and secrets.
> The earthquake discloseth new fountains. In the earthquake of old peoples new fountains burst forth.[44]

OIL

'The empire on which the sun never sets' is a phrase that has been used by countless empires throughout history: from Persian through to contemporary times. Recently the Anglo empire of Britain (and its spin-off America) could be said to be the first empire where the expression transitioned from poetic to literal. Writing against such imperial forces, Persian philosopher and novelist Reza Negarastani, speculates on oil as an ancient sentient monster. Mixing the speculative 'Deep Hot Biosphere' theory of twentieth-century astrophysicist Thomas Gold and Persian esoteric knowledge, Negarestani constructs a sci-fi monster à *la The Thing* as a critique of colonial meddling in the Middle East. In his fictocriticism, the earth's own gravitational energy becomes a chthonic source for emergent life that flows through the underworld, lubricating history and warfare. The empire of the sun on the surface is countered by the autonomy of the underworld. Instead of oil as an inanimate material, Negarerstani proclaims: 'Petroleum definitely plays the role of the alpha-mutineer in Tellurian insurgency against solar capitalism and its neo-Ptolemaic heliocentrism.'[45]

PLASTIC
'In spite of its having Greek shepherds' names (Polystyrene, Phenoplast, Polyvinyl, Polyethylene), plastic, of which the products have just been concentrated in an exhibition, is an essentially alchemical substance [...] more than a substance, plastic is the very idea of its infinite transformation [...] it is less an object than the trace of a movement [...] In the poetic order of major substances, plastic is a disgraced material, lost between the effusion of rubber and the flat hardness of metal: it achieves none of the true productions of the mineral order: foam, fibers, strata. It is a shaped substance: whatever its final state, plastic retains a flocculant appearance, something opaque, creamy, and coagulated, an impotence ever to attain the triumphant sleekness of Nature [...] It is the first magical material that consents to be prosaic; but it is precisely because of its prosaic nature that it triumphs. For the first time, artifice aims for the common, not for the rare [...] A luxury object always derives from the earth, always recalls in a precious way its mineral or animal origin, the natural theme of which it is merely an actuality. Plastic is entirely engulfed in its usage: one of these days objects will be invented merely for the pleasure of using them. The hierarchy of substances is forthwith abolished, a single one will replace them all: the whole world, even life itself, can be plasticized since, we are told, plastic aortas are beginning to be manufactured.'[46]

RIVER
Over the flow of time, Heraclitus's philosophy comes to us as flotsam via various avenues as fragments quoted and requoted. Even his most famous oracular statement about (never) stepping twice into (the same) flowing river has multiple versions from Plato to Plutarch. Textual analysis has attempted to define a voice and perhaps excavate his original words in order to determine his intended meaning. But perhaps the most profound implication of his claim is that we call a body of water a river precisely *because* it consists of changing waters. As one commentator has it: 'Here constancy and change are not opposed but inextricably connected': some things *are* by virtue of their varying constituent matter.[47] Put otherwise, higher-level material realities supervene on lower-level material flux. In a contemporary world of logistical flow – from oil to information – Western philosophy's first process thinker and his theories of flux resurface. From one perspective, Heraclitus's river could be seen as a proto-definition of the algorithm: the content of data is constantly changing, and the algorithm processes this flow, even perhaps dynamically carving new valleys and pathways in the topography. The river has changed because the waters have changed and our interpretations have changed, changing us.

TWIN EARTH
Imagine another world in which everything is the same except for the fact that [...] Other worlds are always possible, and sometimes imagining one can teach you something. The American philosopher Hilary Putnam famously deployed a hypothetical Twin Earth in a thought experiment which concluded that the meanings of words are not purely psychological. He envisioned a planet identical in all respects to our own, save for the fact that our doppelgängers on 'Twin Earth' drink, surf and bathe in oceans made up XYZ (instead of H2O) – a clear liquid that they refer to as *water*. Putnam asks if, at a historical moment before the chemical composition of either substance was known, the inhabitants of both planets *mean* the same thing by this term? In posing this question the philosopher was getting at a deeper issue: are the meanings of our words purely

psychological, or tied to external realities?[48] Today, astrobiologists and astronomers envisage the real possibility of an Earth Twin, somewhere out there. But where? We haven't found one yet. The so-called 'mediocrity principle' suggests that planets very much like ours should be common in the universe. Conversely, the Rare Earth Theory suggests that they are extremely rare. In either case, one doesn't seem like enough. Instead of a single earth, we want two. One to destroy and another to keep.

GARDEN

The garden, despite its construction with plants and terraformed dirt, has always had cosmological aspirations. Whether as an origin myth or an early model of the world, the garden brings together biodiversity and atmospheres normally separated and incompatible within a unified landscape. Beyond any architectonics, the garden as a philosophical imaginary contains layers of meaning mapped onto a controlled plot of land, creating an artificial nature, a process producing a space Michel Foucault calls a 'heterotopia'. Gardens can manifest 'other spaces' through an imaginative practice of incorporating the world within them – a practice that has existed in various cultures since antiquity. As Foucault writes, 'The traditional garden of the Persians was a sacred space that was supposed to bring together inside its rectangle four parts representing the four parts of the world, with a space still more sacred than the others that were like an umbilicus, the navel of the world at its center (the basin and water fountain were there); and all the vegetation of the garden was supposed to come together in this space, in this sort of microcosm.'[49] A triad of vegetative spaces along the spectrum from heterogeneous to homogeneous: the jungle is wild and chaotic, a garden is diverse and structured, a plantation is monolithic and controlled. Appreciating the beauty of diversity found in gardens was challenged by eighteenth-century naturalist William Marsden when describing the pleasure of encountering a colonial plantation, with its symmetrical appearance, amidst the wild foliage of Sumatra.[50] Immanuel Kant, while misunderstanding Marsden on this point in his *Critique of Judgment*, did astutely observe Marsden's appreciation of the land's utility for production.[51] While royal walled gardens expressed the cosmologies of ancient worlds, the monoculture cash crop expresses the logistics of global capitalism.

FOREST FIRE

Arguing for the unification of the many and varied sciences of nature, Otto Neurath invoked a forest fire: '[W]hether a forest will burn down at a certain location on earth depends as much on the weather as on whether human intervention takes place or not. This intervention, however, can only be predicted if one knows the laws of human behaviour. *That is, under certain circumstances, it must be possible to connect all kinds of laws with each other.* Therefore all laws, whether chemical, climatological or sociological, must be conceived as parts of a system, namely of unified science.'[52] The Vienna Circle, a group convened during the interwar period with the aim of shoring up the foundations of empiricism by drawing on logical empiricism (the latest advance in logic and the physical sciences), held the ambition of unifying the sciences. Unification took various forms: the reduction of all scientific laws to laws of physics; the translation of scientific statements into symbolic language; and the publication of a proposed twenty-six-volume tome, the *International Encyclopedia of Unified Science*. The encyclopaedic project was led by Neurath, who also initiated the creation of a language of visual education or ISOTYPE (International System of Typographic Picture Education). In his image of the forest fire as a site of cooperation, we are reminded of the practical aspirations of the philosophy of science that are easily forgotten when one focuses on the evolution of logical empiricism during the era of the Vienna Circle's exile in America. Under the pressure of McCarthyism, European intellectual emigres, many of them Jewish, tended to suppress anything in the contents or application of their research that might be considered communist in its leanings. Indeed, Neurath was a socialist, for whom the unity of science was a political project with overt implications for human welfare. As a philosophical monster, the forest fire holds the promise of transdisciplinary cooperation in the face of complex problems. It is significant that the increase in wildfires today as a consequence of global warming makes the need for this kind of cooperation and mutual recognition of expertise all the more pressing.

SOUTH POLE

Bounded by the Crane Glacier to the north-west, Exasperation Inlet to the north-east, and the Flask Glacier to the south, The Aristotle Mountains are a sequence of ridges that run for 62 km across Graham Land, Antarctica. Their designation honours the ancient Greek philosopher who reasoned that this continent must necessarily exist, some two thousand years before humankind would ever alight on its icy shores. For, if the earth was round, so must the southern hemisphere have a land mass large enough to balance the lands known to exist in the north. He called the probable but undiscovered land mass the opposite of the Arctic: 'Antarktikos'.[53] The postulated southern continent exited the archive of hypothetical entities in the early nineteenth century, verified according to the same anticipatory logic of discovery that would be carried forward with the Higgs Boson, and other phenomena at the edges of our epistemic reach.

1   Friedrich Schlegel, 'Athenaeum Fragments (§34)' in *Philosophical Fragments* (trans. Peter Firchow), Minneapolis and London: Minnesota University Press, 1991, p.22.
2   Patricia Curd (ed.), *A Presocratics Reader* (trans. Richard McKirahan), Indianapolis and Cambridge: Hackett Publishing Co., 1995, p.32.
3   Peter Sloterdijk, *You Must Change Your Life: On Anthropotechnics* (trans. Wieland Hoban), Cambridge: Polity Press, 2018, p.171.
4   P. Curd, *ibid.*
5   F. Schlegel, 'Athenaeum Fragments (§206)', in *op. cit.*, p.45. The German *Igel* was corrected by the authors to 'hedgehog'.
6   William Shakespeare, *The Works of Shakespeare: The Tragedy of Hamlet* (ed. Edward Dowden), London: Methuen and co., 1899, p.107.
7   Gaston Bachelard, *Earth and Reveries of Repose* (trans. Mary McAllester Jones), Dallas: Dallas Institute Publications, 2011, p.11.
8   G.W.F. Hegel, *Elements of the Philosophy of Right* (ed. Allen W. Wood, trans. H.B. Nisbet), Cambridge: Cambridge University Press, 1991, p.23.
9   See Friedrich Nietzsche, *Twilight of the Idols* (trans. R. J. Hollingdale), London: Penguin Classics, 1990.
10 Gary Shapiro, 'The Owl of Minerva and the Colors of the Night', *Philosophy and Literature*, vol.1 no.3, 1977, p.277.
11 Plato, 'Theatetus', in *The Dialogues of Plato. Vol IV* (trans. B Jowett), Third Edition, London: Humphrey Milford, Oxford University Press, 1802, p.264.
12 Farid ud-Din Attar, *The Conference of the Birds* (trans. Fatemeh Kavandi), Tehran: Nazar Art Publications, 2013.
13 Thomas Nagel, 'What is it like to be a bat?', *The Philosophical Review*, vol.83, no.4, October 1974, pp.435–50.
14 Umberto Eco, *Kant and the Platypus: Essays on Language and Cognition*, New York: Harcourt Brace, 2000, p.6.
15 Peter Godfrey-Smith, *Other Minds: the Octopus, the Sea, and the Deep Origins of Consciousness*, New York: Farrar, Straus and Giroux, 2016.
16 Vilém Flusser and Louis Bec, *Vampyroteuthis Infernalis: a Treatise, with a Report*

by the Institut Scientifique de Recherche Paranaturaliste (trans. Valentine A. Pakis), Minneapolis: University of Minnesota Press. 2012, p.69.

17 Donna J. Haraway, *Staying with the Trouble: Making Kin in the Chthulucene*, Durham: Duke University Press, 2016, p.55.

18 Thomas Hobbes, *Leviathan, or the matter, forme and power of a commonwealth ecclesiastical and civil*, p.165.

19 Lorraine Daston and Peter Galison, 'The Image of Objectivity', *Representations*, vol.0, no. 40, Autumn 1992, p.82.

20 Walter Benjamin, 'Theses on the Philosophy of History' in *Illuminations* (ed. Hannah Arendt, trans. Harry Zohn), New York: Schocken, 1968 [1955], pp. 257–58.

21 Jacques Derrida, *Specters of Marx: the State of the Debt, the Work of Mourning, and the New International* (trans. Peggy Kamuf), New York: Routledge, 1994, p.164.

22 Luce Irigaray, *The Forgetting of Air in Martin Heidegger*, Austin: University of Texas Press, 1999, p.80.

23 Luce Irigaray, *Elemental Passions*, London: Athlone, 1992, p.105. Emphasis the authors'.

24 Gaston Bachelard, *Air and Dreams: An Essay on the Imagination of Movement* (trans. Edith R. Farrell and C. Frederick Farrell, Dallas: Dallas Institute of Humanities and Culture. 1988, p.194.

25 Julia Kristeva, *Black Sun: Depression and Melancholia* (trans. by Leon S. Roudiez), New York: Columbia University Press, 1989, p.151.

26 Jalal Toufic, *Radical Disclosures*, Singapore: Singapore Biennial, 2020.

27 Stefano Harney and Fred Moten, *The Undercommons: Fugitive Planning and Black Study*, Brooklyn, New York: Autonomedia, 2013.

28 Gaunilo of Marmoutiers, 'Pro Insipiente' in Franciscus Salesius Schmitt, *S. Anselmi Cantuariensis Archiepiscopi Opera Omni*, Edinburgh: Nelson, 1946–61.

29 Idries Shah, *The Sufis* (intro. Robert Graves), Garden City, New York: Doubleday, 1964.

30 Jacques Lacan, *Seminar XXI: Les non-dupes errent*, unpublished manuscript, 1973–74.

31 Adam Smith, *The Glasgow Edition of the Works and Correspondence of Adam Smith, vol. 1: The Theory of Moral Sentiments*, Oxford: Oxford University Press, 1976, p.184.

32 Adrienne Mayor, *The First Fossil Hunters: Dinosaurs, Mammoths and Myth in Greek and Roman Times*, New Jersey: Princeton University Press, 2000, pp.33–59.

33 George Bataille, *Prehistoric Paintings: Lascaux or the Birth of Art* (trans. Austryn Wainhouse), Lausanne: Skira, 1955, p.35.

34 Cornelius Castoriadis, *Crossroads in the Labyrinth*, Cambridge MA: MIT Press, 1984 pp. ix–x.

35 Michele Serres, *Le passage du Nord-Ouest. Hermès V*, Paris : Éditions de Minuit, 1968. p.18. Translation the authors'.

36 Immanuel Kant, *Critique of Pure Reason* (trans. Norman Kemp Smith), London: McMillan and Co., 1929, p.257.

37 Michèle Le Doeuff, *The Philosophical Imaginary* (trans. Colin Gordon), London and New York: Continuum, 2002, pp.8–9.

38 Gaston Bachelard, 'The Metaphysics of Dust', *Parrhesia*, vol.31, 2019, pp.17–32.

39 Percy Bysshe Shelley., 'Ozymandias', *The complete poetical works*, New York: Hurst Publishers, 1883.

40 Plutarch, 'Lysander', in *Lives, Vol. IV: Alcibiades and Coriolanus. Lysander and Sulla* (trans. Bernadotte Perrin), London: W. Heinemann, 1916 pp.261–65.

41 Maurice Blanchot, *The writing of the disaster* (trans. Ann Smock), Lincoln: University of Nebraska Press.1986, p.2.

42 Karen Barad, 'Transmaterialities: Trans/Matter/Realities and Queer Political Imaginings', *Journal of Lesbian and Gay Studies*, vol.21, 2015, pp. 387–422.

43 Hélène Cixous, 'The Laugh of the Medusa' (trans. by Keith and Paula Cohen), *Signs*, vol.1, no.4, 1976, p.879.

44 Friedrich Nietzsche, *Thus Spoke Zarathustra* (trans. Thomas Common), New York: Dover Publications, 1999, p. 148.

45 Reza Negarestani, *Cyclonopedia: Complicity with Anonymous Materials*, Melbourne: Re:Press, 2008, p.20.

46 Roland Barthes, *Mythologies* (trans. Richard Howard and Annette Lavers), New York: Hill and Wang, 2012, pp.193–95.

47 Daniel W. Graham, 'Heraclitus', *The Stanford Encyclopedia of Philosophy* [online], 8 February 2007, revised 3 September 2019, available at https://plato.stanford.edu/entries/heraclitus/ (last accessed on 2 October 2020).

48 See Hilary Putnam, 'Meaning and Reference', *Journal of Philosophy*, no. 70, 1973, pp.699–711.

49 Michel Foucault, 'Of Other Spaces' (trans. Jay Miskowiec), *Diacritics*, vol.16, no.1, 1986, pp.22–27.

50 William Marsden, *The History of Sumatra: Containing an Account of the Government, Laws, Customs and Manners of the Native Inhabitants, with a Description of the Natural Productions, and a Relation of the Ancient Political State of That Island*, [e-book] [1783], 28 September 2005, available at https://www.gutenberg.org/files/16768/16768-h/16768-h.htm, (last accessed on 2 October 2020).

51 Immanuel Kant, *Critique of Judgement* (trans. Werner Pluhar), Indianapolis and Cambridge: Hackett Publishing, 1987, pp.93–94.

52 Otto Neurath, *Philosophical Papers 1913–1946* (ed. R.S. Cohen and M. Neurath), Dordrecht: Reidel, 1983, p.59.

53 Aristotle, *Meteorologica* (trans. H.D.P. Lee), Cambridge MA: Harvard University Press, 1952.

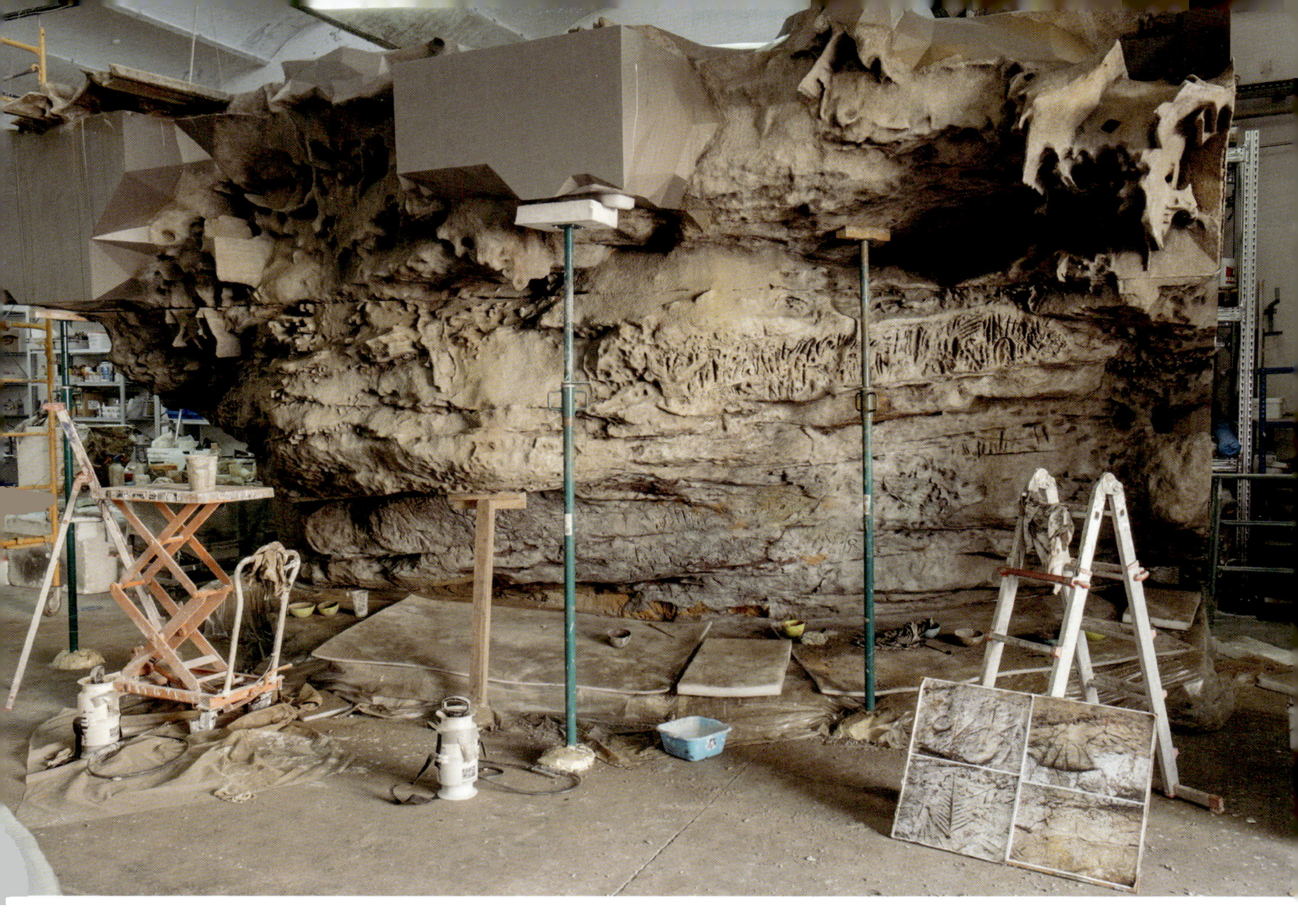

Sacred cave of Kamukuwaká,
section of 3D reconstruction in
Factum Foundation's workshop.
Courtesy Oak Taylor Smith for
Factum Foundation

Dehlia Hannah, Ala Roushan, Nadim Samman, Charles Stankievech

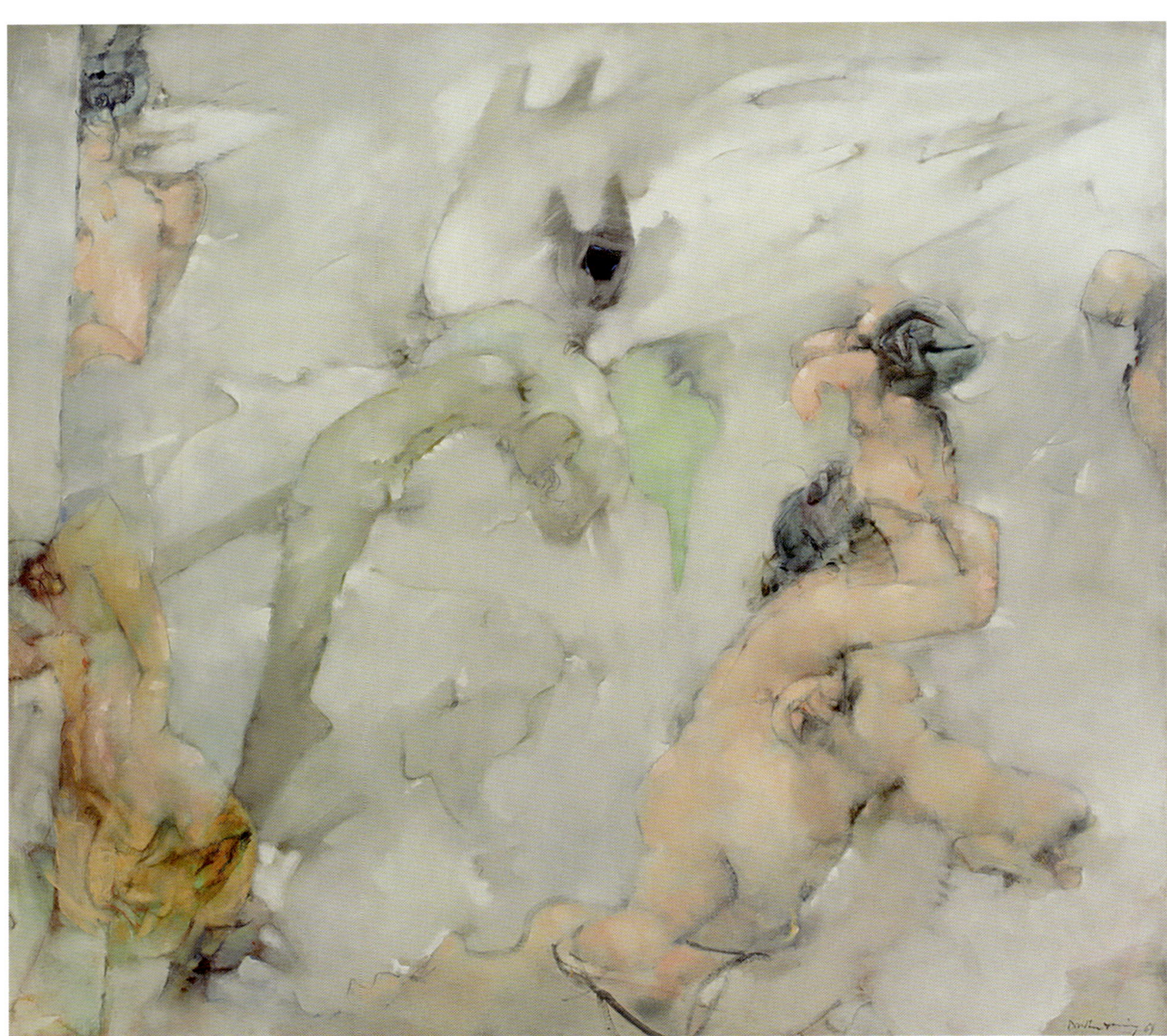

Dorothea Tanning, *Far From*,
1964, oil on canvas.
Courtesy DACS/Artimage

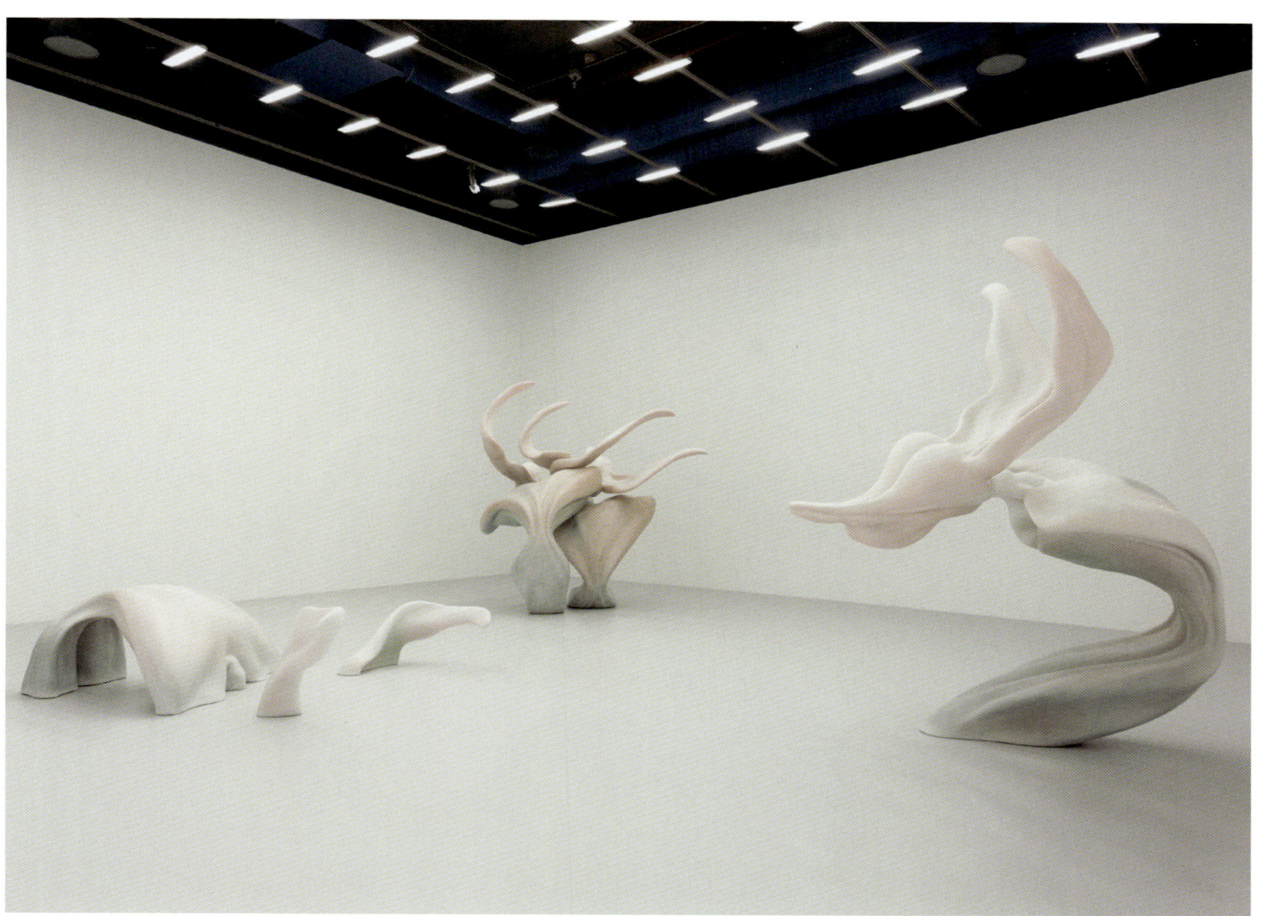

Marguerite Humeau,
High Tide (The Dancer I, The Dancer II,
The Dancers III & IV), 2019.
Exhibition view, Centre Pompidou, Paris. 2019.
Photograph © Julia Andréone.
Courtesy the artist, C L E A R I N G
New York/Brussels

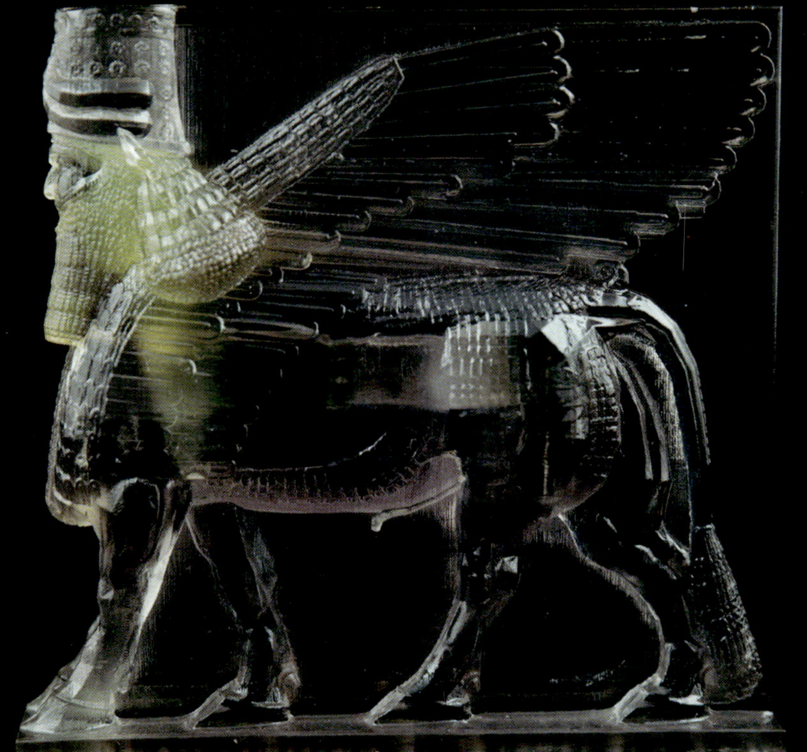

Morehshin Allahyari,
Lamassu from the series,
Material Speculation: ISIS, 2015,
3D-printed sculpture and flash drive,
15.9 x 15.9 x 3.2cm.
Courtesy the artist and
Sapar Contemporary, New York

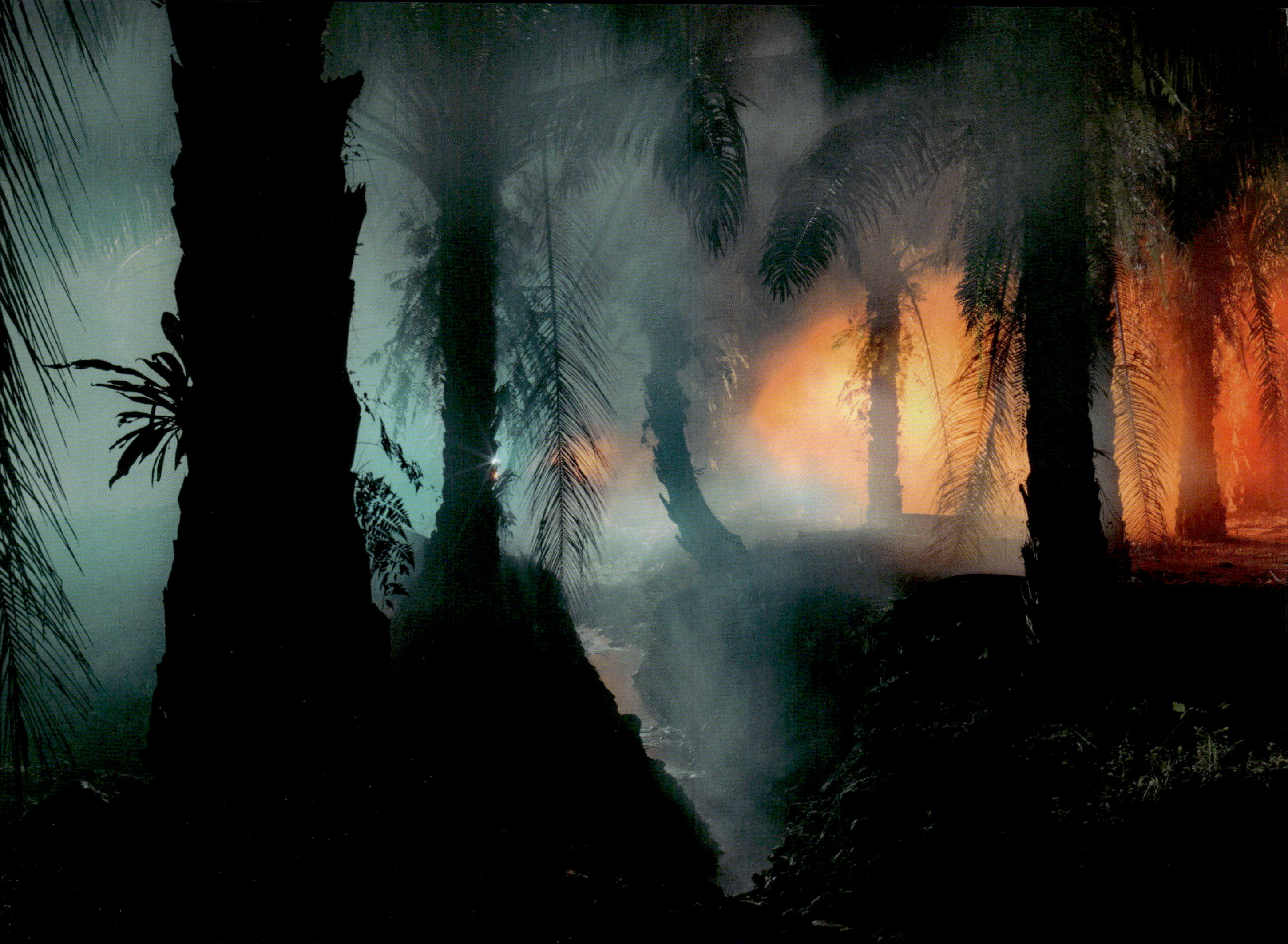

Julian Charrière,
An Invitation to Disappear, 2018, film.
© the artist, VG Bild-Kunst, Bonn,
Germany and Studio Julian Charrière

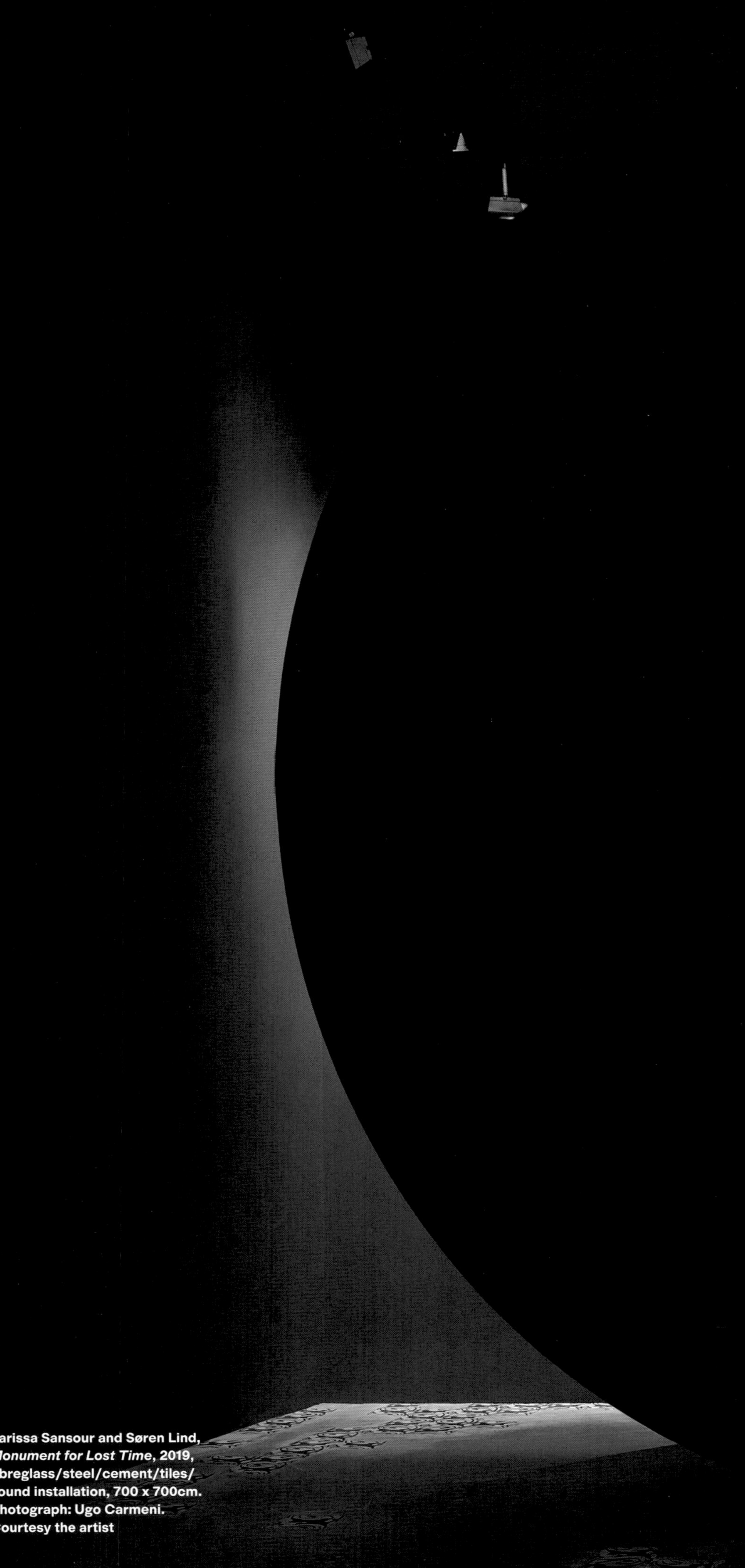

Larissa Sansour and Søren Lind,
Monument for Lost Time, 2019,
fibreglass/steel/cement/tiles/
sound installation, 700 x 700cm.
Photograph: Ugo Carmeni.
Courtesy the artist

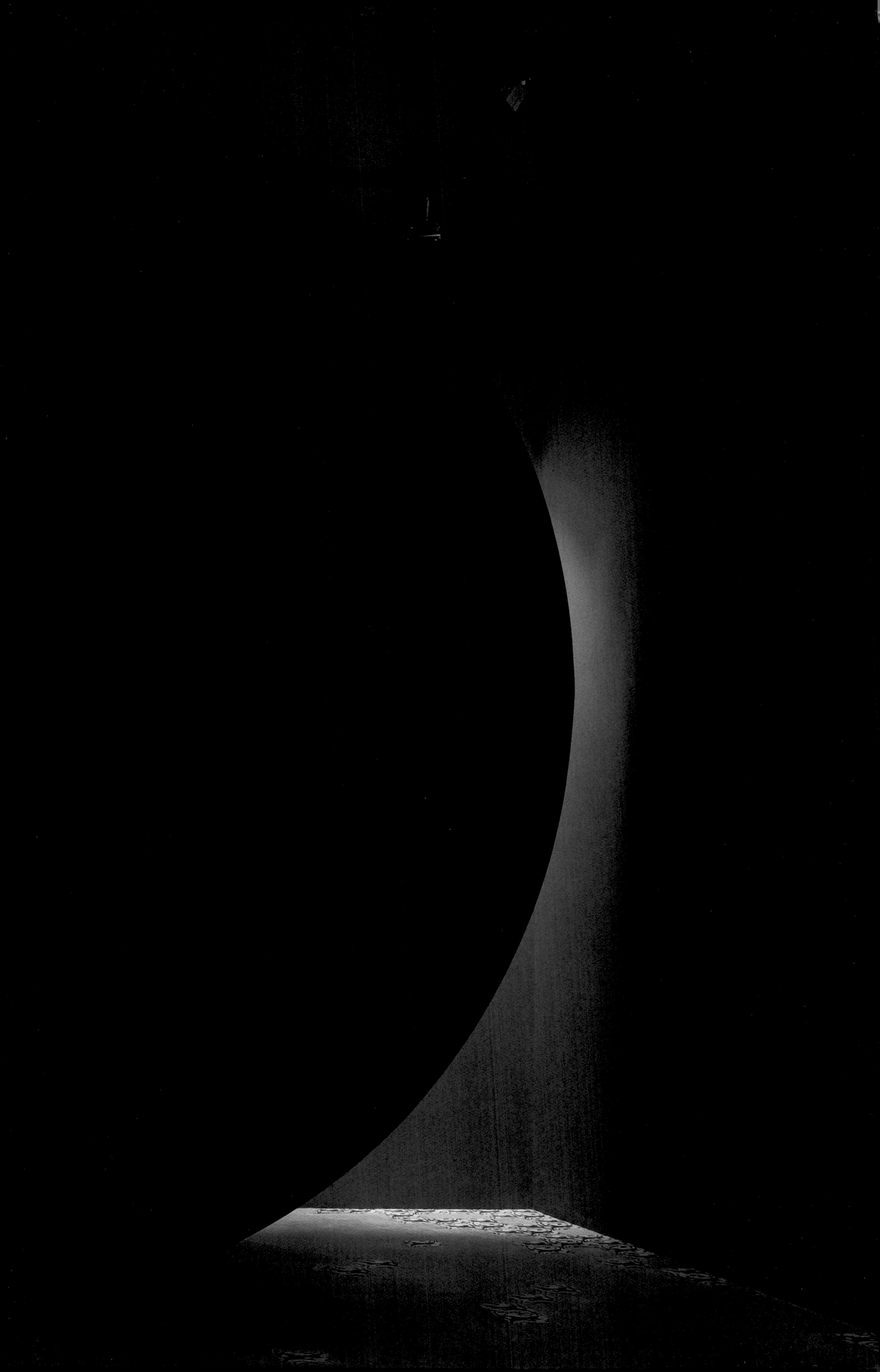

Contributors

UTE META BAUER is the Founding Director of the NTU Centre for Contemporary Art Singapore, and Professor at the School of Art, Design and Media, Nanyang Technological University, Singapore. Previously, she was Associate Professor in the Department of Architecture at Massachusetts Institute of Technology (MIT), Cambridge, where she also served as Founding Director of the MIT Program in Art, Culture, and Technology.

AMANDA CARNEIRO is a researcher. She graduated from São Paulo University and currently works as an assistant curator at the Museu de Arte de São Paulo (MASP) and as an editor of Afterall Journal. She organised the seminars 'Art and Decolonisation' and edited publications including the anthologies *Historias Afro-Atlânticas and Histórias das Mulheres, Histórias Feministas*, as well as the exhibitions 'Sonia Gomes: still I rise' and 'Leonor Antunes: voids, joints and gaps'.

DUNNE & RABY use design as a medium to stimulate discussion and debate about the social, cultural and ethical implications of existing and emerging technologies. Their work has been exhibited at the Museum of Modern Art (MoMA) in New York, the Pompidou Centre in Paris, and the Design Museum in London, and is in several permanent collections including MoMA, the Victoria and Albert Museum, and the Austrian Museum of Applied Arts (MAK). In 2015, they received an MIT Media Lab Award. Anthony Dunne and Fiona Raby are both University Professors of Design and Social Inquiry at the New School/Parsons in New York, where they co-direct the Designed Realities Studio.

LAURA GRACE FORD is a London based artist and writer concerned with the socio-spatial dynamics of class. Drawing on cognitive mapping, hauntology and *dérive*, Ford interrogates the affective contours of the city. Her multidisciplinary practice forges connections with emancipatory forces embedded in the terrain. Ford completed a BA in Painting at the Slade School of Fine Art in 2001 and an MA in Painting at the Royal College or Art (RCA) in 2007. From 2013–14 she was Stanley Picker Fellow at Kingston University. She is author of *Savage Messiah* (2011) and is currently a Somerset House Studios resident and researcher at the RCA.

DEHLIA HANNAH is a philosopher and curator based in Copenhagen. She holds a Ph.D. in philosophy from Columbia University, New York and is currently research curator for the Centre for Environmental Humanities at Aarhus University, Denmark. She is the editor of *A Year Without a Winter* (2019), which was initiated at Arizona State University during her visiting assistant professorship with the School for the Future of Innovation in Society and the School of Art, Media, and Engineering. Her work examines ideas of climate change, nature, and environment through aesthetics and philosophy of science.

NAV HAQ is Associate Director at the Museum of Contemporary Art Antwerp (M HKA) where he is responsible for the development of the artistic programme.

AMBER HUSAIN is a writer, editor and researcher living and working in London. Her essays are published in *The White Review*, *3AM* and *Radical Philosophy*, and her first book will be published by Peninsula Press in 2021. She is a managing editor of Afterall Books.

MARK LEWIS is a Canadian artist and filmmaker. He lives and works in London.

DANA LILJEGREN is a PhD Candidate in Art History at the Graduate Center of the City University of New York. Her specializations and topics of interest include West African art, global contemporary art, postcolonial theory, and environmentalism. Her dissertation examines the repurposing of materials in contemporary Senegalese art and pays special attention to the global circulation of objects. She holds degrees in art history from Brown University, Columbia University, and Université Paris 1 Panthéon-Sorbonne.

VUTH LYNO is an artist, curator and co-founding artistic director of Sa Sa Art Projects, Phnom Penh's only Cambodian artist-run space, initiated by the Stiev Selapak collective. His artistic and curatorial practices are participatory in nature, exploring communal learning and experimentation through multiple voices. As an artist, he works with various media including photography, sound, and video, often resulting in installations and involving project participants in the production of meaning. As a curator, he is interested in the mobility of material and immaterial goods across places and times, and what is produced or transformed from this mobility.

ADEENA MEY is a researcher and curator. He is Managing Editor of Afterall Journal and a lecturer at Lausanne University of Art and Design (ECAL), Switzerland.

ALA ROUSHAN is an Asscociate Professor at OCAD University, Toronto and the co-curator/director of SUGAR, a curatorial platform exploring new trajectories for public art informed by site. Roushan's practice includes research, writing, curating and teaching focused on digital culture. She is a PhD candidate at the European Graduate School in Philosophy, Art & Critical Thought, Saas-Fee, Switzerland and holds a Master of Arts in Advanced Architectural Design from the Städelschule. Her current research navigates the implications of digital technologies as it reveals depth of space beyond the limits of human perception.

ANA SOPHIE SALAZAR is a curator, writer, and co-founder of the Museum for the   Displaced, a cultural and social organisation addressing issues of forced migration, displacement, and statelessness. Through undisciplined explorations of nomadic, poly-lingual, and transcultural subjectivities and expressions, her work proposes inventive ways of challenging current geopolitical world mappings. From 2016 to 2020, she was Assistant Curator for Exhibitions at the NTU Centre for Contemporary Art Singapore. Ana graduated with an MA in Curatorial Practice from the School of Visual Arts, New York, and a BA in Piano from the Music School of Lisbon.

NADIM SAMMAN read Philosophy at University College London before receiving his PhD from the Courtauld Institute of Art. He was Co-Director of Import Projects e.V. in Berlin from 2012 to 2019 and, concurrently, curator at Thyssen-Bornemisza Art Contemporary, Vienna (2013–15). He curated the 4th Marrakech Biennale (with Carson Chan) in 2012, and the 5th Moscow Biennale for Young Art in 2015. He co-founded and co-curated the 1st Antarctic Biennale (2017) and the Antarctic Pavilion (Venice, 2015–). He is currently Curator at KW Institute for Contemporary Art, Berlin.

CHARLES STANKIEVECH is an artist, writer and curator. His award-winning body of work explores the notion of 'fieldwork' in the embedded landscape, the military industrial complex and geopolitics. He is Associate Professor and Director of Visual Studies in the Faculty of Architecture, Landscape and Design at the University of Toronto. He is an editor of Afterall Journal and in 2011 co-founded the art and theory press, K. in Berlin. In 2007 he was a founding faculty member of the Yukon School of Visual Arts in Dawson City, Canada (under joint governance by the Indigenous sovereign nation of Tr'ondëk Hwëch'in).

ELVIA WILK is a writer living in New York. She is author of the novel *Oval* (2019) and her work has appeared in publications including *Frieze, Artforum, Bookforum, Granta, n+1, The White Review, BOMB, Mousse, Flash Art,* and *Ssense.* She is a contributing editor at e-*flux Journal* and a 2020 fellow at the Berggruen Institute.

JOURNAL

Afterall

Subscribe to *Afterall* to receive full electronic access to our back issues, plus two new issues per year in print, on the web and in the new e-book edition.

2020 Subscription Rates
Print and electronic:
$24 ($19 for students)
Electronic: $22 ($17 for students)

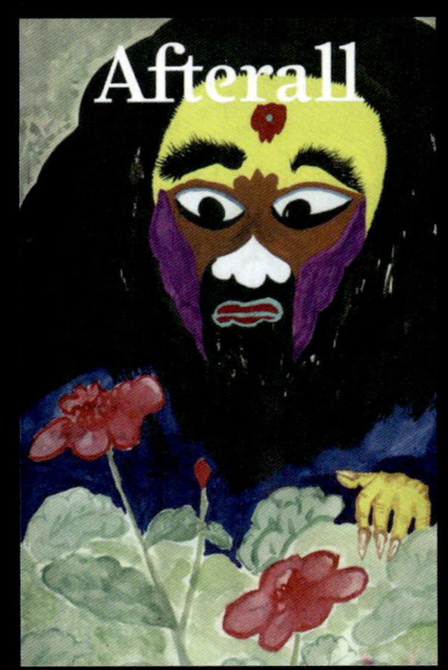

47

GülsünKaramustafa
Naeem Mohaiemen
Araya Rasdjarmrearnsook

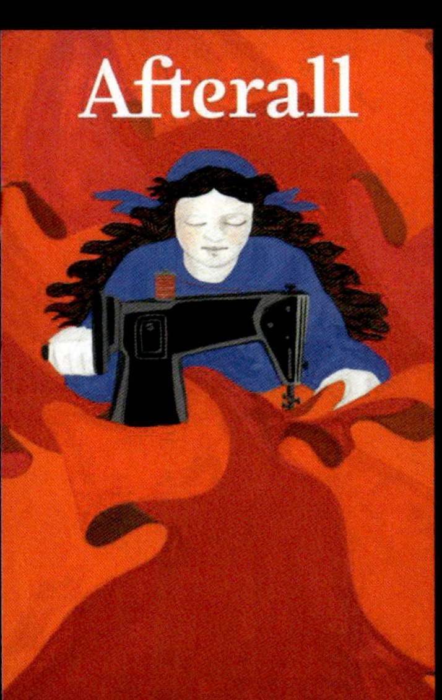

48

Dineo Seshee Bopape
Karrabing Film Collective
Kerry James Marshall
Trinh T. Minh-ha

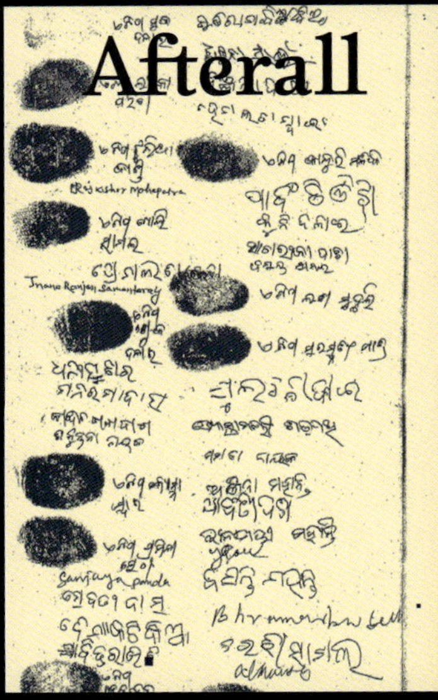

49

Amar Kanwar
Sonia Boyce
siren eun young jung

UNCO-OPERATIVE

不合作的共存：
2000 年的上海
當代藝術展覽

CONTEM-PORARIES:

Art Exhibitions in Shanghai in 2000

Exhibition Histories
展览史系列

Afterall Books

NOW AVAILABLE:
Uncooperative Contemporaries:
Art Exhibitions in Shanghai in 2000

Shanghai's 'exhibition frenzy' in 2000 presented conflicting positions at a transitional moment for 'global' contemporary art. This book explores what was at stake for modernity, contemporaneity, nationalism, internationalism and globalism in the city at the time, while looking back from diverse perspectives today.

With essays by **Jane DeBevoise, Lee Weng Choy, Mia Yu, Carol Yinghua Lu** and **Liu Ding**; archival texts by **Xu Hong** and **Zhou Zixi**; reflections from participants such as **Ai Weiwei, Chen Lingyang, Chen Yanyin, Feng Boyi, Hou Hanru, Li Liang, Li Xiangyang, Li Xu, Liang Shaoji, Xu Zhen, Yang Zhenzhong, Yang Zhichao, Zhang Qing, Zheng Shengtian** and **Zhu Yu**, assembled by **Anthony Yung**; and an introduction by **John Tain**.

Published in association with Asia Art Archive and the Center for Curatorial Studies, Bard College. Distributed by Koenig Books and ARTBOOK | D.A.P.

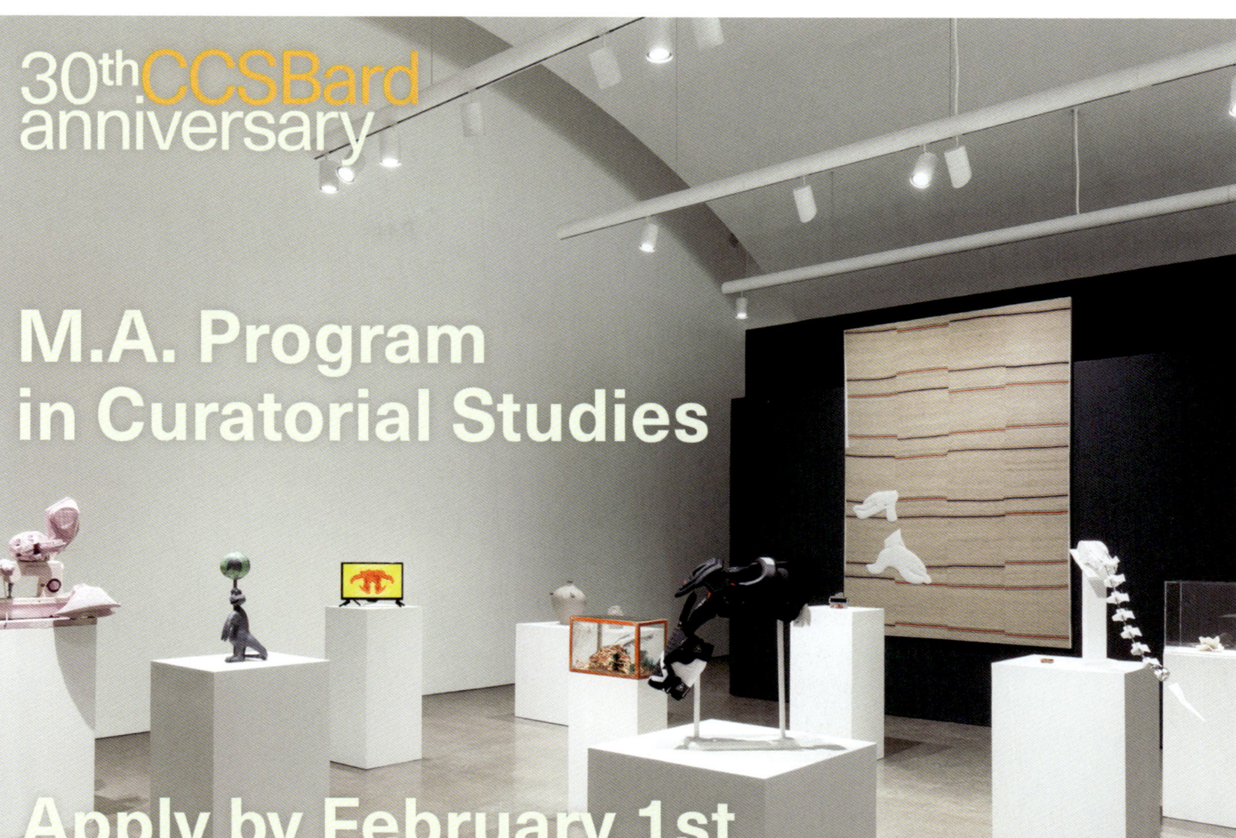

30th CCSBard anniversary

M.A. Program
in Curatorial Studies

Apply by February 1st

ccs.bard.edu

Installation view from Inbetweener, Hessel Museum of Art,
Center for Curatorial Studies, Bard College, Annandale-on-Hudson, NY,
August 20 - September 20, 2020. Master's thesis exhibition curated by
Elizaveta Shneyderman. Photo: Olympia Shannon 2020.

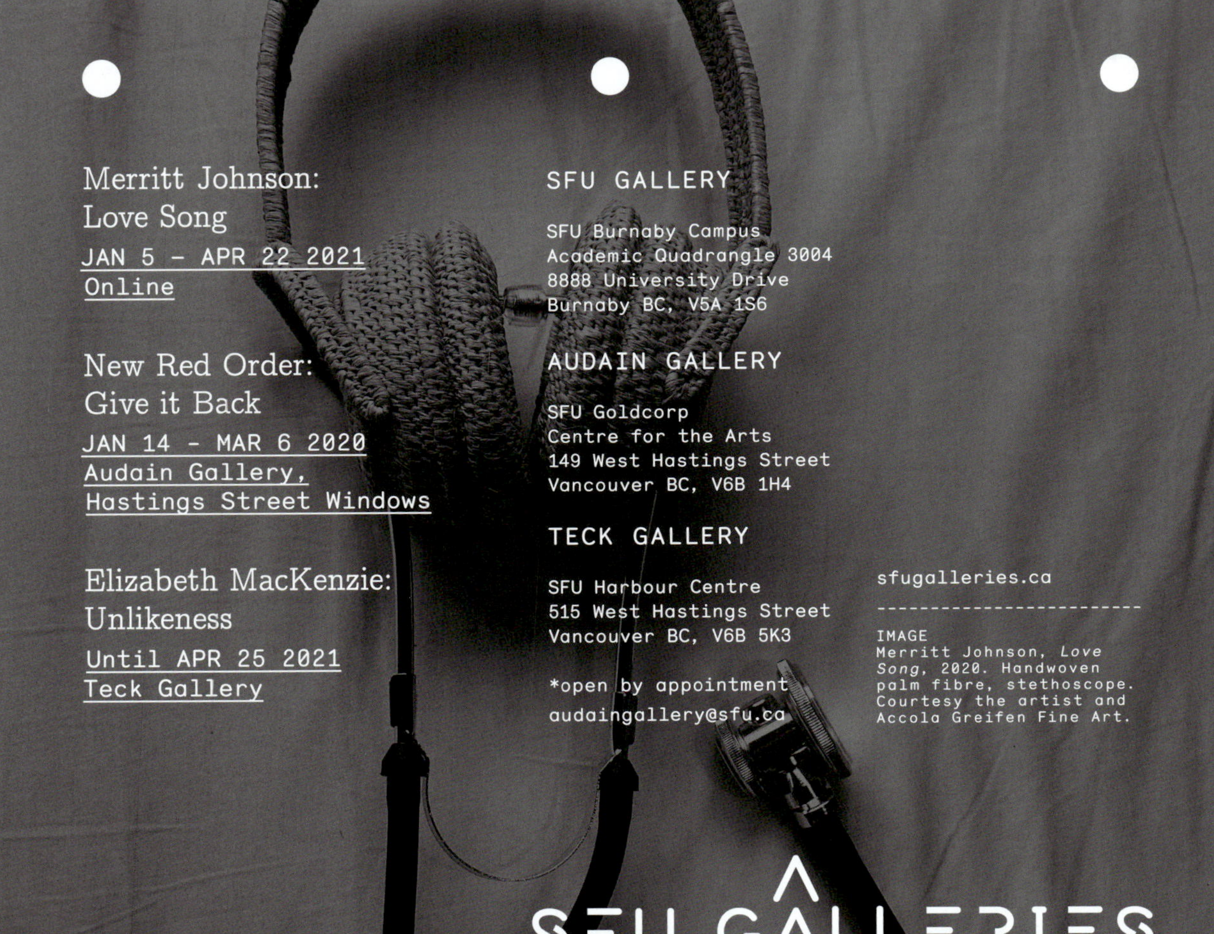

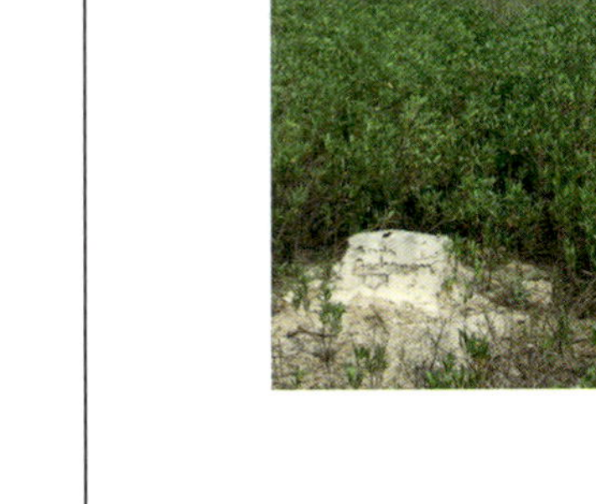

Beverley Buchanan

Marsh Ruins

Amelia Groom

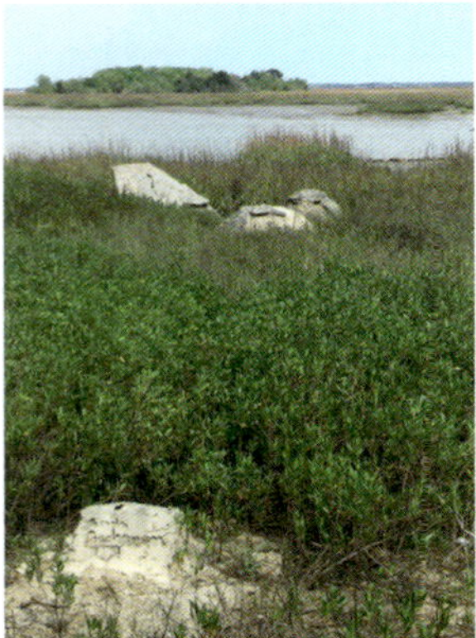

Afterall Books: One Work

Een tentoonstelling met:
An exhibition with:

Hannah Höch
Lovis Corinth
Karl Hofer
Georg Grosz
Carol Rama
Werner Peiner
Belgian Institute for
    World Affairs
Joseph Beuys
Felix Gonzalez-Torres
Andy Warhol
Nicole
Hüseyin Bahri Alptekin

Haseeb Ahmed
Sven Augustijnen
Candida Höfer
Papa Ibra Tall
Maryam Najd
David Blandy
Oxana Shachko
Matti Braun
Jos de Gruyter &
    Harald Thys
Luc Deleu
Jimmie Durham
Catherine Opie

Charlotte Posenenske
Public Movement
Philip Guston
Mladen Stilinović
N. S. Harsha
Lynette Yiadom-Boakye
Rasheed Araeen
Ibrahim Mahama
Kerry James Marshall
Vincent Meessen
Renzo Martens/CATPC
Danny Matthys
Jonas Staal

Sille Storihle
Makhmut Usmanovich
    Usmanov
Nicoline van Harskamp
Dimitri Venkov
Åsa Sonjasdotter

Plus artefacten van
verschillende culturele
archieven.
Plus artefacts from
several cultural archives.

Monoculture

Een recent verhaal
A Recent History

25.09.2020–24.01.2021

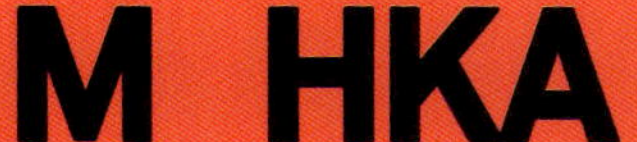

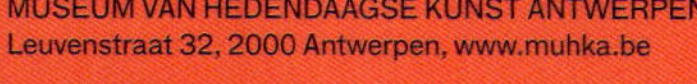

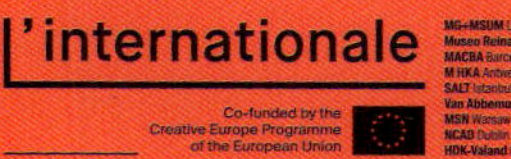

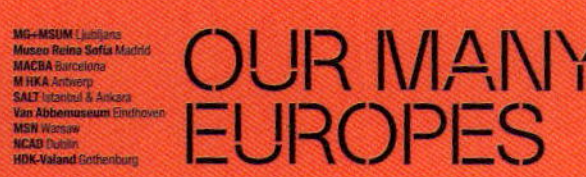

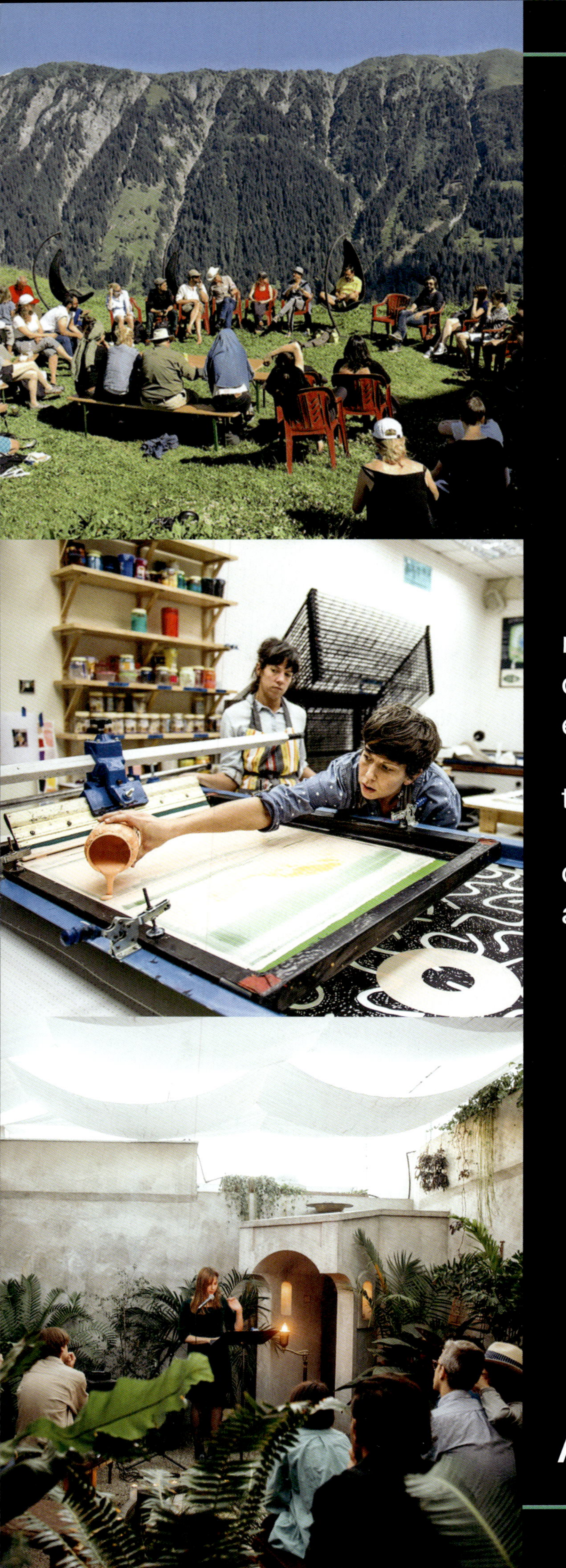

new services
dynamic design
expanded features

the new artandeducation.net

critical perspectives on
art and academia

Art & Education

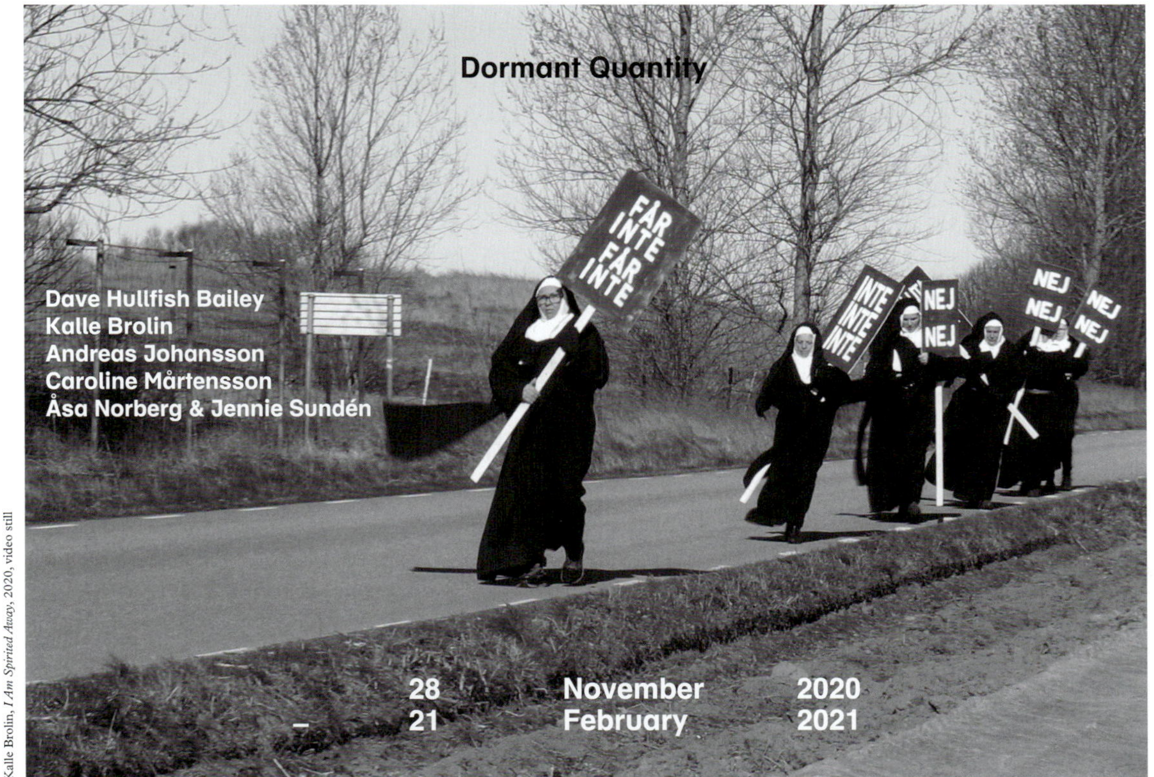

Kalle Brolin, *I Am Spirited Away*, 2020, video still

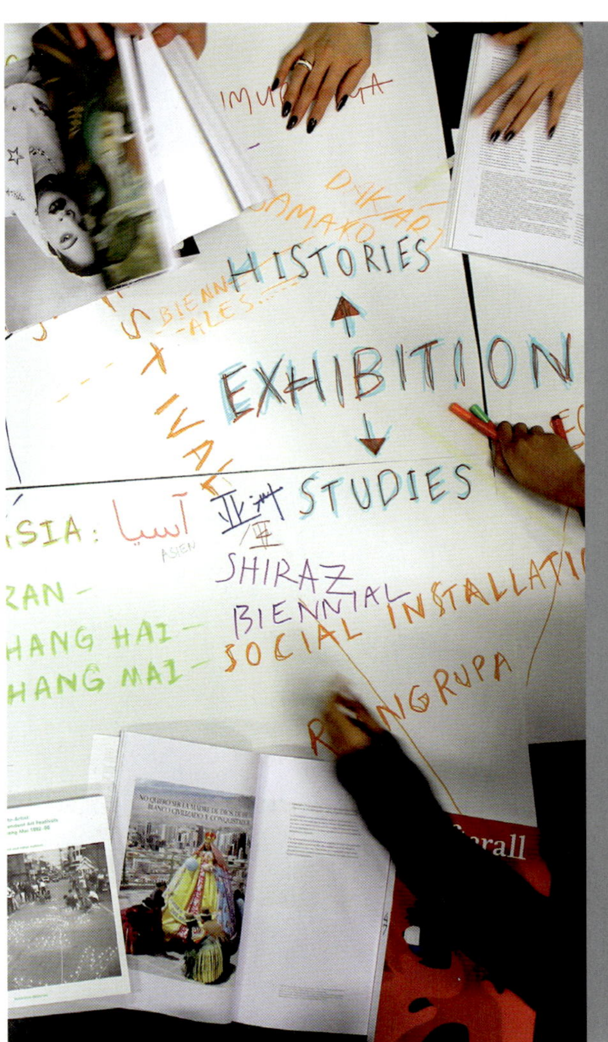

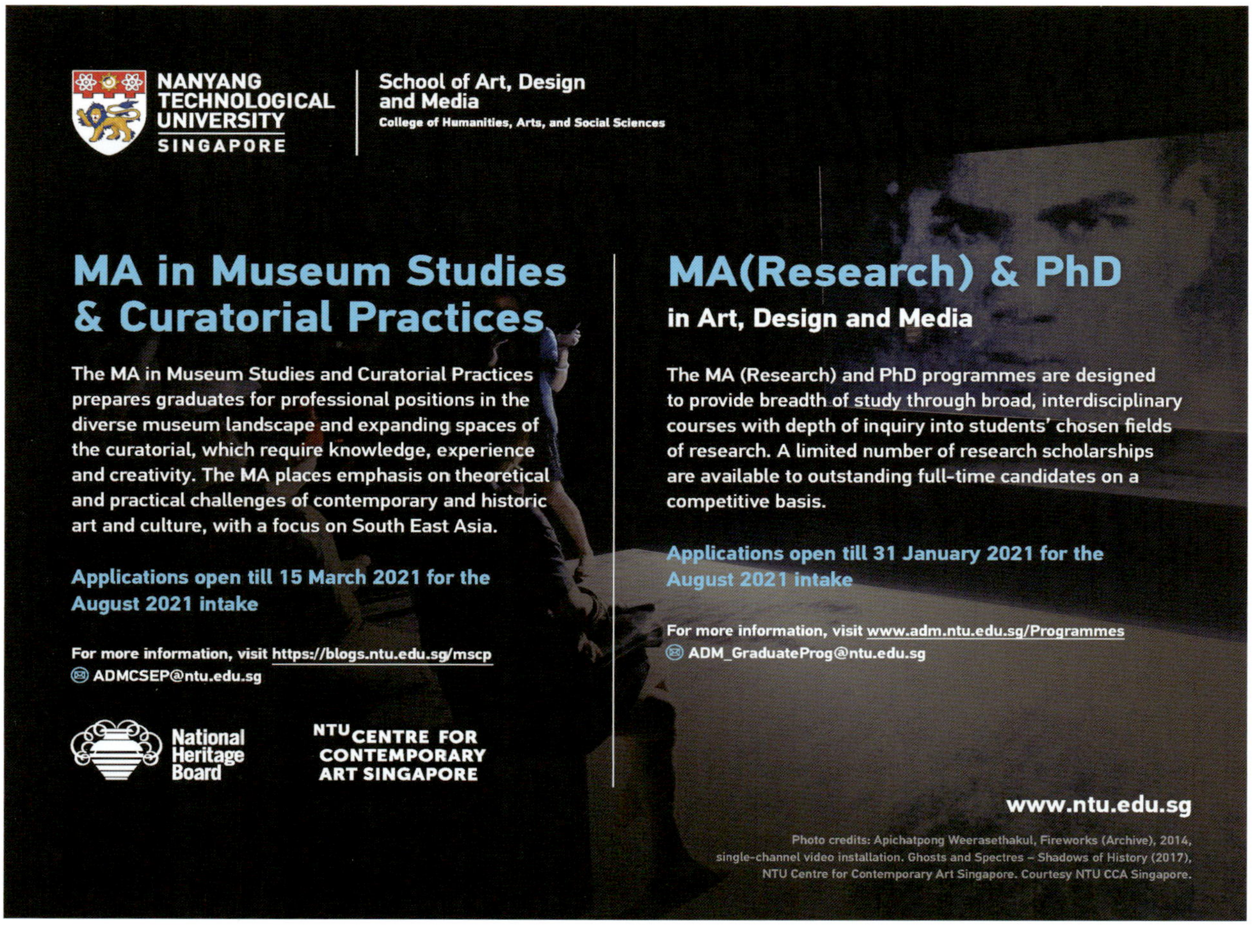

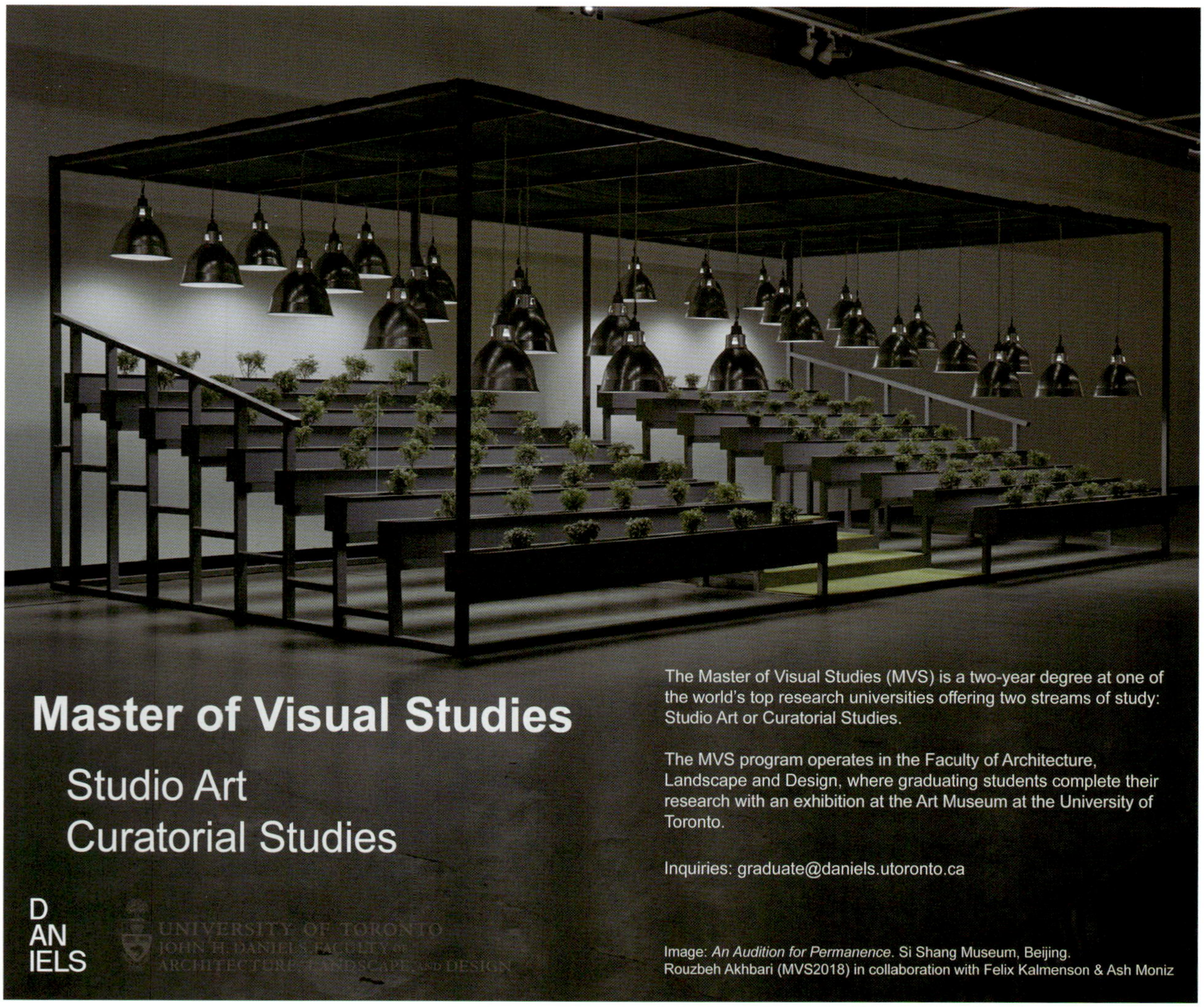

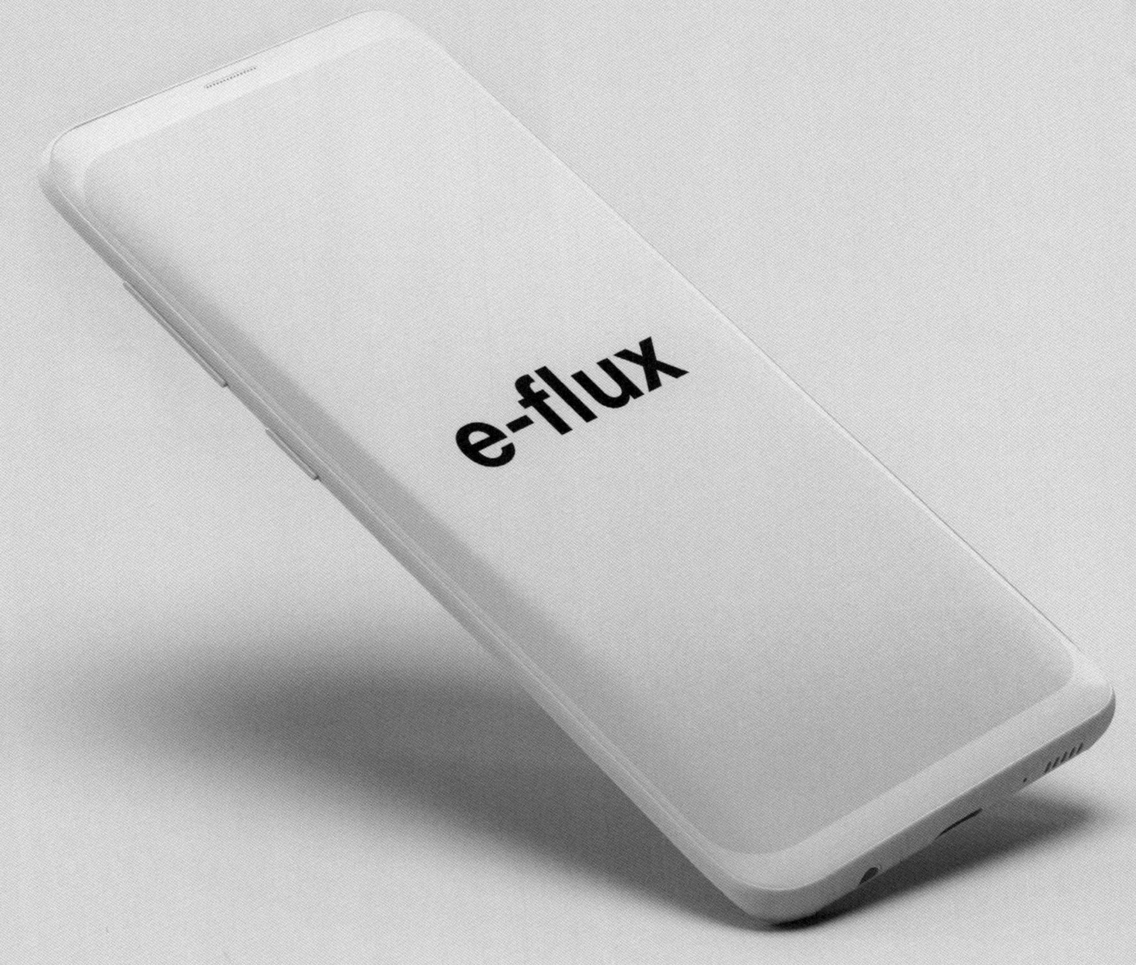

e-flux.com/app

311 East Broadway, New York, NY 10002
www.e-flux.com | 212.619.3356

EXHIBITION
JAN 29 – MAY 2, 2021

EDUCA TION SHOCK

LEARNING, POLITICS AND ARCHITECTURE IN THE 1960S AND 1970S

HKW

Haus der Kulturen der Welt

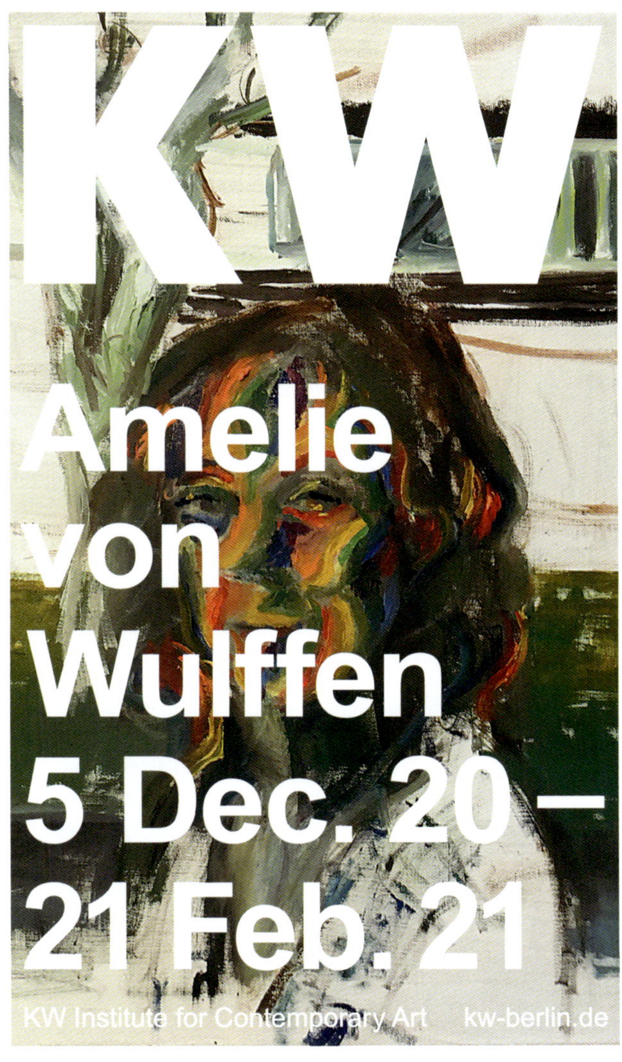

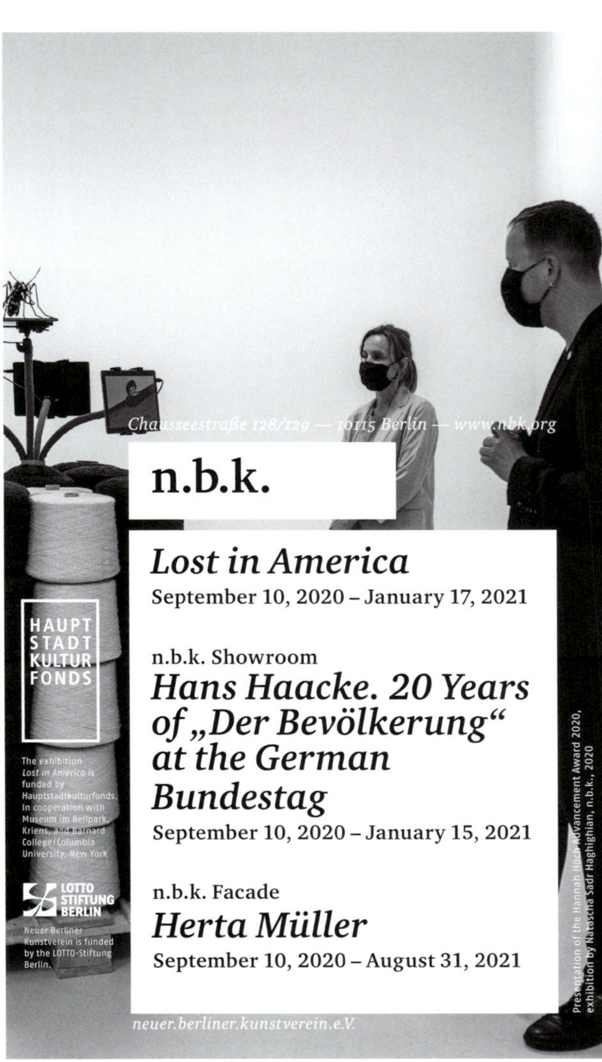

Afterall
ART SCHOOL

Launched at a moment of profound uncertainty for education in general and arts education in particular, Art School is a multi-layered forum for scholars and critics to join with art-workers, students and teachers to collectively reflect on the multiple histories, presents and potential futures of teaching and learning art. Encompassing essay series, live open discussion groups and a reference hub for further reading, watching and listening, Art School engages with the present's most urgent questions around education in art. Art School is a collaboration between Afterall, Central Saint Martins and the Museu de Arte de São Paulo Assis Chateaubriand.

www.afterallartschool.org

A Journal of Art, Context and Enquiry

Colophon

EDITORS
Ute Meta Bauer
Amanda Carneiro
Nav Haq
Amber Husain
Mark Lewis
Adeena Mey
Charles Stankievech

FOUNDING EDITORS
Charles Esche
Mark Lewis

PROJECT MANAGER
Lauren Houlton

PROGRAMME COORDINATOR
Beth Bramich

COPY EDITOR
Janine Armin

CREATIVE DIRECTION & DESIGN
Studio Pacific: Adam Turnbull and
Elizabeth Karp-Evans.

Printed and bound by die Keure, Bruges

ADVERTISING DIRECTOR
Berit Fischer
T +44 (0)20 7514 8173
E adverts@afterall.org

CONTACT
T +44 (0)20 7514 7212
E contact@afterall.org

EDITORIAL BOARD
Elvira Dyangani Ose, Ntone Edjabe,
Barbara Fisher, Vasif Kortun,
Anders Kreuger, Ana Longoni,
André Mesquita, Wanda Nanibush,
Emily Pethick, David Teh,
Christine Tohmé

SUBSCRIPTIONS
Individual and institutional subscriptions
are available worldwide in both print and
electronic formats. Please direct all
subscription enquiries, back-
issue requests and address changes to:
University of Chicago Press Journals
Division
1427 E. 60th Street Chicago, IL
60637–2902, USA
T +1 877 705 1878 (USA & Canada only)
T +1 773 753 3347 (International)
F +1 877 705 1879 (USA & Canada only)
F +1 773 753 0811 (International)
E subscriptions@press.uchicago.edu
www.journals.uchicago.edu

M HKA manages subscriptions in
Belgium, the Netherlands and Luxem-
bourg. Please direct all enquiries for
these countries to Sabine Herrygers:
M HKA
Leuvenstraat 32
B–2000 Antwerp, Belgium
T +32 (0) 260 80 98
E info@muhka.be

DISTRIBUTION
North America: Disticor Magazine
Distribution Services
1000 Thornton Road South, Unit B
Oshawa, Ontario L1J 7E2, Canada
T +1 905 619 6565
F +1 905 619 2903
E dkasza@disticor.com

Europe: Central Books Ltd
50 Freshwater Road, Chadwell Heath
London RM8 1RX, UK
T+ 44(0)20 8525 8825
F+ 44(0)20 8599 2694
E magazines@centralbooks.com
www.centralbooks.com/afterall

Postmaster: send address changes to
University of Chicago Press
1427 E. 60th Street Chicago, IL
60637–2902, USA. Postage paid in
Chicago and additional mailing offices.

All text protected under Creative
Commons Attribution-NonCommer-
cial-NoDerivs 3.0 Unported licence.
Please inform the editors if you intend to
transmit or reproduce any of the articles.

The views expressed by the writers are
not necessarily those of the editors.
Unsolicited material is welcome but will
not be returned.

ISBN 978-184638-249-9
ISSN 1465–4253

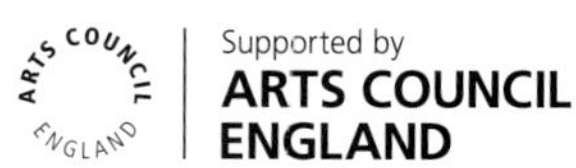

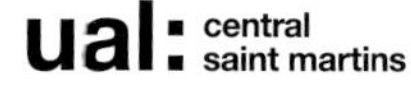

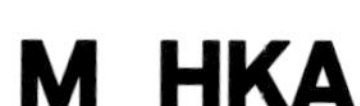

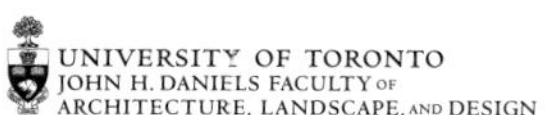

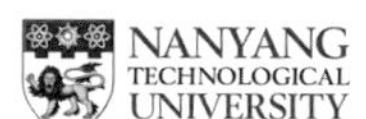